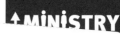

MINISTRY

A Practical Theology of

Dispelling the mystery; Recovering the passion

Eric E Wright

DayOne

First printed 2010

ISBN 978–1–84625–198–6

British Library Cataloguing in Publication Data available

Published by Day One Publications
Ryelands Road, Leominster, HR6 8NZ
☎ 01568 613 740 FAX 01568 611 473
email—sales@dayone.co.uk
web site—www.dayone.co.uk
North American—e-mail—sales@dayonebookstore.com
North American—web site—www.dayonebookstore.com

Cover design by Wayne McMaster
Printed by Gutenberg Press, Malta

A good understanding of biblical theology provides the basis for effective cross-cultural missionary work in A Practical Theology of Missions. *True missionary stories from several continents reflect the author's global perspective that has been nurtured by his development of theological education by extension in Pakistan, followed by his teaching of missions at the Toronto Baptist Seminary, where he was my colleague for twelve years. I highly recommend his effort.*

Rudolph H. Wiebe, lecturer at the Toronto Baptist Seminary for twenty-nine years and a principal lecturer at the Federal College of Education, Pankshin, Nigeria, West Africa since 2004.

This book is the climax of Eric Wright's full life as missionary, pastor and author. It is on a theme he is most qualified to expound, the theology of missions. It distils decades of missionary experience and research, reflection and devotion. The book is thorough and balanced, and yet it is an inspiring book to read. In it the reader will find the threefold calling of the church.

Firstly, the church exists to give praise to God by word, action, prayer and worship. This is the very core of the life of the church, the glory of God constituting the dominating motive in every deed and prayer. Paul declared that grace was given to him to proclaim the unsearchable riches of Christ among the heathen. He says of God, "His intent was that now, through the church, the manifold wisdom of God should be made known to the rulers and authorities in the heavenly realms" (Eph. 3:10). The ultimate goal of the church lies above this world, on another plane. The church exists for God and his glory.

Secondly, the church exists to make known the glory of God's Word to every generation of man. The context of this proclamation is to be through the exercise of loving, pastoral care of its members by opening up and applying to every person all of the Scriptures, individually and on the Lord's Day.

Thirdly, the church exists to encounter and serve the world by bringing to all mankind the good news of Jesus Christ. Through his church Christ stretches forth his hands to those who are outside the light of his everlasting salvation. It constrains the ignorant and lost to come in, as though God were beseeching them by the church.

So Christ uses our words and lives to reveal the glory of his redemptive work to men and women, drawing them to his salvation. The work of mission has received great promises from God. They are our comfort and they also drive us to our knees.

Revd Geoff Thomas, Pastor since 1965 of Alfred Place Baptist Church, Aberystwyth, Wales, UK

This book is dedicated to missionary colleagues on the
SIM team who have served with me in Pakistan

and

All those Pakistani believers who showed such patience in helping
my family and the missionary team adjust to life in the Pakistani culture

and

All the wonderful students who attended my classes at
Toronto Baptist Seminary and who now carry on the work of
the gospel in far-flung corners of the earth.

Contents

Contents

Missionary work doesn't get much press but its heroes and heroines continue to do the impossible, from the garbage dumps of Manila to the boulevards of Berlin. The missionary story pulses with drama and excitement.

Missionaries step over the fallen Iron Curtain to push evangelism into the steppes of Mongolia and the suburbs of Moscow. Persecution cannot blunt the advance of the underground church in China. Over 1,000 Nigerian missionaries fan out in West Africa carrying the gospel torch to communities steeped in Islam. Vicious repression fails to dim the joyful worship of Sudanese Christians while their Ethiopian neighbors struggle to handle mushrooming church growth. Indonesian Bible-school students plant churches of Muslim converts as a course requirement. In South America and black Africa the church continues to expand. Missionary translators keep pushing the linguistic frontiers into new language groups.

As you can tell, I'm upbeat about what God is doing. Stress cracks, however, have begun to appear. A thorough review of missionary theory is necessitated by the condition prevailing in the evangelical church at large. Almost fifty years ago A. W. Tozer diagnosed the problem. He said,

> Much that passes for Christianity today is the brief bright effort of the severed branch to bring forth its fruit in its season. But the deep laws of life are against it. Preoccupation with appearances and a corresponding neglect of the out-of-sight root of the true spiritual life are prophetic signs that go unheeded. Immediate "results" are all that matter, quick proofs of present success without a thought of next week or next year. Religious pragmatism is running wild among the orthodox. Truth is whatever works. If it gets results it is good.[1]

Years later we find ourselves driven even more completely by the engine of pragmatism. "If it works (seems to work) it must be good," has become the touchstone of many in Christian ministry. And if pragmatism is a problem in home churches, it is a plague in missionary circles. The veneer of missionary success in some places is too thin to sustain vibrant churches. Not enough thought has gone into the theological foundations of missionary work. This book is an attempt to return to God's missionary manual to reformulate basic missionary principles.

Pragmatism in its place is valuable. I have tried to make this book pragmatic, by discussing not only theory but also practice. Among other things, we will look at the missionary call, how missionaries adjust to culture and how they should relate to one another and to their sending churches. But my main goal is to suggest ways to strengthen the theological roots of missionary effort. This goal is rooted in the belief that the most pragmatic thing we can do in the long run is to teach what God has revealed, trust his revealed methods and try to apply them in dependence on the Holy Spirit.

This book is about roots, the out-of-sight sources of vibrant life that are needed to sustain real missionary success for generations to come. The beliefs and practices discussed rest upon the assumption that presuppositions matter. Nothing can be more important than to ensure that our missionary presuppositions reflect the principles of Scripture. This will not be true if theology is ignored, because theology brings us face to face with the principles, parameters and priorities that God has revealed.

Notes

1 **A. W. Tozer,** *The Root of the Righteous* (Harrisburg, PA: Christian Publications, 1955), p. 8.

Jesus Christ is doing today exactly what he predicted he would do when he said, "I will build my church, and the gates of Hades will not overcome it" (Matt. 16:18). Christ predicted success: "this gospel of the kingdom will be preached in the whole world as a testimony to all nations, and then the end will come" (Matt. 24:14).

The apostle John foresaw the culmination of this church-building process. "I looked and there before me was a great multitude that no one could count, from every nation, tribe, people and language, standing before the throne and in front of the Lamb ... they cried out in a loud voice: 'Salvation belongs to our God, who sits on the throne, and to the Lamb'" (Rev. 7:9–11).

As predicted, the missionary program of the Master will be a resounding success. However, that does not mean we can relax and leave the results to God. During the interim period between these pivotal predictions the Lord expects us to participate in planting the church among people of every tribe and tongue.

Even a careless reading of the New Testament confronts us with God's commitment to missions. We may call it evangelism, church planting, extending the Kingdom—but whatever we call it, it is the mission of God.

And if we are obedient disciples we cannot ignore the commands "Go into all the world and preach the good news to all creation" (Mark 16:15), "go and make disciples of all nations" (Matt. 28:19). We cannot escape this mandate even at prayer, for Jesus taught us to pray saying, "your kingdom come" (Matt. 6:10). And if we pray for the extension of the kingdom we must "Seek first his kingdom and his righteousness" (Matt. 6:33). Loving God with all of our heart, soul, mind and strength is priority number one. If we love him we will inevitably ask, "Lord, since I love you, what would you have me to do?" The answer in one way or another will involve missions.

Where do we start? First, let us sink our roots into the deep, rich theological soil of the Scriptures. Given prevailing conditions, however, that may be difficult.

Diagnosis: roots

Several modern-day writers have explored the shallowness of our evangelical roots. David Wells, in his book *No Place for Truth: Or*

Whatever Happened to Evangelical Theology?, describes the displacement of theology by a postmodern love affair with therapy, marketing and management technique. He documents how articles on doctrinal or biblical themes have declined to insignificance in two key evangelical magazines, *Christianity Today* and *Leadership*. He shows how the emphasis on the glories of God—the emphasis that produced godly living and passionate social concern in the Puritans—has declined catastrophically in every area of life and society.[1]

He goes on, in *God in the Wasteland: The Reality of Truth in a World of Fading Dreams*, to show the extent to which postmodernity has influenced evangelicals. He uses extensive student survey material to demonstrate how thoroughly seminary students and their training have been affected by this same trend. Missionary training, I might add, has been even more affected. "Evangelicals ... have become enamored of advanced management and marketing techniques, have blurred the distinctions between Christ and culture, and have largely abandoned their traditional emphasis on divine transcendence in favor of an emphasis on divine immanence. In doing so they have produced a faith in God that is of little consequence to those who believe."[2]

Mark Noll also affirms the need for a new reformation in his pivotal book *The Scandal of the Evangelical Mind*. He details the deterioration of evangelical scholarship in North America. In his review of Noll's book, Robert Wuthnow comments, "One wonders if the evangelical movement has pandered so much to American culture, tried so hard to be popular, and perpetuated such a do-it-yourself, feel-good faith that it has lost not only its mind but its soul as well."[3]

Missionary work rests upon divine authority. But the culture that has so influenced evangelicals is postmodern in its denial of external authority. People *subjectively* decide what is true for them at a particular time. Hence what seems pragmatic is thought of as true. Before the Enlightenment most realized that truth was *objective* and authoritative because God made it so. The goal of education was to bring our twisted thinking into conformity with objective external reality as interpreted by revelation. The Enlightenment, however, "shifted this authority from the object to the subject. Now the subject becomes sovereign."[4] Personal preference rules.

Our postmodern age exalts *relativism* and *pluralism* while it categorically denies the kind of propositional truth that we find in the Scriptures. The toxic effects of this lethal mixture have singed the North American church badly. The influence of postmodernism on the church in the United Kingdom, Europe, Australia and New Zealand is no less serious. Indeed, if the rush of the evangelical church in Britain during the 1990s to embrace the experience of the "Toronto Blessing" is any indication, the situation in the UK is far worse.

Concerning missions today, David Hesselgrave writes about the importance of theology in missions and the danger of a pragmatism that he compares to Egyptian gold:

> Christian mission must be undergirded with biblical authority but it must be guided by biblical theology. The most hopeful future for missions and missiology depends on the "re-missionizing of theology" on the one hand, and the "re-theologizing of missiology" on the other.
>
> To accomplish this, a largely new kind of dialogue and synergism will be required. Theologians will need to fight off the infection of an Aristotelianism imported from Egypt centuries ago; devote less time and effort to the erection of theological systems; and, together with missiologists, give more attention to the kind of biblical theology that will arrest the minds and change the hearts of people of various religions and cultures. Missiologists will have to struggle against a pragmatism that is overly devoted to ingenious ways of employing Egyptian gold and put too much stock on the often ephemeral results of alchemized strategies; and they will have to labor alongside theologians in an effort to understand correctly and handle rightly Holy Spirit-inspired Scripture.[5]

The seedbed of missionary concern, our churches, seminaries, Bible colleges and Christian institutions, have not escaped the subtle influence of postmodern thought. From Tozer to Noll red flags are being waved at the runaway engine of evangelical "success." This is sufficient reason to carefully compare modern missionary work with biblical truth. It is my hope that this book will contribute in some small way to the reformation we desperately need.

Diagnosis: outworking

How is mission faring in our local churches? Many church buildings have a bulletin board in the foyer with the pictures of supported missionaries. The budget may include a sizeable amount, perhaps 25 to 35 percent, allocated for missions. At prayer meetings, missionaries may be listed for prayer. A monthly women's missionary society may meet. Once a year the church probably holds a missionary conference, and occasionally visiting missionaries speak in the Sunday service or at the prayer meeting. So far so good.

On closer observation, however, we find that the annual missionary conference is dismally attended. What used to be a week of exciting meetings has shrunk to a Saturday night potluck and a Sunday emphasis. On the surface, members profess interest in missions, but by their actions they seem to be saying, "I've heard it all before—let's get it over with and get back to doing what church is all about." At prayer meetings, specific missionary prayer requests are seldom brought to the throne of grace. "God bless the missionaries. Amen" suffices in many circles. The women's missionary society either has changed its program into a ladies' social night to attract younger women, or is doggedly kept going by a few ladies in their seventies.

At the pastoral and board level much discussion centers on concern about new carpets in the foyer, finding volunteers for the hostess committee, how to revive the flagging Sunday school or how to deal with some crisis of church discipline. Yes, missions is an important part of evangelical church life and part of the budget, but it is just one of many competing programs. Churches are overwhelmingly preoccupied with the day-to-day concerns of their local parish.

In most evangelical churches, considerable concern for evangelism surfaces. Evangelism, however, is viewed as distinct from missions. Members may mumble, "Foreign missions—what about Toronto? Chicago? London?" A legitimate concern. But why are evangelism and missions viewed as competitors? Are home missions and foreign missions really distinct? Is it wise to compartmentalize so thoroughly?

Foreign missions seem romantic. Distant lands, strange foods, unintelligible languages, jungles, snakes, malaria. There is money for overseas missions. A strange anomaly: money to support foreign missionaries, but little interest in understanding what God is doing in foreign lands.

The paradox becomes more puzzling. Any foreign missionaries who return home to reach ethnic groups in their hometowns find that their support soon dries up. Why? The perception seems to be that they are not missionaries anymore. "The budget is tight. Why not remove Joe. After all, he works in LA." It's notoriously more difficult to raise support for the evangelism of Arabs in Detroit than for reaching Arabs in Syria or Lebanon.

Competition and confusion! Somehow we are foggy about the vision of the Master. Perhaps part of the problem is that, as Eugene Petersen laments in *Under the Unpredictable Plant*, most North American pastors are program directors rather than spiritual directors.[6] Pastors are so busy juggling all the activities of local-church life that there is no time left to examine how local concerns dovetail with God's global vision.

Diagnosis: theological preparation

How did this state of affairs come about? George Peters has been a professor of missions at both Trinity Evangelical Divinity School and Dallas Theological Seminary. He traces the fragmentation of our evangelical vision to the compartmentalization of our theological education:

> The study of Christian missions has been for centuries a separate and distinct discipline not usually considered to be material for the theologian or for the pastor. In fact, most theologians and pastors passed by the courses in missions and ignored mission literature and matters of mission organisation. The church, the pastor, and the theologian often remained detached if not aloof from mission studies and mission movements.[7]

In spite of some movement toward integration, Peters, as recently as 1981, wrote, "No formulated theology of missions exists from the evangelical non-ecumenical perspective ... Such a dearth does not exist in the ecumenical world."[8] By ecumenical, Peters means those denominations that are part of the World Council of Churches.

As I look again through my theological textbooks, I have to agree. Sections on Theology, Anthropology, Soteriology, Angelology—but no Missiology! L. Berkhof's extremely helpful *Systematic Theology* has no section on missions—or on spiritual gifts! Neither does Hodge's three-volume set. Why is there more paper about angels than about the mission of God? True, theology has been historically divided into Systematic Theology, Biblical Theology, Pastoral Theology, and so on. But is it wise to omit from systematic theology the central role of missions in God's plan? Is it wise for schools and programs on missions to grow up independently of those committed to preparing pastors? Not if the Bible is what it says it is.

Peters writes, "It is my impression that the Bible is not a book about theology as such, but rather, a record of theology in mission—God in action in behalf of the salvation of mankind."[9] If he is correct, and I believe he is, we face a serious flaw in theological training.

Patrick Johnstone places some of the blame squarely at the feet of the seminaries that prepare pastors. In a tour of North America to introduce a new edition of his excellent prayer guide, *Operation World*, he stepped into the lion's den—the Bible-college and seminary-student world.

During the first week of classes in a bright New Year, Johnstone stood before an audience of seminary students and professors in Toronto. His manner was gentle but his words had bite. He asserted that Western seminaries constitute "one of the greatest hindrances to world evangelization."

Operation World is now in its fifth edition. Probably more missionaries and teachers, pastors and intercessors turn to this book for statistics and information to fuel their prayer lives than to any other book. Why, then, would he make such a statement?

In his talk, he went on to exegete the agonies of Christ as prophesied in Psalm 22. He pointed out how inseparably the Holy Spirit has linked soteriology, God's saving purpose, with missiology, God's missionary purpose. The sufferings of the Son, in this psalm, find their fruition when "All the ends of the earth will remember and turn to the LORD ... and worship" (vv. 27, 29).

Johnstone commented, "Tragically, these two [the doctrine of salvation and the doctrine of missions] have been divorced from each other in the Western world." Seminaries hinder world evangelization precisely because they treat missions as an optional subject in their curricula. "Missiology has become the Cinderella of theological disciplines. Only those committed to missions study about missions. The great majority of students preparing for pastoral ministry have no exposure to what is the heartbeat of God. That ignorance is reflected in their ministry."

He went on to describe the result of this great theological divorce. "Numerous evangelical churches have little meaningful missionary involvement. Many Sunday schools and youth groups fail to grapple with the challenge of world evangelization. Whole congregations focus on local concerns and spend most of their income meeting their own congregational needs."[10]

The problem has been around a long time. Dr. Pentecost spoke on this issue back at the great interdenominational Missionary Conference held in New York in 1900. He said,

> To the pastor belongs the privilege and the responsibility of solving the foreign missionary problem. Until the pastors of our churches wake up to the truth of this proposition, and the foreign work becomes a passion in their own hearts and consciences, our Boards may do what they can, by way of devising forward movements ... yet the chariot wheels of missions will drive heavily. Every pastor holds his office under Christ's commission, and can only fulfil it when, as a missionary bishop, he counts the whole world his fold. The pastor of the smallest church has the power to make his influence felt around the world. No pastor is worthy of his office who does not bring himself into conformity to the magnificent breadth of the great commission, and draw inspiration and zeal from its world-wide sweep.
>
> The problem of the theological seminary is this: not how to train an occasional individual for the foreign field, but *how to kindle missionary passion in every person who passes through the school*, that he may thereby become an able minister of Christ. The essential thing is that there shall be within the school a sacred altar of missionary passion, at which the torch of every man is kindled.[11]

I would be cavalier if I failed to lay some of the blame at the feet of missionaries themselves. In my experience, far too few missionaries understand the concerns of the local church. Since church planting is exactly what missions is all about, this is tragic. Far too many missionaries view a deep grounding in theology as unimportant to their task. I have reasoned at length with missionaries about the danger of listening to the siren song of social sciences, such as anthropology and sociology, while failing to heed the cry of theology—the queen of sciences.

All is not gloomy. God will not allow the failure of his mission. At the chapel service mentioned above, Patrick Johnstone went on to point out that Psalm 22 concludes with a stirring picture of the certainty of missionary success. Using an impressive array of charts and maps, he demonstrated how God is overruling the seemingly random and even hurtful events of history to accomplish his missionary purpose. Evangelicals are growing, worldwide, at a rate of 5 percent, three times the rate of population increase. Asian evangelicals now outnumber their North American brothers and sisters. African and South American church growth is phenomenal. Is our view of missions, as an adjunct, shunting us into a siding while the flow of God's purpose passes us by?

Fortunately, in the West, there remain many who have not allowed their missionary vision to dim. These stalwarts instinctively realize that God is a missionary God.

But what is missions? Before we leave this chapter, let me define several important terms for the sake of clarity.

Definitions

MISSION

By mission I mean the total calling of the church as it reflects the eternal purpose of God. This involves an upward activity—worship, thanksgiving, intercession, fellowship with God. It also involves an inward aspect—the organization of individual believers into local churches, their edification or discipling, their care and comfort, their mutual fellowship and training. Finally, it involves an outward activity—witnessing or evangelism, concern and care for the needs in the community, and particularly missionary outreach, a commitment of the resources necessary to plant churches among the unreached in the community and among all the peoples of the earth.

MISSIONS

By missions, I mean specifically the outward activity of the church—reaching the unreached with the gospel. Missions aims to plant viable churches of mature disciples in every unreached area; among every people, tribe, tongue and nation. This may involve either cross-cultural church planting or church planting in unreached portions of our own cultural groups. Genuine missions always retains both a vision of the whole world and a Christ-inspired passion to reach the gospel-destitute with good news wherever they may be.

MISSIONARY

In keeping with the definition of *missions*, a missionary is a person called and gifted of God for the specific task of planting churches among unreached peoples. He may or may not leave his home area. He may or may not travel to another culture. He is the inheritor, not of apostolic authority and uniqueness, but of the apostolic spiritual gift of church planting. While many who are supported by local churches as "missionaries" are not themselves church planters, they should be involved in some ministry that contributes to church planting to be classified as such. There are a host of ministries that undergird and support the missionary thrust. As long as the overarching vision of planting churches in gospel-destitute areas drives them, we can legitimately call them missionaries.

EVANGELISM

By evangelism, I mean the authoritative proclamation of the gospel in relevant, understandable and persuasive terms—terms that call for a personal response. This may involve personal "soul-winning," in which an individual explains the gospel to a friend, relative or neighbor, or a group activity organized with an aim to harvest the elect from a broader segment of society.

CHRISTIAN HUMANITARIANISM OR SOCIAL UPLIFT

As commanded by Christ, disciples must respond to medical, economic, social, educational and general human needs. Humanitarian activities may undergird church planting but must not supplant it. Such ministry is Christlike, genuine and necessary, but is not to be understood as *missions* as such.

These definitions are meant to help us get our feet wet in the subject. They may leave you with questions. Well and good. They serve as a working introduction to missions but they will be further defined and qualified in the chapters ahead.

Each section of this book begins with a description of missionary work as it is being, or has been, carried on in some particular part of the world. I have compiled these missionary vignettes over the years and they simply represent a slice of missionary activity accurate at the time they were originally written. Many describe the work of SIM (Sudan Interior Mission, now Serving in Mission) missionaries. They are meant to act as a reality check—to keep us from getting too fog-bound in some theoretical ivory tower and to convey what is actually happening in the world. Their use, however, does not mean that every policy they illustrate, or organization they reflect, should be emulated. They serve somewhat like intermissions in a long theater program. Each vignette will highlight some corner of God's global vineyard. So get a cup of coffee or a bowl of popcorn, curl up in a favorite chair and read the first of these descriptions—the exciting story of missions in Paraguay

Notes

1 **David Wells,** *No Place for Truth: Or Whatever Happened to Evangelical Theology?* (Grand Rapids, MI: Eerdmans, 1993).

2 **David F. Wells,** *God in the Wasteland: The Reality of Truth in a World of Fading Dreams* (Grand Rapids, MI: Eerdmans, 1994), front dust jacket.

3 Cited on back dust jacket of **Mark A. Noll,** *The Scandal of the Evangelical Mind* (Grand Rapids, MI: Eerdmans, 1994).

4 **Albert Mohler,** "A Reformed Perspective on a Secular Age," summary by David Brighton, in *Reformation Today*, July–Aug. 1996, p. 12.

5 **David J. Hesselgrave,** "Third Millennium Missiology and the Use of Egyptian Gold," in *Journal of the Evangelical Theological Society*, [n.d], p. 589.

6 **Eugene H. Peterson,** *Under the Unpredictable Plant* (Grand Rapids, MI: Eerdmans, 1992).

7 **George W. Peters,** *A Biblical Theology of Missions* (Chicago: Moody, 1972), p. 25.

8 Ibid. p. 28.

9 Ibid. p. 9

10 Notes from a series of two chapel services taken by Patrick Johnstone at Toronto Baptist Seminary, winter 1994.

11 Quoted in **Andrew Murray,** *The Key to the Missionary Problem* (Fort Washington, PA: Christian Literature Crusade, 1979), pp. 11–13.

Missions in Paraguay

In a shantytown called Plastic Village on the outskirts of Asunción, the capital of Paraguay, South America, a missionary follows Marciano down a muddy lane. Warm smiles and friendly greetings mark their progress. Bits and pieces of plastic cover the roofs of the hovels in an often vain attempt to keep out tropical downpours. The reek of poverty assails their nostrils. After four months of gentle visitation led by Marciano, an untrained Paraguayan believer, at least fifty of the inhabitants of Plastic Village are eager for Bible study. A number already show signs of the transforming grace of God.

In another part of Asunción, the missionary team's associate director and his wife work with the professional class. He builds bridges of friendship with the men while his wife leads a group of professional women in Bible study. With a quarter of their ninety video titles on loan at any one time, it's plain to see that their Paraguayan friends are interested in the gospel.

Paraguayans are a loveable people, carefree and full of humor, and who seem to have a healthier self-image than some other South Americans. Perhaps this can be traced to the blend of indigenous and Spanish cultures in the Paraguayan people. In contrast to other areas where native populations were often wiped out, in Paraguay the aboriginal people were absorbed into the mainstream.

With 97 percent of the people Roman Catholic, Paraguay remains one of Latin America's most unreached countries. Only 2 percent of Paraguayans are evangelical. Until recently, effort had been concentrated among the 50,000 or so tribal Indians who inhabit the desolate Chaco. With about 25 percent of these professing Christ, tribal missionaries are greatly encouraged. But 95 percent of the people live outside the Chaco in Asunción or in the rural towns east of the capital.

The missionary team has found Paraguayans to be receptive to the gospel in both city and village settings. Most response, so far, has occurred in the central area of the country east of Asunción. The team aims to plant churches in this rural area where no evangelical witness exists. They are praying for many more church planters to augment their twenty-member team so they will have the resources necessary to start churches in thirty or forty towns.

The Asian church has greatly enriched the Paraguayan missionary team by sending missionaries from Singapore, the Philippines and South Korea. To support their own missionaries, the Presbyterian church of Dong Myung responded by sending out a team of eleven medical specialists. *ABC*, the popular Paraguayan daily newspaper, bannered their visit "Korean Medical Group Brings Free Attention." The government aided their week-long visit by quickly allowing the import of over 10,000 dollars' worth of medical supplies free of duty.

Two medical doctors, a dentist, six nurses and two pastors made up the Korean team. They treated a total of 1,078 patients in various rural and urban settings. One day, they offered medical attention in a camp of those rendered homeless by the flooding of the Paraguayan River. A sort of mobile pharmacy traveled with them, dispensing medicine in individual packets. Each packet of medicine also contained Bible portions to promote spiritual well-being.

The church-planting team in Paraguay can see the shape of things to come. Their leader explains, "As people come to the Lord, we'll form local groups of believers and disciple them into churches. We'll also disciple Bible-school students by involving them in outreach. Although there hasn't been time for much response from city folk, I'm convinced we're on the verge of a major breakthrough."

The experience in Paraguay illustrates the way the Spirit of God can take North and South Americans, Europeans and Asians and imbue them with a common vision. It also demonstrates the effective way short-term teams, like those from South Korea, can enhance the ministry of career missionaries.

Part 1

The biblical basis of missions

Missions and the nature of God

A passion for God fuels the missionary impulse! As we saw earlier in Psalm 22, soteriology and missiology are handmaidens. In Psalm 46 God urges us to seek quietness to meditate on who he is: "Be still, and know that I am God" (v. 10). He immediately follows up this exhortation with a revelation of the missionary purpose pervading history: "I will be exalted among the nations, I will be exalted in the earth." Theology, the study of God, ought to energize missiology.

David often writes that his greatest desire is communion with God. "O God, you are my God, earnestly I seek you; my soul thirsts for you, my body longs for you, in a dry and weary land where there is no water ... Your love is better than life" (Ps. 63:1, 3).

We are to "Love the Lord [our] God with all [our] heart and with all [our] soul and with all [our] mind" (Matt. 22:37). This in turn leads to loving our neighbors as ourselves, including our cross-cultural neighbors, as demonstrated in the parable of the Good Samaritan. The more we love God, the more we will seek him. And the more we know God, the more we will feel a passion for what is on his heart—missions.

Speaking in 1910, Robert E. Speer made this point:

> The last command of Christ is not the deep and final ground of the church's missionary duty. That duty is authoritatively stated in the words of the great commission, and it is of infinite consequence to have had it so stated by our Lord Himself. But if these particular words had never been spoken by Him, or if, having been spoken, they had not been preserved, the missionary duty of the Church would not be in the least affected.
>
> The supreme arguments for missions are not found in any specific words. It is in the very being and character of God that the deepest ground of the missionary enterprise is to be found. We cannot think of God except in terms which necessitate the missionary idea ... The grounds are in the very being and thought of God.[1]

Deep communion with God, if genuine, inevitably feeds the missionary vision. A passionate love for Christ galvanized generations of Moravians to offer themselves for missionary service. Invigorated by this practical devotion, the Moravians established a twenty-four-hour prayer vigil that they maintained for 100 years. Their devotion contributed to the revival fervor of John Wesley and inspired the Student Volunteer Movement years later.

Under the banner "The Evangelization of the World in this Generation," the Student Volunteer Movement mobilized thousands of students. One of its greatest leaders, John R. Mott, wrote,

> The Moravians have done more in proportion to their ability than any other body of Christians. If members of Protestant churches in Great Britain and America gave in like proportion, missionary contributions would aggregate a fourfold increase.
>
> If we went out as missionaries in corresponding numbers, we would have a force of nearly 400,000 foreign workers, which is vastly more than the number of missionaries estimated as necessary to achieve the evangelization of the world in this generation. I ask the question, *What has there been in connection with their work which is not reproducible?* The worldwide proclamation of the gospel can be accomplished in this generation, *if it has the obedience and determination to attempt the task* [his italics].[2]

With several generations having elapsed since John R. Mott wrote those words, the church finds itself larger and richer—but poorer in determination to attempt the task. A lethargy about missions has spread like a canker through the West. It is the same problem that Andrew Murray addressed in his timeless book *The Key to the Missionary Problem*.

In the Preface included in the modern reprint of this neglected classic we read,

> Murray ... questions why, with millions of Christians in the world, the army of missionaries fighting the hosts of darkness is so small. His answer is—lack of heart. The enthusiasm of the kingdom is missing because there is so little enthusiasm for *the King*. Though much may be done by careful organization and strict discipline and

good generalship to make the best of the few troops we have, there is nothing that can so restore confidence and courage as the actual presence of a beloved King, to whom every heart beats warm in loyalty and devotion.[3]

A. W. Tozer declared,

What comes into our minds when we think about God is the most important thing about us ... For this reason the gravest question before the Church is always God Himself, and the most portentous fact about any man is not what he at a given time may say or do, but what he in his deep heart conceives God to be like. We tend by a secret law of the soul to move toward our mental image of God ... The low view of God entertained almost universally among Christians is the cause of a hundred lesser evils everywhere among us.[4]

Missions is but one of the casualties.

George Peters wrote,

Missions is the progressive objectification of the eternal and benevolent purpose of God which roots in His very being and character and which embraces all ages, races and generations ... Missions is the historic effectuation of God's salvation ... Missions is the practical realisation of the Holy Spirit operating in this world on behalf of the eternal purpose of God ... Missionary theology is not an appendix to biblical theology; it belongs at its very core. No doctrine of God, Christ or the Holy Spirit has been expounded completely according to the Bible until it has established the triune God as the outgoing God of mission ...[5]

So the place to begin clarifying our missionary task is in the throne room of our blessed Sovereign. The proper study of the missionary is always *theology*, the study of God. Let us move immediately, then, to a consideration of God—his attributes and glory—for if what I have been saying is true, they will necessarily reflect God's missionary purpose. Please remember, however, that the study of God extends far beyond the scope of this book. I will sketch the glories of God in a very abbreviated form. For a fuller treatment please refer to a comprehensive systematic theology by L. Berkhof or Hodge. In terms of theology's relationship to missions, I am indebted for some of what follows to George Peters and his book *A Biblical Theology of Missions*.

God as God, his incommunicable attributes

God revealed himself to Moses as Yahweh—"I am that I am." This strange name reflects the fact that in his intrinsic being God is utterly indescribable, transcendent, timeless and self-sufficient. He requires nothing outside of himself for existence or fulfillment.

In the 1689 Confession we read, "God is all-sufficient, and all life, glory, goodness and blessedness are found in Him and in Him alone. He does not stand in need of any of the creatures that He has made ..."[6]

Although self-sufficient, God created the universe. He created us. Clearly, self-sufficiency does not mean isolation or immobility of purpose. The relationship of the unchanging God to his changing, dependent creation remains a paradox. Why did God create the universe when he eternally existed in perfect self-sufficiency? The answer cannot be found by claiming, as some pantheistic philosophies do, that God is the sum of everything. Contrary to the claims of pantheism, creation does not reflect the essential nature of God, for he is transcendent and uncreated. The ultimate answer to the question of why God would create a dependent creation must await his explanation. Creation does not add anything to his infinite glory. Beyond saying that creation and redemption display his glory, we cannot probe the inscrutable motivation of God.

The reality of creation, however, does reflect a significant fact about God—that he is deeply interested in something external to himself. The self-sufficiency of God, then, does not mean that God has determined to remain isolated, incommunicable or distant. As David expressed it in Psalm 139, God reveals himself everywhere one can imagine going. Wherever one may wander or flee, God is found to be nearer than life itself.

As the eternal God, Yahweh exists outside of time. Nevertheless, he has purposed to create time and to reveal himself in the unfolding of history.

Although an infinite, immaterial spirit, God has purposed to fellowship with finite, material beings possessing immaterial souls. They are so important to him that they were created in his image.

Although invisible, God has purposed to reveal himself in visible ways: a smoking furnace and flaming torch to Abraham; the angel of Jehovah to Hagar; a burning bush before Moses. And, of course, in the incarnation.

Although unchangeable in his nature and purposes, God has purposed to reveal himself—not at some eternal point in the future, but through the changing circumstances of history. Redemption is the progressive unfolding of an eternal changeless plan.

All of his actions demonstrate that, instead of remaining isolated, *God reaches out beyond himself*. This remains one of the most amazing things about God. Why he chose to create a world, or time, or you and me, remain mysteries summed up in a baffling phrase: "For his own glory." But the fact that God does reach out beyond himself reflects the reality that *outreach*—missions—is woven into the very fabric of God's self-disclosure. It is part and parcel of every facet of his unfolding redemptive purpose.

God of truth

Obedience to the first and second commandments is central to all Christian faith and expression. "You shall have no other gods before me ... You shall not make for yourself an idol" (Exod. 20:3–4). All other gods are idolatrous fabrications. From Israel's clash with the heathen nations, through Elijah's mockery of Baal's priests on Mount Carmel, to Paul's preaching about the "unknown God" in idolatrous Athens, God's servants have faced the challenge of proclaiming the one true God in the midst of idolatry.

Missions involves the clash of truth with falsehood. Whether people be primitive animists or Buddhists, Muslims, Sikhs, Hindus or even worshipers of Mary or science or money, the missionary message calls them to reject the lie and receive the truth—there is only one true God. "For all the gods of the nations are idols, but the LORD made the heavens" (Ps. 96:5). Isaiah proclaims the foolishness of the craftsman who uses wood from the same tree to make an idol, to warm himself and to bake his bread: "All who make idols are nothing, and the things they treasure are worthless"(Isa. 44:9). As Paul pointed out to the Corinthians who were worried about the power of idols, "We know that an idol is nothing at all in the world and that there is no God but one" (1 Cor. 8:4).

The missionary message declares that Jesus is "the way and the truth and the life," and that "No one comes to the Father except through [him]"

(John 14:6). Nothing could be clearer: "this is eternal life: that they may know you, the only true God, and Jesus Christ, whom you have sent" (John 17:3).

Missions, then, involves calling men and women from the darkness of every kind of deceptive lie, fabrication, false philosophy and counterfeit religion into the light that radiates from the one true God.

God of holiness and justice

God is holy and just. In many places in Scripture God's holiness indicates his transcendent nature. He is the one in Isaiah who declares himself as "the high and lofty One ... whose name is holy" (Isa. 57:15). His majesty sets him infinitely apart from all creation. When we speak of God's holiness, however, we often mean his ethical holiness or moral purity. "Your eyes are too pure to look on evil; you cannot tolerate wrong" (Hab. 1:13).

His moral holiness is revealed in the law written on human hearts and recorded in Scripture. Although non-Jewish people did not have the Scriptures, "they show that the requirements of the law are written on their hearts, their consciences also bearing witness, and their thoughts now accusing, now even defending them" (Rom. 2:15). This law binds all to obedience. The law is neither grievous nor hurtful. "This is love for God: to obey his commands. And his commands are not burdensome" (1 John 5:3). In spite of the glorious benefit to be derived from walking in conformity to God's moral law, everyone—without exception—has sinned against God from childhood. "Even from birth the wicked go astray; from the womb they are wayward and speak lies" (Ps. 58:3); "for all have sinned and fall short of the glory of God" (Rom. 3:23).

Without missions, mankind's condition is grave. Although the creation of the world makes obvious to any unbiased observer "God's invisible qualities—his eternal power and divine nature," people live as if God does not exist (Rom. 1:19–20). "They neither glorified him as God nor gave thanks to him, but their thinking became futile and their foolish hearts were darkened ... they became fools" (Rom. 1:21–22). As a result, "The wrath of God is being revealed from heaven against all the godlessness and wickedness of men" (Rom. 1:18). Mankind stands in terrible danger of facing the judgment of God.

Missions must inevitably bear witness to this fact, warning people to flee from the judgment to come by embracing Christ. Bringing them to that point will likely mean affirming the holiness and justice of God and probably teaching God's moral law. Without reawakened consciences people do not admit their sinfulness nor cry out to God for mercy. Without conviction of sin, few will be prepared to flee to God for mercy and grace—a key goal of missions. Fortunately, the central component of the missionary message concerns actions God has taken to rescue mankind from our own obstinacy.

God of goodness and grace

Missions flows from God's gracious desire to bestow kindness on those who can lay no claim to it. God is a good God. "The LORD is gracious and compassionate, slow to anger and rich in love. The LORD is good to all; he has compassion on all he has made ... You open your hand and satisfy the desires of every living thing" (Ps. 145:8–9, 16). "He causes his sun to rise on the evil and the good, and sends rain on the righteous and the unrighteous" (Matt. 5:45).

More specifically, missions can be traced to God's mercy, longsuffering, love and grace. God's mercy, the tenderness God feels toward those in misery or distress, is extolled throughout the Scriptures. "For the LORD your God is a merciful God" (Deut. 4:31). On the occasion of his sin in numbering Israel, David preferred God's mercy far above that of men: "I am in deep distress. Let us fall into the hands of the LORD, for his mercy is great; but do not let me fall into the hands of men" (2 Sam. 24:14). God "is rich in mercy" (Eph. 2:4). Missions extends God's mercy to lost men and women.

In spite of their rebellion and evil, God is patient and longsuffering with his creatures. On Mount Sinai God came down in a cloud and passed before Moses proclaiming, "The LORD, the LORD, the compassionate and gracious God, slow to anger, abounding in love and faithfulness, maintaining love to thousands, and forgiving wickedness, rebellion and sin" (Exod. 34:6–7). Because he is longsuffering, God waits patiently for the fulfillment of the missionary task.

In Psalm 107 the writer calls for people in all circumstances to "Give thanks to the LORD, for he is good; his love endures forever" (v. 1). Berkhof defines God's love as "that perfection of God by which He is eternally moved to self-communication."[7] Although sin is an abomination to God, he does not withdraw his love completely from rebellious mankind but reaches out to them. "For God so loved the world that he gave his one and only Son, that whoever believes in him shall not perish but have eternal life" (John 3:16). "God demonstrates his own love for us in this: While we were still sinners, Christ died for us" (Rom. 5:8). The missionary message breaks into the lives of lost men and women with the story of God's love.

As we will discuss more fully later, this love is preeminently manifested in Jesus Christ, God's incarnate word of love to the human race. If we would understand the missionary impulse that throbs in the heart of God we must understand something of this love. For this reason, Paul, in his missionary epistle to the Ephesians, prayed that they might be "rooted and established in love, may have power, together with all the saints, to grasp how wide and long and high and deep is the love of Christ, and to know this love that surpasses knowledge—that you may be filled to the measure of all the fullness of God" (Eph. 3:17–19). While God is not only loving but also just and righteous, his love is so central in all his dealings with mankind that John could write, "God is love" (1 John 4:8).

Beyond God's general love is his special love for believers. While preparing his disciples for his coming death Christ explained, "the Father himself loves you because you have loved me and have believed that I came from God" (John 16:27). "In love he predestined us to be adopted as his sons through Jesus Christ" (Eph. 1:4–5). Although those chosen to become his children were, like others, "objects of wrath," yet "because of his great love for us, God, who is rich in mercy, made us alive with Christ" (Eph. 2:3–5). "How great is the love the Father has lavished on us, that we should be called children of God!" (1 John 3:1).

Grace is that aspect of God's goodness that directs his love toward creatures who deserve wrath. Without God's undeserved favor, his grace, none would have hope; "it is by grace you have been saved" (Eph. 2:8). Grace adorns each step in the unfolding of God's great plan of salvation. We are chosen and adopted as his children "to the praise of his glorious grace, which he has freely given us in the One he loves." We are redeemed "in accordance with the riches of God's grace that he lavished on us" (see Eph. 1:6–8).

The fact that we have a missionary message is due to who God is; not only loving and gracious, but holy, just and true. It is also due to the mysterious reality that, although God—within the fellowship of the Trinity—is infinite, eternal and unchangeable in his self-sufficiency, he has chosen to interact with creatures.

God of sovereign purpose

While we cannot trace God's missionary activity to any one attribute alone, it may, perhaps, be ascribed most closely to God's sovereign purpose. The Westminster Confession defines this as "His eternal purpose according to the counsel of his will, whereby for his own glory, He hath foreordained whatsoever comes to pass."[8]

God is no absentee landlord who created the universe then retired into passivity. God actively manages the universe according to his eternal plan. From creation in Genesis to consummation in Revelation the Scriptures make clear that God has a comprehensive plan that he is pursuing throughout human history. Reformed theologians have called God's eternal purpose or plan "the divine decrees," to reflect the fact that whatever happens can be traced to the will of the sovereign God.

While few, especially those of an Arminian persuasion, root missions in the divine decrees, it is important to do so. Paul, probably the greatest missionary who ever lived, affirms this three times in the opening chapter of Ephesians. Every blessing saved people receive from election, through adoption, redemption, forgiveness, sealing of the Spirit to receiving their inheritance in the heavenly realms, is "in accordance with his pleasure and will ... the mystery of his will according to his good pleasure ... in conformity with the purpose of his will" (Eph. 1:5, 9, 11).

Missions, as part of God's sovereign plan, is based on the wisdom of God. Berkhof writes,

> The decree of God bears the closest relation to the divine knowledge. There is in God ... a necessary knowledge, including all possible causes and result. This knowledge furnishes the material for the decree; it is the perfect fountain out of which God drew

> the thoughts which He desired to objectify. Out of this knowledge of all things possible He chose, by an act of His perfect will, led by wise consideration, what He wanted to bring to realisation and thus form His eternal purpose.[9]

In the words of Ephesians: The redemptive plan of God was formulated "in accordance with the riches of God's grace that he lavished on us with all wisdom and understanding" (Eph. 1:7–8).

Missions is no minor church program but a central part of God's comprehensive plan for the universe. "And he made known to us the mystery of his will according to his good pleasure, which he purposed in Christ, to be put into effect when the times will have reached their fulfillment—to bring all things in heaven and on earth together under one head, even Christ" (Eph. 1:9–10). In the words of the Lord's prayer, missions is entrusted with working for the fulfillment of the second and third requests: extending the rule and will of the Sovereign King of the universe. "Your kingdom come, your will be done on earth as it is in heaven" (Matt. 6:10).

Missions, like the divine decrees, is certain of fulfillment. Nebuchadnezzar, the greatest king of his era, after a period of arrogance and then insanity confessed his faith in the sovereignty of God.

> I praised the Most High …
> His dominion is an eternal dominion;
> his kingdom endures from generation to generation.
> All the peoples of the earth
> are regarded as nothing.
> He does as he pleases
> with the powers of heaven
> and the peoples of the earth.
> No one can hold back his hand …
> everything he does is right and all his ways are just. (Dan. 4:34–35, 37)

Even this heathen king recognized that God's sovereignty ensures that whatever he plans will occur and will be good and righteous.

God's decrees are not contingency plans put into place to cover unforeseen circumstances. They reflect his eternal unchanging purposes. How could the plan of the omnipotent and omniscient God be otherwise?

Far from being a doctrine based on a few verses, the truth about God's decrees is found throughout Scripture. "This is the plan determined for the whole world ... the LORD Almighty has purposed, and who can thwart him? His hand is stretched out, and who can turn it back?" (Isa. 14:26–27; see also Job 38; Isa. 53:10; 45:5–6; Jer. 4:28; 23:18; 51:12; Acts 2:23; 4:28; Heb. 6:17).

Many objections are raised against what God has revealed about his sovereign purpose and plan. Some of these objections I will deal with later in the book. For a more comprehensive treatment of this subject go to Berkhof's *The Reformed Doctrine of Predestination.*

Rather than jettisoning a central focus on God's eternal plan—missions—because we have difficulties reconciling diverse truths, we would be wiser to heed Moses' dictum: "The secret things belong to the LORD our God, but the things revealed belong to us and to our children forever, that we may follow all the words of this law" (Deut. 29:29). We can be sure of one thing: God's sovereignty assures us of the success of missions.

God's tri-unity

The 1689 Confession defines the Trinity as follows:

> Three divine Persons constitute the Godhead—the Father, the Son (or the Word), and the Holy Spirit. They are one in substance, in power, and in eternity. Each is fully God, and yet the Godhead is one and indivisible. The Father owes His being to none. He is Father to the Son who is eternally begotten of Him. The Holy Spirit proceeds from the Father and the Son. These Persons, one infinite and eternal God not to be divided in nature or in being, are distinguished in Scripture by their personal relations within the Godhead, and by the variety of works which they undertake. Their tri-unity (that is, the doctrine of the Trinity) is the essential basis of all our fellowship with God, and of the comfort we derive from our dependence upon Him.[10]

The Father, Son and Holy Spirit have eternally enjoyed perfect fellowship within the Godhead. There is no dissatisfaction, no yearning, no hunger that leads God to seek fellowship with created men and women. He is the great "I Am." And yet, each of the persons of the Trinity expresses the divine prerogatives and purposes through intimate involvement with the missionary task.

GOD THE FATHER

The title "Father" is used in different senses in the Bible, some so general as to represent the totality of the Trinity. For example, in some Old Testament passages "Father" expresses God's covenant relationship to Israel (see Deut. 32:6; Isa. 63:16). In the New Testament it is frequently used to denote God's relationship to all his spiritual children: "Love your enemies . . . that you may be sons of your Father in heaven" (Matt. 5:44–45). As Berkhof writes, "In an entirely different sense, however, the name is applied to the first person of the Trinity in His relation to the second person."[11] "The Father loves the Son" (John 5:20).

While all members of the Trinity are equal participants in the divine plan, God the Father is more particularly the God of plan, creation and eternal love. According to Ephesians 1, the God and Father of our Lord Jesus Christ is responsible for having "[chosen] us in him before the creation of the world," "blessed us in the heavenly realms," "adopted us as his sons," and "predestined" us so that everything in our lives would work out according to his plan (Eph. 1:3–5).

The plan of redemption unfolds as things work out "in conformity with the purpose of his will" (Eph. 1:11). In the practical outworking of the Father's eternal plan, missions occupies a central role. To express no interest in missions is to display no regard for the fulfillment of the Father's eternal will.

Such lack of interest also amounts to a lack of appreciation for what God has created. As Creator of the universe, and particularly of the world in which we live, God expresses the intensity of his desire to manifest his glory. God is not like an absentee landlord or a divine clock-maker who abandons what he has created once he has spoken it into existence. He remains intimately associated with his creation. "In him we live and move and have our being" (Acts 17:28).

Indeed, although the love of the members of the Trinity for one another is infinite and unfathomable in its perfection, yet the Father has chosen to express love outside the confines of Triune fellowship. God the Father loves all creatures. He causes "his sun to rise on the evil and the good, and sends rain on the righteous and the unrighteous" (Matt. 5:45). John writes that God seeks worshipers who will "worship in spirit and in truth" (John 4:24).

The intensity of his love focuses on the elect: "In love he predestined us to be adopted as his sons through Jesus Christ" (Eph. 1:4–5). "God demonstrates his own love for us in this: While we were still sinners, Christ died for us" (Rom. 5:8). Paul informs us that nothing will be able to separate us from this love (Rom. 8:38–39). God the Father is so committed to his missionary purpose that his love for his only Son suffered in some unfathomable way when "the Son of his love" died on the cross. His holiness compelled him to turn away.

The whole elaborate plan of salvation demonstrates that God has purposed to seek fellowship with the fallen sons of Adam. He is the God who walked with Adam and Eve in the Garden. He is the God of Abraham, Isaac and Jacob. He is not only the Father of our Lord Jesus Christ, but the God and Father of all who believe. The Spirit leads us to cry, "Daddy," "Abba" (see Rom. 8:15).

The special term "Father" reflects an amazing capacity for communion with his creatures. He is not just the Almighty God or the Lord of Hosts but "Our Father who art in heaven." The word "Father" necessitates a bilateral relationship. This "father–son" relationship is not confined to that between the first and second persons of the Trinity, else he would not have revealed himself to us as "our Father." He would not have given us leave to call him "Daddy." Although God is self-sufficient, in a very real sense the infinite potentiality of his "fatherhood" would not be fulfilled without many sons being brought to glory. Missions, then, is an extension of his relational invitation to lost prodigals to come home.

Without missions the eternal plan of God the Father to create a family of brothers and sisters bearing the image of Christ cannot be fulfilled. Missions is a divinely sanctioned ministry whereby the good news of reconciliation through the blood of Christ is heralded to lost prodigals. Missions is about going into the entire world and calling on men and women to become children of God and joint heirs with Jesus Christ (Rom. 8:17).

While, logically, a consideration of missions in relationship to the Son of God would immediately follow a discussion of the role of the Father, let me postpone that until the next chapter . Instead, next consider how missions are implied by the very nature of the Holy Spirit.

GOD THE HOLY SPIRIT

Although "in the unity of the Godhead there be three persons of one substance, power, and eternity," nevertheless the personal attribute that distinguishes the Spirit is that he is "eternally proceeding from the Father and the Son."[12] The Holy Spirit, like the other members of the Godhead, remains eternally self-sufficient, yet his *procession* indicates that he moves out—reaches out beyond himself. Since missions is fundamentally outreach it would be extremely difficult to understand the operations of the Spirit if we should divorce them from missions.

In space and time, we find the Spirit continually reaching out to execute the decrees of the Father in the world. His activity toward humanity can be considered under two headings: his general benevolent activity and his particular redemptive activity.

THE SPIRIT'S GENERAL ACTIVITY

Long before we find the Spirit coming upon Mary or descending upon the disciples at Pentecost, the Spirit was active on earth. He hovered over the waters at creation (Gen. 1:2). Most probably the Spirit, as the executor of the Godhead, is the one in whom "we live and move and have our being," who "gives light to every man," who "has shown kindness by giving you rain from heaven and crops in their seasons; [and who] provides you with plenty of food and fills your hearts with joy" (Acts 17:28; John 1:9; Acts 14:17).

Berkhof writes,

> It is the special task of the Holy Spirit to bring things to completion by acting immediately upon and in the creature. Just as He Himself is the person who completes the Trinity, so His work is the completion of God's contact with His creatures and the

consummation of the work of God in every sphere ... It includes: (1) The generation of life (Gen. 1:3; Job 26:13; Ps. 33:6; Ps. 104:30). In that respect he puts the finishing touch to the work of creation. (2) The general inspiration and qualification of men ... for their official tasks, for work in science and art, etc. (Exod. 28:3; 31:2–3, 6; 35:35; 1 Sam. 11:6; 16:13–14).[13]

In the latter sense we find that the Spirit who empowered Moses with leadership ability was passed on to the seventy elders and later to Joshua (Num. 11:17; 27:18; Deut. 34:9). The Spirit came upon David (1 Sam. 16:13). The Spirit inspired and guided the prophets.

THE SPIRIT'S REDEMPTIVE ACTIVITY

We also find the Spirit striving with men to halt their slide into sin (Gen. 6:3) and moderating the effects of the Fall by restraining evil (2 Thes. 2:7). He convicts the world of sin and holiness and warns of judgment (John 16:7–8). He prepared Christ for his redemptive work—crafting a body for him, anointing him for ministry at his baptism and gifting him without measure for his ministry (Luke 1:35; Heb. 10:5–7; Luke 3:22; John 3:34).

The Spirit revealed God's Word to selected men. He inspired them to inerrantly record revealed truth (1 Cor. 2:13; 2 Peter 1:21). The Spirit prepares the way for missionary advance by predisposing men and women to see God's love in Christ (Rom. 8:22–23). He creates spiritual thirst and satisfies that thirst (John 7:37–39). He convicts sinners, regenerates the elect, indwells them, illumines the Scriptures to them, conforms them to the image of Christ, enables them to overcome temptation, produces spiritual fruit in them, comforts them and assures them of their acceptance in Christ, and gifts them for service (John 16:7–8; Titus 3:4–7; John 3:5–8; Rom. 8:9–11; Gal. 5:22–23; 1 Cor. 12:4–11). In missions, the Spirit is the vital force; "'Not by might nor by power, but by my Spirit,' says the Lord" (Zech. 4:6). He created the church at Pentecost and he continues to increase the church.

Missions cannot be conceived outside of the empowering and leading of the Holy Spirit, nor should any searching for the fullness or "baptism" of the Spirit be contemplated outside of that missionary impulse. It is a sad fact of our day that thousands of Christians seek some supposed experience of the Spirit—and claim they have received it—who have no practical interest in missions. Much of this search is navel-gazing, the selfish pursuit of some Holy Grail for the purposes, not openly admitted, of self-gratification. How sad that the Holy Spirit who is the Spirit of outreach, "eternally proceeding from the Father and the Son," should become the object of a personal agenda. In reality, the Holy Spirit is the spirit of missions.

Notes

1 Quoted in **George W. Peters,** *A Biblical Theology of Missions* (Chicago: Moody, 1972), p. 55.
2 Quoted in **Andrew Murray,** *The Key to the Missionary Problem* (Fort Washington, PA: Christian Literature Crusade, 1979), p. 30.
3 **Leona F. Choy,** ibid. p. 8.
4 **A. W. Tozer,** *The Knowledge of the Holy* (New York: Harper & Row, 1961), pp. 9, 6.
5 **Peters,** *A Biblical Theology of Missions*, p. 27.
6 *A Faith to Confess: The Baptist Confession of Faith of 1689* (rewritten in modern English; 3rd edn.; Haywards Heath, UK: Carey Publications, 1979), p. 19.
7 **L. Berkhof,** *Systematic Theology* (Grand Rapids, MI: Eerdmans, 1968), p. 71.
8 *The Shorter Catechism of the Westminster Assembly* (Philadelphia: Great Commission Publications [n.d.]), answer to question 7, p. 4.
9 Ibid. p. 102.
10 *A Faith to Confess*, p. 19.
11 **Berkhof,** *Systematic Theology*, p. 91.
12 The Westminster Confession of Faith, chapter 2, part 3.
13 **Berkhof,** *Systematic Theology*, p. 99.

Missions and God the Son

In the light of the perfect communion enjoyed by the Son of God with the Father and with the Spirit, we must ask ourselves why the eternal Son would choose to leave the Father's presence and be born of Mary? The answer can only be, "Because redemption (and its missionary proclamation) is central in the plan of God."

W. O. Carver defines missions as "the extensive realisation of God's redemptive purpose in Christ Jesus by means of human messengers."[1] The name announced by the angel to Joseph enshrines Christ's mission: "you are to give him the name Jesus, because he will save his people from their sins" (Matt. 1:21). Jesus stated clearly that he came "to give his life as a ransom for many" (Mark 10:45). He assured Zacchaeus, "For the Son of Man came to seek and to save what was lost" (Luke 19:10).

Clearly the incarnation was a missionary journey undertaken by the Son of God for the purpose of saving lost men and women by giving his life as their ransom. We need not get into a discussion here on limited atonement. His atonement is sufficient for all but efficient only for the elect.

His mission included not only the salvation of sinners from hell, but also the enrichment of saved sinners so they might enjoy a measure of the communion experienced within the Godhead. In his high-priestly prayer in John 17, Christ talked of glorifying the Father through giving "eternal life to all those you have given him" (John 17:2). This eternal life involves, as Christ expressed it, coming to know the Father and the Son in such a way that they enjoy real communion with God, "in order that the love you have for me may be in them and that I myself may be in them" (John 17:26). Astounding!

From start to finish the coming of Christ was a missionary event. Christmas is a missionary celebration—commemorating the initiation of the Son's earthly mission. Good Friday and Easter memorialize the basis upon which missions will triumph—the historical events that became the essential content of the missionary message. The Ascension and Session celebrate Christ's assumption of his throne. From this position of authority, he directs history irrevocably toward its missionary culmination. "And this gospel of the kingdom will be preached in the whole world as a testimony to all nations, and then the end will come" (Matt. 24:14). Luke implies that, while the Gospels record "what Jesus *began* to do and to teach," Acts records the start of what Jesus *continues* to do (Acts 1:1). Missions is the continuing activity of the Son of God!

At Pentecost he gave birth to the church in the wind and fire of a multi-ethnic, linguistic miracle. The Holy Spirit enabled the apostles to speak in the languages of the people present at that time in Jerusalem. Pentecost is not about personal power—it is a church-planting missionary event. Acts goes on to describe the extension of the Kingdom from the mono-ethnic Jewish culture into the Samaritan, Greek and Roman world.

The names of Christ

The centrality of missions is also reflected in the names of Christ, names that mirror his commitment to reach lost men and women. The Son of God loved to be called the *Son of Man* because this highlighted his identification with those he came to save. *Emmanuel* emphasizes his incarnational journey; God came and dwelt among us. *Jesus* underscores his mission to "save his people from their sins." *Lord* reflects his management of the universe. *Lamb* reveals the atoning role he played in securing redemption. *Master* and *Shepherd* further define his task in terms of giving to lost and foolish men and women the teaching and guidance they need under an umbrella of cosmic authority. He is the universal King of kings and Lord of lords.

The "I am"s

The "I am"s of Christ illustrate how committed Christ is to reaching the lost and how desperately people from every tribe and tongue and nation need the ministry of the Master. By declaring himself to be *the way*, Christ reveals that people can only be saved by rejecting other paths and following the path he has prepared for their salvation. As *the truth* he represents what people must know to be saved. As *the door* he is the only way to enter heaven. As the *resurrection and the life* he alone can breathe new spiritual life into dead sinners. As the *living water*, he alone can quench spiritual thirst, and as the *bread of life*, he alone can sate spiritual hunger. As the *Shepherd* he alone provides, protects and cares for foolish straying humans. As the *light of the world* he has a universal mission to bring spiritual comprehension to eyes blinded by the darkness of this world's selfishness and lust. The "I am"s demonstrate how inseparably missions is woven into the life and teaching of Christ.

Christ the missionary model

The descent of Christ into our midst illustrates outreach in its truest form. In the version of the Great Commission found in John's Gospel, Jesus commands all his followers to demonstrate in their service an outreach model based on his relationship to the Father: "As the Father has sent me, I am sending you" (John 20:21). The way Christ came into the world is the way we should go among the nations. While on earth he showed us how to act. Consider some of the ways he demonstrated model missionary work.

BEING SENT BY GOD

In John's Gospel we find Christ referring thirty-two times to the fact that the Father sent him. For example, "As long as it is day, we must do the work of him who sent me. Night is coming , when no one can work" (John 9:4. The work, of course, is gospel proclamation with the goal of reaping an eternal harvest—in a word, missions. See also 5:24, 37; 6:40, 44; 7:28–29). Missionaries, according to the root meaning of the word, are "sent ones"—not those who make a calculated career move or desire adventure.

God sent his only Son into the world. God sent John the Baptizer to preach repentance. Christ sent out the Twelve and then the Seventy on missionary journeys. He did not stop sending when he ascended! Today he continues to send men and women to the nations with the gospel (John 1:33; 3:28; 20:21). God is the one who initiates the genuine missionary impulse.

A CALLING ROOTED IN SUBMISSION TO THE FATHER'S WILL: OBEDIENCE

Ongoing submission to God's will authenticates the initial call (Rom. 12:1–2). Jesus said, "My food is to do the will of him who sent me and to finish his work" (John 4:34). "I always do what pleases him [the Father]" (John 8:29). Even when facing death he responded, "... not my will, but yours be done" (Luke 22:42).

Christ modeled for us the open and obedient attitude toward the

Father's will that must characterize all missionary activity. Every step is to be taken with a prayerful sensitivity to the desires of the Father. This will mean devotion to prayer and a careful search of the Scriptures at every juncture. "Jesus often withdrew to lonely places and prayed" (Luke 5:16). Without thoughtful prayer on a continuing basis, even the most valid missionary organization may become a fossilized institution.

A CALLING TOTALLY VOLUNTARY

Although Christ was sent by the Father and continued to do what pleased the Father, yet whatever he did, he did voluntarily. The Father did not compel him to come to earth or force him to die for our sins. In describing the difference between his ministry and that of a hireling among sheep Christ said, "The reason the Father loves me is that I lay down my life—only to take it up again. No one takes it from me, but I lay it down of my own accord. I have authority to lay it down and authority to take it up again" (John 10:17–18). While no one has the freedom Christ had, missionary work is meant to be voluntary. Compulsion, manipulation or pressure must never be used.

In Philippians 2 the attitude of Christ is the model of missionary volunteerism: "Your attitude should be the same as that of Christ Jesus: Who, being in very nature God, did not consider equality with God something to be grasped [clung to], but [voluntarily] made himself nothing ... being made in human likeness" (Phil. 2:5–7).

Christ emptied himself by leaving behind, in some mysterious way, the conscious enjoyment of his divine prerogatives to adopt servanthood. While this passage continues to perplex scholars, at the very least it must reflect the way Christ voluntarily surrendered the independent exercise of his divine attributes and muted his enjoyment of Triune fellowship. As the Son of Man the intensity of his fellowship with other members of the Godhead must have been masked in some way. Without voluntarily leaving behind this divine privilege, he could hardly have identified with mankind in a genuine way.

A LEAVING OF ONE'S OWN PEOPLE

Clearly, the Son of God did not cease to be God but he did become man. In a similar way, missionaries, when they leave home, don't stop being citizens of their home country, nor do they stop being members of the family they were born into. Missionary activity, however, does involve a leaving behind of one's kith and kin. Missionary service requires a voluntary muting of one's ethnic or national pride. The mission field is no place to brag about London or Toronto. One should also note that this leaving behind of what is familiar and friendly usually means that missionaries must be ready to embrace loneliness.

A HUMBLE ADOPTION OF THE SERVANT ROLE

Although Christ had a perfect right to express his superiority over all creatures by virtue of his deity, he voluntarily masked his equality with God. He was born into a human family and grew up to become a servant. As a servant, Jesus washed the disciples' feet—and told them to do likewise. He went further; he "humbled himself and became obedient to death—even death on a cross!" (Phil. 2:8).

Paul calls upon us to "Do nothing out of selfish ambition or vain conceit, but in humility consider others better than yourselves" (Phil. 2:3). Missionaries have not always resisted the temptation to parade their imagined (or real) superiority. Paternalistic imperialism dogged the footsteps of colonial missionaries, many of whom went out with the "white man's burden to civilize" more than the Master's burden to win the lost. Genuine missionary ministry requires a humble setting aside of any sense of cultural, educational, technological or economic superiority.

AN IDENTIFICATION WITH ANOTHER PEOPLE

Christ identified with us, "being made in human likeness. And being found in appearance as a man ..." (Phil. 2:7–8). "The Word became flesh and made his dwelling among us" (John 1:14). His identification was so extensive that the book of Hebrews states that he has been "tempted in every way, just as we are—yet ... without sin." The extent of his identification enabled him to "sympathize with our weaknesses" (Heb. 4:15).

COMPASSION

The book of Hebrews explains Christ's ability to understand our frailties and identify with our weaknesses and temptations by referring to the way he incarnated himself in our midst (see Heb. 4:14–5:10). His identification fostered real sympathy and compassion. "When he saw the crowds, he had compassion on them, because they were harassed and helpless, like sheep without a shepherd" (Matt. 9:36). His compassion moved him to heal the sick, teach needful truths, feed the hungry, give sight to the blind and comfort the grieving (Matt. 14:14; Mark 6:34; Matt. 15:32; 20:34; Luke 7:13). His parables frequently illustrated the importance of compassion. Without compassion missionary work is merely work.

SACRIFICE

Missions involves sacrifice. In the course of preparing his disciples to carry on his mission, the Lord spoke of his coming death and their own suffering. He urged them not to be ashamed of him and his words. "If anyone would come after me, he must deny himself and take up his cross daily and follow me. For whoever wants to save his life will lose it, but whoever loses his life for me will save it" (Luke 9:23–24). Here too Christ preeminently led the way. He set his face to go up to Jerusalem even though he knew it meant death; "he humbled himself and became obedient to death—even death on a cross!" (Phil. 2:8). A twentieth-century missionary martyr accurately applied this concept to his own life: "If Christ died for me, then no sacrifice I make for him can be too great."[2]

COMMUNICATION

The central activity of missions is the communication of the gospel. Although Christ healed, cast out demons, raised the dead and fed the hungry, these activities gave way more and more in his second and third years of ministry to teaching. Indeed, the Spirit revealed to John at the beginning of his Gospel that communication was so central to the mission of Christ that one of Christ's most important names is "Word." "In the beginning was the Word, and the Word was with God, and the Word was God ... The Word became flesh and made his dwelling among us" (John 1:1, 14). How can we explain the mystery of the eternal *logos* without admitting that God has been eternally committed to communication—and that this communication centers on the incarnate Christ?

Missionary activity that fails to focus on, or support in some way, the proclamation of the gospel fails to be missionary. Philanthropy, perhaps; missions, no.

DIRECTED FOCUS ON A LIMITED GROUP

What puzzles many about the ministry of Christ are his statements about being called to reach the lost sheep of Israel (e.g. Matt. 15:24). In these sayings he actually models another crucial aspect of missionary strategy. Although his vision was universal, his earthly ministry was largely confined to Judea and Galilee. At the beginning of this ministry, he forbade his disciples from going beyond the confines of Israel (Matt. 10:5–6; 15:24; 10:5–6). Even after his resurrection, when he commissioned them to reach the world, he mentioned stages: Jerusalem, Judea, Samaria.

So today, missionary church planters, while they retain a vision of reaching the world for Christ, must learn to confine their activities to one culture, or fail as missionaries. To try to do more, with rare exceptions, is to fail to establish deeply rooted, culturally sensitive churches able to disciple converts and evangelize the people in a particular linguistic and cultural grouping. Any person who is so caught up by a vision of reaching the whole world for Christ that he or she races off in a hundred different directions cannot but produce a shallow result. Missions, while universal in scope, is particularistic in practice.

Jesus focused his ministry on Israel. This was practical and wise. Of course, he also came at a transitional period of history. He was the Messiah, the expected fulfillment of Old Testament prophecy. He kept the law. He fulfilled the Old Testament Mosaic code to prepare the way for Gentiles to become part of the family of God. As the fulcrum of history, he led the people of God to abandon the Jerusalem-centered approach of calling on the nations to come there for salvation. This centripetal method, intrinsic to Old Testament history, was replaced by a centrifugal method—going out to the ends of the earth to reach the lost.[3]

UNIVERSAL IN VISION

Although Christ largely confined his ministry to Israel, his teaching and actions abundantly heralded the universal nature of his mission. He ministered to the Samaritan woman and the people of Samaria, the Canaanite woman, the Roman centurion of Capernaum, the Gaderene and the deaf man of Decapolis (John 4:1–42; Matt. 15:21–28; Matt. 8:5–13; Mark 5:1–20; 7:31–37). Angels announced his birth as "good news of great joy that will be for all the people" (Luke 2:10). Simeon praised God, saying that the child in his arms was "a light for revelation to the Gentiles and for glory to your people Israel" (Luke 2:32). John the Baptizer declared that he was "the Lamb of God, who takes away the sin of the world" (John 1:29).

ALLUSIONS BY CHRIST TO HIS WORLDWIDE MISSION

Christ alluded to the universal scope of his mission in many ways. He said that the temple "will be called a house of prayer for all nations" (Mark 11:17). He called believers "the salt of the earth … the light of the world" (Matt. 5:13–14). In his model prayer we are taught to pray, "your will be done on earth as it is in heaven" (Matt. 6:10). He specifically predicted that Gentiles would overtake Jews in the Kingdom (Matt. 21:43; Luke 13:28–29). Parables indicate that the field is the world (Matt. 13:36–43; 21:28–32). John multiplies references to the *kosmos* as the focus of God's love and the target of Christ's mission (John 1:9, 29; 3:16–17, 19; 4:42; 6:33; 12:47; 16:8; 17:21). Jesus said, "I am the light of the world" (John 8:12; see also 9:5; 12:46).

The Great Commission explicitly puts world missions on the front burner for this whole age (see Matt. 28:19–20; Mark 16:15; Luke 24:47–48; John 20:21; Acts 1:8). We will look at this specific mandate in more detail later.

We have seen how missions is illustrated by the activity of the Triune God—particularly by the commitment of the incarnate Christ to the worldwide missionary purpose of God. Let us turn next to the missionary vision of the biblical text itself.

Notes

1 Quoted in **George W. Peters,** *A Biblical Theology of Missions* (Chicago: Moody, 1972), p. 26.

2 C. T. Studd.

3 See **Peters,** *A Biblical Theology of Missions*, p. 23.

Missions in the Old Testament

The Bible reveals a God whose concerns are universal in scope. The early chapters of Genesis establish this fact. The rest of the Old Testament, however, focuses the cosmic purpose of God on one nation in order to prepare the way for the coming of the Messiah. The final book, Revelation, predicts the climax of history in terms of the defeat of evil and the worship of people from every tongue and tribe and nation around the throne of God. History is linear—moving toward its culmination. The missionary impulse is its driving force.

Biblical universalism

By "biblical universalism" I do not mean the sense defined by Webster: "the theological doctrine that all souls will eventually find salvation in God."[1] This kind of liberal theology, far from inspiring missionary work, cuts the nerve of missionary passion. Why reach the world for Christ if all people will eventually be saved anyway?

Biblical universalism, as defined by George Peters, "connotes that God's purpose is comprehensive rather than particularistic, including the total human race rather than being national or merely individual."[2] On the surface this could be disputed. After all, does not the Old Testament largely deal with one nation, the nation of Israel? Is the Old Testament a missionary backwater—a historical footnote? We cannot dispute that God had a purpose for the nation of Israel, but that this purpose was universal and not particularistic has been widely misunderstood, or de-emphasized. In the pages ahead we will ponder this seeming paradox. But whatever we may find from Genesis 12 to Malachi, the universal scope of God's redemptive purpose is clearly seen in the first eleven chapters of Genesis.

Genesis 1–11

CREATION

"In the beginning God created the heavens and the earth" (Gen. 1:1). The creation of a universe establishes the fact that God has determined to express his purpose in something external to himself. And the result of God's creative genius became the object of God's comprehensive care through his ongoing providence.

Although the entire universe mirrors God's creativity, only mankind reflects his image. "So God created man in his own image, in the image of God, he created him" (1:27). The *imago dei* comprises the human capacity to reason, decide, feel, communicate and relate in the context of "righteousness and true holiness."[3] Since God delegated to his image-bearers the responsibility to demonstrate creative initiative in caring for the earth's resources, that image must also include mankind's creativity and leadership potential. This astounding "image" that all men and women possess demonstrates God's concern and care for the whole human race.

THE INVASION OF EVIL

Upon the cataclysmic Fall of Adam and Eve, sin invaded the human race as a dynamic toxin that destroyed their relationship with God and doomed their posterity: "... sin entered the world through one man, and death through sin, and in this way death came to all men, because all sinned" (Rom. 5:12); "... in Adam all die" (1 Cor. 15:22).

The toxicity of sin is so virulent that every human being born since the Fall is infected with evil. Since all of us live our lives "dead in [our] transgressions and sins ... disobedient ... gratifying the cravings of our sinful nature and following its desires and thoughts ... by nature objects of wrath" (Eph. 2:1–3), we have no hope unless God initiates a rescue operation—in a word, missions.

Fortunately, even in the midst of Adam's shattered righteousness, God proclaimed the *protoevangelium* which promised in shadowy form a scheme of redemption: "And I will put enmity between you and the woman, and between your offspring and hers; he will crush your head, and you will strike his heel" (Gen. 3:15). Peters finds six facts about the outworking of God's redemptive plan in this prophecy: (1) Salvation is God-wrought; (2) Evil is neither permanent nor inevitable. Satan's scourge will be destroyed. (3) Victory over Satan will affect all mankind. (4) "Salvation will come through a mediator who, in an organic way, is related to mankind. He is the seed of the woman." (5) Salvation will involve the suffering of the redeemer, the "striking of the heel" of this seed. (6) Salvation will be experienced in history, just as the Fall occurred in space and time.[4]

Throughout history there will be those who are related to the woman, her "offspring," who struggle with the "offspring" of Satan. This cosmic conflict between good and evil, between the children of God and the children of the devil, defines much that unfolds in history. Because of missions' avowed purpose of restoring those who have fallen to renewed fellowship with God, missionary activity became one of the most hated targets of Satan. Just as the national redemption of God's chosen people remained the focus of fiery opposition in the Old Testament, so the church continues as this target. Wherever church planting is promoted, Satan will rage.

THE EVOLUTION OF SIN

Genesis 4 and 5 describe the progressive intensification of evil from disobedience to outright rebellion. Eve's unbelief encourages Adam's disobedience. Cain's carelessness about worship degenerates into jealousy, anger, hatred and, ultimately, fratricide. The solitary murder of Abel promotes brutality and escalates into the serial murder of Lamech. The marital fidelity of Adam degenerates into the polygamy of Lamech.

Chapter 6 begins with an assessment of human degradation: "The LORD saw how great man's wickedness on the earth had become, and that every inclination of the thoughts of his heart was only evil all the time" (Gen. 6:5); a description of lust and immorality on a huge scale.

Genesis continues to unfold the sorry saga of human brutality, polygamy, incest, intemperance, immodesty, rebellion and idolatry. The descriptions of universal sin found in these early chapters of Genesis, and filled out as the Bible develops, provide the dark backdrop against which the bright hues of God's redemptive activity shine. This contrast throws into stark relief the need for an emergency missionary rescue operation.

JUDGMENT ON SIN

The urgency of this need is further heightened by the righteous judgment of God manifest in the flood described in chapters 6 through 8. Clearly, human sinfulness throws mankind into imminent danger of judgment. The biblical text makes clear that "Every living thing on the face of the earth was wiped out" (Gen. 7:23).

The flood again brings us face to face with the universality of God's purposes. It typifies the danger of judgment that all face from the righteous wrath of God. Although God has promised never again to send a universal flood, a cataclysm of fire is predicted for the end of time. Just as Noah warned the people of his day about the judgment to come, so must missionaries take this warning to the ends of the earth.

A COVENANT WITH NOAH

Not only was the judgment universal in its scope, but the covenant God made afterward with Noah was comprehensive as well. The rainbow is an "everlasting covenant between God and all living creatures of every kind on the earth ... all life on the earth" (Gen. 9:16–17). How may that promise be known without missions?

Unfortunately, Genesis 9 also describes the revival of sin in Noah's family. Noah becomes drunk and immodest. His son Ham uses this occasion to titillate his fallen pornographic instincts (see Gen. 9:18–28). This episode reminds us that periodic judgments of an earthly nature cannot eradicate or restrain sin. Sin is internal and must be dealt with by an internal remedy—which came in the missionary gospel.

NATIONS AND LANGUAGES

Chapter 10 describes a diversity of nations, while chapter 11 records the lengths to which their inventive pride takes them in building alternative structures of worship. (Towers were used in Mesopotamia to view the stars, which were objects of worship.) The resulting dispersion of peoples into competitive language groups ensures that the spread of sin will be somewhat contained.

Although learning another language is a tedious part of missionary work, the reality of multiplied languages has been a divine mercy designed to inhibit the virulence of evil. It ensures that one group of people can be isolated from the evil in another group. Imagine a world in which no ethnic or linguistic barriers existed to stem the flow of moral filth. When the evil unite, the good suffer. Today we see serious breaches in the dikes that stem the spread of moral pollution. The information age and the spread of English as a language of communication may promote world trade but they also promote the spread of evil.

The first eleven chapters of Genesis therefore introduce us to the universality of God's concern for his creation. In Genesis 12 he begins to narrow his work of redemption through the appointment of a special people. But first he reiterates the worldwide scope of his redemptive plan.

Israel, God's chosen people

From Genesis 12 to the end of the Old Testament, God seems to turn from his universalism to exhibit favoritism toward one nation, Israel. How can this narrowing of his focus further his broader goals? The content of the covenant introduced in chapter 12 introduces the answer. His concern for a lost world is furthered through choosing a man and his descendants to become the focused vessel of redemptive outreach.

ABRAHAMIC COVENANT

Abraham obeyed God's call to leave behind his pagan nation, his people and his family in order to go to an unknown land where he would become the father of a great nation. The covenant God established with Abraham contained the promise of a land peopled by an abundant population. But at the very end of the covenant statement God appended words that would be fulfilled sometime after Christ came. He said, "and all peoples on earth will be blessed through you" (Gen. 12:3). These words of universal promise are repeated four more times (Gen. 18:18; 22:18; 26:4–5; 28:14). This repetition signals God's intent to use the nation that would be raised up from Abraham to become a blessing to all the ethnic peoples of the earth.

What is the "blessing"? It can only be understood as a gospel blessing. The saving relationship that God gave to Abraham through his justifying faith would become available to all nations through the gospel. This could only be accomplished through the seed of the woman (Gen. 3), the seed of Abraham (Gen. 12), that is, the Messiah. "All peoples" clearly foreshadows "every tongue and tribe and nation" that becomes, in the New Testament, the target of missionary outreach.

ISRAEL AND GOD'S MULTI-ETHNIC PURPOSE

That God had a purpose for Israel larger than the confines of the nation itself is clear from many texts, besides those that describe the Abrahamic covenant. In Exodus 19 God declares, "Now if you obey me fully and keep my covenant, then out of all nations you will be my treasured possession. Although the whole earth is mine, you will be for me a kingdom of priests and a holy nation" (vv. 5–6). Holiness would prepare the nation to be God's ambassadors to the whole earth.

Priests occupied a mediatorial role between God and other people. The whole nation was to exhibit, through its holy worship, this priestly or mediatorial function. They were to be the vehicle through which God would call the nations to worship and obedience and shower them with blessings.

In Deuteronomy 26:19 we read, "... he will set you in praise, fame and honor high above all the nations." The nations would then see the exaltation of Israel and be attracted. When they came to search for the reason for Israel's greatness they would discover a theocracy with God at the center. This very thing occurred when the queen of Sheba came to Jerusalem to inquire of Solomon's wisdom. It would have happened many times over if Israel had become a consistent demonstration of God's holiness and redemptive love. Unfortunately, the paganism of surrounding nations acted more as a magnet to Israel than its covenant position with God acted as a magnet to the nations.

Nevertheless, many of Israel's leaders recognized their missionary role. They often based their appeal for God's help on the possibility of God's glory being diminished by Israel's defeat. Moses, for example, prayed in the wilderness for God to stay his hand of judgment lest Israel perish: "... then the nations which have heard of Your fame will speak, saying, 'Because the LORD was not able to bring this people to the land which he swore to give them, therefore He killed them in the wilderness'" (Num. 14:16, NKJV; see also Exod. 32:12; Deut. 9:28; Josh. 7:9). Isaiah prays, "Now therefore, O LORD our God, save us from his hand, that all the kingdoms of the earth may know that You are the LORD, You alone" (Isa. 37:20, NKJV). Clearly what happened to Israel affected the impact of God's Word on pagan nations.

ISRAEL AS A DIVINE COUNTER-CULTURE

The relentless and lightning spread of evil following the Fall and again after the flood necessitated the establishment of an island of righteousness in a sea of depravity. With paganism and idolatry pervading the earth in the time of Abraham, God established a "divine counter-culture designed both to arrest evil and unfold the gracious plan, salvation and purpose of God."[5]

It makes pragmatic sense, when faced with widespread spiritual apostasy, to choose one place, one person or one town in which to establish a beachhead. This is exactly what God did in choosing Abraham and establishing a covenant nation with a unique set of laws. By doing so, God demonstrated ideal missionary strategy—the need to concentrate effort and avoid being distracted by a thousand evils crying out for correction.

ISRAEL'S UNIQUE RELIGION

Israel was to serve as a beacon of moral and religious strength. In a polytheistic world full of idols, they bore witness to the one true God, the self-sufficient I AM. God is no local deity. He is the Creator and Sustainer of the universe, sovereign in glory and power. He manifested his presence in their midst in the Shekinah glory and in the pillar of cloud and fire. He smote the rock and divided the Red Sea; he stopped the sun in its tracks and fed his people manna. The tabernacle in the midst of the camp illustrated the centrality of Jehovah's worship in Israel. The layout of the camp and later, of the city of Jerusalem, symbolized "God in the midst."

Surrounded by loose and licentious nations whose worship involved prostitution, Israel bore witness to an elevated moral code delivered by divine revelation. The Decalogue and allied statutes of a social and ceremonial nature reflected unparalleled religious insights backed up by rigid penalties and broad promises.

The revelation given to Israel came to no other nation. To them alone he revealed his creative majesty and his righteous will. He spoke to patriarchs and to prophets, to kings and to warriors. The Old Testament collection of these revelations stands unique among the nations of history.

ISRAEL AS A DEMONSTRATION OF HUMAN IMPOTENCE

Israel is also a historical demonstration of the impotence of every human avenue of salvation. Although the people of Israel enjoyed privileges bestowed on no other nation, they repeatedly reverted to human schemes of redemption. They failed every time!

The rescue of Israel through the miraculous intervention of God in Egypt ultimately did little to reform the nation. Rather it became a bright backdrop against which their rebellion stood out in stark relief. Numbers tells the sordid story of their grumbling and rebellion. Miracles failed to save them. Peerless leadership on the part of Moses was not enough. A body of amazing laws and regulations proved fruitless. Visible manifestations of God failed to save them. Amazing provision of their needs proved inadequate to move them to unswerving devotion.

Even when they achieved miraculous victory over the Canaanites and inherited a prosperous land, the Israelites failed to walk with God in holiness. Judges records the repeated cycle of sin and rebellion.

Even under great kings like David, Solomon, Hezekiah and Josiah, depravity was not contained.

Suffering and persecution failed to purify them. Their repeated sufferings under the Philistines, the Syrians, the Assyrians, the Babylonians and others did not purge them of evil. Israel became a cesspool of iniquity, a sponge absorbing the evils of surrounding nations.

The history of Israel in the Old Testament is a historical parable meant to teach us the impotence of anything but the sacrifice of Christ. Politics, ethics, social uplift, miracles, good leadership, poverty and persecution cannot produce changed hearts. Only a new heart produced by the Spirit, as foreseen in Ezekiel and other prophets, can break the power of human depravity. In a sense, the history of Israel demonstrated to all the surrounding nations that salvation could only come through the gracious provision of sacrificial atonement. In the same way the church should demonstrate that only the atoning blood of Christ can arrest the depraved slide of a sinner.

Israel demonstrated in concrete terms the universal need of missionary outreach. Sociologically and politically, the nations have no hope. Wars will never cease. Greed will not be satisfied. Violence will not stop. The only hope of the world is in the transformation of individuals from the inside out through the salvation that Christ alone can give.

ISRAEL AND DIVINE SOVEREIGNTY

Not only does the Old Testament demonstrate the hopelessness of human solutions, it also illustrates the thrilling way God fulfills his purposes. Modern missionaries under the stress of government fiat, municipal corruption or legislated oppression can find in its pages a God who laughs at impossibilities.

Hope shines from the pages of the Old Testament wherever we turn. Whether we consider the hundred-year task of Noah or the hundred-year body of Abraham, the slavery of Joseph or the inadequacy of Moses, we discover the triumph of Jehovah. From the Garden of Eden to the palaces of Persia, Satan weaves an evil web—a web, however, that is blown away by the wind of God. Hebrews 11 catalogues the glittering story of triumph through faith in a God who can use storm or sea, snakes or stones to accomplish his sovereign will. Nothing can stay his hand.

Jehoshaphat faced a vast army and yet exulted, "O LORD, God of our fathers, are you not the God who is in heaven? You rule over all the kingdoms of the nations. Power and might are in your hand, and no one can withstand you ... We do not know what to do, but our eyes are upon you" (2 Chr. 20:6, 12).

We've already alluded to the humbling and transformation of King Nebuchadnezzar, the mightiest king of his time (Dan. 4:34–35).

Further Old Testament missionary texts

MOSAIC PERIOD

The specific provision in the law for the acceptance of the alien demonstrates God's universal love. Although the people of Israel became proud of their own ethnicity they were exhorted from the beginning, "Do not mistreat an alien or oppress him, for you were aliens in Egypt" (Exod. 22:21).

Israel was reminded that "the LORD your God is God of gods and Lord of lords, the great God, mighty and awesome, who shows no partiality and accepts no bribes. He defends the cause of the fatherless and the widow, and loves the alien, giving him food and clothing. And you are to love those who are aliens, for you yourselves were aliens in Egypt" (Deut. 10:17–19).

According to Deuteronomy 29:11, the alien was to be included in the terms of the covenant.

DAVIDIC PERIOD

The book of Psalms contains at least 175 references to the universal implications of God's unfolding plan. See especially Psalms 2, 33, 66, 67, 72, 86, 98, 117, 145.

Solomon's understanding that God had a purpose far beyond the scope of his own nation is clear from his prayer at the dedication of the temple:

> As for the foreigner who does not belong to your people Israel but has come from a distant land because of your name—for men will hear of your great name and your mighty hand and your outstretched arm—when he comes and prays toward this temple, then hear from heaven, your dwelling place, and do whatever the foreigner asks of you, so that all the peoples of the earth may know your name and fear you, as do your own people Israel, and may know that this house I have built bears your Name.
>
> (1 Kings 8:41–43)

Solomon describes what George Peters terms "the centripetal method." According to this missionary method, God used the happenings and testimony of Israel to attract the nations to Jerusalem, that they might be saved by joining with God's covenant people there (2 Chr. 6:32–33). The law made provision for aliens to be covered by the covenant through undergoing the rite of circumcision. Compare Exodus 12:48 with Numbers 9:14.

Solomon concludes his great prayer by mentioning what he perceives to be the missionary purpose given by God to Israel: "so that all the peoples of the earth may know that the LORD is God and that there is no other" (1 Kings 8:60).

PERIOD OF THE KINGS

Throughout this period there are unusual stories of God's interest in the nations. A foreign widow cares for Elijah. The priests of Baal are confronted. The Syrian commander Naaman is healed of leprosy.

PROPHETIC TEXTS

As the prophets begin to turn the eyes of Israel toward the future hope of a Messiah, the role of the nations becomes more prominent. The prophets reveal that God is the God of the nations, not just the God of Israel. Nebuchadnezzar is God's servant (Jer. 25:9; 27:6; 43:10). Cyrus is his shepherd and his anointed (Isa. 44:28–45:13). The Assyrian is the rod of his anger and the staff in his hand (Isa. 10:5). The kings of the Medes are his battle-axe and weapons of war to destroy Babylon (Jer. 51:11, 20).

God is repeatedly portrayed as the God who will judge the nations. Isaiah, for example, contains a large section (from chapters 13 to 23) dealing with the coming judgment of Babylon, Moab, Syria, Cush, Egypt and Tyre. Amos repeats the refrain, "for three sins of ... even for four, I will not turn back my wrath" in warning Syria, Gaza, Tyre, Ammon, Moab, Judah and Israel of coming judgment (see Amos 1:3–2:3). Each of the major prophets has a large section devoted to the nations (see Isa. 10:5–34; 13:1–23:18; Jer. 42–51; Ezek. 25–32; 38–39; and most of Daniel). Obadiah's whole prophecy concerns Edom (see also Obad. v. 1).

Many specific texts also portray the Messianic hope in multi-ethnic, universal terms: "In the last days ... Many peoples will come and say, 'Come, let us go up to the mountain of the LORD, to the house of the God of Jacob. He will teach us his ways, so that we may walk in his paths'" (Isa. 2:2–3); "the earth will be full of the knowledge of the LORD as the waters cover the sea. In that day the Root of Jesse will stand as a banner for the peoples; the nations will rally to him" (Isa. 11:9–10); "And afterward, I will pour out my Spirit on all people" (Joel 2:28); "My name will be great among the nations, from the rising to the setting of the sun" (Mal. 1:11). Jonah especially illustrates God's compassion for the nations (see also Joel 3:9, 11–12; Isa. 43:21; 49:2; etc.).

Clearly, the Old Testament lays a solid foundation for the superstructure of New Testament missionary concern.

Notes

1 **David B. Guralnik,** (Gen. ed.), *Webster's New World Dictionary of the American Language* (New York: Avenal Books, 1978), p. 818.

2 **George W. Peters,** *A Biblical Theology of Missions* (Chicago: Moody, 1972), p. 20.

3 *A Faith to Confess: The Baptist Confession of Faith of 1689* (rewritten in modern English; 3rd edn.; Haywards Heath, UK: Carey Publications, 1979), 4:2, p. 22.

4 Ibid. pp. 85–86.

5 Ibid. p. 90.

Missionary preparation in the intertestamental period

The bulk of the Old Testament concerns the establishment of, and God's dealings with, one nation, Israel. This exclusivity, however, served as a beacon designed to draw the nations to Jerusalem. Light in Israel failed as the nation repeatedly corrupted its theology and practice through introducing paganism. The nation split into two and finally both were conquered and dragged into captivity. Throughout this period of Jewish missionary failure, the prophets warned of judgment and promised a renewal. A rising crescendo of prophetic hope focused on a coming day when all peoples would be blessed through the Messiah.

Long before that day dawned God providentially prepared the way for the coming of Messiah. The Assyrian and Babylonian captivities scattered Israel. In this way God seeded the nations with Jewish theistic ideas and dreams. Only 42,000 Jews returned from captivity during the time of Ezra and Nehemiah (see Ezra 2:64; Neh. 7:66). Vast numbers of Jews of the Diaspora remained in Persia and ultimately spread to many other countries of the Mediterranean world. Wherever the apostolic missionaries traveled, they found synagogues. Where Jews settled, "There arose circles of proselytes who, for the most part, did not permit themselves to be circumcised, yet held to the Jewish law and sent their gifts to Jerusalem ... such are mentioned as worshipers of God."[1] As the apostles later discovered, God had been preparing an audience for their preaching.

Bavinck points out that, while many Greeks and Romans misunderstood Jews and held them in contempt, others were powerfully impressed by their strong monotheism, high moral ethics and the cohesiveness of their communities. Their spiritual concept of God and the teaching of the Old Testament which had been translated into Greek, as the Septuagint, made an impact on a number of pagan philosophers. "Judaism was a legitimate religion within the Roman Empire. A Jew enjoyed many civic advantages. The Jews who lived in the cities had a sort of government of their own and were states within the state."[2]

God not only set up centers of Old Testament witness with a predisposition to listen to the coming Hebrew evangelists, he also prepared a cultural climate conducive to missionary advance. Adolf Harnack lists a number of first-century conditions that aided the spread of the Christian faith. Howard Snyder places them alongside modern parallels and points out how strategic is the age in which we now live: "Some of the parallels with today's conditions are striking, particularly when Harnack speaks of 'blending of different nationalities,' 'the comparative unity of language and ideas,' and especially, 'the rising vogue of a mystical philosophy of religion with a craving for some form of revelation and a thirst for miracle.'"[3]

During the period leading up to the New Testament, Roman power enforced Pax Romana throughout the empire. Peace promoted trade and paved the way for ease of travel and communication. The system of Roman roads (52,000 miles of them according to one estimate) further expedited travel. The Greek language predominated as a lingua franca throughout the empire. In these ways God prepared for the early missionaries to bypass the often painful and lengthy process of linguistic and cultural assimilation.

Snyder writes that it was a time of

> pervasive social change, with a tendency toward a humanizing, universalist, "one world" outlook; a feeling that mankind is essentially one and shares a common destiny. A broad movement of men and ideas tends to unravel the fabric of tradition and produce social change ... Ancient life had by this time begun to break up; its solid foundations had begun to weaken ... The idea of universal humanity had disengaged itself from that of nationality. The Stoics had passed the word that all men were equal, and had spoken of brotherhood as well as the duties of man toward man. Hitherto despised, the lower classes had asserted their position. The treatment of slaves became milder ... Women, hitherto without any legal rights, received such in increasing numbers. Children were looked after. The distribution of grain ... became a sort of poor-relief or welfare system, and we meet with a growing number of generous deeds, gifts, and endowments which already exhibit a more humane spirit.[4]

In spite of this, there was widespread moral degeneration:

> Widespread religious and philosophical ferment; the mixture and "relativization" of world views; the rise of new religions; a practical atheism and disbelief in the gods, coupled with an existential mysticism. Latourette notes, "This ethical, philosophical, and religious ferment is one of the chief reasons for Christianity's remarkable spread" ... The rise of new, intensely emotional religions and the resurgence of some of the older oriental faiths ...[5]

The Great Missionary Strategist, through the operation of his sovereign providence, perfectly prepared the way for his ultimate Missionary, the Incarnate Christ. He used three means: (1) The failure of Israel, even under its greatest leaders, intensified a longing for someone greater than Moses, David or Solomon; (2) The dispersion of Israel among the nations created the base for further revelation to the Gentiles; (3) The cultural and political climate in the Roman Empire prepared fertile soil for the coming gospel seed.

No wonder Paul wrote to formerly pagan Galatians who "were slaves to those who by nature are not gods," that "we were in slavery under the basic principles of the world ... when the time had fully come, God sent his Son, born of a woman, born under law, to redeem those under law, that we might receive the full rights of sons" (Gal. 4:8, 3–5).

Notes

1 **J. H. Bavinck,** *An Introduction to the Science of Missions* (Grand Rapids, MI: Baker, 1960), pp. 26–27.

2 Ibid. pp. 26–29.

3 **Howard A. Snyder,** *The Problem of Wineskins: Church Structure in a Technological Age* (Downers Grove, IL: Inter-Varsity Press, 1975), pp. 26ff.

4 Ibid.

5 Ibid. p. 30.

Chapter 5

Missions in the New Testament

God is the perfect strategist and the ideal teacher. As such he progressively unfolded his eternal missionary purpose—dimly to Adam and Eve in the *protoevangelium* and more clearly to Abraham in the promise to bless all nations. To Moses God revealed the importance of Israel as a beacon to all peoples. Then throughout the prophetic Scriptures we find men such as David and Isaiah searching

> intently and with the greatest care, trying to find out the time and circumstances to which the Spirit of Christ in them was pointing when he predicted the sufferings of Christ and the glories that would follow. It was revealed to them that they were not serving themselves but you, when they spoke of the things that have now been told you by those who have preached the gospel to you by the Holy Spirit sent from heaven. Even angels long to look into these things. (1 Peter 1:10–12)

God's unfolding missionary purpose perplexed and fascinated not only prophets but also angels. However, it became clear that a new covenant would include the whole non-Jewish world—the Gentiles.

At the most appropriate point in history, God sent his incarnate Son. In his birth, ministry, Passion and continuing Session, Christ reveals God's redemptive purpose in its new-covenant manifestation.

Overview

THE KINGDOM

During his ministry, Christ talked of *the kingdom of heaven* or *the kingdom of God*. Indeed, he began his ministry by declaring, "Repent, for the kingdom of heaven is near." "Blessed are the poor in spirit, for theirs is the kingdom of heaven." We are to pray, "your kingdom come." We are to "seek first his kingdom and his righteousness" (see Matt. 4:17; 5:3; 6:10,

33). In talking to Nicodemus, Christ said, "... no one can see the kingdom of God unless he is born again" (John 3:3). Two kingdoms are not meant—a kingdom of heaven and a kingdom of God—but one kingdom described variously as "heavenly," because it is ruled from heaven, and "of God," because God is the one who rules it from his throne in heaven. Obviously, then, New Testament success hinges upon the growth or extension of that kingdom.

THE SPIRITUAL KINGDOM

The Kingdom is dissimilar to all earthly organizations in that it is the invisible, spiritual rule of God in the hearts of believers. When he was asked when the Kingdom would come Christ answered, "The kingdom of God does not come with your careful observation, nor will people say, 'Here it is,' or 'There it is,' because the kingdom of God is within you." This phase of the Kingdom comes when the Holy Spirit regenerates a sinner. In the new birth a rebel is born into the Kingdom of God. Christ told Pilate, "My kingdom is not of this world. If it were, my servants would fight to prevent my arrest by the Jews. But now my kingdom is from another place" (Matt. 7:21; Luke 17:20–21; John 3:3–8; 18:36–37).

The Kingdom, however, is not present in those who merely profess Christ as Lord but fail to do "the will of my Father in heaven" (Matt. 12:50).

THE KINGDOM AND THE CHURCH

The common name for the new-covenant manifestation of this organization is "the church." "I will build my church, and the gates of Hades will not overcome it" (Matt. 16:18). Paul describes this entity as "the kingdom of light." He goes on to explain, "For he has rescued us from the dominion of darkness and brought us into the kingdom of the Son he loves" (Col. 1:12–13). This image of two warring kingdoms takes us back to the *protoevangelium* of Genesis 3:15 and hints at the fact that in some sense the church is not new.

Since God has always been King of a kingdom, this organization—in some sense at least—has always existed wherever there were believers. Abraham is the father of the faithful. (We can properly speak of the Old

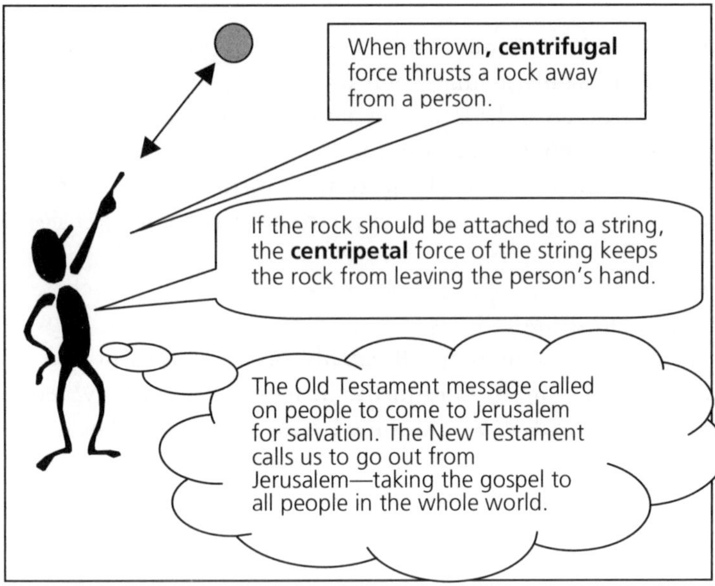

Testament church.) In his peerless epistle on the church, Paul describes how God has broken down the wall of separation between Jew and Gentile, "to create in himself one new man [the church] out of the two … to reconcile both of them to God through the cross" (Eph. 2:14–16). In this sense the church is new. Without becoming circumcised Israelites, all men and women can now join it. The body of Christ is a new creation of which Christ is the cornerstone (Eph. 2:20).

The church, although new, has roots in the old organization. The New Testament family of God is part of the family of God that has existed from the beginning. Paul explains, "… you are no longer foreigners and aliens, but fellow citizens with God's people and members of God's household, built on the foundation of the apostles and prophets" (Eph. 2:19–20). In this sense the new manifestation of the "holy temple in the Lord" (Eph. 2:21) is but a new dispensation of the old reality—that all men and women who have come to God by faith have been citizens in one household, the household of God. In this sense the Kingdom of God is a more universal concept than the church, embracing as it does the old dispensation. How will men and women hear this wonderful news of their invitation to join a multi-ethnic family in which they can enjoy unity and equality free from prejudice? Only through missions!

MISSIONS AS CENTRIFUGAL NOT CENTRIPETAL

New-covenant disciples are responsible to contribute to the fulfillment of God's missionary purpose. "As the Father has sent me, I am sending you"; "Go into all the world and preach the good news to all creation" (John 20:21; Mark 16:15; see also Matt. 28:18–20, etc.). As explained by Peters, this is the centrifugal force of the Great Commission.

In the Old Testament dispensation God's missionary purpose operated centripetally; that is, Israel was to be a beacon of testimony to Yahweh by attracting the nations to Jerusalem, the center of God's redemptive activity during that period. Now God's missionary method operates centrifugally; that is, all New Testament believers are expected to go out into the highways and byways with the gospel. We are to take the good news to all the world that all peoples may respond where they are, without traveling to some geographic center. Wherever they respond they become part of the invisible kingdom of God—the church.

So missions is *outreach* involving the extension of the Kingdom through planting the church in every nation.

Missions and the composition of the New Testament

The New Testament, in its entirety, is a missionary document whose writers were missionaries communicating with missionary churches. George Peters writes, "The New Testament is a missionary book in address, content, spirit and design."[1]

The four Gospels contextualize the life, ministry and Passion of Christ in different cultural styles suited to different audiences. Matthew, Jewish in style and language, exalts Christ as King and refers frequently to the Old Testament Scriptures. Mark, with its active story form, appeals to a Roman audience. Luke provides a more complete biography, but with more of an emphasis on Christ the Man of compassion, the Savior of all. John, with its philosophical portrayal of Christ as the eternal *logos* of God, appeals to Greek sensibilities.

Acts is the first missionary history of the church. Christ ascends, sends forth the Spirit, creates the church and continues to supervise the expansion of that church from his position at the Father's right hand. He meets Saul on the road to Damascus, blinds him and commissions him for missionary service. The book concludes without a conclusion—because the story of missions continues to unfold. In the final chapter, Paul is in Rome, "boldly and without hindrance" preaching "the kingdom of God" and teaching about "the Lord Jesus Christ" (Acts 28:31).

Paul, Peter, James, John and Jude wrote epistles dealing with issues and problems affecting the missionary churches they had been used to establish.

John, in his Revelation, talks of the state of seven missionary churches and brings prophetic comfort from the risen Christ that the mission of God will culminate in resounding success. The twenty-four elders sing a new song to the Lamb "because you were slain, and with your blood you purchased men for God from every tribe and language and people and nation. You have made them to be a kingdom and priests to serve our God" (Rev. 5:9–10).

Missions woven into the content of the New Testament

Peters writes,

> To establish the theology of missions in the New Testament one simply accepts the New Testament for what it is ... There is perhaps little theology of missions as such in the New Testament because it is in its totality a missionary theology, the theology of a group of missionaries and a theology in missionary movement. Thus it does not present a theology of missions; it is a missionary theology.[2]

Missions is interwoven so completely into the New Testament text that any attempt to extract missionary texts or the missionary impulse would destroy it. And isolating every missionary text is a task too large to attempt in a book of this size. Rather let us sample this missionary smorgasbord by selecting some choice morsels from Matthew and Acts.

MATTHEW

The New Testament opens with Matthew closely linking the life of Christ, through the genealogy, with the Old Testament. Christ is to "save his people from their sins" and "be the shepherd of my people Israel" (Matt. 1:21; 2:6). But devotion from other nations is immediately introduced in the form of fervent adoration from pagan Magi. Joseph and Mary flee to Egypt for safety from Herod's rage. In chapter 3 John the Baptizer calls down wrath on the Jewish establishment.

In chapter 4 Christ fulfills Scripture by coming from "Galilee of the Gentiles," where "the people living in darkness have seen a great light." He begins his ministry by declaring in universal terms, "Repent, for the kingdom of heaven is near" (vv. 15–17). As described earlier, this kingdom is not a restoration of the Jewish kingdom but a universal rule of God in the hearts of people from all nations.

In the Sermon on the Mount (chapters 5–7) Christ proclaims a message with cosmic overtones in which the meek inherit the earth and the people of God are the "salt of the earth ... the light of the world" (vv. 13–14). The sermon continues to compare and contrast the teaching he is delivering with that of the Jewish establishment—clearly indicating that a new kind of righteousness is necessary to enter the kingdom of heaven.

From this point Christ begins to expound an aspect of God little revealed in the Old Testament—the fatherhood of God. He uses the relational and comforting term "father" over 173 times in the Gospels, beginning with the marvelous model prayer he introduces to his disciples. "Father" becomes his controlling image of God.

Following the healing of the man with leprosy in Matthew 8, he commends the faith of a Gentile—the Roman centurion whose servant is suffering: "I have not found anyone in Israel with such great faith" (Matt. 8:10). At this point Christ makes a startling announcement: "I say to you that many will come from the east and the west, and will take their places at the feast with Abraham, Isaac and Jacob in the kingdom of heaven. But the subjects of the kingdom will be thrown outside ..." (Matt. 8:11–12). With this announcement he proclaims the end of an exclusive relationship between God and Israel and the beginning of a new universalism in which Gentiles from east and west join patriarchs and prophets in God's family—the kingdom of heaven.

As the book unfolds, Christ's identification with sinners intensifies and his healing ministry expands. Scarcely a chapter passes without some allusion to the expanding missionary ministry he foresees. He sends out his disciples, commanding them, "Do not go among the Gentiles or enter any town of the Samaritans. Go rather to the lost sheep of Israel." Far from indicating a restriction of the gospel to Jews, this commission fulfills the condition that his message might first be preached to Israel. But in the same instructions, while forewarning them about persecution, he declares, "On my account you will be brought before governors and kings as witnesses to them and to the Gentiles" (Matt 10:5–6, 18).

Chapter 11 compares Korazin, Bethsaida and Capernaum unfavorably with Tyre, Sidon and even Sodom (Matt. 11:20–24). In chapter 12 he compares his resurrection to the missionary Jonah's experience in the fish. He speaks of the fulfillment of Isaiah's prophecy of the suffering servant in whose name "the nations will put their hope" (Matt. 12:40, 21). In chapter 13, the field where the gospel seed is sown is the world. In chapter 15 he goes to the region of Tyre and Sidon and praises the faith of a non-Jewish woman.

Throughout the next chapters he repeatedly corrects the prevailing teaching of the Pharisees and Sadducees. His exchanges with them culminate in his statement that since they reject the capstone (himself) "the kingdom of God will be taken away from you and given to a people who will produce its fruit," that is, the Gentiles (Matt. 21:43).

The parable of the wedding banquet enforces this same lesson (Matt. 22). As with other parables we are introduced to an interval when "the servants went out into the streets and gathered all the people they could find" (v. 10). In this parable, the interval of grace before the wedding is our missionary age, the period in which we are to labor to win the lost. In the same way, the time that elapses before the Master returns in the parables of chapter 25 represents our missionary period.

The signs of the end of the age in chapter 24 are cosmic in extent. Crucial to the culmination of time is the clear statement of Christ, "This gospel of the kingdom will be preached in the whole world as a testimony to all nations, and then the end will come" (Matt. 24:14).

Matthew next proceeds to record the events of the Passion and concludes his book with the explicit command of Christ, "All authority in heaven and on earth has been given to me. Therefore go and make disciples of all nations" (Matt. 28:18–19).

Nothing could be clearer! Christ came to die for elect believers from every nation. "And surely I am with you always, to the very end of the age" (Matt. 28:20).

If the first and most Jewish of the Gospels is so clearly missionary in thrust, what of the others? In each of the other Gospels—Mark, Luke and John—we will discover the same vision of the Master.

Mark is apparently written for a Roman audience. In Mark 11:17, the temple is meant to be "a house of prayer for all nations."

From the outset of Luke its universality is implied in the salutation to a Gentile, Theophilus. Although Christ comes to receive "the throne of his father David," Luke explains that "his kingdom will never end." The angel choir sings to the shepherds of peace to all men. Simeon takes up the child into his arms in the temple and praises God for the babe "which you have prepared in the sight of all people, a light for revelation to the Gentiles and for glory to your people Israel." John the Baptizer's ministry is spoken of as the fulfillment of Isaiah when he predicts one who will "Prepare the way for the Lord ... And all mankind will see God's salvation" (Luke 1:1, 32–33; 2:14, 31–32; 3:4, 6).

John begins with the cosmic significance of the Word who "was with God, and ... was God. He was with God in the beginning ... Through him all things were made ... In him was life, and that life was the light of men" (John 1:1–4). "He gives light to every man"; he "takes away the sin of the world"; he "is the Savior of the world"; "God so loved the world" (see John 1:9, 29; 4:42; 3:16). Much more could be said about the missionary melody that pulses beneath the surface of the Gospels. This rises to a sustained crescendo in the book of Acts.

ACTS

Into the maelstrom of Greek civilization and Roman oppression the risen Christ sends his apostolic band. They have no organization, no money, no buildings, no power and no influence. All they have is a message about a Jewish man who was crucified but who, they claim, rose from the dead. Humanly speaking, the expectation of their success is nil. And they take the gospel into the world at a time when a myriad of mystery religions and mystical ideas vie for the attention of people.

However, their mission is clear. The disciples were to wait until the promise of the Holy Spirit was fulfilled. "But you will receive power when the Holy Spirit comes on you; and you will be my witnesses in Jerusalem, and in all Judea and Samaria, and to the ends of the earth" (Acts 1:8). They did wait. The Holy Spirit did descend at Pentecost and that very day 3,000 were converted. From that explosive beginning, Acts records the growth of the church in a very candid and realistic way that has a multitude of ramifications for the exercise of missions today. We will return to those lessons later.

IN JERUSALEM (ACTS 1–7)

Pentecost was a multi-cultural missionary event that planted the seeds of the church among many ethnic groups. "Now there were staying in Jerusalem God-fearing Jews from every nation under heaven" (2:5). These Jews, perhaps proselytes, spoke many languages. "How is it that each of us hears them in his own native language? Parthians, Medes and Elamites; residents of Mesopotamia, Judea and Cappadocia, Pontus and Asia, Phrygia and Pamphylia, Egypt and the parts of Libya near Cyrene; visitors from Rome (both Jews and converts to Judaism); Cretans and Arabs" (2:8–11). What a cross-cultural explosion!

The revival continues. "The Lord added to their number daily" (2:47). Peter and John heal a man crippled from birth and then preach to the people about Jesus, explaining that what is happening is the fulfillment of "all [that] the prophets from Samuel on" have said concerning how "Through your offspring all peoples on earth will be blessed" (3:24–25). Obviously, Peter understands at this point the relationship between God's plan for all the nations and his covenant with Abraham and the Jewish people. The vigor of their witness immediately arouses persecution from the Sanhedrin, who thrust them into jail. "But many who heard the message believed, and the number of men grew to about five thousand" (4:4).

Although further witness and healings bring down even more persecution, nothing can stop them. Peter responds to the Sanhedrin's strictures, "We must obey God." As a result of their fearless witness, "the number of disciples was increasing" (5:29; 6:1). After organizing to overcome possible division through the neglect of Grecian widows, "The number of disciples in Jerusalem increased rapidly, and a large number of priests became obedient to the faith" (6:7).

However, in spite of the instructions of Christ to take the gospel beyond Jerusalem to Judea and Samaria, the early Christians concentrated their efforts in the city. Their understanding of the global dimensions of the Master's mission developed slowly. The spread of the gospel to the Samaritans, to Greeks in Antioch and even later to a whole spectrum of Gentiles caught the early church by surprise. Their natural Jewish reticence rendered them slow to accept what God was doing. Most of the early disciples were Galileans, naturally reluctant even to go beyond Jerusalem into Judea, let alone into Samaria. Only after the Spirit had produced signs and wonders among the Samaritans, in Cornelius's household, in Antioch and in Ephesus were their doubts about Gentile conversion allayed. Finally, at the Council of Jerusalem most believers accepted the multi-ethnic dimensions of the church. Notice how this understanding developed.

MISSIONARY EXPANSION DUE TO PERSECUTION (ACTS 8–12)

During this stage God himself drove the missionary vehicle without the cooperation of the apostles. With the church confined to Jerusalem but spreading like wildfire, Stephen was martyred and "a great persecution broke out against the church at Jerusalem, and all except the apostles were scattered throughout Judea and Samaria ... Those who had been scattered preached the word wherever they went" (8:1, 4). Philip evangelized Samaria.

The apostles sent Peter and John to check on the authenticity of the Samaritan experience (8:14). Then Philip was called to the side of the Ethiopian eunuch and through his conversion God established another non-Jewish church.

In chapter 9 Saul, the persecutor, was converted and commissioned by Christ. "This man is my chosen instrument to carry my name before the Gentiles and their kings and before the people of Israel" (v. 15). Peter had his vision of the lowered sheet in chapter 10, as a result of which he reluctantly concluded, "I now realize how true it is that God does not show favoritism but accepts men from every nation" (vv. 34–35).

Still unable to accept a global mission, "circumcised believers criticized him [Peter]" for mixing with Gentiles. Peter explained the vision he received and the outpouring of the Spirit on Cornelius's household (11:2–18).

Meanwhile, "those who had been scattered by the persecution in connection with Stephen traveled as far as Phoenicia, Cyprus and Antioch, telling the message only to Jews. Some of them, however, men from Cyprus and Cyrene, went to Antioch and began to speak to Greeks also ... a great number of people believed and turned to the Lord" (11:19–21).

Imagine the excited, but very traditional, Jerusalem saints trying to understand all these outbreaks of the Spirit beyond the boundaries of Judaism. They sent Barnabas to Antioch to check it out. When he arrived he "saw the evidence of the grace of God" (11:23).

These early Christians seemed stuck on a centripetal view of missions, the Old Testament pattern—"If anyone wants to come to God, let him come to us"—rather than the New Testament pattern of outreach—"Go into all the world and preach the gospel to the whole creation." (We should not be complacent. Too often Christians today have the same outlook, expecting people to come to church to be saved.) It took a sovereign and overruling act of God—the waves of persecution—to move the early Christians into outreach mode. Finally, in the new church of Antioch, where believers were first called Christians, a more organized form of missionary outreach was initiated.

MISSIONARY EXPANSION THROUGH PLANNED JOURNEYS (ACTS 13–28)

During this stage, apostles empowered by the Spirit drove the missionary vehicle. Organized missions under the umbrella of a local church come into focus. This pattern was initiated when the Holy Spirit led the leadership group at worship in Antioch to appoint Barnabas and Saul for missionary work. They fasted and prayed, placed their hands on them and sent them out as the first formal cross-cultural missionary team.

The team set out on a tour that took them to Cyprus and Asia Minor.

They adopted a pattern of first visiting the Jewish community. This invariably aroused persecution. They then turned their attention to Gentiles. Groups of believers were converted in Pisidian Antioch, Iconium, Lystra and Derbe. Before leaving the area they revisited each group, "strengthening the disciples and encouraging them to remain true to the faith ... [They] appointed elders for them in each church and, with prayer and fasting, committed them to the Lord, in whom they had put their trust" (14:22–23).

In fifteen years the four most populous provinces of the Roman Empire were evangelized. The three main missionary journeys mentioned in Acts led to the planting of churches in the provinces of Galatia, Asia, Macedonia and Achaia (Greece). At this point Paul could say, "From Jerusalem all the way around to Illyricum, I have fully proclaimed the gospel of Christ." We also know that unknown missionaries had planted a strong church in Rome.

Our overview of the book of Acts has brought us face to face with Paul, who—after Christ—was the premier missionary.

PAUL, THE MODEL MISSIONARY

Almost eighty years ago, Roland Allen wrote that his years of missionary service in China led him to conclude that "in the careful examination of Paul's work, above all in the understanding and appreciation of his *principles*, we shall find the solution of most of our present difficulties."[3] Although Church Growth theory was unknown in his day and a multitude of other methodologies have sprouted since then, a study of the apostle Paul remains more essential than ever. In the chapters that follow we will return again and again to his life and principles. But at the outset let me summarize some of the ways in which Paul, after Christ, remains our model.

A study of his journeys in Acts, his missionary epistles and the summary of his ministry in Acts 20 shows the importance of the following:

- a clear conversion to Christ
- a definite call to missionary service
- a thorough education, in his case, in Jewish theology and Greek culture
- a careful, not hasty, embracing of the missionary call

- a deep grasp of God's ultimate and unifying purposes (Eph. 1:15–23) and their connection to the church (Eph. 3:2–11)
- a focus on the central missionary tasks: verbal proclamation of the gospel, reaching the unreached and planting churches (Rom. 15:19–20)
- freedom from cultural bias through an understanding of the revolutionary multi-ethnic nature of the church (Eph. 2:11–22)
- cultural adaptability (1 Cor. 9:19–23)
- flexibility of methodology
- an ability to work with teams
- a realization of the importance of discipling (Acts 20:18–20, 26–27, 31; Titus, 1 and 2 Tim.)
- a commitment to training and encouraging leaders through the delegation of responsibilities to elders and deacons (Acts 20:17–18)
- a humble passion for godliness, including a freedom from materialism (Acts 20:18–19)
- a willingness to endure suffering and persecution (Acts 20:22–25)
- an absolute faith in God
- through everything else, a pervasive sense of the importance of love for God and others (Rom. 12:9–10; chapters 13–15; 1 Cor. 13; Eph. 3:14–19).

Paul embodied the genuine missionary compulsion—the urge to move on rather than to settle into a ministry of shepherding and edification. He wrote, "It has always been my ambition to preach the gospel where Christ was not known, so that I would not be building on someone else's foundation" (Rom. 15:20). Although martyred around AD 64, Paul's theology became the most formative of that of all the apostles, and his life and practice the most important sources of missionary principles.

MISSIONS IN THE EPISTLES

Among a multitude of passages that reflect missionary themes, let me mention several in Romans. Paul writes of his missionary obligation "both to Greeks and non-Greeks," his desire "to preach the gospel also to you who are at Rome" (Rom. 1:14–15). Paul was not ashamed of the gospel because of its cross-cultural power to save: "it is the power of God for the salvation of everyone who believes: first for the Jew, then for the Gentile" (Rom. 1:16).

In chapters 9, 10 and 11 we glimpse something of the heart-passion of the apostle, the passion that ought to characterize all missionaries: "my heart's desire and prayer to God for the Israelites is that they may be saved" (Rom. 10:1). Desire, however, is not enough. If lost men and women are to be saved, someone must be sent with the gospel: "how can they believe in the one of whom they have not heard? And how can they hear without someone preaching to them? And how can they preach unless they are sent? As it is written, 'How beautiful are the feet of those who bring good news!'" (Rom. 10:14–15).

Before concluding Romans with a list commending his fellow-workers, Paul describes the essence of the missionary calling: "to be a minister of Christ Jesus to the Gentiles [to any unevangelized peoples] with the priestly duty of proclaiming the gospel of God, so that the Gentiles might become an offering acceptable to God, sanctified by the Holy Spirit" (15:16). Clearly the missionary stands as a priest, between heaven and earth, mediating the only message that can save and preparing those who respond—through the Holy Spirit—to be an ongoing offering of praise to God.

Paul goes on to highlight another aspect of healthy missions, the impulse "to preach the gospel where Christ [is] not known" (Rom. 15:20). Missions means reaching the unreached and moving on as soon as a church is planted. (For further references on missions see 1 Cor. 9:9–23; 2 Cor. 5:9–21; Eph. 3:1–12; 1 Tim. 2:1–7; 1 Peter 1:1–2; 2:9–11.)

MISSIONS IN REVELATION

The book of Revelation presents the victorious culmination of God's missionary program. In one vision the twenty-four elders fall down before the Lamb with golden bowls full of incense, the prayers of the saints. They sing a new song that highlights the missionary implications of Christ's sacrifice: "You are worthy to take the scroll and to open its seals, because you were slain, and with your blood you purchased men for God from every tribe and language and people and nation. You have made them to be a kingdom and priests to serve our God, and they will reign on the earth" (Rev. 5:9–10). Amen. Even so, Lord, fulfill your purposes throughout our world!

MISSIONS IN THE APOSTOLIC TRADITIONS

Early church traditions reflect how dominant was missionary outreach in the lives of the apostles. "The oldest traditions seem to indicate that the Apostles made among themselves a division of their respective spheres of witnessing much after this fashion: first, in the region of the Black Sea, Peter, Andrew, Matthew, and Bartholomew; second, in Parthia, Thomas, Thaddeus, and Simon the Canaanite; and third, in Asia Minor, John and Philip."[4]

During the first century the gospel spread from Jerusalem and Judea to Samaria, Syria, the provinces of Asia Minor, Cyprus, Macedonia, Achaia, Rome, Spain, Alexandria, North Africa, Parthia, and possibly to India.

Notes

1 **George W. Peters,** *A Biblical Theology of Missions* (Chicago: Moody, 1972), p. 131.

2 Ibid.

3 **Roland Allen,** *Missionary Methods, St Paul's or Ours?* (London: World Dominion Press, 1956), p. ix.

4 **V. Raymond Edman,** *The Light in Dark Ages* (Wheaton, IL: Van Kampen Press, 1949), p. 69.

Key missionary questions

Before we can move on to a consideration of the missionary task, several nagging questions need to be put to rest. Without resolving these questions, missionary motivation may be lukewarm at best.

Gospel missions: fulfillment or alternative plan?

In a benighted attempt to protect God from charges of culpability for the presence of evil and accidents in the world, some thinkers have proposed that God is neither omniscient nor omnipotent. According to this view, while mega-powerful, all he can do is moderate unforeseen consequences as they occur. In this view—commonly called "Open Theism"—the New Testament mission is God's attempt to remedy the failure of his experiment with the people of Israel.

Such a view is neither reasonable nor faithful to the biblical text. As we have already seen in our survey of the Old Testament, God's choice of Israel was to prepare the way for the coming of the Messiah, a new covenant and a salvation that would be for all nations. New Testament missions is fulfillment, not Band-Aid.

The apostles came to realize that Jesus Christ's death and his mission was a determinate part of God's plan as promised in the Old Testament. In his sermon in Acts 2, Peter interprets Pentecost as the fulfillment of Joel's prophecy, ushering in an era in which "everyone who calls on the name of the Lord will be saved" (Acts 2:21). Peter notes that David had fellowship with Christ and predicted his resurrection, enthronement and Session (Acts 2:25–35).

In the temple Peter declared,

> The God of Abraham, Isaac and Jacob, the God of our fathers, has glorified his servant Jesus ... But this is how God fulfilled what he had foretold through all the prophets ... Indeed, all the prophets from Samuel on, as many as have spoken, have foretold these days. And you are heirs of the prophets and of the covenant God made with your fathers. He said to Abraham, "Through your offspring all peoples on earth will be blessed." (Acts 3:13, 18, 24–25)

In Romans, Paul points out that Abraham was chosen and justified by faith before circumcision, before the law which formalized Israel as a nation. This happened so that "the promise ... may be guaranteed to all Abraham's offspring—not only to those who are of the law but also to those who are of the faith of Abraham. He is the father of us all ... 'a father of many nations'" (Rom. 4:16–17). Open Theism questions the certain fulfillment of prophecies such as those quoted by Peter.

In Acts 10 God jolted Peter out of his ethno-centricity through the vision of the lowered sheet with unclean animals that Peter was to kill and eat. Following this revelation, he went to minister to Cornelius, a Roman. This experience profoundly affected the early, largely Jewish, church. When Paul and Barnabas's work among the Gentiles was criticized, James used Peter's experience to silence opposition to universal outreach. "Simon has described to us how God at first showed his concern by taking from the Gentiles a people for himself. The words of the prophets are in agreement with this, as it is written: '... that the remnant of men may seek the Lord, and all the Gentiles who bear my name'" (Acts 15:14–15, 17).

New Testament missions, far from being a divine attempt to remedy an earlier failure, is the fulfillment of God's eternal plan. Indeed, Peter cried that "Jesus of Nazareth ... was handed over to you by God's set purpose and foreknowledge; and you, with the help of wicked men, put him to death by nailing him to the cross. But God raised him from the dead" as David predicted (Acts 2:22–25). When the church prayed together they declared of the death of Christ, "They did what your power and will had decided beforehand should happen" (Acts 4:28). "He was chosen before the creation of the world, but was revealed in these last times for your sake" (1 Peter 1:20). Foreknowledge! Power and will! Eternal decision! Certainty of fulfillment!

Bavinck summarizes the Gospels' view of missions as follows: "The very idea of missions in the teaching of Jesus is carefully and slowly derived from the Messianic expectation of salvation. Old Testament prophecy regards Messianic salvation as including both the spiritual renewing and glorification of Israel, and also the spontaneous coming of the heathen and the radical transformation of the world order."[1]

Indeed, as New Testament missions develops, believers become clear that of the two, Jew and Gentile, God has determined to form one new body. As already noted, Paul writes that God has made Jew and Gentile one (Eph. 2:11–14). God has created one new household, "built on the foundation of the apostles and prophets" (Eph. 2:20), one temple, one dwelling place of the Spirit, one body. This is a mystery, "that through the gospel the Gentiles are heirs together with Israel, members together of one body, and sharers together in the promise in Christ Jesus" (Eph. 3:6).

In his first epistle, Peter explains that God's elect, who were "strangers in the world," who "were not a people," are now "a chosen people, a royal priesthood, a holy nation, a people belonging to God" (1 Peter 1:1; 2:10, 9).

Far from being a rescue mission put together by God to salvage victory out of the failure of earlier attempts, New Testament missions was in the mind and plan of God from the very beginning. Prophecy and history through Old Testament times weave together a pattern that can only be understood in terms of New Testament fulfillment.

Are the heathen really lost?

An even more urgent question concerns the lost condition of those who are outside Christ. As A. T. Pierson pointed out more than a century ago, "Behind the shameful apathy and lethargy of the church, that allows one thousand millions of human beings to go to their graves in ignorance of the Gospel, there lies a practical doubt, if not denial, of their lost condition."[2] This serious issue can be broken down into several related questions,

IS MANKIND LOST?

If mankind were not lost, Jesus would not have come, for he came to seek and save the lost (Luke 19:10). Everyone who believes on Jesus, who repents, has everlasting life; whoever does not is lost (John 3:15; Luke 13:5). "Whoever does not believe stands condemned already because he has not believed in the name of God's one and only Son. This is the verdict: Light has come into the world, but men loved darkness instead of light because their deeds were evil" (John 3:18–19). The verdict is in: Without Christ mankind is lost.

In the first three chapters of Romans Paul proves that "Jews and

Gentiles alike are all under sin … There is no one righteous, not even one … for all have sinned and fall short of the glory of God" (Rom. 3:9–10, 23). All men and women are alienated, separated from God (Eph. 4:17–18). From birth we are all "dead in … transgressions and sins" (Eph. 2:1).

WHAT IS THE ETERNAL DESTINY OF LOST MEN AND WOMEN?

It is the universal teaching of Scripture that "The wrath of God is being revealed from heaven against all the godlessness and wickedness of men" (Rom. 1:18). Only those who have been justified by faith in Christ can escape the wrath of God. We need go no further than the teaching of Christ to discover that the eternal destiny of the lost is everlasting punishment in the fire, darkness, wailing and torments of hell. "Gehenna" is found twelve times in the New Testament, falling eleven times from the lips of Jesus. Hell is a place "where the fire never goes out … where 'their worm does not die, and the fire is not quenched'" (Mark 9:44, 48).

Herbert Kane summarizes well the two destinies of mankind:

> One involves everlasting happiness in the presence of God and the holy angels (Lk 15:10; Re 22:3–5; 1 Th 4:17); the other involves everlasting misery in the company of the devil and his angels (Mt 25:41) … Two gates—one strait and the other wide; two ways—one broad and the other narrow; two destinies—one life and the other destruction (Mt 7:13–14). In the day of judgement the sheep will be separated from the goats (Mt 25:31–46), the wheat from the tares (Mt 13:36–43), the good from the evil (Jn 5:29). And in the resurrection there will be a separation between the just and the unjust (Acts 24:15).[3]

DOES MANKIND HAVE ANY HOPE OF SAVING ITSELF?

This question can be subdivided into two parts: Does anyone have the ability to save him- or herself, and does anyone have the inclination—the desire?

Paul writes that people are steeped in ignorance about the gospel and are unwilling to seek God due to their bias against him. "They exchanged the truth of God for a lie, and worshiped and served created things rather than the Creator" (Rom. 1:25); "there is no one who understands" (Rom. 3:11). They live "in the futility of their thinking. They are darkened in their understanding and separated from the life of God because of the ignorance that is in them" (Eph. 4:17–18).

This ignorance is not an innocent lack of knowledge but a deliberate rejection of God through "the hardening of their hearts" (Eph. 4:18). In their natural state, humans willfully reject God in spite of the fact that he has revealed himself in creation and in their own consciences. They "suppress the truth by their wickedness ... For although they knew God, they neither glorified him as God nor gave thanks to him" (Rom. 1:18, 21). There is "no one who seeks God. All have turned away ... there is no one who does good ... There is no fear of God before their eyes" (Rom. 3:11–12, 18).

Lost men and women became enslaved to their own passions. "God gave them over in the sinful desires of their hearts ... God gave them over to shameful lusts" (Rom. 1:24, 26). "All of us also lived among them at one time, gratifying the cravings of our sinful nature and following its desires and thoughts" (Eph. 2:3). The resulting enslavement is something from which mankind, unaided by God, can never escape. "Everyone who sins is a slave to sin," and only the Son of God can set a person free (John 8:34, 36). Christ declared that the enlightened Jewish leaders he confronted were carrying out the desires of their father, the devil (John 8:42–47).

Even if a person had the desire to be saved, he or she would not have the ability. God is holy, just and good. To be justified by what we do requires perfection. And yet, no one can keep God's commandments perfectly. All our works are rendered defective because they arise from motivations that are proud and selfish. The law was given to show our inability to save ourselves: "so that every mouth may be silenced and the whole world held accountable to God. Therefore no one will be declared righteous in his sight by observing the law; rather, through the law we become conscious of sin" (Rom. 3:19–20).

Paul points out to Titus that Christ "saved us, not because of righteous things we had done [all of which are defective], but because of his mercy" (Titus 3:5).

DOES MANKIND HAVE A SECOND CHANCE AFTER DEATH?

Nowhere in the Scriptures do we discover any second opportunity to be saved. The parable of the rich man and Lazarus teaches us that "a great chasm has been fixed" between those who die in faith and those who, like the rich man, go to "hell, where he was in torment" (Luke 16:26, 23). Repentance is possible only in this life, for immediately following death people face the judgment. "Just as man is destined to die once, and after that to face judgment ..." (Heb. 9:27).

WHAT ABOUT THOSE WHO HAVE NEVER HEARD THE GOSPEL?

Many might object that it is not fair to condemn those who have never had a chance to hear and reject the gospel. Rejection of the gospel, however, is not the basis upon which unevangelized people will be judged. As Paul points out in Romans 1, wrath comes upon men and women for rejecting natural revelation in the form of creation and conscience.

"For since the creation of the world God's invisible qualities—his eternal power and divine nature—have been clearly seen, being understood from what has been made, so that men are without excuse" (Rom. 1:20). Creation clearly portrays the fact that there must be a Creator, that he is a being of infinite power and wisdom and thus completely different from humanity; an infinite creative deity. Paul argues that, although these facts are clearly acknowledged by lost men and women, they willfully turn away from him. Instead of worshiping the Creator, they foolishly worship images and ideas that they themselves create. They exchange truth for an obvious lie. They exchange natural relationships, such as between a man and a woman in marriage, for immoral relationships. (See the development of Paul's argument in Romans 1:18–32.)

People will also be judged by reference to their own consciences: "when God will judge men's secrets" (Rom. 2:16). "Gentiles, who do not have the law ... show that the requirements of the law are written on their hearts, their consciences also bearing witness, and their thoughts now accusing, now even defending them" (Rom. 2:14–15).

The finality of Christ: Is Christ the only way?

In the West tolerance of all beliefs is exalted—except the belief that there is only one way of salvation. It is considered intolerant to claim that Christ is the only way to God. Opponents of Christ's uniqueness claim that there is much good in all religions—that there are many ways to God, through Zoroaster, Buddha, Confucius or Muhammad.

In Old Testament times, Israel was repeatedly warned to "Get rid of the foreign gods you have with you" (Gen. 35:2). That Old Testament period was an extended polemic against the gods of Egypt, Canaan, Assyria, Babylon and Persia (see Exod. 20:1–6, 22–23; Deut. 32:16–18; Ps. 115:4–8; 135:15–18; Isa. 41:21–24; 44:6–20; Jer. 10:1–16). The New Testament carries on the polemic against the idolatry of Rome and Greece. Paul warns that "the sacrifices of pagans are offered to demons, not to God, and I do not want you to be participants with demons" (1 Cor. 10:20).

An examination of non-Christian religions shows that they are human fabrications that break the first two commandments. They are beliefs designed to save mankind from bowing in submission to the Lord and Creator of the universe. They profess to provide a way for men and women to save themselves, because they deny mankind's lostness, our irremediable fallen nature. In the view of non-Christian religions, "There is something we can do to be saved." But, biblically, we know that "There is nothing we can do to save ourselves."

Although there are some laudable principles in a variety of world religions, the mixture is toxic. Where we find admirable principles in non-Christian religions and cultures they are due to the influence of God's common grace. As Paul noted in his address to the Athenians, God has not left himself without witness (see Acts 17:22–31). Taken as a whole, however, non-Christian religions are morally bankrupt and infinitely dangerous, preparing people, not for heaven, but for hell. The false sense of security they engender, and the self-righteousness they encourage, lead men and women away from the true God into further bondage and even demonism.

Erich Sauer has summarized man's religiosity as follows:

> Heathenism as a whole rests not only on error and deceit but at the same time also on a spiritistic foundation ... Through all this the heathen, under demon influence, became the "creator of his gods."
>
> The Grecian says: Man, know thyself.

The Roman says: Man, rule thyself.

The Chinese says: Man, improve thyself.

The Buddhist says: Man, annihilate thyself.

The Brahman says: Man, merge thyself in the universal sum of all.

The Moslem says: Man, submit thyself.

and in HIM the Christian says: "I can do all things through Christ who makes me mighty" (Phil. 4:13). [Or "apart from me you can do nothing" (John 15:5).]

In his religion the heathen expresses his *godlessness*. Religion is *the* sin, namely, the sin against the first command, the replacing of God by the gods ... the most powerful expression of the opposition of man against God and contradiction within himself.[4]

When asked about other ways to God we need but quote Christ, who said, "I am the way and the truth and the life. No one comes to the Father except through me" (John 14:6). "Salvation is found in no one else, for there is no other name under heaven given to men by which we must be saved" (Acts 4:12; see also 1 Tim. 2:5).

The way to God provided by Christ is a solitary way, because Christ who provides it is absolutely unique. As he said, "You are from below; I am from above. You are of this world; I am not of this world" (John 8:23). He alone was virgin-born. He alone was sinless (Luke 23:41; John 19:4, 6; 2 Cor. 5:21; 1 Peter 2:22; 1 John 3:5). He alone died an atoning death in order to save lost men and women (1 Peter 1:18–20; 2:24; 3:18). His sacrifice alone can save us. He alone rose from the dead. He is alive. Other religious founders are dead. He alone governs the universe from the throne of God. He alone will return to judge the earth.

There can be no doubt in the missionary's mind: There is only one way to God and that way is through Christ. Hence the absolute necessity of worldwide missions.

Notes

1 **J. H. Bavinck,** *An Introduction to the Science of Missions* (Grand Rapids, MI: Baker, 1960), p. 35.

2 **A. T. Pierson,** *Evangelize to the Finish* (New York: Robert Carter, 1886), p. 12.

3 **J. Herbert Kane,** *Understanding Christian Missions* (Grand Rapids, MI: Baker, 1979) p. 130.

4 **Erich Sauer,** *The Dawn of World Redemption*, trans. by G. H. Lang (London: Paternoster, 1951), p. 85.

Elvin, a quiet young man from the wheatlands of Saskatchewan, Canada, and Lolita, a vivacious young woman from the sophisticated city of Montreal: The narrative of these intrepid pioneers, from their courtship to their retirement, makes very unlikely but fascinating reading.

Elvin and Lolita Harbottle arrived in the dusty town of Madaoua, Niger, for a six-month stint in January 1953. They stayed for over thirty years. In 1984, when they left Niger for retirement in Canada, the fruit of their years of trekking and teaching seemed meager and scattered. They had no way of knowing that a change would come.

How did they endure so cheerfully the heat and dust? How did they persevere year after year in the face of Muslim antagonism and scanty response? Let's trace their story.

Both were Presbyterians heading toward missionary service in India when they enrolled in what became Tyndale College in Toronto. In spite of having so much in common, their paths seldom crossed at Bible college. Then, unknown to each other, a concern for Africa replaced their interest in India.

The Sudan Interior Mission, now renamed Serving in Mission (SIM), sent Elvin out to Nigeria in May 1950. Meanwhile, Lolita also applied to SIM for service in Africa. Asked by the council if she had a special male friend, she easily replied, "No, I'm not interested in anybody at all." She meant it, too. She and Elvin were barely acquainted.

Lolita, however, must have made an impression on Elvin. She explains, "He had a letter waiting for me in every port of call. Of course, I didn't answer them. I wasn't interested. After all, we were like chalk and cheese. I couldn't see it at all. But the senior missionary on the boat did call me in to ask why I had told the council that I had no special interest in any man and yet I was receiving letters at every port."

In October 1950 Lolita arrived in Nigeria. Before long the mission, aware of her knowledge of French, sent her across the border into Niger to serve as a secretary. Elvin proved persuasive. Lolita explains, "Of course, we were extremely compatible. Our beliefs and our concern for Muslims were identical."

They married in October 1951 and spent a year at Tsibiri, a station in Niger not far from where Lolita had served as secretary. Soon a vacancy developed further down the road and the mission transferred the Harbottles to Madaoua for a temporary stay of six months that lasted for over thirty years.

Their simple home in Madaoua had no electricity and no pump. Until they had a well dug, water came from a barrel in the back yard. Deadly vipers inhabited the hedge along one side of the property. Along the front ran a trail, rather pretentiously named "The Trans-African Highway." During their early years there, this highway was nothing more than a track in the sand running from Senegal on the West African coast inland to Lake Chad.

The terrain around Madaoua must have been daunting to a couple used to green fields and forests. A visitor once described the area as a moonscape. Vast tracts of undulating sand, dotted here and there by the occasional thorn tree or stunted bush, stretch in every direction. During the dry season, from October into June, the harsh hot winds veil the landscape with a shroud of powdered sand from the desert.

The few thousand inhabitants of Madaoua live in mud houses reminiscent of Sudanese architecture. The poorer huddle under thatch. Donkeys bray in the shimmering heat. Mysterious robed Tuaregs from the northern desert and stately Fulanis from the ruling class mingle with the predominant Hausas in the open-air market. The vast majority are Muslim. Indeed, to have any status at all in Niger society one must demonstrate open adherence to the rituals of Islam.

Jim Lucas, the missionary preceding them, had encountered bitter antagonism. After years of labor he could not point with confidence to any one person in Madaoua and say that he or she was a Christian. Malam Sule, one of the most powerful Muslim priests of the area, made Madaoua a hotbed of anti-Christian propaganda and Islamic indoctrination.

A visitor commented, "Everywhere I went I saw groups of *malams*, disciples of the renowned older man, sitting together laboring over the Arabic characters of the Koran, or copying, by hand, entire commentaries, or the Koran itself." She went on, "My disappointment deepened day by day, for the dire threat issued by the *malams* had preceded me into every home."

Into this situation the Harbottles brought their mix of tenacity and stubborn cheerfulness. Taking a leaf from the Lucases, they began focusing on villages. They soon estimated that some 200,000 Hausa of the Gobir clan, living in hundreds of scattered villages, inhabited what they took to be *their parish*. The base of their enormous pear-shaped parish sat on the Nigerian border. The narrower neck extended north into the encroaching desert.

The daunting size of the task led them to strategize. They concluded that if they split up the work they would be able to reach twice as many villages. Consequently, Elvin went to the more distant villages while Lolita visited the ones nearer to Madaoua.

But how to get there? There were no cars or buses, trains or taxis. Bicycles wouldn't do. They had no money for a motorcycle until later. So … they walked. They rode shank's mare—they trekked, tramped and hiked.

Elvin would begin his trek at the break of day. With his great prairie stride he covered about twenty-five miles the first day, stopping here and there to talk to those he met. Arriving at a cluster of mud huts he would make the traditional greeting, "Peace be upon you!" If the villagers proved friendly, they would respond, "And peace be upon you." Setting out straw mats, they would invite him to sit and share their communal bowl of *tuwo*, pounded millet. Before long, Elvin would begin to speak about Jesus.

When Elvin found a friendly village, he made it his base. He would stay there a week or ten days. Every morning he would go out, like the spokes on a wheel, to a different village. At night he returned to share the communal meal at his base village.

Meanwhile, Lolita set off on her own. She spent four or five days a week trekking to nearby villages along the main road. At weekends she returned to Madaoua. While her quiet-spoken husband excelled in personal work, she felt more comfortable teaching groups. Lolita soon developed a bewildering array of ministries. She conducted worship services, preached, taught Bible classes for men, women and children, and drilled them in Bible memory and singing. She held literacy classes and tended various maladies. She took in orphans and nursed them to health.

Other missionaries sometimes shook their heads at this unlikely pair—Lolita the teacher-preacher and Elvin the personal worker. They could not fault her husband's thoughtfulness. Elvin felt he had the easier job, trekking to distant villages. When he returned home, after a week or so away, he would often insist that Lolita take the weekend off at a mission station 100 miles away. After packing her off on the ramshackle bus for Maradi, he set to work. He would bake his famous mini-cakes and other staples so she could get on with the Lord's work when she returned.

Before long, a fellow-missionary, impressed with their outreach, gave Elvin a motorcycle. With this new mobility, their travels multiplied. On a map tacked up on the wall, they pinpointed some 115 villages. Concentrating on those that were the most responsive, they developed a regular itinerary. In a station report from that period they wrote, "Twenty villages and hamlets have been visited regularly once a month. At least twelve others have been visited often enough so that we feel they have had ample opportunity to understand the gospel."

During the wet season they were forced to stop their treks. People were too busy to listen to their teaching. Overnight, grass sprouted in the sandy washes. Subsistence farmers rushed to plant their hoarded seeds. Nomadic Tuaregs and Buzus scoured the washes for the lushest grass as they sought to fatten their herds against the dry season ahead. While thirty inches of rain might fall in a good year, the thirsty soil and parched winds soon made the moisture vanish. When the rains failed, drought and famine stalked the land.

Besides evangelism, Elvin assisted with agriculture. At the onset of the dry season, many of the men left home and sought work in nearby countries. To help stem the hemorrhage of men, Elvin helped dig wells, introduced dry-season crops and encouraged them to plant fruit trees such as guavas and papayas. As crops of red peppers, tomatoes, onions and sweet potatoes took hold and found a ready market, fewer men migrated. Family life improved.

As resilient as the desert grass, the Harbottles persevered. Early on, the people nicknamed Elvin "*Langa Langa*," "scrap-metal banding." To their nickname the people added the honorary title "*Malam*," meaning "teacher." The nickname described both his skinny appearance and his resilient character. Although Elvin faced daunting discouragements, the Hausa soon realized that *Malam Langa Langa* always sprang back.

Lolita they honored by nicknaming her "*Bahaushia*," meaning "Hausa woman." Lolita and Elvin adapted to the culture long before the word "contextualization" was invented. They lived among the Hausas, as much like Hausas as they could. Her language skills developed so well that in later years Lolita became the Hausa Language school teacher.

Madaoua would hardly seem to be the place to raise a family. The Harbottles, however, believed it was a fine place to raise children. After all, didn't the Hausas have lots of children? Hadn't Jesus grown up in a dusty hamlet in Palestine?

In due course their family increased to include four girls. When the girls were small, Lolita took them with her on her treks. As the children grew, Elvin and Lolita took turns, alternately trekking and caring for the family.

When first Kathleen, then Linda, Joyce and Karen reached school age the SIM plane came in to fly them to Kent Academy, the missionary boarding school 300 miles away in Nigeria.

When asked if their four girls didn't complicate ministry, Lolita exclaimed, "Absolutely not! Kids attract kids. They broke down barriers. As soon as they learned to read we set them the task of teaching younger children to read Hausa."

Since the children's summer holidays coincided with the onset of the wet season, their arrival proved providential to the running of the summer vacation Bible school. Unable to trek, the Harbottles used this period to run almost continuous Bible studies and literacy classes. The girls pitched in to help. Looking back on those days, their daughter Linda commented, "We felt as if we were really part of the work."

Weather permitting, Elvin and Lolita kept on trekking. Elvin traded for a heavier motorcycle and Lolita got one of her own. From time to time villagers here or there assured the Harbottles that they believed. Pockets of animistic Hausas, who had not yet succumbed to Islam, were the most interested. None, however, gave evidence of real faith. Finally, in 1966—thirteen years after they arrived—they baptized their first real convert and arranged his marriage to a Christian Hausa girl. The rejoicing proved short-lived. The girl's family insisted on the annulment of the marriage of their daughter to one from an inferior clan.

Ten years later, in 1976, several struggling groups of believers had begun to meet. By 1983, there were five or six small congregations. Overjoyed at seeing churches develop in such a difficult setting, several Christians from other tribes pitched in with money and expertise to help the Hausa Christians build the first tiny church buildings. Nevertheless, to an outside observer, the fruit of a lifetime of dogged toil seemed pitifully stunted.

In December 1983 Lolita returned to Canada to retire. At the airport an official asked her about a re-entry visa. "Oh, we're retiring. I won't be returning," she explained. The officer protested, "Anyone who speaks Hausa as well as you must return. I'll give you eight months." The official was prophetic.

Elvin followed Lolita back to Canada a few months later. Traveling in a truck from Madaoua, he arrived late at the outskirts of Niamey, the capital of Niger, where he was to catch a flight. He wondered how he would get a ride to the mission compound. Just then a Tuareg taxi driver pulled up. He cried, "*Malam Langa Langa*, where do you want to go? I'll take you anywhere. You may not recognize me. I was one of the children who came to your house every morning during the famine. The peanut balls you gave us kept us alive." When drought and famine had swept through the Sahel in 1974, they had fed a thousand people a day with high-protein balls made from the residue of peanuts crushed for oil and mixed with spices. But that's another story ...

The Harbottles left Niger content in knowing they had fulfilled their task. When asked if Elvin ever got discouraged, Lolita replied, "No. He didn't feel it was necessary to see results. He felt fulfilled just doing what he knew he should do."

Settling into a retirement lifestyle didn't prove easy. Two years later the pull of the Hausa drew them back to Maradi, Niger, for a short-term assignment. Lolita taught new missionaries Hausa and Elvin worked with bush Fulanis. While driving to Madaoua to pick up their language books, they stopped briefly at Tumba, one of the villages they had particularly targeted. Soon a crowd came running toward them. "*Malam Langa Langa*

... *Bahaushia* ... You return. We remember. Just last night we were talking about you. See, now we follow Jesus."

Elvin and Lolita were astonished as they visited the places where they had trekked. In village after village they discovered groups of believers. Many of the children they taught had become disciples of the Master. Now a good number of tiny churches have sprung into being—in the very places where they persevered in sowing gospel seed.

Elvin died in February 1992. Lolita lives in Listowel, a small Ontario farming community, where she keeps almost as busy as she was in Niger. She would love to get a motorcycle like they had in Niger, but her daughters won't let her. Even so, she manages to hold Bible studies in two apartment buildings and a retirement home, as well as spend time counseling.

The Hausas remember Elvin and Lolita. While preaching near Madaoua, Gerry Swank once asked some villagers if they knew any missionaries. "No," they replied sullenly. "Well, do you know Elvin Harbottle?" he persisted. "No," came the chilly answer. Finally, someone asked, "Do you mean *Malam Langa Langa*?"

When Gerry replied in the affirmative, the change was dramatic. "Oh, he's not a missionary, he's our brother," the Hausa tribesmen smilingly exclaimed. "We didn't realize you were one of his people." The thaw in their attitude spoke volumes about the continuing place the Harbottles have in the hearts of the Hausas.

Part 2

The missionary task

A brief historical overview of missionary practice

Lest we theorize about missions in a practical vacuum, I want to give an overview of missionary practice from post-apostolic time to our day. We will range broadly, and briefly, from the Celts to Carey and from the Moravians to McGavran. Against that background we will then move on to define the main missionary task.

The early Christians commonly endured severe persecution, which worked to keep the church relatively pure during its first three centuries. The *Didache*, dating from the second century, indicates that the basic practices of the church founded by the apostles continued in the post-apostolic church. The ease of travel and the peace ensured by Roman power encouraged the itineration of lay leaders and missionary apostles. (Missionaries were still called apostles in the second century.) Travel between the churches became so prevalent that rules for hospitality and guidelines for discerning genuine faith had to be circulated.[1]

Raymond Edman quotes Justin and Harnack to assert that

> In the earliest centuries of the expansion of Christianity the messengers and the methods of evangelization began with the spontaneous and unplanned enthusiasm of those who had themselves come out of spiritual darkness into the light and only gradually did ecclesiasticism and priestly professionalism replace the powerful preaching and witnessing of the primitive church ... The great bulk of the work was accomplished by laymen ... [W]hile leaders were chosen by the individual groups for the oversight of the work, the task of evangelization was assumed by the believers.[2]

The simplicity of organization found in the early churches, the way they mobilized all to the task, the unity they enjoyed and the purity of their life and message were gradually compromised as the second century passed.

Emperor Constantine's accession to power encouraged a new era of church expansion. After his Edict of Toleration in AD 313, the church became popular, powerful and wealthy but increasingly nominal. Ecclesiastic mechanisms and the rise in power of bishops replaced widespread lay involvement. A view of the sacraments as magical displaced faith in the simple truth and ordinances described in the New Testament. With increasing superstition came the spreading blight of moral evil. From this point on the Roman Church advanced as much by the sword as by the Spirit. Political power was wielded to effect the conversion of pagan peoples to Latin religious rites through mass baptisms.

The Byzantine, Coptic, Syrian and Armenian segments of the church developed along similar lines. Almost alone in these centuries the Byzantine missionary Ulfilas—a converted Visigoth—sought to indigenize missionary work among the wild Goths. He translated the Scriptures in their tongue, conducted worship in their language, preached and trained disciples. His missionary band constructed a wagon church that could go wherever these nomadic people went. In this and other ways Ulfilas showed the innovative skills essential in missionaries who seek to "become all things to all men ... [to] save some" (1 Cor. 9:22).

From the fifth century until the ninth, while Latin Christianity languished, Celtic missionaries kept the torch of missions burning bright in Britain and Northern Europe. In 432 Patrick began his missionary work in Ireland.

Patrick sought, first of all, to win influential leaders to his cause by demonstrating that he was a mightier Druid than their own pagan priests, a practice today called a "power encounter." By this is meant the overwhelming of pagan superstition and magic by a head-to-head demonstration of God's power.

Although Patrick's commitment to the evangelical faith, his preaching and his intense discipling are almost without peer, this early compromise doomed the Irish church to tolerate an underlying framework of superstition.

Nevertheless, Celtic missions flourished for several centuries during a time when Latin mission practice further deteriorated. The Celtic missionary bands emphasized reaching unreached countries through teams of missionary teachers and evangelists. They were completely independent of Rome and free to marry. Teamwork characterized Celtic missions. A band of twelve missionaries would be sent to an unreached area to establish a missionary village. In the village they would build a simple church, huts for their own accommodation and schoolrooms for teaching. They cultivated fields to produce their own food.

With language learning a priority, they concentrated on translating the Scriptures, writing hymns and teaching interested people in their own language. Baptism was delayed until those professing faith had received adequate instruction and showed some proof of their faith.

Boniface, Roman Catholic missionary to Germany in the eighth century, also believed in the efficacy of a "power encounter." His felling of the sacred oak of Thor, without Thor's retaliation, awed the pagans among whom he ministered. In other ways, his methodology characterized all Roman, Byzantine and Russian Orthodox missionary endeavor up to and including Francis Xavier in the sixteenth century. "When a group, often under the influence of a chieftain or ruler, had decided to become Christian, it was customary to baptize the catechumens without any long delay ... Then followed the long and patient process of trying to make Christians in deed of those who had become Christians in name."[3]

Roman Catholic missionary advance was greatly enhanced by a series of religious orders established in the twelfth century: the Franciscans, the Dominicans and the Augustinians. In the sixteenth century another society, the Jesuits, was founded. It became one of the most zealous of all the missionary orders. A considerable number of other missionary orders also sprang up in the centuries that followed. These bands of celibate, committed men and women took their Latin faith to the far corners of the earth.

The Reformation introduced one of the most intense missionary periods in history. During a relatively short period a mighty revival of faith in the cardinal doctrines of Scripture loosed Europe from the darkness and superstition of mediaeval Romanism. The Protestant Reformation won much of Europe for Christ. As an example, consider John Calvin, who trained and sent eighty-eight missionary evangelists back to his native France. Many became martyrs.

In common with other periods, much occurred that was unworthy of the gospel. We look in vain in the great confessions for clear statements of missionary strategy. Misunderstandings about the universal application of the Great Commission and the role of the State, together with prejudices about Jews and Muslims, can be discovered in the writings of Reformers such as Martin Luther. These must be understood, however, against the superstitious darkness that prevailed at that time. Despite having a limited view of the missionary task, the Reformers did understand the essentials: the authority of Scripture, the glory of Christ's atoning work, and justification by faith alone through grace alone. These rediscovered truths became the rallying cry of the Reformation—which, in the sovereign hand of God, became a mighty missionary outreach to a darkened Europe.

Pietism injected new devotion into Protestant churches which, in the inevitable march of the years, grew stultified by nominalism. Hermann Francke preached a return to personal piety and devotion that inspired Count Zinzendorf and many others. Under persecution by Roman Catholics in their home state of Moravia, thousands of Moravian Brethren took refuge on Zinzendorf's estate in Germany. His vision of missions and the Moravians' burden for the lost spearheaded a missionary thrust almost unparalleled since the time of the apostles. After a time of revival around a communion observance, they instituted a twenty-four-hours-a-day, seven-days-a-week missionary prayer meeting that lasted for a hundred years.

Tucker claims that, in the two decades following this revival, the Moravians sent out more missionaries than had the whole Protestant church during the preceding two centuries.[4] (I must temper this claim by pointing out that, although the Reformers and their stepchildren were not self-consciously missionary, the Holy Spirit used their outreach to produce astounding results.)

Under Zinzendorf's leadership the Moravians adopted the following principles:

- All Christians should witness through their daily vocations. For this reason all were to be trained in evangelism.
- One in sixty of their number should go as foreign missionaries.
- All missionaries were expected to become self-supporting by working at their trades in their countries of service.
- They were to witness by spoken word and example.
- They were to avoid all involvement in politics.

- The driving motivation of missions was personal devotion to Christ, an emphasis on the cross and absolute surrender to him.

After the religious wars with Rome ceased, the Protestant nations began to expand their influence globally. In their colonies, Britain and the Netherlands adopted diverse missionary philosophies. Britain paid for chaplains to accompany its trading companies but tried to outlaw any missionary work among its clients lest it hinder trade. The Dutch, on the other hand, paid preachers in their colonies not only to care for expatriate Dutchmen, but also to Christianize the indigenous population. This policy in Indonesia led to a large but nominal church.

While colonial opposition to missionary activity gradually moderated, a feeling of superiority infected much missionary activity. Many of the early British and Dutch missionaries carried with them "the white man's burden to civilize the heathen." This colonial attitude created both a deep-seated resentment and a paternalistic dependence within converts. Gradually, however, missionaries became more biblical, the servant-disciplers described in the Scriptures.

In 1706 Plütschau and Ziegenbalg, the first non-Roman Catholic missionaries to India, arrived in Tranquebar. These men, members of the Danish-Halle Mission, had been deeply influenced by pietism. They carried out their work under five principles:

- Christians must be able to read the Word of God. For this reason they sought to establish both a church and a school together.
- The Bible must be available in the local language.
- To be effective, preaching must be based on an accurate knowledge of the mind of the people, their religious beliefs and cultural mores.
- The aim must be personal conversion.
- As early as possible an Indian church with Indian ministry must be established.

William Carey, widely viewed as the father of modern missions, arrived in India in 1793. He operated under five basic principles:

- The gospel should be preached by every possible means as widely as possible.
- The Bible should be translated into the languages of the people and distributed widely.

- A church should be established at the earliest.
- Missionaries should carry on a profound study of the culture and thought of the people among whom they were to minister.
- As early as possible indigenous leaders should be trained to carry on the ministry of the new churches.

In 1890 Dr John L. Nevius, a missionary in Chefoo, China, visited Korea and passed on what he believed were four indispensable missionary principles:

- When people become Christians, they should not leave the calling and place where they were before they were converted. Instead, they should support themselves with their own work and be witnesses for Christ where they live.
- Church methods and organizational structures should only be developed as far as the Korean church can take responsibility for them.
- The church should call out for full-time work those who are best qualified and whom the church is able to support.
- Church buildings should be built by the Christians themselves from their own resources and in the local style.

Building upon this developing body of missionary methodology a series of writers in the early part of the twentieth century began to describe the missionary task in terms of the establishment of indigenous churches. Melvin Hodges defined the missionary goal as the establishment of churches that are self-governing, self-propagating and self-supporting. Roland Allen wrote a series of influential books calling for a return to apostolic missionary methods (*The Spontaneous Expansion of the Church*; *Missionary Methods: St Paul's or Ours?*).

But it was left to Donald McGavran to take these various insights and compose a comprehensive missionary theory called "Church Growth." As a missionary in India, McGavran pondered why certain groups seemed to respond to the gospel while others remained resistant. In 1955 he wrote *Bridges of God* and soon after collaborated with others to write *Church Growth and Group Conversion*, both of which became epochal books in the movement.

Most of what McGavran emphasized in Church Growth strategy can be summarized under the following principles:

- Numerical church growth, not just qualitative development, is God's will and thus should be sought.
- Missionaries should concentrate on church planting not on perfecting those who are already saints or on maintaining institutions.
- The bulk of missionary effort should be concentrated on responsive peoples, leaving resistant peoples with a skeleton crew of missionaries.
- Since "birds of a feather flock together," missionaries should target homogeneous groups and not seek to plant churches that manifest ethnic diversity.
- Evangelism should be culturally sensitive.
- Scientific disciplines such as statistics, sociology, anthropology, linguistics, etc., should be used to deepen our understanding of the missionary task.
- Strategy should be carefully planned.
- People are more likely to make "group decisions"—later called "multi-individual group decisions"—when evangelists are members of their own group or tribe.

McGavran frowned on the establishment of institutions. He felt that they detract from church planting—the primary missionary focus. Nevertheless, missionary institutions begun in the nineteenth century have continued to expand in many parts of the world. Indeed, some view missionary work as primarily the establishment and promotion of schools, hospitals, universities, literacy programs, public-health ministries, agricultural projects and relief efforts.

Ralph Winter further clarified the missionary task. In 1976 he established the US Center for World Missions as a missionary think tank and resource center. Along with the William Carey Library this has become a catalyst on the missionary scene. Throughout its young life focus has remained on the unreached, hidden peoples of the world. Gradually the center has amassed data on thousands of languages and cultures. Churches have been encouraged to adopt an unreached people group. For example, in one issue of their magazine, *Mission Frontiers*, 815 "untargeted peoples ... a subset of some 4,000 [least-evangelized people]" are listed to draw attention to their gospel poverty. Every serious missionary, mission or church should subscribe to the magazine.[5]

The twentieth century has seen missionary strategies multiply. Bible translation has thrived, along with evangelism-at-a-distance through radio, TV, correspondence courses, literature distribution, newspaper evangelism and phone-book follow-up. Missionary aviation and gospel ships have been added to the missionary line-up. Relief efforts have mushroomed in the belief that "you can't tell a hungry person about the gospel until you fill his or her stomach." "Tent-making ministries" have been invented in an effort to reach countries that have closed their doors to traditional missionary outreach. Christian engineers, doctors, nurses, technicians and teachers of English as a second language (ESL) have gone out under secular companies or on government contracts to many of these countries with the express aim of presence evangelism, living in the midst of non-Christians. Other ministries, such as Open Doors, have sought to brainstorm ways of getting the message into closed countries. Some, such as Partners and Christian Aid, exist to support national workers. More recently, the Internet has become a fruitful sphere of ministry.

Fortunately, diversity and innovation further the modern missionary expansion of the church. We face unparalleled need—the immense population of the unreached world—and a unique opportunity—the thrilling possibility that we have within our grasp the tools necessary to evangelize the whole world. Unfortunately, the number of Westerners volunteering for missionary service has been greatly reduced. Hopefully, the rising missionary commitment of the two-thirds world will offset this dearth.

No matter how many volunteers we have, there will never be an abundance. Trying to respond to all of the options before us could easily dissipate our limited resources. We must conserve the missionary personnel pool by putting our emphasis where it can contribute most to the divine plan. And so we turn to the New Testament to uncover the central task of missions.

Notes

1 **Philip Schaff,** (ed.), *Didach, The Oldest Church Manual called the Teaching of the Twelve Apostles: The Didache and kindred Documents in the Original with the Translations and*

Discussions of Post-Apostolic Teaching, Baptism, Worship, and Discipline (2nd edn; New York: Funk and Wagnalls, 1886), pp. 198–200, 204–5.

2 **V. Raymond Edman,** *The Light in Dark Ages* (Wheaton, IL: Van Kampen Press, 1949), pp. 32–33.

3 **Stephen Neill,** *A History of Christian Missions* (New York: Penguin, 1964), p. 77.

4 **Ruth Tucker,** *From Jerusalem to Irian Jaya* (Grand Rapids, MI: Academie Books, 1983), p. 71.

5 *Mission Frontiers*, Jan.–Feb. 2002. *Mission Frontiers* is published six times a year by the US Center for World Mission. Visit missionfrontiers.org for more information.

Chapter 8

The central missionary task

A mélange of concepts about missions has engaged Christian thinkers down through the centuries. In our day as well, a confusing smorgasbord of ideas about missions is laid before the missionary theorist. There is talk of contextualization, bonding, redemptive analogies and homogeneous units. While the size of the missionary task is so great and varied that a diversity of approaches must be adopted, yet we desperately need an understanding of the unchanging biblical principles before we dare embark on missions. Confusion here will have disastrous long-term consequences.

Part of the confusion exists because of a failure to distinguish between two separate commissions: the cultural commission and the Great Commission.

The cultural commission

In the Garden of Eden, God commissioned Adam and Eve to populate, nurture, subdue and rule over creation: "God blessed them and said to them, 'Be fruitful and increase in number; fill the earth and subdue it. Rule over the fish of the sea and the birds of the air and over every living creature ... The LORD God took the man and put him in the Garden of Eden to work it and take care of it" (Gen. 1:28; 2:15).

God gave to his image-bearers the responsibility to be stewards over creation. This mandate implies that earth and its creatures need governing and organizing. It also involves the responsible exploitation of the resources and habitat of the earth. Later, the Mosaic code laid down specific principles to guide Israel in the care of animals, land, and the administration of human society.

Although God gave this mandate to Adam and Eve before the Fall, he continues to call all mankind to the responsible and moral use of the habitat in which we all live. This cultural mandate calls for man to apply his best creative abilities to nurture and develop the earth for the benefit of all. In a sense, many facets of human culture find their origin here:

agriculture and animal husbandry, mining and forestry, industry and scientific study, health, education and government, music and art.

The violation of God's principles for earth and society brought on the universal flood of Noah. Even after this terrible warning, destructive exploitation continued. God raised up prophets to continue to warn against evil. Under the new covenant Jesus calls us to be salt and light—in the broadest possible terms. Christians are urged to obey governments whose authority is established by God to promote order and human welfare (see Rom. 13).

The cultural commission holds all mankind responsible. The missionary commission, however, comes to a limited group within society at large: God's new creation, the church. This Great Commission mandate calls disciples of Christ to evangelize the nations and to gather disciples into churches. It is a clarion call to apply the gospel to the spiritual problems of sin and guilt. Only through the establishment of churches can the most basic of all human problems, sin and rebellion, be dealt with on an ongoing basis. Those who are born again by the Spirit attack endemic evils because their new allegiance to God as King requires them to live holy lives—lives that are morally consistent in all areas, including areas of ecology and culture. While the second commission or mandate calls Christians to a ministry totally distinct from that of the first, it reintroduces a renewed commitment to be good stewards of the earth—and the power to effect change.

The two mandates, or commissions, must be carefully distinguished if confusion is to be avoided. A clear and burning vision of the most basic human need of all—salvation from sin—necessitates a narrow focus. George Peters writes,

> It must be emphasized that both mandates originated in God and are designed to serve mankind. Together they meet every need of man. It may sound irreligious but it nevertheless is a fact that the gospel does not serve all the needs of mankind. It was never designed to do so. While metaphysically it is true that all good originates in God, existentially and practically it does not all emanate directly from the gospel. When man is hungry he needs bread; when he is naked he needs clothes; when he has a serious infection he needs antibiotics first of all to remedy the situation. Man needs culture as well as the gospel; there is urgent need for both.

> Care must be taken, however, not to confuse the two mandates. If the two are disassociated unnaturally and unhealthily, a dichotomy arises which will work negatively upon society. If the mandates are too closely interrelated or blended, a culture-religion arises. The gospel suffers, divine priorities become blurred, and man's spiritual welfare is imperiled. The last-named is the case in the social gospel and liberalism where biblical evangelism is practically eclipsed.[1]

The cultural commission *is* distinct from the missionary commission, and *must be kept distinct*. The church, as the church, has not been called to do what individual citizens, as citizens, must do. The marching orders of the church are to pursue worldwide evangelization, not philanthropy or humanitarianism. George Peters warns, "Because the two mandates have not been distinguished, serious confusion has resulted in our assignment, work, and the choice of workers for mission fields."[2]

Consider the precedent of the apostolic missionaries recorded in the book of Acts. The apostles expressed their concern for the plight of widows by arranging for their care. Acts records the concern of early Christians for those suffering from famine. Gentile churches were urged to collect an offering to alleviate the suffering of those in Jerusalem. Apostolic tenderness toward those in dire straits is written large in the New Testament.

We must ask ourselves, however, whether the works of mercy demonstrated in the early church occurred as the natural outworking of Christian love or as the result of strategic evangelistic planning. I am convinced that the former is the case.

In Acts 6 the apostles came to a crossroads. They were faced with the choice of either pitching in to create a full-scale Christian ministry to widows or of maintaining their preaching ministry. They concluded, "It would not be right for us to neglect the ministry of the word of God in order to wait on tables" (v. 2).

They were not trying to avoid servanthood. They didn't think that serving tables was beneath them. The image of Jesus washing their feet had burned into their subconscious a commitment to servanthood. No, they based their conclusion on an analysis of priorities. They realized that "[We must] give our attention to prayer and the ministry of the word" (v. 4), without overlooking the needs of widows. To care for the widows, they suggested that "seven men ... known to be full of the Spirit" be put in charge of this task (v. 3).

The apostles wisely chose not to be diverted from their primary task by laying aside their preaching and prayer ministries to alleviate physical need. The main task—the proclamation of the Word of God—and the central goal—the extension of God's Kingdom through the establishment of churches—remained their focus. As a result of their conscious choice, local churches grew up wherever they went. The apostles knew what we often forget: that Jesus's mandate called for church planting not philanthropy.

Missionary church planting is not the enemy of works of mercy. These are not two competing preoccupations. But they must be addressed in a specific order of priority. When we evangelize according to the apostolic model, local churches spring up where converted sinners can gather to worship, pray, fellowship with one another, learn apostolic doctrine and break bread together (Acts 2:38–47). Once established, local churches become centers of salt and light. As outposts of the Kingdom of God, they radiate, in a dark and selfish world, a new climate of love and concern. As sinners grow in grace they increasingly manifest both love for God and love for their neighbors. Works of concern and compassion spring up as believers see neighbors in need.

Growing Christians supernaturally radiate neighborly love. This becomes the catalyst for all kinds of individual and corporate social programs. It is no accident that Christians have fought against slavery and child labor, have started orphanages and homes for battered women. It is no coincidence that the African church in Burkina Faso collects grain to help alleviate suffering in the yearly round of drought. It is no accident that churches in Khartoum take in refugees or that North American churches collect grain to ship to Sudan and Ethiopia.

Genuine churches demonstrate social concern. Churches, however, must first be planted! If we do not give priority to the planting of organized churches, centers of compassion and concern cannot be established in needy places. The apostles clearly understood their priorities: that evangelism precedes, and produces, social action. In this area at least, the Church Growth school of missionary thinking has done us the valuable service of challenging God's people to correct their priorities.

God has not called us (in the missionary mandate) to go into all the world and improve agriculture, relieve medical distress or build schools. He has called us to go and plant churches, which in turn become centers of improved agriculture, health and education. Educational, relief and medical work must take their place behind church planting in order of priority. True, where missionary vision remains steadfast, medical, agricultural and other philanthropic ministries can and have resulted in the planting of churches.

Please understand that I have the greatest respect for Christian works of compassion: hospitals, schools, literacy programs, relief projects, agricultural efforts. These important ministries, however, do not constitute missions as such. We must never again allow social action to usurp the place of evangelistic ministry. Ambivalence here spawned the social gospel of a previous generation. It is rearing its head again to create fuzzy thinking in church and missionary circles concerning the exact nature of our mission. Let's remove all ambivalence by looking carefully at what Jesus declared in the Great Commission.

The Great Commission

Before he ascended to Mission Control, Christ left explicit instructions with his disciples in what has been widely called "the Great Commission." Each of the five texts where the mandate is found has certain individual distinctives. They are summarized in Table 1.

Before examining the chart, you would do well to open your Bible and read each occurrence of the Great Commission: Matthew 28:16–20; Mark 16:14–20; Luke 24:44–49; John 20:19–23; Acts 1:1–11.

Summarizing the Great Commission

MISSIONS IS A TRIUNE UNDERTAKING

From this summary of these passages it is clear that each person of the Godhead is involved in missions. Missions carries on under the authority

References	Matthew 28:18–20	Mark 16:15–18	Luke 24:45–49	John 20:21–22	Acts 1:8
Context	The risen Christ addresses the Eleven at the mount in Galilee—some doubted	Best texts omit this passage. Eleven at meal, after which Christ ascends	In Jerusalem. To Eleven plus. Jesus dispels doubt by eating, explains events, leads to Bethany and ascends	Appearance after resurrection in locked room	Near Jerusalem. Much said about Kingdom during forty days of appearances. Told to wait for Spirit; ascends
Grammatical form	Command	Command	Prophecy	Promise/ statement	Prophecy/ promise
Divine dimension	"All authority"; Triune baptism; Jesus's presence	Lord worked with them and confirmed his word by signs	The promise of the Father and of the Holy Spirit	"Receive the Holy Spirit"	Power after Holy Spirit comes on them
Scope	All nations	Whole world	Among all nations		Jerusalem to whole world
Central task	Make disciples	Going and preaching	Preaching about sins' remission after repentance	Forgive sins or not	Witness
Strategy or method	Going, discipling, baptizing, teaching	Preaching	Wait for power from on high, then preach, beginning with Jerusalem	"Go as I have been sent"	Begin in Jerusalem, then go to Judea, then Samaria, then world
Time period	To the end of the age	From this time on	Near future	Present	Near future
Message	"Everything I have commanded"	The good news	Death and resurrection of Christ	Forgiveness of sins	"my witnesses"
Appeal of message	Make disciples, baptize, obey	Whoever believes and is baptized will be saved	Repentance and remission		
Signs and wonders		Exorcism, new tongues, snakes, poison, healing			
Special emphasis	Involvement of the Trinity, the authority of Christ, focus on discipleship	The urgency of the task and its extent	The Christocentric nature of the message and its effect; forgiveness	How missions is modeled on the Father–Son relationship; forgiveness	The role of the Holy Spirit, power for witness, the strategic process of advance

Table 1

of Jesus Christ, in whose name we are to preach. Indeed, Acts can be understood as "what Jesus continued to do," through his promised presence with his people to the end of the age. Missionaries are sent in the same way as the Father sent Christ. Missionaries are to be "clothed with power from on high," the Holy Spirit, who is promised by the Father. Those who respond to the gospel are to be baptized in "the name of the Father and of the Son and of the Holy Spirit."

THE SCOPE OF MISSIONS IS UNIVERSAL

Four of the five texts stress our obligation to take the gospel to the whole world: "Go into all the world and preach the good news to all creation." This will involve the planting of viable churches in every ethnic group: "make disciples of all nations."

MISSIONS IS THE DUTY OF ALL BELIEVERS

While not all are gifted as missionary church planters, it is assumed that all believers will contribute in some way to the fulfillment of Christ's final command. Many more than the eleven apostles were present in the contexts of Luke and Acts, when this command was reiterated. All believers are to "Seek first the kingdom of God." All are to pray, "Your kingdom come." The New Testament stresses the priesthood of all believers, not the creation of an elite. All believers must be involved in missions in some way.

MISSIONS IS A SPIRITUAL TASK

Three of the five texts stress the importance of the Holy Spirit in missions. Since the conviction, regeneration and edification of sinners can only occur under the influence of the Holy Spirit, his presence and power are vital in every step that is taken. "'Not by might nor by power [personal charisma, ability or training— or political influence, for example], but by my Spirit,' says the LORD Almighty" (Zech 4:6). This puts prayer in a central place.

MISSIONS REQUIRES ACTIVE OUTREACH

Every single text emphasizes the necessity of going. Missions cannot be accomplished by staying in one place. Travel, cross-cultural visitation and itineration must remain high on any list of missionary priorities.

THE MISSIONARY MESSAGE

The initial missionary message calls for an acknowledgement of sinfulness leading to repentance accompanied by faith in the gospel facts about who Jesus is, his death, burial and resurrection, and the purpose of those historical events—to make available remission of sins. But it also includes an appeal to discipleship involving "all that Jesus commanded." An analysis of the content of the apostolic message will be carried out in Part 3.

THE MISSIONARY TASK

What are missionaries called to do?

PREACHING

First on the agenda we find *evangelization*, bearing witness to the person and works of Christ with a view to calling men and women to repentance for forgiveness from sin. By his use of "witnesses," Christ underscored the importance of missionaries having a personal experience of Christ. Without that, "witness" is meaningless. Another word used for this primary task is "preaching," emphasizing the authoritative declaration of a message revealed from God himself. Under the blessing of the Holy Spirit, the natural fruit of this primary task is the conversion of sinners.

DISCIPLING

Following on naturally from the work of evangelization is the work of discipling. Matthew states that our goal must be to disciple the nations to the point that they know and obey all that Jesus has taught. Obviously, it is important to understand the nature of a disciple, which we will seek to clarify later in this chapter. Genuine disciples adopt a lifestyle in which they follow Christ in everything they do.

GATHERING DISCIPLES INTO CONGREGATIONS

Those who evidence even the rudimentary marks of genuine discipleship are to be baptized. Baptism is an entry ritual by which converted sinners publicly proclaim their identification with Christ and his church. While the Great Commission texts do not spell out in any great detail the necessity of gathering disciples into congregations, the precedent of Acts and the teaching of the rest of the New Testament make this clear. Disciples must be gathered into organized churches where the ordinances of baptism and the Lord's Supper can be celebrated.

TEACHING

Teaching must continue throughout the life of disciples and churches. Teaching involves helping people to understand and obey the instruction of Christ. In this sense, missions calls for a very thorough and comprehensive communication process. In the context of John's Gospel, Christ made the point of urging Peter to "take care of my sheep," "feed my sheep" (John 21:15–17), adding the dimension of pastoring to teaching. Discipling involves not only a pedagogical process but also the nurturing of those being taught.

MISSIONARY SUCCESS IS PREDICTED

Success is sure: "repentance and forgiveness of sins will be preached in his name to all nations"; "you will be my witnesses ... to the ends of the earth." Of course, not all will respond positively.

The book of Acts records what the apostles actually did in fulfillment of the Great Commission. Our practice ought to resemble theirs as closely as possible. The pattern they adopted can be formulated into seven steps, as noted below.

The early church model of missionary advance

ITINERATION

In practice, the missionary passion of reaching out to the unreached through exploring new areas of missionary activity is commonly sidetracked. While all Christians conceive of missions in terms of foreign outreach, it has been my sad experience that few cultivate the New Testament passion for the unreached. Instead, the Old Testament centripetal pattern of outreach seems to control people's minds: that sinners should be invited to an established local church and there be evangelized by preaching. In the West, when the culture was more open to the gospel, many did come to evangelistic services in local churches. Many were saved. That day has largely disappeared.

If Christ had intended that this pattern be promoted, he would not have repeatedly stressed the importance of "going." He sent out the Twelve and the Seventy. In spite of his example, however, the early Christians in Jerusalem continued to adopt the Old Testament pattern of expecting the unsaved to come to them in Jerusalem. Only when the persecution of Stephen scattered the church did believers begin to witness everywhere—eventually among the Gentiles. From that point on, missionary journeys occupy the attention of Luke in his story in the book of Acts. The journeys of Peter and John as well as those of Barnabas and Paul, and of Paul and Silas, also illustrate this pattern. The missionary impulse is to itinerate, not to settle down for long periods in one place (see Mark 16:15, 20; Acts 8:4–5; 9:32; 13:4). [Note: The extreme difficulty of evangelism in some contexts—for example, in Muslim nations—may require a lengthy period of residence. Assimilating a culture also takes time, something Paul and his colleagues had perfected since their childhood.]

PROCLAMATION

From the day of Pentecost onward, the book of Acts makes clear that the proclamation of the gospel occupied first place among the activities of the early missionaries. After the healing at the temple, Peter explained to the astonished crowd that "the God ... of our fathers, has glorified his servant Jesus. You handed him over to be killed ... but God raised him from the dead. We are witnesses of this" (Acts 3:13–15). Next Peter preached to the Sanhedrin.

Stephen's preaching so enraged his hearers that they stoned him to death (Acts 7). As a result of this persecution we read that "Those who had been scattered [lay Christians, not the apostles who remained in Jerusalem] preached the word wherever they went" (8:4). Philip preached in Samaria with powerful result. After confirming the work of the Spirit done through Philip, "Peter and John returned to Jerusalem, preaching the gospel in many Samaritan villages" (8:25). And so the text continues, describing the ministries of Barnabas and Paul until the book concludes with Paul in Rome, where "Boldly and without hindrance he preached the kingdom of God and taught about the Lord Jesus Christ" (28:31). (See also Mark 16:15, 20; Acts 20:20–21.)

ORGANIZATION

Church organization gradually developed with simple patterns of leadership. The formation of churches did not follow the Old Testament pattern where God gave elaborate details about the construction of the tabernacle. No detailed blueprint of church organization was given to the apostles. Instead, church organization evolved as the Holy Spirit guided the early Christians to make wise and practical organizational decisions. As problems arose, a structure evolved to handle them.

For example, the apostles asked the congregation in Jerusalem to choose from their own number seven men to care for neglected widows. This developed into the diaconate. While the apostles were recognized as leaders appointed by Christ, other leaders were needed as new groups of believers sprang up. James was recognized as a leader among leaders in Jerusalem—not an autocrat or pope (Acts 15:12–21). In Lystra, Iconium and Antioch "Paul and Barnabas appointed elders for them in each church and, with prayer and fasting, committed them to the Lord" (14:23). Timothy and Titus indicate that the appointing of elders and deacons was central to early church organization (see 1 Tim. 3:1–13; Titus 1:5–9).

While we would be hard put to prove an Episcopal, Presbyterian or Congregational form of organization as we know them today, certain elements of each appear. On the one hand, the apostles chose and appointed leaders. On the other hand, the whole congregation was asked to choose deacons. What of treasurers, committee chairmen, etc., etc.? The pragmatic and flexible nature of New Testament church organization ought to warn us to avoid exporting denominational models to missionary churches. Within the general revealed guidelines of the New Testament, a minimum of organization should be developed lest flexibility be sacrificed.

TEACHING

Teaching scarcely needs re-emphasis here. Christ was the Master who came teaching. He sent out his disciples to teach (see Matt. 28:20; chap. 10; Acts 20:20, 27). In obedience to his command, every missionary apostle or evangelist in the early church was committed to teaching. Acts concludes with Paul teaching about the Lord Jesus Christ (28:31). Elders are to be able to teach (1 Tim. 3:2). Titus and Timothy, as apostolic emissaries, were urged to be adept at teaching. Every epistle warns about the importance of recognizing and rejecting false teaching.

DELEGATION

Since missionaries evangelize, disciple and then move on to other places, the delegation of local responsibilities is a crucial facet of biblical missions. Good leaders always delegate. Humanly speaking, leaders may want to do things themselves and retain authority over others—a pattern that must be resisted. Throughout his ministry Jesus delegated responsibilities. He chose twelve that they might become his apostles. He sent out the Twelve and then the Seventy. He even gave Judas responsibility over the joint purse. He had the disciples find the colt upon which he rode into Jerusalem. He had disciples prepare the upper room. The Great Commission illustrates Christ's commitment to delegation. His delegation of authority was so complete that he was able to say, "whatever you bind on earth will be bound in heaven, and whatever you loose on earth will be loosed in heaven" (Matt. 16:19).

Except in their tardiness to delegate authority to Gentile believers, Jesus's disciples showed that they had learned the "delegation lesson" well. The choice of seven men to deal with problems in Jerusalem and the appointment of elders and deacons in every church demonstrate this reality. The limited time that Paul's missionary teams stayed in any one place also shows that he understood that disciples grow, not when overshadowed by older believers, but when given responsibility and left to develop. To the Ephesian elders Paul said, "I commit you to God and to the word of his grace, which can build you up and give you an inheritance among all those who are sanctified" (Acts 20:32). He directed Timothy not to do everything himself but to take his teaching and entrust it "to reliable men who will also be qualified to teach others" (2 Tim. 2:2).

PROTECTION AND NURTURE

The early missionaries also followed the pattern of Jesus by committing themselves to care for disciples as shepherds care for sheep (see John 10). In each of the New Testament epistles there is evident concern that disciples be nurtured in the faith and protected from evil. "Like newborn babies, crave pure spiritual milk, so that by it you may grow up in your salvation ... abstain from sinful desires, which war against your soul ... Be self-controlled and alert. Your enemy the devil prowls around like a roaring lion looking for someone to devour" (1 Peter 2:2, 11; 5:8).

The repeated visits of the early missionaries to new churches demonstrate this same concern. When Paul reviewed his ministry among them, he took pains to prepare the Ephesian elders to protect the sheep under their care: "You know that I have not hesitated to preach anything that would be helpful to you but have taught you publicly and from house to house ... in every city the Holy Spirit warns me ... Keep watch over yourselves and all the flock ... I never stopped warning each of you night and day with tears" (Acts 20:20, 23, 28, 31).

MOVING ON TO THE NEXT UNREACHED GROUP

Why not stay for a lengthy period in one place? Paul did stay for three years in Ephesus, but that was an exception. His normal pattern was controlled by the missionary impulse "to preach the gospel where Christ was not known" (Rom. 15:20). This passion is perfectly illustrated in the book of Acts, with its extensive missionary journeys. Once they got over their "Jerusalem complex" the apostles began to itinerate broadly. Tradition tells us that they went as far as Britain, Persia, India and North Africa. Although Christ's first priority was Israel, even he kept moving from one place to another: Judea, Galilee, Tyre, Decapolis.

This sevenfold model is similar to the cycle of outreach described by Dr. Paul Hesselgrave of Trinity Evangelical Divinity School in Chicago. He conceives mission as a self-perpetuating pattern of church planting. Led by the Holy Spirit, the process includes everything from commissioning for service to church planting and beyond, when a newly planted missionary church then commissions missionaries of its own.

The nature of a disciple

Missionary evangelism involves making disciples, hence the need to identify the characteristics of a genuine disciple. This is particularly important in the light of the proliferation of professing Christians who show no evidence of real conversion.

George Peters defines a disciple as follows:

> A disciple of Christ is a believing person: 1. living a life of conscious and constant *identification* with Christ, a. in life, death and resurrection; b. in words, behavior, attitudes, motives and purposes; 2. fully realizing Christ's absolute *ownership* of his life; 3. joyfully embracing the *saviorhood* of Christ; 4. delighting in the *lordship* of Christ; 5. living by the abiding, indwelling *resources* of Christ; 6. according to the imprinted *pattern* and *purpose* of Christ; 7. for the chief end of *glorifying* his Lord and Savior.[3]

Although Peters' definition is quite comprehensive, there are several discrepancies. One missing element may be due to the Western perspective it betrays. Genuine disciples don't live isolated lives They feel themselves part of a family and as such seek out fellowship with other disciples. They worship and minister with others as members of some local church.

Secondly, Peters did not mention the sense of servanthood that leads disciples to engage in some aspect of ministry in which they can use their spiritual gifts.

Thirdly, the work of the Holy Spirit is not mentioned.

I cannot fault Peters too much for these omissions. A comprehensive definition may be impossible without quoting the length and breadth of the New Testament! What we need is a simple definition that covers the essentials and takes into account the imperfections that remain in all disciples.

Using Matthew 28:19–20, Luke 9:23, and John 13:14–17, 34, I would define a disciple as: *A follower of Jesus Christ who lives in conscious and progressive dependence upon the Holy Spirit to overcome his or her sinful tendencies and to walk in joyful obedience to the commands of Christ, and to use his or her spiritual gifts to serve fellow believers in a local church and further the Kingdom beyond it.*

More briefly: *A disciple is a sinner who has been regenerated by the Holy Spirit, justified by faith in Christ's atoning death, and who is being progressively sanctified through following and serving Jesus Christ and his church.*

Disciples are not perfect, but they are growing in grace and holiness. Disciples are not just professing Christians; they possess a genuine relationship with Jesus Christ. As his followers, disciples are obedient to Christ. Disciples are learners and servants. Disciples love the Father, trust in the Son of God and depend on the Holy Spirit. Disciples sympathize with the passion of the Savior.

The nature of the New Testament church

Since missions is church planting, we need to be very clear on just what missionaries are expected to plant! How can we define the church? How many people constitute a church? How is it organized? Early in their ministry, missionaries must have clear answers to questions such as these.

Peter Wagner defines the church as follows: "I would suggest that there are five basic things that you must have to be a church as a visible, social institution: (1) Scripture (in oral form perhaps for non-literate culture); (2) leadership; (3) the *sacraments* (baptism and communion or their equivalents, as in Quakerism); (4) giving; and (5) consensus of belief."[4]

Errol Hulse writes that an ideal church will have: biblical preaching, scriptural church government, the sacraments of baptism and the Lord's Supper, and spiritual life evidenced by spiritual worship, holiness of life, brotherly love, evangelism and good works.[5] On the subject of church government he writes that there must be scripturally appointed elders who see that the ministry of the Word is carefully carried out and applied, and that members are biblically screened and disciplined if necessary.

Using Acts 2:38–47, 4:23–37, and 20:18–35, I would define the church as follows: *The church is a local group of baptized believers who come together in an organized way under biblically qualified leadership. An authentic local church maintains commitment to apostolic doctrine and practice by celebrating two ordinances; gathering to worship, pray, hear the Word and fellowship; and demonstrating a growing godliness and love in personal and community life and outreach.*

Although the church in Jerusalem was a new church, it was characterized by all of these marvelous qualities. Amazing! We would be wise to remember, however, that it is very unlikely that any one local church, or denomination, will approach this ideal except in the throes of revival. Each will manifest weaknesses. We need patience with real churches and with one another. Authentic churches will strive to improve those weaknesses through prayer and a deepening commitment to Christ and his Word. New churches will need to manifest the most fundamental characteristics, such as those outlined by Errol Hulse, while they continue to develop toward maturity.

Notes

1 **George W. Peters,** *A Biblical Theology of Missions* (Chicago: Moody, 1972), p. 168.

2 Ibid. p. 170.

3 **Peters,** *A Biblical Theology of Missions*, p. 188.

4 **C. Peter Wagner,** *Church/Mission Tensions Today* (Chicago: Moody Press, 1972), p. 34.

5 **Errol Hulse,** "The Ideal Church," in *Local Church Practice* (Haywards Heath: Carey, 1978), p. 23.

Pioneering in Senegal

How do you catch cockroaches? Well, Steve Vannah, a missionary team leader in the West African nation of Senegal, read about King Solomon allowing lizards the run of his palace (see Prov. 30:28). He thought he would give it a try. So he caught a lizard, christened it "Lizzy," and turned it loose. Eureka! Lizzy had a feast.

Barbara Vannah expects the unusual from her husband, Steve. His daughters, Esther and Sarah, look forward to having another story to impress friends back in the USA! Other missionary wives were not too thrilled, however, when their kitchens were targeted for the lizard solution!

Adaptability is the name of the game for church planters in Senegal. But can flexibility be carried too far? Suppose you are a woman and want to get your hair cut. What do you do when you can't speak a word of Wolof? Well, you try to explain what you want to the hair stylist but you may come back with a *very* short "French haircut," as Tammy Simpson did! Fortunately, the Senegal team has a great sense of humor. But where is Senegal, and who are the Wolofs?

Suppose you are basking on a beach in Jamaica. Imagine sending a mythical arrow arching high into the stratosphere to plunge to earth due east of Jamaica in Africa. It would bury itself in the sandy soil of Senegal, the most westerly point in Africa. If your imaginary arrow was off course to the north it would be lost in the howling emptiness of sun-smitten wilderness, that is, the Saharan country of Mauritania. If too far south, it would plunge into the rich swamps or lush jungle of equatorial Africa.

Just at the point where your imaginary arrow strikes the soil of Africa you would find the bustling capital and seaport of Dakar. Ships from all over the globe offload their cargoes here at the gateway of Africa. Ocean-going trawlers from Russia and Europe fish the rich waters offshore. Consumer goods from the four corners are found here. Beautiful buildings, luxurious French villas and intriguing restaurants grace the city. Almost a quarter of Senegal's seven million people inhabit this modern city.

The US State Department has rated Senegal as the most democratic of all the sub-Saharan states and the safest place to live in that sphere. Missionaries working with SIM have found the people to be friendly and open, hospitable and interested.

Since 1984 a handful of SIMers have been hard at work among the industrious Wolofs who dominate Senegalese society. Although the Wolof tribe comprises only a third of the population, its language and influence permeate society. Some two million non-Wolofs from other tribes, such as the Fula, Serer, Tukulor, Mandingo and Jola, speak the Wolof language.

In spite of their friendliness, however, most Senegalese have proved to be resistant to the gospel. Portuguese and French colonial influence permeated Senegal for centuries. Nevertheless, the Roman Catholic Church has been unable to win more than a meager 3.5 percent of the people. Most of these have come from animistic tribes in the south.

Among Protestants the situation is similar. While a couple of hundred Protestant missionaries from twenty different agencies labor here, there are only a couple of thousand evangelical believers in the whole nation. Among the Wolofs the situation is even gloomier. Only twelve Wolof believers were known in 1994! Why have missions found the Wolofs so unresponsive?

To find out, we need to take the train inland from Dakar over the sparsely treed and semi-arid plain that comprises most of Senegal. Clumps of niim (a tree common in India, Pakistan and this part of Africa) and eucalyptus trees punctuate fields of millet and peanuts. Here and there we notice plots of vegetables and massive old boabob trees.

We continue east through the savannah. Suddenly, a cluster of slender towers that seem to defy gravity rises like a mirage from the dusty plain. We have arrived at Touba, the center of Muslim Senegal. The five minarets, one of which rises fully 280 feet into the azure sky, represent the five pillars of Islam. The Senegalese claim that this mosque is the largest in Black Africa.

We join a stream of pilgrims leaving the train. Many wear the clothes of poor farmers. Several Mercedes thread their way through the throng. Pilgrims nod their heads deferentially to the occupants who wear expensive imported suits. These must be Marabouts, leaders of the Wolof Mourides sect, whose brotherhood is such a power in Senegal.

Bill and Tammy Simpson, who have chosen to travel with us, explain that the Mourides sect sprang up 110 years ago when the French defeated the Wolof king. Scholars view the Mouride movement as a violent reaction against the French breakup of Wolof power. While the French built railroads and great buildings the Mouride leaders, called Marabouts or Sheikhs, completely displaced the former Wolof chiefs in both power and prestige. To be a Mouride today is to be a true Wolof, unbroken in spirit against foreign and "Christian" nations. No wonder the Wolof are resistant to the gospel.

As we push on toward the mosque complex, a group of young boys beg us for money. About six thousand young men from twelve to fifteen years of age study Islam from the Marabouts around Touba. They swell Mouride coffers by begging money from visitors.

Gothic arches decorated by Moroccan artisans with beautiful Islamic calligraphy grace the huge complex of buildings. The sound of loud singing and chanting permeates the whole area. Here and there we come on groups of Mourides seated on the floor with their hands over their ears as they sing. A leader sings a verse and the men repeat it, yelling as loudly as they can. I can understand why they cover their ears!

In a courtyard a group of disciples gathers around a Sheikh. We pause to watch. A disciple kneels before the Marabout and says, "I submit my body and my soul to you, both in this life and in the next. I will do everything you order me, and abstain from anything you forbid me." The Sheikh then pronounces a brief benediction and spits into the hands of the disciple. The disciple passes his hands over his face, symbolizing that he is in the hands of his Sheikh "like a corpse in the hands of the embalmer."

A stream of men and women propels us toward the tombs of the five dead Khalifa—that is, supreme Islamic rulers—of the sect. As non-Muslims, we are not allowed to enter Bamba's tomb, but we peer through the ornate iron gates. Gold-leaf decorates the ceiling. A huge French chandelier glitters above the mausoleum. As worshipers come in and out of his tomb they touch the gates or lintels. Then, as if to rub in the blessing, they wipe their hands over their faces.

We travel back toward Dakar to Senegal's third largest city, Thies, where the SIM team has its base. As we travel, we ponder the significance of what we have seen. Amadu Bamba, who spent the last three years of his life in the construction of this great mosque, died in 1927 … but his influence permeates Senegalese society.

Amadu Bamba was an ascetic Muslim mystic. During his life, the mere sight of Bamba at prayer was said to plunge the faithful into hysterical outbursts. Disciples would roll at his feet, kiss his sandals and hold out their hands for his saliva. When he spit into their hands they would rub their faces and body and fall into convulsions.

Bamba promised salvation to all who would become his disciples. "Any Mouride who seeks refuge with me shall go to paradise and shall not know the burning embers of hell." When asked for a blessing, he would simply reply, "Go and work." Work in this context meant working every Wednesday for the Marabout (religious leader of the society). Their work ethic has enabled the Marabouts to corner the peanut farming economy and become extremely wealthy.

No wonder Wolofs resist the gospel of free grace when they have been taught that salvation comes through work. Even then it can only be received through a chain of mediation leading from disciple to Sheikh to Amadu Bamba to the prophet Muhammad to Allah.

When we arrive in Thies, we find the missionary team is gearing up to present the *Jesus* film. Every Wednesday night they show it in one of the fifty districts of the city. This evening, over 1,200 gather under the stars. As the life of Christ unfolds before their eyes a hush descends. The crowd claps when Jesus performs a miracle. It bursts into applause at the appearance of the risen Christ before the disciples. After the film some buy Gospels of Luke in French or Wolof.

In the days that follow film showings, interested people trickle into the SIM boutique in the market area of the city. Decorated, not by pictures that would be anathema to Muslims, but by symbols, the book room offers a variety of religious books and Bibles. A cassette corner allows non-readers to listen to Bible stories. Some days, visitors fill the boutique. Discussions often develop.

After this Wednesday's film showing three come to the boutique to sign up for correspondence courses on the Old Testament. Fifty or more study by correspondence. Interest is building.

As friends are made, they are invited to a variety of evangelistic opportunities. About twenty men and women who show sustained interest come together for a time of singing, Bible study and discussion on Sunday afternoons. Some sixteen women, drawn by friendship evangelism, gather on Wednesday afternoons. A group of teens also meet on Wednesdays. Twenty men and women assemble on Friday nights.

Music plays an increasing role in Wolof outreach. Slip into the back of the Sunday afternoon Bible study group with us. A mixture of men and women, believers, inquirers and curious Muslims comprise the group. Accompanied by drums, tambourine and guitar, a recent Senegalese convert sings his way through John 11. As soon as he finishes, the group burst into explosive applause.

Barbara Vannah talks with animation of the fifty songs they have made up in Wolof. She has either re-worked praise songs borrowed from the French or taken local African melodies and put new words to them. She intends to write a series of teaching songs that follow the story of the Bible. Her first songs concern Adam, Abraham, Moses and David. When missionaries visit inquirers they often find them humming the tunes and whispering the words they have learned.

A small congregation is beginning to develop. A handful of believers gather Sunday mornings for worship. George (not his real name) suffers intense persecution. A second young man, originally attracted by the film showings, committed himself to Christ after a vivid dream. A young woman, very active in the church, has been baptized but fights the onslaught of spiritual warfare inspired by her non-Christian father. Another believer stands firm in spite of the threats of her belt-wielding husband. Discipleship is costly in Senegal!

When we ask the Vannahs if they need more workers, they emphatically reply, "Absolutely! If we had more workers, we could send them to three more villages that have requested Bible studies; we could show the *Jesus* film to many unreached villages around the city of Thies, thus opening up more Bible studies; we could show the *Jesus* film and open another evangelistic room in a nearby city of one million people that has no Christian witness whatsoever; we could start a radio ministry with correspondence courses; and so much more!"[1]

Note

1 The preceding cameo accurately describes the way missionary work in many Muslim countries progresses. I wrote it in July 1992 of SIM International church-planting work in Senegal, and it was accurate at that time.

Part 3

The missionary message

Chapter 9

Methodology or message?

Christians widely assume that the message presented by present-day evangelists and missionaries corresponds exactly to that handed down by the apostles. With that assumption reigning, focus today is most commonly not on a recovery of the apostolic message but on the search for relevant methodology. Viewing the lost in the light of insights on marketing, we are urged to adopt a marketing strategy for the church so that felt needs may be met.

While I don't want to detract from the laudable motives of Christian communicators nor the valid insights afforded by marketers, I believe our research ought to be more basic. While freshness and novelty of speech may aid communication, we ought to ensure that our message conforms to apostolic doctrine. I don't believe it is safe to assume it does.

Noting the danger, John Piper writes,

> I have been pondering a possible relationship between the minimizing of the Bible in so-called seeker-driven churches and in some of the radical forms of contextualization that have emerged in missions ... The common denominator that I am pondering is the loss of confidence that declaring what the Bible says in the power of the Holy Spirit can create and sustain the church of Christ.[1]

In the same article Piper describes numerous saints coming to him to complain that their pastor "doesn't proclaim to us what the Bible says and means. The messages are not revelations of the glory of Christ. They are advice-talks with a religious twist."[2]

I have found the same trends prevailing. To remedy this situation we need a robust return to the Bible. In particular, let me suggest a careful analysis of the book of Acts, a book which is full of methodology—but much more.

I have read and re-read the book of Acts in an attempt to discover the precise nature of apostolic witness. In Luke's history, I have found the record of fourteen messages, testimonies, addresses and statements of defense. Some are lengthy. Many are short.

Apostolic terms for the Christian message	Times used
"Jesus," "Jesus as the Christ," "the whole message of his life," "the name of Jesus Christ," etc.	16
"The word of God," "the word of the Lord"	13
"The gospel," "the good news"	9
"The way," "way of the Lord," "way of salvation"	9
"The hope of Israel," "the things announced beforehand," "the good news of the promise," etc.	7
"The kingdom of God"	6
"Forgiveness," "repentance toward God," "faith in our Lord Jesus Christ," etc. (various responses to and results from the message)	5
"The resurrection"	4
"The word of this salvation"	2

Table 2. Variety of expression

Table 2 lists the terms actually used by the apostles and their followers. These words and phrases reflect their understanding of the message Christ had commissioned them to share. Since the Spirit inspired Luke to record in the book of Acts these specific terms, we would do well to carefully evaluate their import. Subsequent chapters will deal with some of the most important implications.[3]

Early Christians, as expected, referred to "the gospel" and the "word of God." But even more frequently, they referred to their message as "Jesus" or "the whole message of his life," or they talked about "Jesus as the Christ." Not only so, but they ranged far afield in talking about the gospel as "the way," "the hope of Israel," "the kingdom of God," "the resurrection," "the word of this salvation" and the message of "forgiveness."

The variety of terminology found in words as diverse as Jesus, kingdom, resurrection, way, hope and gospel is arresting to say the least. Such a variety of expressions might indicate that the apostles were imprecise in their communication; however, this is not the case, as we can tell from Table 2.

I also searched through the text of Acts to come up with some idea of the scope of the apostolic message. The next table contains a summary of the subject matter in apostolic proclamation. Before looking closely at this summary, consider several relevant points.

Apostolic proclamation manifests a notable breadth of content. There is also a basic underlying unity from person to person and place to place. No discernible difference surfaces between the message of apostles, such as Peter and Paul, and of deacons, such as Stephen, or of evangelists, such as Philip.

For this reason, I have chosen to include not only what the apostles said, but also all the recorded messages and witnesses found in the book of Acts. These include defenses given in the courts of the day which demonstrate a conscious effort on the part of the Christian prisoners to use creativity in declaring the Christian message. All the messages, except the one given by Paul to the Ephesian elders in Acts 20, were to non-believing audiences.

Consider another matter. Dr. Luke does not quote the messages verbatim. We know that the apostles often preached lengthy sermons. (Paul preached all night at Troas—Acts 20:7!) Without a doubt, Acts gives us shortened summaries of the important messages. (The Athenian address can be read slowly in two minutes.) The abridged nature of the records contained in Acts renders their content of special importance. These abstracts form an inspired summary of the most important content elements.

In spite of space limitations, Luke is not content to summarize the messages in terms of a few key phrases. At least thirty-three different elements, perhaps more, can be isolated. These facets of apostolic communication touch almost the whole breadth of revelation. They can be listed under three headings: About God; About man; About Christ.

Table 3 summarizes the topics covered. The numbers that follow the different topics give the number of messages or witnesses—out of a total of thirteen—that mention a particular topic. The message to the Ephesian elders is not included in this study because it summarizes, not Paul's message, but his ministry in general. While I have sought to demonstrate

About God	No.	About man	No.	About Christ	No.
God of covenant and Israel	10	Ignorance	3	Connection with John the Baptist	2
God's decree (purpose, plan, ordination, predestination, etc.)	8	Sinfulness	5	Related to OT promises	9
Holy and glorious character	2	Responsible for Christ's death	5	Holy character	4
Graciousness	4	Need of salvation	3	Lived a life of attesting signs	2
Judge of sin	6	Promise of inheritance and Holy Spirit	3	Trial	2
Creator and Ruler	3	Should repent	6	Death, blood	9
Father	1	Needs forgiveness	6	Burial	1
One who raised Jesus	5	Should believe	4	Resurrection	9
Holy Spirit	3	Should be baptized	4	Exaltation	3
		About sanctification and good works	5	Present continuing ministry	6
		Resurrection and hope	1	Sender of Holy Spirit	2
				Second Coming	1

Table 3. Breadth of apostolic content: The content elements found in apostolic communication

the frequency of each topic, nevertheless it is very difficult in chart form to show the actual weight given to any topic.

This table illustrates, in summary form, the message of the apostolic band in the first century. Since there is one gospel (Gal. 1:6–10) and one faith (Eph. 4:5), which has been once for all delivered to the saints (Jude 3), their message must also be our message.

The aim of evangelism remains the expansion and building up of "God's household," the church. The church, in turn, can only be genuinely built up if it is "built on the foundation of the apostles and prophets ..." (Eph. 2:20).

Since the New Testament gives us God's perspective on missions, we must assume that its message is our message, and the pattern it lays down ought to be our pattern. In the chapters that follow, we will extract relevant principles from the practice of the apostles—as summarized by these two tables—in order to establish a framework in which missions ought to operate.

Notes

1 **John Piper,** "Minimizing the Bible? Seeker-Driven Pastors and Radical Contextualization in Missions," in *Mission Frontiers*, Jan.–Feb. 2006, p. 16.

2 Ibid. p. 17.

3 The material in chapters 10–14 is adapted from that contained in my book *Tell the World* (Welwyn: Evangelical Press, 1981).

Bandwagon or balance?

The apostles proclaimed a message in which a number of different ideas were held in delicate balance. Our Lord Jesus occupies a major portion of their messages, but not without reference to God the Father. Man's condition is thoroughly sketched, but so is redemption. No single word or phrase predominates as the favorite term they used to designate their messages. It is not only the "gospel" but also the "word of God," "the way," "the word of this salvation" and "the things concerning the kingdom."

The three main categories of content (God, man and Christ) demonstrate the breadth and balance of apostolic proclamation. It is first of all Trinitarian. Apostolic preaching resonated with the vibrant presence of the Father, Son and Holy Spirit. The apostles talked about "the times or dates the Father has set by his own authority" (Acts 1:7) and about what the "Father promised" (1:4).

Mention of the Holy Spirit occurs frequently. Jesus promised that they would receive power "when the Holy Spirit comes on you" (1:8). Jesus's reference to the Spirit did not take them by surprise; evidently, they understood his role in the history of Israel. They spoke of Old Testament Scripture as that which "the Holy Spirit spoke long ago through the mouth of David concerning Judas" (1:16; also 4:25).

On the day of Pentecost we find them speaking "as the Spirit enabled them" after having been "filled with the Holy Spirit" (2:4). Luke records Ananias lying to the Holy Spirit (5:3–4). To the Sanhedrin, the apostles bore witness that Jesus, who died on the cross, was raised by God and "God exalted him to his own right hand as Prince and Savior ... We are witnesses of these things, and so is the Holy Spirit, whom God has given to those who obey him" (5:31–32). Note that the indwelling presence of the Holy Spirit is not a gift God gives to an elite few as a second blessing. God promises this gift to all whom he calls to salvation (2:38–39).

The apostles' teaching and personal faith were so transparently Trinitarian that this fact stamped all they did and said, especially when they faced the peril of death at the hands of the Jewish Council.

Of course, the person of Jesus Christ occupied a central place. The good news they preached was new and it was about Christ. The angel who released the apostles from prison told them to go out and "tell the people the full message of this new life" (5:20). In response, the apostles "never stopped teaching and proclaiming the good news that Jesus is the Christ" (5:42). Philip proclaimed Christ in Samaria and preached Jesus to the Ethiopian (8:5, 12, 35). This emphasis continues throughout the book of Acts, which concludes with Paul in Rome as he "taught about the Lord Jesus Christ" (28:31).

Their messages convey an overwhelming preoccupation with Christ. They did not, however, reduce their proclamation to include only the barest essentials—for example, the three elements of 1 Corinthians 15: death, burial and resurrection. They heralded many aspects of Christ's ministry and character. Apostolic practice would lead us to conclude that the three historical facts of 1 Corinthians 15 are meant to be summary in nature. Their redemptive centrality does not mean that the gospel is a message limited to the proclamation of these three facts.

We should also note the emphasis on the resurrection. While the resurrection of Christ is mentioned in the same number of passages as the death of Christ, it takes up a proportionately larger portion of the messages in which it figures. The apostles did not state that Christ arose, which was true, but that "God raised up Jesus." By using these words, they emphasized their belief that the resurrection was a bold intervention of Almighty God into history. God wrested Christ from the last enemy, death.

The resurrection was the glory of their faith. It attested the reality of their claim that the death of Christ brought the forgiveness of sins within the grasp of lost men. It was an evidence of God's power, giving them confidence that those bound in sin could be delivered from the grip of spiritual death.

The full title "the Lord Jesus Christ" demonstrates the balance manifest in the apostolic message about this Person. He is Jesus, the man who lived, taught, performed miracles, died, rose again and ascended to the Father's right hand, from which position he continues to rule.

He is also Christ, the Messiah who came in accordance with the promise of the law and the prophets. This is he whom God anointed to be the King-

Deliverer. Fittingly, apostolic preaching concerned a kingdom. The *International Standard Bible Encyclopedia* emphasizes the importance attached to the usage of "Messiah": "The substantive use [of 'Messiah'] is restricted to the King. He only is called 'the Lord's anointed.'"[1]

Lastly, Jesus was proclaimed as "Lord." Apostolic usage of "Lord" shows the apostles equated him with Jehovah of the Old Testament, normally translated there as "LORD" (see Acts 2:34). This usage emphasizes Christ's deity. While the Greek word for "Lord" does not in itself indicate deity, nevertheless, finding this title in contexts that connect it with "Jehovah" requires us to come to such a conclusion.

"Lord" also indicates Jesus's role as teacher. The Gospels frequently refer to Jesus as the "Master," a related term.

Besides these implications, his title "the Lord Jesus Christ" portrays his three main offices. As "Lord," he occupies the prophetic office—ministering as Teacher and Prophet. As "Jesus," he, by his own perfect sacrifice and intercessory ministry, fulfills the office of Priest. As "Christ," he holds the position of King, at God's right hand.

The three titles also illustrate the three periods and the three spheres of his ministry. As "Lord," he is the *eternal* Son of God. As "Jesus," he is the incarnate Son of Mary who was born, died and rose again during a *specific period* of time. As "Christ," he is *presently* ruling as King at the Father's right hand, from where he will return in the future.

As we turn our attention from that era to this, we need to ask ourselves whether we manifest apostolic balance or a penchant for climbing on the latest bandwagon. On the whole, conservative Christians today believe each of the truths heralded by the apostles. Modern messages, however, do not always manifest the same balance. We have a tendency to seize one facet of truth and hold it out as a panacea for all ills. This love affair with the latest fad presents subtle dangers.

Imbalance opens a window for error that eventually leads to throwing the door wide open to heresy. Error often flits into our assemblies on the gossamer wings of innocence—a naive attraction to some exciting trend or program. At first, some aspect of the truth is emphasized. As time passes, an emphasis becomes an overemphasis. That one facet gradually takes center stage and a new group is born.

History is replete with examples. We can read of imbalance introduced by Arius, Pelagius and Arminius. Hyper-Calvinists sought to discourage William Carey from his missionary vision. Concern about neglect of the law, particularly of the Sabbath, led the Seventh-Day Adventists to slip into legalism.

Today we are as susceptible to imbalance as ever. Christian Reconstructionists seem bent on forcing on modern societies the very Old Testament law that Peter warned believers about at the Council of Jerusalem. Third-Wave Charismatics would have us re-establish the institution of the prophet and inaugurate a new day of miracles. Others who claim to be evangelical promote a prosperity gospel of health and wealth. Still others would persuade us to adopt a positivist gospel of self-affirmation.

Society at large swings wildly from one extreme to another, and too often the church seems to follow along. Most trends are basically humanistic, focusing on some preoccupation of men and women with themselves. Feminist studies lead us to de-emphasize the uniqueness of the sexes and to empty the home of the female nurture God intended. Sociological studies tracing family abuse to male dominance demand that the state, not parents, control childhood development. New laws threaten families that exercise biblical child discipline. Psychological writings decry codes of morality as inhibiting and guilt producing. Adultery, immorality, homosexuality and abortion are redefined and sold to the mainstream as if they represent normality. Biological studies trace all problems to genetics or chemicals. Some social scientists claim that governments ought to provide health care, guaranteed income and housing to all and sundry, irrespective of any commitment to work. Some champion euthanasia.

Innovative Christian writers are tempted to climb on the current secular bandwagon, pick up the reins and lead the wagon at a gallop into our midst. They persuade us to invent a Christian approach to self-fulfillment, ecology, violence, homosexuality, sexual fulfillment, female leadership, etc., etc. Every year a torrent of "relevant" books pours from the presses.

Lest you misunderstand, let me assure you that I am not calling for an uninformed retreat from the burning issues of the day. We live in the world, not in some holy ghetto. Each secular emphasis deserves careful study and response.

However, when we fail to maintain a correct balance in our worship, witness and walk, we inevitably invite distortion. If all our attention is taken up by responding to every current issue, we cannot possibly maintain the balance necessary to demonstrate genuine Christian maturity. No wonder many of the basics of the Christian life—devotion to Christ, prayer, Bible study and holiness, for example—excite lukewarm interest. They are not novel enough.

A random survey of many leading Christian magazines, particularly in North America, will yield very few feature articles on the Trinity, the person of Christ, the character of God, creation, providence or Christian discipleship. It is fortunate for our study of the Lord that we have the holidays of Easter and Christmas to stimulate articles on his incarnation and Passion!

Take your own survey of the Christian media. You will find a myriad of items about fitness, family, self-image, gifts, ecology and politics. Granted, horrendous social problems have rightly galvanized Christians into writing about abortion, euthanasia, genetic engineering, abuse, divorce, incest, pre-marital sex, drugs and suicide. As long as we maintain biblical essentials, we should address these issues.

The temptation to be trendy, however, cannot all be traced to secular thinkers. Down through the years, Christian innovators have called for a new emphasis on visitation, Sunday school, church growth, Christian counseling, small groups and body life. More recently, writers have sought to persuade us to embrace power evangelism, seeker services, market-driven churches, upbeat worship or spiritual gifts.

Missions, too, has gone through a long series of permutations. Indigenous church planting, tribal evangelism, Evangelism in Depth, church growth, hidden peoples, native missions, relief, final frontiers, the 10/40 Window and Vision 2000 come to mind.

This is not an exercise in sour grapes! I deeply appreciate the insights of many of these emphases. In the context of perpetual imbalance in the church, we need continual self-examination. It is terribly true that the church that fails to continually renew and reform itself is doomed to slow death.

And multitudes of traditional churches have slid down the slippery slope of imbalance into deep ruts. Imbalance becomes particularly stultifying where tradition rules. If change is intrinsically stigmatized as evil, then the perpetual renewal and development that Scripture itself demands becomes suspect. Too many groups whose theology is biblical and balanced have fallen into practical imbalance.

Frankly, many churches and missionary societies are in a deep rut. The response "But that's the way we've always done it" is too commonly heard. Failing to realize that imbalance in practical living and witness is as dangerous as imbalance in doctrine, many accept evangelistic lethargy as the status quo. In such circumstances, we desperately need many of the writings that I have mentioned to shock us out of our ruts.

Nevertheless, too often an emphasis becomes the primary focus of this or that Christian group. Perceiving deadness in our worship, charismatics call us to lively praise. Any reader of Psalms will agree that there is nothing inherently wrong in such a concern. Para-church groups may call us to a particular method of evangelism in order to reach, for example, high-school teens. Who can fault such a crucial concern! But too often the concern of a para-church group develops into tunnel vision. We all know those who perpetually play only one chord. They are single-issue people. Modern Christendom has too many of these. Any truth overemphasized may lead to distortion.

Salvation messages may subtly de-emphasize the role of all members of the Trinity. The holiness of God, which rendered the cross essential, may not even be mentioned. Justification, by which the legal demands of an outraged law are met, may be only dimly proclaimed. Christ as the coming Judge may not be stressed. Dependence on the convicting and converting work of the Spirit may be lacking.

Evangelists often present "receiving Christ," a biblical but hardly central concept, as if Christ is outside just waiting for us to invite him in. We can't escape the image of an impotent Christ, sentenced to wait until a person is reluctantly persuaded by the evangelist to open his or her heart's door.

The Holy Spirit is frequently recognized not so much as the agent of regeneration and ongoing sanctification, but as the bearer of gifts and power. An ego-booster!

Christ's position as Savior is almost exclusively emphasized to the detriment of his Lordship. In truth, conversion involves unconditional surrender to Christ as Lord.

Imbalance can be found also in teaching about the response we are to make to conversion. Assurance of salvation is more often connected with a raised hand in a meeting, a verbal response made to a set of questions or to going forward at an altar call than to an ongoing demonstration of obedience to Christ. Counselors encourage people to look back on what they did (again the man-centered approach) for comfort, rather than to the objective reality of what Christ has done or is doing in their lives.

The crucial relevance of the Old Testament is another victim of this fixation with what is current. The decline in use of the Old Testament has led to a corresponding decline in the presentation of Christ in his historical context. The apostles presented the Lord as the culmination of a historical process of revelation—the fulfillment of the promises made to the fathers. The frequency with which the apostles made mention of this aspect of the gospel is only exceeded by that of their mention of his death and resurrection.

Note too the space given in New Testament preaching to a consideration of God as the God of Israel. Stephen, in his defense, spent his entire testimony describing Old Testament revelation before concluding with a reference to Jesus. In Antioch, Paul proclaimed good news about the promise made to their fathers. He pointed to Jesus as the offspring of David. In Athens the bulk of Paul's message related to Old Testament truths about God. Only after having laid down the basics of biblical truth did he introduce the resurrection of Christ as evidence of God's coming judgment (Acts 17:22–31).

Consider also the modern ignorance of Christ's threefold office. Post-Reformation Protestants almost universally acknowledged his three offices of Prophet, Priest and King. Today his role as a presently reigning King is well-nigh denied or relegated to an eschatological future. The glory of his person has been diluted, albeit unconsciously. We are left with a one-dimensional Sunday-school figure. Injustice is done to his eternal deity, the historical progress of revelation leading up to his incarnation, the incarnation itself, his reigning majesty and his coming judgeship.

One aspect of his ministry is, of course, emphasized—his Second Coming. In fact, eschatology is emphasized and elaborated to such an extent that views on end-time events become the touchstone of fellowship. In a meeting in Pakistan one mission had to exclude itself from participation in a joint Bible-training ministry because of its inability to subscribe to a pre-millennial timetable of events surrounding the return of Christ.

In the light of the fact that Christ's return is mentioned only once in the messages of the apostles in Acts, such dogmatism is astounding. (Besides this one reference, a coming day of judgment and the certainty of bodily resurrection are mentioned several times.) Why are we so dogmatic where the book of Acts, in common with the rest of Scripture, is the least specific?

Bandwagons! Trends! Novelties! Like a flock of starlings they settle on our spiritual gardens and gobble up the balanced nourishment that we need to face the challenges of today. Novel approaches to missionary strategy or church growth, if not sifted with great care, siphon off energies and leave us starving for the truth.

If missionaries perpetuate the imbalance present in their sending societies, the result will be doubly damaging.

Note

1 **James Orr,** (General Ed.), *The International Standard Bible Encyclopedia*, vol. iii (Grand Rapids, MI: Eerdmans, 1955), p. 2039.

Mini or maxi message?

The preaching of the apostles manifested not only balance but also breadth of content. They communicated at least thirty-two elements concerning God, man and Christ. These themes touch all the main subjects of the Bible. Paul's description of his ministry as a heralding of "anything that would be helpful" and "the whole will of God" reflects the unparalleled scope of apostolic teaching (Acts 20:20, 27).

The apostles' message spanned the Old Testament as well as the New. In fact, their preaching was so steeped in the Old Testament that they talked about the gospel as "the hope of Israel" (Acts 28:20), "What God promised our fathers" (13:32) and "the word of the Lord" (13:49). In Pisidian Antioch Paul linked the gospel and the Old Testament hope in the following terms: "We tell you the good news: What God promised our fathers" (13:32).

In most cases their audiences contained a large proportion of Jews to whom such an Old Testament link would particularly appeal. It is plain from messages given to purely Gentile audiences, however, that this practice was not simply to accommodate Jewish hearers. Peter explained to Cornelius, the Roman, that his message was the one that "God sent to the people of Israel" (10:36). We would expect this, for, in talking to the Gentile Corinthians, Paul defined the gospel as the death, burial and resurrection of Christ "according to the Scriptures" (1 Cor. 15:3–4). This implies that we must present the gospel as historical events that fulfilled Old Testament prophecies. While when preaching to Gentiles the apostles didn't explicitly quote Old Testament references as frequently as with Jewish audiences, yet in their presence they went further back into Old Testament content to teach concerning creation, sin and the character of God.

In this broader sense the gospel should be set in the context of the whole Bible. Did not Christ expound to the two men on the road to Emmaus the things concerning himself in all the Scriptures? The statement of Paul, "I resolved to know nothing while I was with you except Jesus Christ and him crucified" (1 Cor. 2:2), might lead us to wonder if his preaching exclusively dealt with the death of Christ. We must take such statements, however, in the greater context of the book of Acts and of the Epistles. They serve not to limit proclamation but to focus it. Since Scripture is one progressive unified revelation, Old as well as New Testament truth should be proclaimed.

As already mentioned, Acts contains the least teaching about the eschatological aspects of the Kingdom. There are references to a coming judgment (10:42; 17:31; 24:25) and to a future "time ... for God to restore everything, as he promised long ago through his holy prophets" (3:21), some references to the resurrection of the righteous and the wicked (24:15), and mention of "an inheritance" (26:18). The apostles' messages did not, however, contain details of eschatology relating to heaven, the rapture, the tribulation or the millennium. They took seriously Jesus's rebuke, "It is not for you to know the times or dates the Father has set by his own authority" (1:7). The stress on a coming judgment day, and the resurrection of the just and the unjust, enabled them to call their audiences to repentance and faith. The book of Acts leaves us with an exuberant sense of the present kingdom of God. They were not preoccupied with a future kingdom.

In short, the apostles, far from reducing the gospel to barest essentials, strove to expose their hearers to as broad a spectrum of content as possible. They knew that breadth of content would lead to balance and spiritual maturity.

This maximizing tendency of the apostles contrasts sharply with two modern inclinations. The first is the tendency to present the gospel in too narrow a context. Much evangelistic material centers too narrowly on certain of the gospel facts without laying adequate groundwork in Old Testament teaching. We could safely say that the vast majority of popular evangelistic materials present a message divorced from the Old Testament. Perhaps this might be somewhat excusable if the populace exhibited widespread knowledge of God, man's nature, and the law as taught in the Old Testament. In reality, whether in a Western context or in a mission situation, most people today live and die abysmally ignorant of basic biblical facts. In Paul's day the worshipers at Jewish synagogues that he visited in his missionary travels knew the Old Testament quite well. Even so, Paul did not minimize the content of his messages.

Why is much of modern evangelism and missions carried on in terms of the irreducible minimum needed for conversion? Evidently, the *Four Spiritual Laws* of Campus Crusade has been printed in most of the major world languages to the tune of over 2.5 billion copies.[1] This booklet is presented as an indispensable aid to evangelism. In Pakistan some Muslims have assented to its simplistic message without any evidence of subsequent interest. The damage done by methods such as this, in terms of "gospel-hardening" masses of people, is incalculable.

The increasing role various kinds of media play in evangelism may have contributed to this minimizing trend. Personal face-to-face ministry is time-consuming. Evangelism by radio, TV or by using the printed page seems to offer considerable saving in time and effort. These media, however, restrict the amount of content that can be communicated. A tract has a specific number of pages, a radio program a standard length, a TV spot an even more limited time, a mass evangelistic meeting a closely restricted format, a stylized pre-planned witness one specific goal.

Media and methods such as these force programmers to trim and shave the content to a minimum. To gain attention and keep interest up, they must allow considerable space for illustrations and stories. Doubtless many of us need to cut a lot of dead wood out of our messages. Sometimes what we say is boring. And the pressure to orient programming to meet specific goals can help us clear away the fuzziness present in too much Christian communication. But before we cut content we need to be clear about essentials.

Paul E. Little, in a book that has much to commend it, nevertheless defines the gospel in narrow terms. There is little reference to Old Testament truth. His diagnosis of man as a sinner sadly lacks the early church's concepts of sin as legal guilt and personal wickedness. He recommends that we present sin as the reason "we suffer all the frustrations, problems, loneliness and boredom that we see around us."[2]

Many materials translated or written in the Third World (and in the West) are superficial popular works. The exegetical and historical heritage of the ages is deemed too heavy and unpopular to warrant printing. Breadth and depth of content are media-induced casualties of our over-entertained age.

The minimizing trend results also in neglecting convert instruction. The urgency and size of the unfinished task distract evangelists from completing what they begin. In Pakistan I've run into a number who conceive of evangelism as a series of whirlwind tours. As a result the growth of scattered converts remains stunted.

If we, like Paul, are to be free of the blood of all men, we too must arrange for the instruction of converts in the whole counsel of God. An experienced Pakistani co-worker traced most of the ills afflicting the present Pakistani church to a lack of thorough teaching in the church's infancy.

Terry Hulbert, who at the time was Dean of the Columbia Bible College Graduate School of Bible and Mission, lamented the theological confusion and disunity represented by 1,000 different church groups in Africa. He wrote, "I think that behind all of this movement, however, there lies a significant lack of Bible teaching of the great mass of believers."[3]

We must not let worries about delaying calls for commitment, caricatured as "search theology," deter us from thorough proclamation.[4]

Another modern tendency contrasts sharply with early church practice. A trio of urgent friends—*methodology*, *activism* and *pragmatism*—have tended to dethrone the foundational place of biblical content. Many treat hermeneutics, exegesis, acquaintance with the original languages and biblical theology as options in training for missionary service. Church history, which screams lessons for missions and evangelism, is often viewed as irrelevant. Missiologists frequently dismiss systematic theology as an ivory-tower pursuit of little practical use for missionary training. By contrast, the Reformers—who rode a wave of renewal and evangelism unparalleled since the first century—looked upon theology as the queen of sciences. They realized that theology is not the enemy of evangelism but its handmaiden, arranging as it does biblical truth in convenient topical categories for ready use.

A sincere sense of missionary urgency may have contributed to this trend. Besides the pressure to achieve instant results, there are demands to shorten and streamline procedures. On every hand we face a hesitancy to commit time to what some regard as dry and impractical studies. And yet, adequate training in a Bible school or seminary is not a waste of time—it is a must!

A technological mindset has invaded Christian circles. Ever more complex evangelistic programs are planned. The latest marvels of technology are harnessed. Market researchers study pragmatic situations in order to adapt outreach methods to current contexts. Sociology, psychology and anthropology are brought to bear.

Missionary pundits coined a new word, "missiology," to capture the new emphasis and another word, "contextualization," to dramatize the need to suit the message to the audience. As theology and exegesis are shunted aside, the message itself emerges in new—and sometimes unrecognizable—forms. Imperceptibly, media guru McLuhan's analysis of our age comes true: *the medium becomes the message*.

There is no denying that technology should be harnessed to the cause of Christ. But not if it distorts content. Unfortunately, the voice of technology is often so urgent and compelling it drowns out the quiet voice of Scripture.

Bernard Ramm warns us,

> Technology has a way of shaping the mentality of a population that uses it, creating a surface view of life ... The technological instrument is the thing! ... Soon it moulds a mentality that finds anything absolute as static and unpalatable ...
>
> Furthermore, the mentality produced by a technological society finds it impossible to believe in the transcendent, the supernatural or the miraculous. Again it is not sheer coincidence that contemporary philosophy has given up the grand tasks of the past ... In a technological age nobody can believe any more in a "Great System" like a comprehensive philosophy or a great system of theology ...
>
> My point is that the world of theologians is not exempt from the influence of the technological mentality. If a theologian assumes the technological mentality (in varying degrees, of course) then the historic Christian theology will seem all wrong. The mentality of sophisticated technology is at total odds with the mentality of Christian revelation ...
>
> That which does appeal to him are the larger problems of our society coupled with world politics. He becomes an issue theologian. Granted, we do have serious issues in ethnic theology, third world theology and feminism. They are valid issues. But my

complaint is that too much of current issue theology is based upon the loss of historic Christian doctrine. If we deal with such distressing issues let us always do so from the center of our historic Christian theology.[5]

In this area, Ramm is right on target. A love affair with technology joined to an impatience with theology accelerates the minimizing trend. Add to this a concern for the multitude of distinct peoples who need the message presented in relevant and contextual terms and we face serious competition for study time. Pressure to short-circuit biblical studies mounts. But how can we contextualize the gospel in every culture if our knowledge of Scripture is superficial?

Missionaries and evangelists should be theologically better prepared, not less prepared than pastors. Continuing education for missionaries is a must, We would do well to heed the caution of J. I. Packer: "When evangelism is not fertilized, fed and controlled by theology, it becomes a sterilized performance seeking its effect right through manipulative skills rather than the power of vision and the force of truth."[6]

Statistics dethrone theology. Art Glasser described what he called "the ambivalence of a majority of the delegates" at a mission conference in a main denomination.[7] This ambivalence led to the uncritical acceptance of whichever statistics emerged from the four corners.

Perceived results become the authority used to affirm a given method. This type of mentality constructs new theological parameters based on pragmatics rather than biblical revelation. But where evaluation criteria are not scriptural but pragmatic, the real interpretation of data is unknown. We can count statistics but we can never tell who is genuinely converted. Statistical inaccuracy will increase exponentially as we minimize content. Only biblical prophets and apostles possessed the ability to inerrantly interpret what took place around them. In their absence, Scripture alone contains the principles we need to evaluate people movements. If we fail to dig deeply into the systematic arrangement of scriptural principles that we call theology, we cannot hope to interpret what we may bravely call "the pragmatic situation." And yet, activists treat missionary statistics as if they were inspired.

To minimize or maximize? The answer must be: to maximize! We must restore apostolic thoroughness. In the event we ignore their maximizing ministry—a commitment to present the whole counsel of God—we will find ourselves left with nothing but chaff. If we don't reverse the trend to present the gospel in its irreducible minimum, we will see a further acceleration in the spread of nominalism.

Notes

1 The "Four Spiritual Laws" are: (1) God loves you and has a wonderful plan for your life; (2) All of us sin, and sin separates us from God; (3) Jesus is the only provision for our sin; (4) We must receive Christ.

2 **Paul E. Little,** *How to Give Away Your Faith* (Downers Grove, IL: IVP, 1966), p. 60.

3 **Terry Hulbert,** "Missions Dialogue," in *Ce Be Cequel*, Spring–Summer 1978, p. 7.

4 "Search theology" is a term used to describe those who are everlastingly sowing the gospel seed but not reaping any harvest. This is due, it is claimed, to lack of proper methodology, goal orientation and cultural relevance.

5 **Bernard Ramm,** "Radical Theology Grows," in *Eternity*, May 1979, p. 17.

6 **J. I. Packer,** "What is Evangelism?", in **Harvie M. Conn,** (ed.), *Theological Perspectives on Church Growth* (Nutley, NJ: Presbyterian & Reformed, 1977), p. 91.

7 **Art E. Glasser,** "Power Encounter in Conversion From Islam," The North American Conference on Muslim Evangelization, a research paper, 1978.

Chapter 12

Absentee landlord or reigning King?

The truth of God's past, present and future rule (Kingdom) forms the warp and woof on which the variegated gospel message is woven. Since the Gospels refer to the Kingdom 124 times, it is not surprising that Jesus's post-resurrection ministry, as described in Acts, echoed that theme. Dr. Luke says the message was "about the kingdom of God" (Acts 1:3). Philip proclaimed to Samaritans "the good news of the kingdom of God and the name of Jesus Christ" (8:12).

The text of Acts reflects the whole fabric of biblical revelation. The Old Testament portrays Jehovah as the King not only of Israel, but of all nations, indeed, of all creation (see 1 Sam. 8:7; Ps. 24; 145:13; etc.). Jeremiah called Jehovah "King of the nations" (Jer. 10:7). Nebuchadnezzar, king of Babylon, learned this fact the hard way. After a terrible period of insanity, he finally affirmed God's authority: "His dominion is an eternal dominion; his kingdom endures from generation to generation ... He does as he pleases with the powers of heaven and the peoples of the earth" (Dan. 4:34–35).

Under Christ's tutelage, the apostles developed a thorough understanding of the Kingdom of God and God's sovereignty. Their word choice illustrates this belief: "appointed," "plan," "purpose," "ordained," "predestined" and "foreknowledge" (Acts 2:23; 4:28; 3:20; 20:27; 21:14; 13:48–49). Without an understanding of God's sovereignty from the beginning of time, they would not have used phrases such as "what your power and will had decided beforehand should happen" (4:28).

Their messages echoed this belief. "He himself gives all men life and breath and everything else. From one man he made every nation of men ... and he determined the times set for them and the exact places where they should live ... 'For in him we live and move and have our being'" (Acts 17:25–28). They realized that God's influence affects all of mankind's past, present and future. God alone gives "rain from heaven and crops in their seasons" (14:17).

The apostles particularly enjoyed meditating about God's ongoing role in human salvation. They described salvation as a gift received by "all whom the Lord our God will call" (2:39). Since "the Lord added to their number daily those who were being saved" (2:47), they knew that real church growth depended upon him. No wonder they carefully drew their hearers' attention to the fact that it is God who turns men from wickedness (3:26) and grants repentance and forgiveness (5:31; 13:48). Please note that they did not deliver these (decidedly theological) pronouncements in lecture form to seminary students. Far from it! They proclaimed the deepest theological issues in the course of ministry to everyone, whether mature saints or raw unbelievers.

It is no accident that both Christ and his Kingdom are central themes in the book of Acts. One cannot legitimately think of Christ without considering the Kingdom. The Kingdom has, in itself, no substance without the presence of King Jesus.

Dr. Luke describes his Gospel as a summary of that which "Jesus began to do and to teach" (Acts 1:1). This necessarily signifies that Acts was written to describe what Jesus continued to do and teach. We must deduce that Christ continues to be actively involved in the growth of his church. In what sense is this true?

Christ rules his Kingdom from the right hand of the Father: "Exalted to the right hand of God, he has received from the Father the promised Holy Spirit and has poured out what you now see and hear" (Acts 2:33); "God exalted him to his own right hand as Prince and Savior that he might give repentance and forgiveness of sins to Israel" (5:31). Stephen, on the point of martyrdom, "looked up to heaven and saw the glory of God, and Jesus standing at the right hand of God" (7:55).

While our Lord tenderly stood to welcome Stephen, he is now seated on a throne of authority at the Father's right hand. From that position he rules the universe. In his sermon at Pentecost, Peter quoted David's prediction that Christ would rise from the dead, ascend, and then sit on David's throne (2:29–31). Jewish antagonists plainly understood apostolic teaching on the subject. They dragged Christians before the city authorities in Thessalonica with the accusation that "They are all defying Caesar's decrees, saying that there is another king, one called Jesus" (17:7).

Early disciples knew Jesus as "Lord of all" (10:36). They talked of him as the coming Judge (10:42; 17:31). In the power of his name Peter said to the beggar at the gate of the temple, "Walk!" (3:6, 16). They boldly asserted to the priests and Sadducees, "know this, you and all the people of Israel: It is by the name of Jesus Christ of Nazareth, whom you crucified ... that this man stands before you healed ... Salvation is found in no one else ... there is no other name under heaven" (4:10, 12). They prayed that signs and wonders would take place in the name of Jesus (4:30).

Paul would later write, "God exalted him to the highest place and gave him the name that is above every name, that at the name of Jesus every knee should bow, in heaven and on earth and under the earth, and every tongue confess that Jesus Christ is Lord, to the glory of God the Father" (Phil. 2:9–11).

Why do we find this theme so pervasive in apostolic preaching and witness? It had to be so! The apostles realized that the Kingdom is part of the very matrix of reality. Their preaching had meaning and power because they spoke out of a position as subjects of the King. They wielded the gospel as a divine sword crafted by God specifically to rescue men and women from an infernal kingdom, the dominion of darkness. Their lives were always on a war-time footing; their churches were outposts of the expanding Kingdom. They stood before kings and priests as ambassadors of the King of kings.

For almost a century there has been a lack of proclamation of the Kingdom of God. Too many treat God more as an absentee landlord than as a reigning King. The grand themes of God's Triune majesty, his glorious character, his mighty acts and his sovereign rule need heralding as the setting in which we present the gospel gem.

Many find terminology concerning Christ and his Kingdom offensive. Its unpopularity can be traced to the influence of the humanism that began to invade the church with the Enlightenment. Humanism places mankind on an imaginary pedestal high above the influence of any supernatural being. Modern people want no King, especially one who decrees and ordains.

In this day of idolatrous humanism, the shell of man's self-sufficiency and independence can only be cracked by the King's hammer. Our generation needs a dose of reality, the reality of our utter dependence upon God for life and breath. Sinners living an illusion must be made to face reality by being confronted with the thrice-holy God of Isaiah. Then, when men and women realize their impotence and peril, let us herald from the housetops that the God who pulled Jesus from the bands of death can deliver them from the thralldom of darkness. God's Kingdom is! "Salvation ... comes from the LORD" (Ps. 37:39)!

Sad to say, this fuller context of the gospel is often shunned, whether by oversight, or out of the fear that such belief is hyper-Calvinistic, or from a view that God's Kingdom is wholly future. What a loss!

How can we preach Christ if we conclude his story at the empty tomb? He did ascend. He is now seated in glory. He does rule. Without appeal to these facts, any proclamation of the gospel must be tentative and incomplete.

How can we understand his role in missions, in evangelism, in the week-by-week operation of our local churches, even in family counseling, without a conscious awareness of his Kingship?

Our loss of a sense of awe reflects this lost emphasis. A. W. Tozer highlights this issue in his book *The Knowledge of The Holy*:

> The Church has surrendered her once lofty concept of God and has substituted for it one so low, so ignoble, as to be utterly unworthy of thinking, worshiping men ... This loss of the concept of majesty has come just when the forces of religion are making dramatic gains and the churches are more prosperous than at any time within the past several hundred years. But the alarming thing is that our gains are mostly external and our losses are wholly internal; and since it is the quality of our religion that is affected by internal conditions, it may be that our supposed gains are but losses spread over a wider field.[1]

Missions must recover this concept of the Majesty on High in the setting of his ongoing Kingdom. If the reality of God's Kingdom became the warp and woof of missions, then instead of the perpetual search for innovative methods there would be a worldwide search for evidences of God's providential preparation of peoples for the gospel. This, in turn, would give us a head start in interpreting the events going on around us. For if Christ is King, then we know that he has a strategy for the extension of his Kingdom. Inevitably, we would commit ourselves to study providential events in order to respond to them in a biblical way. If we adopt this procedure, we will be able to advance in step with the outworking of God's providence, his plan.

Fortunately, there are some signs of a revival of interest in the Kingdom of God. An issue of *Asian Challenge* analyzed present-day evangelistic preaching. It concluded that there was a lamentable lack of emphasis on the sovereignty of God.

In another context Bruce Nicholls pondered what truths would be most appropriate for Muslim evangelism. He was struck by the relevance of the Kingdom message. In a paper written for a consultation he said,

> I am suggesting that we explore the biblical concept of the Kingdom of God as the one that effectively meets both the religious and cultural needs of the Muslim ... Evangelicals have not always taken seriously enough the fact that the framework for our Lord's ministry was the proclamation of the Kingdom of God ... Jesus' concept of the kingdom was cosmic ... Wherever Christ reigns within the visible church there the Kingdom of God has come to earth.[2]

The concept of the Kingdom of God not only speaks to Muslims and Americans, Asians and Brazilians, but it also forms an irreducible part of the message once and for all delivered to the saints. If we would preach the gospel, we must preach the Kingdom!

Notes

1 **A. W. Tozer,** *The Knowledge of the Holy* (New York: Harper and Row, 1961), pp. 6–7.

2 **Bruce J. Nicholls,** "New Testament Approaches in Muslim Evangelism," The North American Conference on Muslim Evangelization, a research paper, 1978.

Evangelistic persuasion or divine intervention?

Appropriately, our discussion of the apostles' message concludes, as most sermons conclude, with an appeal for a response. To what degree did apostolic missionary bands seek to evoke a response in their hearers?

The apostles were not reticent in proclaiming mankind's addiction to sin, man's darkness and man's bondage to Satan (Acts 26:18). Every single message in some way drew attention to man's lost condition. This reflected, not a gloomy fixation with the dark side, but a passion to see men and women delivered from sin's yoke. They labeled their messages "the forgiveness of sins" and "the message of salvation (13:26, 38; 28:28).

The apostles realized that all people should seek God: "From one man he made every nation of men ... that men would seek him" (17:26–27). They knew, however, that many would both shun this option and reject the good news. No wonder they frequently warned their hearers about the dangers of rejection. Concerning Jesus Christ, the prophet like Moses, Peter declared, "Anyone who does not listen to him will be completely cut off from among his people" (3:23). Paul warned, "Take care ..." (13:40).

Of course, they also delighted in freely offering the grace of forgiveness to all who would respond with repentance and faith. In his address to the Ephesian elders, Paul succinctly summarized the response expected of sinners: "repentance and ... faith in our Lord Jesus" (Acts 20:21). The apostles sought to awaken sinners so they could be ready to face the Judge of all the earth.

Repentance

In the course of appealing for repentance, the apostles first endeavored to provoke *conviction of sin* by showing how sinners had broken God's law, prostituted God's character by worshiping idols (Acts 14:15), committed wickedness (3:26) and lived without self-control (24:25). In this sense, repentance involves the opening of a sinner's eyes (26:18) so he or she can see God in a new way. Genuine repentance is a new awareness of, and accountability to, the Majesty on High. Where God illumines the mind of the sinner, this dawning conviction involves fear (24:25) and godly sorrow.

Secondly, the apostles repeatedly described repentance as *turning from* wickedness (3:26; 14:15; 26:18). A sinner who "turns" from sin demonstrates confession of, sorrow for and a repudiation of his or her sinful ways.

Thirdly, repentance includes *turning to* God in submission (3:19; 14:15; 26:18, 20). Apostolic preaching on repentance called sinners to turn completely around and begin to walk with God in the opposite direction.

The apostles carefully distinguished between genuine and counterfeit repentance. True repentance inevitably results in transformation of life as evidenced by outward signs such as restitution, obedience, good deeds, and so on (11:18; 26:20; 5:32).

Faith

Repentance is not enough. The New Testament message challenged awakened sinners to respond to the gospel in faith as well as repentance. The apostles mentioned faith slightly less frequently than repentance, not because it is of less importance but because it is implicit in the message itself. The apostles expected unbelievers to respond with "faith in our Lord Jesus" (20:21). Preaching necessarily aims to inspire men and women to believe. The apostles were seldom disappointed. In common with many others, the people of Samaria "believed ... the good news of the kingdom of God and the name of Jesus Christ" (8:12).

What does biblical faith involve? The repeated use of words such as "proving," "persuade" and "reasoned," combined with the sentence "Those who accepted his message were baptized," demonstrates that genuine faith contains a large intellectual element (9:22; 17:2–4; 18:4; 2:41). Their preaching challenged men and women to think. Besides the mind, the apostolic preachers also engaged the will and heart of their hearers: "If you believe with all your heart ..."(8:37[1]).

Baptism

Repentance and faith led naturally to baptism. Baptism, as the necessary external demonstration of inward repentance and faith, is commanded of all new believers (Acts 2:38; 8:12; 8:38; 22:16). Some texts closely link forgiveness of sins with baptism.

Without the clarification of the Epistles, we might be tempted to assume that the baptismal waters have some mystical power to bestow forgiveness. The didactic portions of the New Testament, however, explain that it is the "washing of regeneration" and not water baptism that cleanses us from all sin.

Appeal

We find abundant evidence that the early disciples realized that sinners needed to repent, believe and be baptized. Strangely, however, we do not find them concluding their messages with an appeal, as we are prone to do today. In only one or possibly two instances did the apostles conclude their message with a persuasive appeal. (This is not to say that the need to respond was not clearly presented in the body of their messages.)

Amazingly, we find no instance of them asking their hearers to come forward, to raise their hands, to make a decision for Christ or to receive the Lord. Our modern tradition of concluding a message with an appeal is strangely missing from their practices. The cause cannot be traced to the nature of their audiences. In all but one of the instances recorded in the book of Acts, the audience addressed consisted of unbelievers!

We cannot find an appeal to "receive Christ" in the book of Acts. While such an appeal has some scriptural support, it is far from central in the New Testament.

Instead, we find the apostles calling sinners to bow to Christ's authority. The record indicates that they expected sinners to respond by turning from sin to submit to the authority of Christ—the reigning King. For a sinner to pass into the sphere of Christ's recognized authority obviously requires that sinner to make some acknowledgement of Christ's Lordship. In this context, "receiving Christ" into one's life is not as appropriate a response as bowing in awe and submission to his authority. The sinner does not receive the King—rather, the King receives the sinner!

New Testament preachers did not need to issue lengthy or emotional appeals. The strength of their faith in the sovereign glory of God, as manifest in his developing Kingdom, was too great for that. They didn't look within the hearts of their hearers for the strength to respond. Instead they looked to God to work in hearts by the power of the Holy Spirit. They knew that sinners could only be rescued from the thrall of Satan by virtue of a mighty intervention of the King. They didn't generate regeneration, conversion, repentance or faith by extended and elaborate appeals. These dramatic changes came as a result of the mysterious working of God in their hearts.

Apostolic expectations were not dashed. God intervened mightily, with 3,000 converted at Pentecost and 5,000 converted later. No wonder they talked so much about the resurrection. When hearers came face to face with the person of the risen Christ, they experienced firsthand the force of God's sovereign power. Consequently, these early missionaries appealed to sinners to look in faith to God who had raised Jesus from the dead.

As we study Acts we find that the apostles did not so much ask for a response; rather they were asked. In most cases people in the audience interrupted their messages to ask what their response ought to be. Such was the case at Pentecost and in the Ethiopian's chariot: "When the people heard this, they were cut to the heart and said to Peter and the other apostles, 'Brothers, what shall we do?'" (2:37). In the case of Cornelius's conversion, the Holy Spirit descended on Cornelius's household while Peter was speaking. This sovereign interruption bears eloquent testimony to the role God fulfills in the evangelistic process and the care that needs to be exercised concerning altar calls.

On at least three occasions these early preachers were interrupted by adverse actions. Jewish anger cut short Stephen's testimony. A jeering Athenian crowd interrupted Paul's address on Mars Hill. An angry mob stopped Paul from completing his impromptu defense in Jerusalem. How many of us today would tell the truth so forcefully, or in such unpopular terms, as these early Christians? Indeed, modern communicators advise us to avoid any content that might be confrontational. But when we note that modern preaching rarely arouses anger, we may conclude that something is probably missing.

Incentives to respond

We now turn to the matter of incentives. To what extent did the apostles offer their hearers incentives designed to persuade their hearers to respond to the gospel? Do we find the apostles promising certain benefits to those who repented and believed?

A search through Acts reveals that they never promised healing. Nor did the promise of deliverance from frustrations, boredom, meaninglessness, difficulties, loneliness, fears or poverty ever constitute a part of the apostolic message. Peace is mentioned once.

Most frequently they urged their audiences to consider the outcome of their sins. In such a context the offer of the forgiveness of sins becomes a most wonderful boon. Twice they promised the Holy Spirit (2:38; 5:32). They talked twice of believers receiving a spiritual inheritance (20:32; 26:18). (This did not occur in the course of evangelistic preaching. One mention occurs in a message to Christians, the other in Paul's address to Agrippa.) Four messages contain no promise of a reward or blessing of any kind. What is offered relates to forgiveness for sin and deliverance from judgment.

I conclude that the apostolic band did not use an array of promised blessings to entice their hearers to respond. They appealed for their hearers to face their legal guilt before the bar of divine justice. They proclaimed Christ as Savior from sin, Lord over repentant sinners and Judge of the unrepentant.

In our day repentance and the preparation that leads to it are widely neglected. Faith is emphasized. Those who profess faith are quickly assured of their salvation without waiting to see if their profession is attested by "works appropriate to repentance" (see Acts 26:20).

Superficiality is the result. When we dogmatically assure all who make a profession of faith that they are saved, before we see credible evidence of faith, we create a congregation of cardboard saints. If repentance is an essential ingredient of conversion—and it is—then the absence of repentance means the absence of conversion. The absence of conversion, in turn, means the absence of transformation. The absence of transformation, dependent as it is on regeneration, results in a host of professing Christians who continue to live as they have always done. They feel no inner compulsion to obey Christ—no overwhelming sadness when they sin.

Nominalism curses both mission churches and those in the homelands—which are themselves fast becoming needy mission fields. We can trace much of the carnality of professing Christians to an appeal for sinners to believe without any corresponding appeal to repent. Campus Crusade's *Four Spiritual Laws* makes scant mention of repentance! Paul Little, in his book *How to Give Away Your Faith*, does include a diagnosis of man as a sinner, but fails to appeal for repentance! In his view, the clearest statement on how to become a Christian is the appeal in John 1:12 to "receive Christ."[2] The almost universal use of John 1:12, out of context and without the balance of the rest of the New Testament, is a serious defect. This neglect of repentance is very, very serious.

The widespread use of false incentives in evangelistic appeals also indicates a dysfunctional understanding of the gospel. Much evangelism, rather than proclaiming the demands of the King—that men and women repent and believe in order to receive the grace of forgiveness—instead appeals for sinners to accept Christ in order to get what they really want. Preachers offer peace, joy, health, wholeness, improvements in our marriages and success in business as incentives to respond. I am not denying that the side-effects of the gospel are wonderful! Without Christ we can never know real peace or lasting joy, but should we appeal to people's selfish desires in order to win a hearing for the gospel?

We find that the apostles, who understood the exceeding deceitfulness of human hearts, seldom mentioned the benefits to be derived from conversion. They remained steadfast in directing their preaching to the problem of human sin. They spoke as representatives of the Judge of all the earth. How inappropriate for representatives of a judge to offer incentives for the accused to attend court! No, the accused are commanded to face their Accuser, to acknowledge their crime, and to accept the reality of their guilt.

Admittedly, it is extremely tempting to preach in such a way as to awaken the natural desires of our hearers. I'm not denying that there is a place for that. But preachers who appeal to sensed needs must do so with great care. Blessings may be offered after a carefully balanced explanation of the unpleasant facts of our sinfulness and the real demands of discipleship. Jesus offered abundant life, living water and spiritual bread. But Jesus always offered these attractive gifts in the context of the most costly discipleship: "Follow me"; "Leave your father and you mother"; "Deny yourself"; "Take up your cross daily." Following the Master's method, the writers of the Epistles explain how the gospel meets all of our genuine human needs, but only as rebellious sinners become real disciples.

Much modern evangelistic literature reflects a different mixture. I've already mentioned *The Four Spiritual Laws* and Paul Little's writings. In his sovereign grace, God often graciously overrules methods that seem questionable. And God frequently arouses spiritual hunger in those he leads to seek him. Nevertheless, we should maintain a biblical balance that emphasizes repentance.

This consideration of the role of motivation in conversion leads us to ask some serious questions about the Church Growth school of missionary thinking.

In their book *Principles of Church Growth*, Weld and McGavran discuss favorably a study carried out in India by Waskom Pickett.[3] Pickett evaluated 3,947 individuals. He concluded that, in the long run, there is no real difference between the use of spiritual or carnal motivation in evangelism. He felt that people who became Christians for spiritual motives, such as finding salvation or forgiveness of sins, did not differ from those who became Christians for educational, monetary, social or family reasons. According to Pickett, both groups made about the same spiritual progress. He deduced that the quality of instruction received after baptism was more important than the motive for conversion.

No doubt many serve the King who were first attracted to Christ from unworthy motives. There are two flaws, however, in Pickett's deduction.

Firstly, all the criteria Pickett used to identify spiritual progress, with the possible exception of a desire to be free of the fear of evil spirits, are external criteria. External characteristics such as church attendance, financial giving and abandonment of idolatry are subject to peer pressure. He failed to factor in the reality that a desire to conform nominally to a given group may lead a person to do certain things to achieve acceptance. External indices, such as these, are inaccurate indicators of internal qualities such as faith in Christ, devotion to the Lord, love for God's people and hunger for holiness. Nominalism already runs rife in the Indo-Pakistan subcontinent—as it does in much of the rest of the world. We should not encourage more nominalism! But if we blur the distinctives that set genuine believers apart from nominal Christians we will do just that.

Secondly, the observation that post-baptismal instruction was the crucial factor may only hide the fact that actual evangelism occurred at this point. I suspect that, during the process of instruction following baptism, many who had been attracted to the faith for unworthy reasons experienced a genuine conversion. Even if we admit that the end result appears to be genuine, this should not condone preaching in such a way that masses of people will be attracted to Christ from the wrong motives. While the instruction given to these candidates following their baptisms may have been of a high quality, instruction given either before or after baptism is, in many places, either completely lacking or sadly defective. We cannot depend upon churches making up for what evangelists may have neglected. From the very outset, we need to present a whole gospel that calls for faith, repentance and discipleship.

Many sober Christians wake up at night troubled by a nightmare of a whole generation becoming "gospel hardened" by evangelistic techniques that are sub-biblical. It is a vision of masses of people living unchanged, carnal lives while they insist they are children of God because they have registered a "decision." In fact, their failure to produce the fruit of the Spirit affirms their real family allegiance: They are children of the devil! Giving people false assurance insulates them from the convicting power of the Word. How unspeakably cruel to naively affirm the faith of those who show no evidence of repentance!

Many of those who profess faith disappear. Others occupy church space but ignore pleas to take instruction in the faith. As already mentioned, Tozer wrote, "… since it is the quality of our religion that is affected by internal conditions, it may be that our supposed gains are but losses spread over a wider field."[4]

In the past chapters we have considered the terms used for and the content of apostolic preaching. We've noted its delicate balance and amazing breadth of content. We've discovered a message set in the context of the Kingdom presented without appealing to the carnal desires of fallen men and women.

The apostolic faith is no mythical Excalibur suited to another age but an Imperial Sword forged in the divine smithy that is as powerful today as it ever was. We must preserve it from the corroding influences of our humanistic age. It alone "is living and active. Sharper than any double-edged sword, it penetrates even to dividing soul and spirit, joints and marrow; it judges the thoughts and attitudes of the heart" (Heb. 4:12).

Even here a word of caution is needed. The obvious role of divine sovereignty in the conversions recorded in Acts reminds us that there is no method that will guarantee evangelistic results. Indeed, not even perfect conformity to the apostolic message can be counted upon. For people to be converted, God must sovereignly work through the intervention of the Holy Spirit. A humble and prayerful dependence on God ought to continually characterize God's servants.

Notes

1 See NKJV, which includes this verse, since it is found in Western texts including the Latin version.

2 **Paul E. Little,** *How to Give Away Your Faith* (Downers Grove, IL: IVP, 1966), pp. 58–60.

3 **Waskom Pickett,** *Christian Mass Movements in India* (1933), cited by **Wayne Weld** and **Donald A. McGavran,** *Principles of Church Growth* (South Pasadena, CA: William Carey Library, 1971), pp. 7–19.

4 **A. W. Tozer,** *The Knowledge of the Holy* (New York: Harper and Row, 1961), p. 3.

A ladder up to literacy and new life

Your name is Rani. You're a teenage girl in a mud-walled village surrounded by the irrigated wheat fields of the Punjab in Pakistan. You're trapped in a downward spiral of poverty. You're illiterate. Ahead looms an early marriage arranged with some man you've never met, in a place you've never been, to begin a lifetime of drudgery unrelieved by hope. Your youthful bloom will soon wilt under an unrelenting barrage of orders from your mother-in-law: water you must carry, meals you must cook, clothes you must wash, babies you must bear so they can carry on the same endless cycle. Of course, someday you'll be a mother-in-law yourself!

On Sundays you join others in singing lustily the plaintive Punjabi songs in the little church building at one corner of the village. You don't understand much that the pastor says. You can't read the Bible he holds aloft. Occasionally, the verse of a hymn or a fragment from a psalm strikes some tinder deep within your heart and begins to smolder. Monday dawns. A blur of duties quickly snuffs out the longing for something higher, something finer.

Then one Sunday a strange foreign woman wearing Punjabi clothes arrives in your little church. At the pastor's invitation, she comes to the front. Trying in vain to keep her head covering in place, she launches into an animated appeal. Holding aloft a colorful little booklet she exclaims, "Using these simple booklets, every one of you can learn to read. Next week we're starting a literacy class in this village. We want you to join the class."

You and your friends look at one another in disbelief. You have no school in your village. How can you learn to read? Older women frown in disapproval. Wiry farmers mutter their doubts.

Undeterred, "Miss Ann," as you will learn to call her, beckons for a girl who has accompanied her to come forward. With a confident spring in her step a girl about your age almost bounds to the front.

She mentions her village. You know that village; it has no school either. She radiates excitement as she describes how she learned to write her own name and read the colorful booklets "Miss Ann" holds aloft.

Miss Ann passes her a Bible and asks her to read. With a strong and confident voice she reads a passage from John's Gospel. Your mouth hangs open in astonishment. Even the pastor raises his eyebrows in surprise.

Learn to read! A tender sprig of something tenuously like hope begins to sprout in the eager soil of your young heart. A vision of something better tantalizes your thoughts as you file out after church. "With all the field work to do, will Mother allow me?" you speculate. "I'll work extra hard this week and plead with Mom to go."

On the way home you linger at the little shop to stare at the advertisements with new interest. "Will I soon be able to read what they say?" you wonder.

Ann Wiltshire poured all her Welsh energy into pushing back the frontiers of illiteracy. In this instance, she ministered among nominal Christians in the area around Sahiwal, a hundred miles south of Lahore in Pakistan.

On a three-month work term in Pakistan my wife, Mary Helen, and I had occasion to see for ourselves the results of Ann's work. We were deeply impressed.

Some years ago, a large group of Presbyterian churches sent out an SOS. Their literacy program needed a massive transfusion of missionary encouragement. Although 1,500 were enrolled, tests showed that many had not even progressed enough to write their own names.

The need was critical. In Pakistan only 26 percent can read and write. Among women the figure drops to 16 percent. Village Christians fare far worse, with Christian women at the bottom of the literacy scale.

As a stopgap, Ann came to help them conduct short courses for supervisors and teachers. She soon realized that they needed more help than she could give in a few days. Field administration agreed and loaned her to the Associate Reformed Presbyterian (ARP) mission to supervise their literacy work (the ARP is an evangelical group of churches mainly found in the southern USA).

She first concentrated on reducing the number of students enrolled. Although difficult, this inspired a dramatic increase in the quality of teaching. Soon there were 550 students studying under twenty teachers. Ann guided three supervisors who encouraged teachers laboring in three different districts.

Back in your village, you go about your tasks with a new eagerness. "Waste of time," your mother snaps. "I never needed to read. You'll be getting fancy ideas."

The cold water your mother throws on the fire of your enthusiasm fails to quench your hope. With water pots balanced on your head you glide down the dusty track toward the village well. For once, a subject other than boys animates the girls who gather there.

Finally Friday comes. You join ten or so other girls in the church. Several boys cast shy glances your way. The teacher, a woman from a neighboring village, arranges a blackboard and charts on the side wall.

At the beginning of the class a short time of worship and prayer reminds you of God's love. The teacher reads a passage from the Bible and talks about how much you need its comfort in your daily lives. She promises that if you work hard, you will soon be able to read it for yourselves.

She passes out colorful primers and slates. Then she turns to the blackboard and draws the first two letters of the Urdu alphabet. Aleph—A; Be—B. "Draw these letters on your slates," she says.

"Now let's combine these two letters. Here's how you write water—AB. This is father—ABBA. See how B changes when it joins other letters? See how it is different at the beginning and end of a word? Copy these words on your slates. Now, how would you write old man, BABA? Write it on your slates."[1]

And so it went on. You progressed slowly through the first year of classes. Not everyone kept at it. In spite of the pastor's encouragement, several girls dropped out when field work increased. The boys stopped coming as soon as they learned enough to write their names. Boys seem motivated mainly by a desire to write enough to get a basic job.

"Rani, you're doing very well," Ann comments one day. At first it seemed impossible, but now you have progressed through several levels of literacy spread over two years.

By the end of the first year you were able to struggle through passages in John's Gospel. In the evenings, with your work finished, you loved to light the lamp, open your shiny new Bible and read about the Samaritan woman or the women at the empty tomb.

Before long you realized that you needed Christ to become your personal Savior. One day, as you led the water buffalo to the canal, you haltingly confessed your need and asked Jesus into your heart.

During the second year you learned to answer the seventy catechism questions about the Christian faith that "Miss Ann" had prepared. The answers frequently come to mind as you work in the fields or help mother prepare the evening meal. The teacher has asked you to help some of the newer students with their catechism.

With a view to introducing nominal Christians to the basics of the faith, Ann Wiltshire had developed a catechism with seventy questions and answers. Churches and Christian schools in various parts of the country soon realized its potential. It has proven its usefulness.

Besides her catechism, Ann was able to incorporate existing materials into a carefully structured literacy program with five distinct levels spanning three years. She challenged students about their need of salvation through a series of correspondence courses used throughout Pakistan. They introduce non-Christians to the Bible. Teachers use ten of these basic courses to lead new-literates through the study of Old Testament stories and prophets as well as the life of Christ.

Not content with giving new literates the basics, Ann also included several of the introductory courses of the Open Theological Seminary (OTS). Fortunately, the OTS has developed courses for entry-level students with a view to leading them up the ladder of biblical literacy to active ministry. Ann used their Abundant Life course to confront literacy students in their second year with the glory of living for Christ.

Those who stay with the program for three years enjoy many exciting options in their last year. Ann hand-picked motivated students to attend a week or two-week Bible camp in town. The brightest went away for a month's training in a Bible institute for young women. All plunged into another entry-level extension course on Bible doctrine.

"Hallelujah!" you shout as you run home. Ann has chosen you along with two other girls from your village to attend the two-week Bible camp in Sahiwal. But suddenly your excitement turns to gloom. You have only a couple of patched outfits to wear. "What will I do?" you wail to your mother.

Both your mom and dad, who initially complained about you wasting time learning to read, have commented on the changes literacy has brought. You were able to read your dad the notice about water use from the canal department. You explained how Daraprim protects from Malaria. You showed your brother the ad about the factory where he now has a steady job. You've become more buoyant and helpful.

"Never mind," your mother consoles. "We'll get you a new outfit somehow."

She goes over to the corner of the one-room mud home and rummages in the big tin trunk set up on bricks. Pulling out some satins from her wedding outfit, she says firmly, "We'll get the village tailor to remake these to fit you." Your father brings out the milk money he has been saving to buy another goat to pay for the tailor.

The weeks crawl by until finally you join the chaperone and the other two girls on the ramshackle rural bus. Your new outfit is safely folded in the battered case you carry. Two weeks in the city!

The sputtering rickshaw drops you at the mission compound. You glance shyly at the other girls gathering from distant villages. The pang of homesickness soon departs as you plunge into a whirlwind of activities.

Three meals a day—even fruit to eat! Meat two or three times a week! Heartfelt singing that shakes the shutters of the old building. Catechism drills and Bible studies. Practice reading difficult Old Testament passages. Lectures on health and hygiene. Games in the afternoon sun. Crafts in the evening. Laughter and chatter with new friends after the lights blink out.

Yes, your name is Rani—"princess"—but you never felt like a princess until you learned to read. Reading has helped you climb out of the prison of ignorance to breathe the fresh air of hope. Marriage still frightens you, but you can face it.

Christ now lives in your heart and he has given you a place in his Kingdom. Every Friday you gather the village children and tell them the Bible stories you have learned.

Literacy has changed the lives of many of your new friends, too. A number have gone to school. Several are already married and now teach their children from the primer. A number hold classes for children. You've met other girls who have become nurses and teachers. You have decided that you will become a nurse and work in the mission hospital. You know it is possible![2]

Notes

1 Although the process is much more complicated than this sequence seems to indicate, this imaginary exchange gives some idea of the process of teaching literacy.

2 After her retirement Ann Wiltshire, an SIM missionary, lived in Wales, where she encouraged her church to reach out to South Asian immigrants until she passed away in 2007.

Part 4

The missionary

Chapter 14

Searching for the elusive missionary

We often hear well-meaning preachers declare that every believer is a missionary. While it is true that Christ calls all Christians to seeking first his Kingdom, concluding that all believers are called to missionary service confuses the issue. What then, if anything, distinguishes an active Christian, or even a full-time Christian worker, from a Christian who is engaged in *missionary* work?

Could it be the possession of the skill or training required to fill a specific missionary position? The roster of any large mission board includes people with an extremely varied mixture of skills and training.

In the annual recruiting magazine of one of the largest interdenominational mission boards a bewildering array of opportunities is listed under ten categories.[1] These include under "Evangelism and Church Growth": rural and urban church planters, youth outreach workers, women's outreach workers, refugee ministry, international church pastors, and so on; "Theological Education": religious education teachers for public schools, Bible-school teachers, seminary lecturers, Theological Education by Extension (TEE) tutors, disciplers; "Development": agronomists, entrepreneurs and veterinarians; "Health": doctors, nurses, dentists, midwives, drug- and alcohol-abuse administrators. Likewise a host of other specialists are required under headings such as: "Education," "Technical Services," "Business and Administration," "Media," "Support Ministries" and "Translation and Literacy." Given such a wide range of opportunities for service, we might conclude that being technically qualified to serve in any capacity in a country at some distance from one's home church qualifies a person as a missionary.

Such a conclusion would be erroneous. In this chapter, and in those that follow in this section, I discuss the convergence of suitability in five areas of missionary qualification. They include the importance of apostolic passion, spiritual giftedness, consistency of life, practical qualifications and divine calling. Consider first the preeminent need to model apostolic passion.

Missionaries in the apostolic mold

Our word "missionary" derives from the Latin *mittere* which means "to send." Our word "apostle" comes from the Greek words *apo stellein* meaning "to send away." The similarity of these two words suggests that missionaries are those who are sent to carry on the apostolic task.

The exclusive *office* of the twelve apostles no longer exists. But the apostolic *work* of church planting continues wherever pioneer missionaries labor. The *Didache*, describing early church ministry, was written near the beginning of the second century. This manual uses "apostle" in two senses. It recognizes the unrivaled position of the original Twelve. But it also mentions the presence at that time of itinerant apostles akin to present-day missionaries. "Concerning apostles and prophets, so do ye according to the ordinance of the gospel. Let every apostle, when he cometh to you, be received as the Lord; but he shall not abide more than a single day, or if there be need, a second likewise; but if he abide three days, he is a false prophet."[2] Since the Twelve had died by this time, this text must refer to traveling ministers who carried on a work similar to that begun by the apostles.

Leslie B. Flynn quotes the *International Standard Bible Encyclopedia*: "In the New Testament and in the other literature of the early church, the word 'apostle' is used in a narrower and in a wider sense. The wider use of the word has descended to the present day. Apostles or 'holy apostles' is still the name for missionaries in some parts of the Greek church."[3] He concludes, "Officially, the apostolate ended with the apostles; unofficially the apostolic gift persists to our day as the missionary gift."

"The apostolic gift is still being given today," maintains Ray Stedman, "though in a secondary sense. It is part of the apostolic gift to start new churches. We call those who do this 'pioneer missionaries.'"[4]

It is of great importance that we do not confuse the prerogatives, and unique place in history, of the Twelve. Modern-day missionaries are not apostles in that sense. And yet, missionaries, in turn, must not be confused with pastors or teachers in an established church situation. They are specially gifted individuals sent out by God to labor in the extension of his Kingdom.

I would define missionaries as *those unique individuals sent out by the Spirit with both the vision and gifts to plant churches among unreached peoples*. Missionaries in the apostolic mold are pioneer church planters.

Consider six aspects of this definition:

VISION

The apostles' actions were increasingly governed by a missionary vision. They knew Jesus's desire—"I have other sheep that are not of this sheep pen" (John 10:16)—and his marching orders—"make disciples of all nations" (Matt. 28:19). And yet, in the beginning, their burden was limited to Jewish evangelism. Then Peter's vision of the sheet let down from heaven spurred them on to reach into Roman society. The bestowal of the Spirit as manifested in four distinct cultural Pentecosts—to Jews in Jerusalem, to Samaritans, to Gentile God-fearers at Cornelius's house and then to pagans in Ephesus—must have deepened their missionary vision. As their understanding developed they connected this vision with the covenant promise to bless all nations through Abraham's seed. While the vision of the early apostles was faltering and parochial at first, it gradually developed until it found mature expression in the missionary teams of the apostle Paul.

Today, those with a missionary vision view the world in terms of the marching orders of the Master. Where this understanding of our task prospers, a concern for the unreached parts of the earth prevails. Churches owe their origin and continuing spiritual health to the maintenance of this apostolic vision. Unfortunately, in too many cases, churches exhibit profound concern about buildings, programs and budgets, but little about the mission fields of the world. And yet the Lord of the harvest still calls us to look upon the fields of the world. Those individuals who hear his call and feel his passion may inherit the apostolic vision.

BEING SENT OUT

The missionary calling involves the willingness to be sent out by a local congregation. This sending is inherent in the very meaning of the word "missionary."

Barnabas sought out Paul's help to teach the new converts in the infant church at Antioch. After about a year of ministry there the church sent them with a gift of money to relieve the famine-stricken saints in the Jerusalem church. Returning to Antioch, they continued serving the local church for some time. Later, while engaged in corporate worship, "the Holy Spirit said, 'Set apart for me Barnabas and Saul for the work to which I have called them'" (Acts 13:2–4).

Missionaries, just like Barnabas and Paul, are:

- set apart for ministry *in* a local church
- sent out *from* that church
- return or report *to* that church.

Missionaries are neither adventurers who love to travel nor eccentric individualists who find local church life too confining. They are visionaries who develop within a local-church setting and whose calling and missionary gifts are recognized by church leaders.

The New Testament record teaches us, however, that a home church cannot closely supervise missionaries in distant lands. Like the apostles, missionaries must have the freedom and flexibility to do their work on the field. The genius of missionary endeavor can be stifled if a distant home church seeks to administer every detail of the work where their sent ones labor. Although free, missionaries in the apostolic mold are accountable to their sending church.

A good example of this principle of accountability is found in the great William Carey. Although his missionary vision was not shared by his denominational colleagues, he patiently prepared himself for service and continued to pray about his call and concerns until a small group arose to send him out. Missionaries are "sent ones."

MESSENGERS

Missionaries go bearing a message. Thayer defines an apostle as "a delegate, messenger, one sent forth with orders."[5] In Luke 9 Jesus called the twelve apostles to his side. He gave them power to drive out demons, to cure the sick and "to preach the kingdom of God." At his command "they set out and went from village to village, preaching the gospel and healing people everywhere" (vv. 1–6).

Although the early Christian missionaries were well known for their good works, these acts of mercy did not constitute their message. While the apostles healed, cast out demons and encouraged relief work, they never lost sight of their main task. They had been commissioned to bear witness to the risen Christ. The proclamation of the gospel was paramount (Mark 1:38; Acts 6:2). They were messengers of the Word, not social workers, in terms of their calling. As compassionate Christians they no doubt expressed their love for others in a multitude of ways that were not verbal.

Missionary work, in the apostolic mold, will always focus on evangelism (the announcing of the good news) because man's need for salvation is more desperate than any other need.

PIONEERS

As already noted in this chapter, the needs of the unevangelized grip the heart of the missionary (Rom. 15:20–24). Pastors and teachers minister where there is already a foundation laid, while those with the missionary calling lay the foundations for new churches in unchurched, pioneer situations. (As we shall see later, this does not mean that missionaries do not exercise teaching or shepherding/pastoral gifts.)

When God gave Peter the vision of the lowered sheet he said, in effect, "Peter, stop being concerned only with the Jewish people while the Gentiles remain unreached" (see Acts 10). A burden to reach out to the unreached is a distinguishing feature of apostolic missions. Missionaries who have this burden feel compelled to take the gospel into the unevangelized parts of the earth.

It has always been so. During the past three centuries we have seen three great missionary thrusts into the dark places of earth, all fueled by a burden for the unreached. Firstly, William Carey and his contemporaries pioneered work in the unevangelized coastlands of India, China and Africa. Secondly, Hudson Taylor and a host of "faith missionaries" led the thrust further into the vast unreached inland portions of these countries. This era spawned the China Inland Mission, the Sudan Interior Mission, the Africa Inland Mission and a number of other groups. More recently, men such as Cameron Townsend recognized the presence in all parts of the world of unevangelized tribes. Linguistic or cultural isolation had hidden them from view. Wycliffe Bible Translators, Gospel Recordings and the New Tribes Mission, to name but a few, were founded to reach these overlooked tribes and peoples.

In recent decades the research of Ralph Winter at the US Center for World Missions and of others like him has uncovered a new frontier. While most modern nations have churches, hundreds of distinct ethnic groups, *peoples*, have been overlooked in each nation. These *hidden* or *frontier people groups*, distinguished by dialect, custom, religion, residence and caste, cannot be reached without a team specifically aimed at them. This is today's task, planting churches among every one of the people groups of our world.[6] Todd Johnson and Peter Crossing constructed a list of 395 of the world's ethno-cultural families, 13,509 languages, 6,600 cultures and 12,600 ethno-linguistic peoples. An ethno-linguistic people is defined as "a people in one country with a unique race code and a specific language as a mother tongue ... e.g. Turks in Turkey speaking *osmanli*." Analysis uncovered 815 untargeted peoples—a great improvement in the last few decades.[7]

CHURCH PLANTING

Church planting, more than any other task, distinguishes the missionary gift. Paul wrote to the Corinthians to remind them that their very existence was evidence of his apostleship (1 Cor. 9:2; 2 Cor. 3:2; see also Rom. 15). In his parting speech to the Ephesian elders, Paul reviewed the various ministries that had engaged his attention while he was among them. Essentially he tabulated different facets of church planting—from evangelism to the nurture of converts and the appointment of leaders. Paul's church-planting success is written large in the pages of Scripture.

Missions *is* church planting. Nothing—not even relief work or Bible translation, not the establishment of hospitals or schools—nothing must distract us from the main missionary task. These diverse activities have missionary validity only as they contribute to building the kingdom through the establishment of local churches. Local churches, in turn, become centers where compassion will be displayed in many diverse ways.

ITINERATION

Both Peter and Paul were travelers. Missionaries who follow in their footsteps are not prone to settle down, a policy that has important implications for leadership development. New leaders rarely develop if more mature and gifted leaders overshadow them. Good leaders delegate and nurture future leaders by moving out of church plants that have developed satisfactorily. One of the effects of the scattering of the early Jewish church was that strong new leaders, such as Philip, developed when they were forced out from under the shadow cast by the Twelve.

The missionary should not sink permanent roots in any one place. Once a church was sufficiently established Paul moved on. He realized that, while there was much yet to do in Greece and Asia Minor, the foundation had been laid. To the Romans he wrote, "So from Jerusalem all the way around to Illyricum, I have fully proclaimed the gospel of Christ ... now that there is no more place for me to work in these regions, and since I have been longing for many years to see you, I plan to do so when I go to Spain" (Rom. 15:19, 23–24). Once a foundation is laid, missionaries should move on.

The amount of time necessary to lay a foundation is not easy to determine and will vary greatly from place to place. Gaining facility in language takes much time. In the Muslim world this might mean staying for decades. Tribes may require fifteen years or more. On the other hand, churches might spring up in a year or two among responsive peoples. But, in most cases, the time to move on will come. One of the defects of missions has been the construction of great mission stations which are a practical denial of this principle. Historically, long-term residence in the countries of Asia and Africa gave missionaries the time to construct beautiful missionary compounds and elaborate medical and educational institutions. This "mission station" approach usually led to paternalism and dependence and tended to stunt indigenous leadership development.

In summary, those who receive the missionary gift possess vision, are sent out by local churches as messengers of the gospel and are commissioned to itinerate with a view to planting churches among unreached people.

The preeminent missionary gift was modeled by Paul and those he mentored, such as Silas and Timothy. In any missionary society and on any missionary committee, missions must be inspired and directed by a vision of the unreached. Unless the focus of a missionary organization rests firmly on pioneer church planting, a host of other competing needs will tend to smother its primary calling.

Notes

1 Fall 1994 issue of *SIMNOW*, the magazine of SIM International.

2 Quoted in **Leslie B. Flynn,** *19 Gifts of the Spirit* (Wheaton, IL: Victor Books, 1981), pp. 43–44.

3 Ibid. p. 42.

4 **Ray Stedman,** *Body Life* (3rd edn.; Ventura, CA: Regal Books, 1981), p. 74.

5 **J. Thayer,** *Greek–English Lexicon of the New Testament* (New York: American Book Company, 1889), p. 68.

6 According to Steve Hawthorne, there are 24,000 people groups in the world, with approximately 14,000 of these reached. (The exact number of ethnic groups changes as research develops.) Steve Hawthorne, "Laying a Firm Foundation for Mission in the Next Millennium," in *Mission Frontiers*, Special Issue, January 2000, p. 11.

7 **Todd M. Johnson** and **Peter F. Crossing,** "Which Peoples Need Priority Attention?," in *Mission Frontiers*, Jan–Feb. 2002, p. 16.

Chapter 15

Spiritual giftedness

Besides the clear direction generated by apostolic vision, missionaries require the equipping of the Holy Spirit for their task. Vision is not enough. Passion is not enough. Sincerity is not enough. We all know examples of godly and passionate ministers who lacked the practical abilities needed to function effectively in their spheres of influence. Few things are more lamentable than seeing a person laboring away trying to do what he or she is not gifted to do. The following story illustrates the situation from the perspective of pupils in a rather unusual school.

Once upon a time, the animals decided they should do something meaningful to meet the problems of the new world. So they organized a school. They adopted an activity curriculum of running, climbing, swimming and flying. To make it easier to administer the curriculum, all the animals took all the subjects.

The duck was excellent in swimming; in fact, better than his instructor. But he made only passing grades in flying and was very poor in running. Since he was slow in running, he had to drop swimming and stay after school to practice running. This caused his web feet to be badly worn, so that he was only average in swimming. But average was acceptable, so nobody worried about that—except the duck.

The rabbit started at the top of his class in running, but developed a nervous twitch in his leg muscles because of so much make-up work in swimming.

The squirrel was excellent in climbing, but he encountered constant frustration in flying class because his teacher made him start from the ground up instead of from the treetop down. He developed "charlie horses" from overexertion and so only got a C in climbing and a D in running.

The eagle was a problem child and was severely disciplined for being a non-conformist. In climbing classes he beat all the others to the top of the tree, but insisted on using his own way to get there ...[1]

How frustrating to be a rabbit who is expected to climb, or a Christian who is expected to serve as a missionary without the requisite gifts! Both Paul and Peter stressed the necessity of giftedness in Romans 12, 1 Corinthians 12–14, Ephesians 4 and 1 Peter (see especially Rom. 12:3–8; 1 Cor. 12:4–11; Eph. 4:7–16; 1 Peter 4:7–11).

The twenty or so gifts of the Holy Spirit mentioned in these verses constitute the spiritual endowments needed by God's people to serve Christ. Every Christian has a gift-mix different from that of other Christians. "We have different gifts, according to the grace given us" (Rom. 12:6). In 1 Corinthians Paul writes, "There are different kinds of gifts, but the same Spirit. There are different kinds of service, but the same Lord. There are different kinds of working, but the same God works all of them in all men" (1 Cor. 12:4–6). Neither zeal nor passion can produce fruit unless the Holy Spirit endows a person with the requisite gifts. And diverse fruit will be produced by diverse gifts in different situations. The Spirit is sovereign.

Not only is every Christian a gifted Christian, but every church needs the exercise of every one of the continuing gifts[2] of the Holy Spirit. A spiritual church cannot exist without, for example, those who encourage, evangelize or extend mercy. Each spiritual gift has been specifically designed by God to produce specific effects. The gift of teaching leads to understanding and application of the Word of God. When someone exercises the gift of encouragement, sad, discouraged, weary believers are uplifted. Mercy leads to helping the poor, the sick and the lonely to find what they need. Each believer has a different sphere of service and will see diverse results through the use of his or her gifts. No two people possess the same gift-mix.

I consider the essential, continuing gifts of the Spirit to be the following: preaching, evangelism, shepherding, knowledge, teaching, discernment, wisdom, mercy, hospitality, practical helpfulness, leadership, giving, faith and encouragement (the reasons behind this list are contained in my book *Church: No Spectator Sport*).[3]

From this larger list of gifts we can extract five or so that may be considered the foundational gifts necessary to plant churches in pioneer situations. Ephesians 4 highlights the endowments given by the ascended

Christ to "prepare God's people for works of service, so that the body of Christ may be built up until we all reach unity in the faith and in the knowledge of the Son of God and become mature ..." (Eph. 4:12–13). This goal, creating a mature church in which God's people are prepared to do all necessary works of service, is the missionary goal. We can conclude, then, that the gifts that have special relevance for missions are the gifts of evangelism, shepherding and teaching (assuming that the gift of apostles and prophets was limited to the apostolic age).

To these three foundational gifts we should add preaching and leadership. Every New Testament church planter demonstrated leadership gifts. It makes no sense to constitute a missionary team without one or more who have the ability to plan, organize and lead the team—the gift of leadership or management. As to preaching, previous chapters have already established the primacy of preaching in any missionary activity that seeks to follow in the footsteps of the apostles.

Every missionary team needs to have members who demonstrate giftedness in at least these five areas. Further gifts, such as mercy, giving, faith, discernment, wisdom or encouragement, will also be present in the gift-mix of team members. I am not denigrating those gifts. However, without a mix of members possessing leadership, preaching, evangelism, shepherding and teaching gifts a missionary team will be hampered in winning the lost and discipling those who respond to the gospel; the team will be hindered from organizing new believers into a church that becomes self-governing, self-supporting and self-propagating.

Normally, spiritual gifts are discovered and developed in the local church, the special nursery God created for the nurture of new believers.[4] Church leaders, indeed all those whose hearts beat with a missionary passion, should be on the constant lookout for those with these five foundational gifts. Consider each in turn.

The gift of preaching

The gift of preaching is that spiritual ability to communicate biblical truth in powerful and relevant ways so that people sense a word from God directed to them in their situation.

J. I. Packer writes that

History tells of no significant church growth and expansion that has taken place without preaching (significant, implying virility and staying power, is the key word there). What history points to, rather, is that all movements of revival, reformation and missionary outreach seem to have had preaching (vigorous, though on occasion very informal) at their center, instructing, energizing, sometimes purging and re-directing and often spearheading the whole movement. It would seem, then, that preaching is always necessary for a proper sense of mission to be evoked and sustained anywhere in the church.[5]

According to Packer, biblical preaching has five qualities:

- Preaching is presenting God's message to man and is thus biblical in content.
- Preaching has the purpose of informing, persuading and calling forth an appropriate response.
- Preaching always has the perspective of being life-changing in its application.
- Preaching is the declaration of the Word with authority.
- Preaching effects an encounter with God in his presence and power.[6]

The gift of evangelism

The gift of evangelism is that concern for lost men and women which moves the gifted person toward outreach wherever that may lead. This concern is combined with a Spirit-produced ability to communicate the gospel so effectively that people respond in faith and repentance. (Please note that only the Holy Spirit can regenerate lost men and women. This is a sovereign act of God. Nevertheless, the Holy Spirit uses means, and the means he frequently chooses to use is an individual whom he endows with the gift of evangelistic persuasion.)

On his way to Jerusalem, Paul stayed in Caesarea at the "house of Philip the evangelist" (Acts 21:8). Sometime during the period between Saul's violent persecution of the church and the conclusion of his third missionary journey, Philip, one of those chosen to wait at tables, had become known as "Philip the evangelist." Evangelism became the main focus of his life.

While Acts frequently alludes to witnessing Christians, Philip is the only witness specifically described in the Bible as an evangelist. He could not, however, have been unique.

Jesus predicted that his disciples would become "fishers of men," that is, evangelists noted for their success in catching souls. Success in fishing for men presupposes effectiveness in drawing men and women to faith in Christ.

This harvest image drawn from the sea indicates that God gifts some with the ability to draw people to Christ. We can equate the gift of evangelism with success in soul-winning, a vital aim of missions.

The gift of shepherding

The gift of shepherding is a spiritual sensitivity and concern for the care of Christians which leads the gifted person to draw near believers in order to protect them from danger, understand their spiritual needs and suggest steps to take to develop vigorous spiritual health. The shepherd is the spiritual General Practitioner whose skill in diagnosis, prescription and treatment helps maintain believers in good spiritual health.

In my own experience, and in that of many missionaries I have known, weakness is often exhibited in missionary organizations in the area of shepherding. Missionaries themselves, and those God uses them to pluck from antagonistic cultures, desperately need ongoing pastoral care.

The word *poimen* is translated "pastor" only once in the New Testament. The word, which denotes a "shepherd," is much more commonly used for Christ. In John 10 he is the "good shepherd" who calls his sheep by name, who goes ahead of them so they can follow him and, most particularly, is the one who gives his life for them. Once his sheep receive eternal life, he protects them so they will never perish. "No one can snatch them out of my Father's hand" (v. 29).

While the New Testament uses the word "shepherd" sparingly, nevertheless the concept commonly arises whenever church leadership is discussed. Paul exhorted the Ephesian elders to "Keep watch over yourselves and all the flock of which the Holy Spirit has made you overseers. Be shepherds of the church of God" (Acts 20:28). Pastoring is like shepherding a flock.

This involves protecting the flock from danger: "wolves will come in among you and will not spare the flock ... be on your guard!" (Acts 20:29, 31). Wolf-like false teachers and divisive leaders insinuate themselves into the midst of believers to cull out a flock of their own. True shepherds constantly "help the weak" by watching for signs of error or division in the immature and unstable (Acts 20:35).

In that poignant episode when Christ asked Peter about his love, our Lord instructed him to "take care of my sheep" (John 21:16). Years later, in Peter's first general epistle he echoed what he had learned by saying, "Be shepherds of God's flock that is under your care, serving as overseers" (1 Peter 5:2). Oversight of a flock involves a shepherd's care and concern. This is especially true of a flock recently rescued from Satan in a mission situation. And if Peter needed pastoral care, so do missionaries who don't have the benefit of Peter's firsthand experience with the Master.

As a spiritual diagnostician, the shepherd "watches for souls, as one that must give account" (Heb. 13:17). Charles Bridges describes the shepherd's diagnostic work well:

> He "watches for souls," lest a root of bitterness should spring up to the trouble and defilement of the church—lest unchristian tempers and practices should mar the profession of Christ—lest a lukewarm spirit should paralyze exertion, or a spirit of contention hinder Christian love. The indolent are slumbering—the self-dependent are falling back—the zealous are under the influence of spiritual pride—the earnest are becoming self-righteous—the regular, formal. Then there is the inquirer, asking for direction—the tempted and perplexed, looking for support—the afflicted, longing for the cheering consolation of the Gospel—the convinced sinner, from the slight healing his wound, settling in a delusive peace ...[7]

The gift of teaching

The gift of teaching is that Spirit-endowed ability to instruct others in the Word of God in such a way that God produces in those taught present and lasting changes in understanding, attitude, will and behavior.

Since Jesus Christ was called "the Master," which means "Teacher," it is no wonder that Christianity has always been, and always will be, a teaching faith. While on earth, Jesus went about teaching. In his final commission he said, "go and make disciples of all nations, baptizing ... and teaching them …" (Matt. 28:19–20). Following his lead, the disciples went everywhere teaching and preaching the gospel. Paul, although preeminently thought of as a flaming missionary evangelist, characterized his ministry as preaching and teaching publicly and from house to house (Acts 20:20). The four Gospels, the Epistles—indeed, all the books of the Bible—are great didactic documents. Teaching will always occupy a crucial place in missionary work.

The gift of leadership (administration)

The gift of leadership (administration) is a Spirit-endowed ability to serve the Lord and his people by taking a vision of what should be, evaluating the present situation, planning what to do, and motivating, organizing and directing until a plan is brought to completion.

The apostle to the Gentiles twice mentions leadership as a gift, for example, "We have different gifts … if it is leadership, let him govern diligently" (Rom. 12:6, 8). In 1 Corinthians Paul writes about "those with gifts of administration" (1 Cor. 12:28).

The Greek word *proistemi* used in Romans "means 'to stand before,' hence, to lead, attend to (indicating care and diligence)."[8] Leaders stand before a group charged by God with the responsibility of caring for them through diligently attending to their needs and directing their progress. Note: Leaders do not stand above others to dominate or boss them, but before them to lead the way.

A second Greek word, *kubernesis*, occurs in the Corinthian list. Translated "governments" by the KJV and "administration" by the NIV, the word comes from a root meaning "to guide."[9] It denotes "steering, pilotage"; and thus "metaphorically … governings, said of those who act as guides in a local church."[10] In this sense the leader, like the captain or pilot of a ship, guides others through dangerous waters to a safe harbor.

Paul's choice of these two words from among many available to him underscores the qualitative difference which Jesus declared must exist between Christian and worldly leaders. Christian leaders are foot-washing servants. Paul could have chosen words more freighted with power, authority and domination, such as those from which our English words "despot" or "hegemony" originate, or terms used by the Romans to describe their absolute power. Instead, he chose milder words that highlight a leader's responsibility more than his authority. (I am not denying the realities of spiritual authority.) The gift of leadership, in this sense, would indicate a call to go before a group of people to steer them in a productive direction or to guide them safely through treacherous waters to a safe haven.

The discovery and development of spiritual gifts is of crucial importance. This book, however, is not the place to enter into a lengthy discussion on these divine enablements. Instead, I would again refer you to my book on the subject: *Church: No Spectator Sport. Discovering and Developing Spiritual Gifts.*

Notes

1 Quoted in **Charles Swindoll,** *Growing Strong in the Seasons of Life* (Portland, OR: Multnomah, 1983), p. 312.

2 By "continuing gifts" I mean to exclude those five charismatic gifts concerning which there is great controversy: the gift of inspired prophecy, the gift of tongues, the gift of interpretation of tongues, the gift of miracles, the gift of healing. For a discussion of this matter read my book *Church: No Spectator Sport. Discovering and Developing Spiritual Gifts* (Darlington: Evangelical Press, 1994).

3 **Eric E. Wright,** *Church: No Spectator Sport. Discovering and Developing Spiritual Gifts* (Darlington: Evangelical Press, 1994).

4 If you are interested in a booklet describing six steps to take in discovering and developing spiritual gifts, contact me through the publisher.

5 **J. I. Packer,** in **Samuel T. Logan,** (ed.), *The Preacher and Preaching* (Phillipsburg, NJ: Presbyterian and Reformed, 1986), p. 21.

6 Ibid. pp. 8–13.

7 **Charles Bridges,** *The Christian Ministry* (London: Banner of Truth, 1967), p. 350, footnote.

8 **W. E. Vine,** *An Expository Dictionary of New Testament Words* (1st edn. 1939; [n.d.]: Lynchburg, VA: The Old Time Gospel Hour), p. 979.

9 Ibid. p. 498.

10 Ibid. p. 979.

Chapter 16

Missionary qualifications

Some missionaries on deputation have had children come up to them and exclaim, "Wow! Are you a real live missionary?" Others have been introduced as a cross between Superman and Wild West hero Wyatt Earp. A past generation almost universally regarded the missionary as a hero. "It was assumed that he was an intellectual and spiritual giant, more dedicated, more courageous, and more spiritual than his counterpart, the pastor here at home."[1]

Fortunately, most people today realize that the missionary doesn't wear a halo. We live in a more open, more transparent era. Missionaries can now, more than before, "tell it like it is." In my own experience I have found that the tactful but frank sharing of spiritual challenges and even weaknesses mobilizes prayer more than it inspires disdain.

However, the pendulum may have swung too far. In many segments of the church, "today's missionary is in danger of being reduced to a humdrum worker in the vineyard of the Lord."[2] Attendance at missionary conferences is down. In some circles young people view missionaries as hopelessly "out of it." The romance of missions is gone!

While missionaries are not superheroes, neither are they naive and plodding dolts. They are the salt of the earth! In our attempt to demythologize the mysterious missionary we dare not gloss over the very real excitement involved in serving at the cutting edge of the kingdom!

Some years ago Stephen Neill wrote,

> I may place on record my conviction that the needs of the mission field are always far greater than the needs of the Church at home, that no human qualifications, however high, render a man or woman more than adequate for missionary work, that there is no career which affords such scope for enterprise and creative work, and that in comparison with the slight sacrifice demanded, the reward is great beyond all measuring.[3]

What, then, qualifies a person to become a missionary? This will vary widely depending upon the person's destination, specific ministry and the duration of his or her service. George Peters states that the degree of preparation necessary and the qualifications required for missionary service will depend on: (1) the government of the country involved; (2) the missionary society; (3) the state of the church in the country of service; (4) the task to be fulfilled.[4]

Further, short-term service requires less rigorous preparation than commitment to a lifelong career. Missionary work in a familiar culture that does not require language study calls for somewhat less rigor in preparation than does cross-cultural missionary activity. Church planting will call for a different kind of preparation than will commitment to a support ministry such as aviation or radio. Health will be a factor as well.

While qualifications will vary, certain basic qualities ought to characterize every missionary. Many of these are no different from those we should expect in any genuine follower of Christ. Hudson Taylor listed the following as indispensable missionary equipment:

- a life yielded to God, controlled by his Spirit
- a restful trust in God for the supply of all needs
- a sympathetic spirit and willingness to take a lowly place
- tact in dealing with people and adaptability toward circumstances
- zeal in service and steadfastness in discouragements
- love for communion with God and for the study of his Word
- some experience and blessing in the Lord's work at home
- a healthy body and a vigorous mind.[5]

George Peters, in his chapter on the subject, lists seven indispensable qualifications:

- unreserved commitment to Christ demonstrated in abiding discipleship
- a deep and abiding consciousness of call either to the ministry of the Word or to become a helper in that ministry through being a doctor, nurse, teacher, etc., combined with a sense of being led to a place of assignment and labor
- a settled conviction that the Lord has committed to us a message of salvation necessary for the destiny of man that can only be communicated under the qualifying power and equipping of the Holy Spirit
- a servant attitude that leads the missionary to seek identification with those to whom he is called, and to be flexible and open to sacrifice of any kind

- an ability to relate graciously and lovingly with co-workers and nationals
- a demonstration of a pure and honest motivation to serve Christ, although perfection of motivation can never be attained
- a high view of and deep loyalty to the church of Jesus Christ.[6]

Let me comment briefly on some of the qualifications that I deem essential.

Spirituality

No qualification for missionary service is more basic or more necessary than consistency of life. While those with limited language ability or ordinary gifts may stumble somewhat in their attempts at communication or ministry, if the quality of their walk with Christ is high, they may be mightily used of God.

Especially important here is devotion to Christ and total submission to the Holy Spirit. Since missions is a Triune enterprise, a loving relationship with the Triune God will immerse the prospective missionary in an atmosphere conducive to spiritual success. As will be discussed in Chapter 25, this puts worship and intercession front and center.

Discipleship is another way of describing this qualification. Since missions is making disciples, the missionary must first *be* a disciple, as defined in Chapter 8. One cannot be a spiritual leader without first being a follower of Christ. As a disciple, the prospective missionary embraces a learning lifestyle that commits him or her to a lifetime of growth in the spiritual disciplines of prayer, Bible study, meditation, ministry, and so on. However young the candidate may be, there must be a sense of development—a growth in grace and in the knowledge of Christ.

Discipleship presupposes discipline, the governing of the tongue, the control of one's temper. Once, in a meeting with church leaders, one missionary suddenly got up and stormed out of the building. He refused to return. The national Christians present read from his actions that he wanted his own way and would refuse to work with them unless they gave in to his desires. Since he held the purse strings, they learned to appease him. He obviously knew little about being crucified with Christ.

In another case a missionary exploded in a meeting between town officials and church leaders. The polite stalling of the officials was more than he could stand. His angry language, in a culture where expressions of anger are anathema, destroyed any progress the group had been making toward gaining permission for a program they planned.

Permanent damage might not have resulted in the cases of the two missionaries mentioned above had they been humble enough to confess their sinful actions. If they had asked for forgiveness it would have been granted to them. True spirituality calls for openness, transparency, meekness and humility. The fields of the world need humble, godly missionaries even more than gifted missionaries. Of course, we know that the Spirit can combine both in one person.

Perseverance and stability

Hudson Taylor highlighted the importance of steadfastness in the face of discouragement. Planting churches among the unreached is one of the most challenging tasks on earth. This work requires the ability to endure frustration, loneliness and disappointment without giving up even though years elapse. The information age with its constant stimulation and focus on entertainment ill-prepares people to stick with tedious tasks over a long period of time.

The emphasis in our Western culture on frequent career changes also militates against those who would give their whole lives to missionary service. The trend toward short terms also makes it more difficult to recruit lifelong, career missionaries.

For this reason, recruiters would do well to look for signs of maturity. Has the person demonstrated the ability to stick with one church through thick or thin? Has he or she drifted from job to job? Has the candidate been a Christian long enough to have a seasoned faith? Or is the romance of missions blinding the person to the trials ahead? Zeal and youthful energy are needed, but they must be harnessed by the maturity of approach that is found in those who have already endured problems, trials, challenges and disappointments with a measure of stability.

Ability to get along with people

The second great commandment is to love our neighbor as ourselves.

Without this kind of self-effacing love, the challenge of getting along with missionaries and national believers will be impossible. One of the greatest problems my wife and I encountered in our missionary career was somewhat unexpected: How to get along with missionaries from different cultures, how to deal with conflict, how to build a team spirit?

People are all different. They come from different cultures. When we first arrived, we were astonished to realize that our habit of having peanut butter for breakfast offended our British senior missionaries. Americans come across differently compared with Canadians. Germans and Australians have their distinctives. When we add to the cultural mix the cultural mores of our host country, we face serious challenges to harmony.

Often, differences in temperament go unrecognized. The Scriptures describe impetuous Peter, doubting Thomas, thundering James and John, timid Timothy, encouraging Barnabas and driving Paul. These temperaments—sanguine, melancholic, choleric, phlegmatic, however we classify them—present us with a challenge that makes team unity difficult to achieve.

Missionary candidates, then, need to be realistic people who understand human differences, celebrate diversity, have a healthy understanding of their own strengths and weaknesses and demonstrate the ability to get along with others. Care should be taken to beware of the inflexible, dogmatic "I'm always right" type of personality; "the Lord's servant must not quarrel [strive]; instead he must be kind to everyone" (2 Tim. 2:24).

Has the person demonstrated the ability to work as a team member in the local church or ministry? Or is the person a Lone Ranger? Teamwork will be crucial to missionary success. Even Paul, the dynamic and driving pioneer, insisted on working with a team.

We cannot expect new churches to demonstrate unity if church planters can't get along with one another. Too often, petty jealousies damage teamwork. I could document many sad cases. A gifted missionary refusing to forgive a co-worker. Immature workers going off on a tangent because they chose to ignore the valuable advice of more experienced laborers.

In one missionary team, a particular missionary insisted that the field council approve his pet program. The council knew that failure to approve it would anger him and alienate his family. They gave in, even though they knew that it was not in the best interests of the whole team.

Breaches of fellowship occur much more often than any of us would like to admit. And wherever there is a breakdown in fellowship, the work of the kingdom suffers. I am not saying that disagreements will never arise. But how we handle disagreements distinguishes genuine discipleship from carnality. Godliness of character exudes humility and openness to others. In evangelism, just as much as in any other sphere of human activity, "Blessed are the peacemakers."

Flexibility

We must distinguish stability from a stubborn inability to adapt to changing circumstances. Biblical missionaries have the ability to look at seemingly impossible circumstances and come up with some innovative way to communicate the gospel. Bazaar preaching, TV evangelism, correspondence courses, film evangelism, mobile book vans; missionaries use a great variety of methods.

We live in a world of accelerating change. Add to this the challenge of being set down in a culture distinct from your own, and no wonder missionaries need to be adaptable. Interruptions, changing bureaucracies, diverse cultural patterns: all call for flexibility. Missionaries need to be people who use time wisely without being slaves to their schedules.

Faith and vision

Besides adapting to current situations and people, missionaries need to bring a vision of the future to their task. Balanced missionary work is neither a blind denial of traditional ways of doing things nor an undiscerning adoption of novelty for the sake of change. All change is not good. It has been my experience, however, that both in home churches and in many missionary organizations there is an aversion to healthy change.

And yet missionaries are change-agents. As pioneers, they envision how a seemingly impossible situation can be overcome to extend the kingdom. They are committed to maintain the unchanging integrity of the message while inventing innovative ways to advance the cause of Christ. Vision led Hudson Taylor to go inland when his compatriots were content to work on the coast. Vision led Joy Ridderhof to invent Gospel Recordings as a way to train her disciples when sickness kept her from being at their side. Vision led Ralph Winter, and others, to invent Theological Education by Extension (TEE) when traditional methods of training church leaders failed.

In a sense, missionaries ought to be spiritual entrepreneurs. This requires not only wisdom and inventiveness but also faith. When we think of great missionaries from the past, we think of their visionary faith: Carey, Judson, Taylor, Carmichael, the Auca martyrs.

Candidates ought to have some experience of living by faith in the sovereign God. For this reason Hudson Taylor wisely introduced the "faith principle" to evangelical missions. While rarely applied as a support principle today, missionaries need faith just as much as they ever have done. My wife and I were greatly helped in our missionary training by the emphasis of Columbia Bible College (now Columbia International University) on faith goals. We learned practical lessons in how to trust God to provide for us, lessons that stood us in good stead in the years ahead.

Servanthood

Jesus came "not ... to be served, but to serve, and to give his life as a ransom for many" (Mark 10:45). Before his death he washed the disciples' feet. Few characteristics are as important as a servant spirit. Missionaries go to minister, not to be ministered to, not to enhance their egos or enforce their will. Has the candidate got his or her hands dirty? Does he or she shy away from mundane jobs? Has he or she washed dishes and cleaned toilets? Humility and openness to serve are absolute prerequisites for this job—more so than ever in a world that remembers imperialism and reacts against the know-it-all foreigner.

Bible training

Russ Irwin, a veteran missionary who offered helpful suggestions on the text of this book, said to me, "Emphasize, emphasize and emphasize Bible training. It is needed in every type of missionary work and in all situations." The view that a couple of years of Bible school is adequate for a missionary while a pastor needs post-graduate seminary training is erroneous. Missionaries should be among our best-trained professionals.

They represent Christ in new churches. They must know the Scriptures thoroughly, as well as have facility in missionary methodology.

Church integration

Since missions is church planting, a candidate without home-church membership and involvement raises immediate questions in the minds of recruiters. And yet I have often talked to young people who show interest in foreign missions but no desire to root themselves in a local church. A most mysterious paradox! The Lord of the church expects us to be part of the visible church.

Granted, many of our home churches have problems. Granted, they may be stodgy. But without learning how to relate to other believers in a real church setting, how can candidates hope to relate to those in mission churches?

Ministry skill

Certain spiritual gifts are crucial to the missionary task. Depending on the type of work for which they are recruited, candidates should show some developing ministry skills, especially in the areas of evangelism and teaching. They should have already been heavily involved in ministry in their home churches. Perhaps they have been preaching or participating in visitation or evangelistic programs, or in Sunday school or youth programs. Perhaps they have been involved in summer outreach. Their training should not all be cerebral; they need practical experience. Are they adept at visiting, shepherding, encouraging? Even if they go as support staff to a mission hospital or college, or minister through teaching English as a second language, some facility in personal evangelism is necessary. Even missionary mechanics should seek to stir up the gift of evangelism.

If they plan to minister cross-culturally, they should show some facility in languages. Have they taken French or German, Greek or Hebrew? Do they speak a second language?

Health

Since missionary work requires vigor, candidates should be in good health and demonstrate a balanced approach to rest, recreation, diet and exercise.

No one can duplicate the array of qualifications found in Peter or Paul. Missionary candidates are not going to be perfect! In some measure, however, all should demonstrate devotion, a commitment to spiritual disciplines, humility, the ability to get along with others, vision, faith, persistence, flexibility, adequate training, ministry skills, good health and involvement in a local church.

Notes

1 **Herbert Kane,** *Understanding Christian Missions* (Grand Rapids, MI: Baker, 1979), p. 73.

2 Ibid.

3 **Stephen Neill,** *Builders of the Indian Church* (London: Edinburgh House Press, 1934), p. 4.

4 **George W. Peters,** *A Biblical Theology of Missions* (Chicago: Moody, 1972), p. 293.

5 Ibid. pp. 297–298.

6 Ibid. pp. 294–297.

The missionary call

Whenever people talk about who should serve as missionaries, the need for a clear sense of divine call is usually mentioned most frequently. The importance of the call has been exaggerated to such an extent that many look for some mystical experience mirroring that of Gideon, Isaiah or Saul.

Once we hear the words "God called me to serve in Germany" (it could be Detroit), we may feel loath to ask any further questions. If we did, wouldn't we be questioning God? Who wants to throw cold water on the Spirit? But did the call come from the Holy Spirit or from the person's own spirit?

There is a sense in which this traditional approach to the call of God has not served us well. C. Griffiths, former General Director of OMF, comments, "The high percentage of people who feel called to glamorous fields makes one a little skeptical."[1] Dr. Raymond Davis, a former General Director of SIM International, writes, "The concept of a 'call' as a necessary introductory experience for serving God cannot be Scripturally substantiated." Dr. Ian Hay, who succeeded him at SIM, says, "Actually the use of the word bothers me. There's a lot of misunderstanding regarding a 'call.' The word has assumed overtones that I think we can do without."

The problems surrounding a *call* as noted by Griffiths, Davis and Hay are rooted in misunderstandings about the role of subjective feelings in discerning God's will. The interpretation of what we feel to be *a sense of peace* given by the Holy Spirit may be unreliable and due more to our desires than to God's direction. Garry Friesen, in his excellent work *Decision Making and the Will of God*, urges us to make decisions based on both God's revealed moral will and the wisdom and judgment that we develop as maturing Christians.

I would urge readers to delve more fully into this subject, either in Friesen's book or through considering the summary at: gfriesen.net/sections/willofgod_principles.php.

To approach this subject from a fresh perspective, let's review what the Bible teaches about "calling."

An overview of biblical teaching on the "call" of God

First we note that the terminology is used of God's general invitation to sinners: "I have not come to call the righteous, but sinners" (Matt. 9:13). The parable of the wedding banquet and the reluctant guests in Matthew 22:2–14 describes God's universal invitation for sinners to partake of his mercies. We also find it in his compassionate invitation, "Come to me, all you who are weary and burdened, and I will give you rest" (Matt. 11:28).

Besides this general call, however, there is God's effectual call. At his effectual call the rebellious repent, the unbelieving believe and even the dead are raised. It is an irresistible call that never fails in its effects: "those he predestined, he also called; those he called, he also justified; those he justified, he also glorified" (Rom. 8:30).

The word translated "call" is used only three times in the New Testament to indicate the appointment of someone to ministry. In Romans 1:1, Paul was "set apart for the gospel of God." In Antioch the Holy Spirit said to the church leaders, "Set apart for me Barnabas and Saul for the work to which I have called them" (Acts 13:2). The vision of a Macedonian led Paul to conclude, "God had called us to preach the gospel to them" (Acts 16:10). This is not a very strong basis for asserting that all who preach the gospel receive a call as distinct and objective as that received by Barnabas and Paul.

Besides these instances, the Bible does record a number of spectacular callings in the Old Testament: God's covenant with Abraham; Moses and the burning bush; Isaiah's vision of God in the temple; Jonah's call to Nineveh. These Bible characters, however, were divinely inspired prophets and leaders. These dramatic episodes impress us but do not give us sufficient reason to declare that everyone who is called of God must have a dramatic sense of that call.

When we turn to other passages in the New Testament we find there is considerable precedent to emphasize more ordinary means of calling. Mark was chosen to accompany the first missionary team without any unusual manifestations of the Spirit. Barnabas and Paul were acquainted with him and decided he would be helpful (Acts 12:25).

After the Council of Jerusalem the whole church met and decided whom to send to Antioch. "Then the apostles and elders, with the whole church, decided to choose some of their own men and send them to Antioch with Paul and Barnabas. They chose Judas (called Barsabbas) and Silas, two men who were leaders among the brothers" (Acts 15:22). Their joint decision proved to be wise. As a result of that exercise of congregational wisdom, Paul became impressed with Silas and asked him to accompany him on his journeys (Acts 15:36–41).

The choice of Timothy, who became such a valuable minister that two books are addressed to him, occurred in an even more ordinary way: "The brothers spoke well of him," and "Paul wanted to take him along on the journey" (see Acts 16:1–5). Besides episodes as dramatic as the burning bush and the light on the Damascus Road were a host of more ordinary "callings." Many men were "called to ministry" without dramatic manifestations.

The book of Proverbs highlights the importance of making wise decisions. For that reason, I believe that the "missionary call" owes more to wise decision making on the part of the candidate, and wise use of discernment on the part of those in his or her home church, than on a mystical, subjective "call."

Steps in missionary preparation equals steps any disciple follows

The steps to confirm or deny a "missionary call" can be equated with the steps any obedient Christian should take in the course of his or her normal Christian walk. At some point, the growing Christian whom God intends to use as a missionary comes to a guided decision that missionary service is the right choice. Let me outline the steps that he or she might take. Note how similar they are to those of any growing Christian.

POSITIVE REACTION TO THE GREAT COMMISSION

Jesus has called all Christians to respond obediently to his final command to expedite the extension of his kingdom into all the world. All Christians are to "seek first his kingdom and his righteousness" (Matt. 6:33). All are called to be world Christians (Matt. 28:19–20). Every believer is to pray in the terms of the Lord's prayer, "Your kingdom come." Every single disciple is to work toward quantitative and qualitative church growth (Matt. 6:10; Eph. 4:11–16).

UNCONDITIONAL SUBMISSION TO CHRIST

No disciple is exempt from the command of Christ to "deny himself and take up his cross daily and follow me" (Luke 9:23–27). Yieldedness and sacrifice come with the territory—being a citizen of the kingdom. "I urge you, brothers, in view of God's mercy, to offer your bodies as living sacrifices, holy and pleasing to God—this is your spiritual act of worship" (Rom. 12:1). In the process of this submission of ourselves to God as living sacrifices we "test and approve what God's will is—his good, pleasing and perfect will" (Rom. 12:2). There would be no shortage of missionary volunteers if all of us yielded ourselves unconditionally to Christ for his service.

ACTIVE OBEDIENCE TO ALL THE COMMANDS OF CHRIST

All disciples, including all missionaries, are called to live a life of ongoing obedience. We must obey whatever command we read in the Scriptures. Whether it is to tell the truth or to love our neighbor, to give generously or to help the lonely, our only valid choice is to obey. "If you love me, you will obey what I command ... Whoever has my commands and obeys them, he is the one who loves me" (see John 14:15–21).

ACTIVE GIFT DISCOVERY, DEVELOPMENT AND EXERCISE

All believers have a function to fulfill in the body of Christ. The health of the body depends on the participation of all its members. The New Testament contains no category for spectators. All must give themselves to the discovery, development and use of their spiritual gifts in the context of a local church (read 2 Tim. 1:6; 1 Cor. 12:4–7; Rom. 12:6–8).

The thin ranks of missionaries would be swollen with volunteers if it was the norm in our churches for every believer to participate in ministry. Some would develop latent gifts of evangelism, shepherding, administration, mercy, teaching, and so on, but would find limited scope for their use in their own church. Like Philip in Samaria, some might be led to use their gifts beyond the borders of their own church. They might feel a burden to reach recent immigrants or visitors, or to start a Bible study in a new neighborhood. In the course of using their gifts they might begin to feel more deeply a burden for missions.

We must not only discover our spiritual gifts, but also use them. That may involve teaching a Sunday school class, visiting someone in hospital, tidying up the church, writing notes of encouragement—there are countless possibilities. Where gifts are not exercised, they atrophy.

ACTIVE SEARCH FOR KNOWLEDGE

We are living through an information explosion. Most of us grapple with information overload. But if we are learners (a basic meaning of disciple), we will develop the curiosity that God intends us to have about the world in which we live. This curiosity will move us to want not only to master the Word of God, a basic given, but also to understand news, the geography of nations, the diversity of human cultures and so on. Every Christian should fight tooth and nail the tendency to become contented, slothful and indifferent. We should be readers. We should have some basic interest in world news. If we do, God's Spirit may burden our hearts for the world beyond our shores—as he did with Carey, who pored over the maps and travel literature of his day.

GROWTH IN PRAYER

Throughout the Scriptures the Lord exhorts us to pray. Wherever we go we find Christians lamenting the lack of prayer. And yet there is a growing movement toward prayer retreats and days of prayer. The struggle to maintain a prayer life and to develop more discipline in this area is something each of us must grapple with daily—but especially missionary candidates. As we grow in our devotion to prayer individually, we will naturally grow in our concern for the things that are on the heart of God: local concerns, world concerns, missionary outreach.

GROWTH IN FAITH

Allied with exhortations to prayer are invitations to trust God. Every Christian needs experience in trusting God to overcome impossible situations. Without some acquaintance with the trustworthiness of God, one cannot become an effective missionary. Missionaries, more so than local Christians, need visionary faith.

So far, the steps a prospective missionary must take do not differ from those embraced by any serious disciple. These steps are basic. They reflect one's devotion of Christ—the quality of one's relationship with God. Without having walked along this pathway, in some measure at least, a person considering missions should not proceed. If, however, a believer comes to this point and finds an interest in missions beginning to catch fire within, he or she should embrace the further steps outlined below.

Passion, more than anything else, will motivate the prospective missionary. Floyd McClung has written, "Apostolic passion, therefore, is a deliberate, intentional choice to live for the worship of Jesus in the nations. It has to do with being committed to the point of death to spreading His glory. It's the quality of those who are on fire for Jesus, who dream of the whole earth being covered with the Glory of the Lord." [2]

McClung goes on to explain that choosing to move out beyond the reached world requires a deliberate decision:

> Apostolic decision-making starts with a passion for God's glory in the nations, then asks: "Where shall I serve you?" Most people do the opposite. They ask the where-and-when questions without a revelation of His glory in the nations. Is it any wonder they never hear God say "go!" They have not cultivated a passion for the passions of God. All kinds of lesser desires can be holding them captive.[3]

Passion, however, can be a passing feeling. It requires confirmation.

Confirmation of a missionary calling

PERSONAL EVALUATION

A prospective missionary candidate should engage in prayerful self-examination. This will involve considering the qualifications listed in the previous chapter and asking questions such as the following:

- Do I have a strong devotional and prayer life?
- Am I growing spiritually?
- Have I the ability to persevere in one place, doing one task? Am I stable?
- Do I get along with people?
- Am I adjustable or do I demand a well-defined and inflexible setting in which to work?

- Am I willing to be a servant or do I have to be recognized, praised?
- Do I have the Bible training necessary for the missionary calling I envision?
- Have I been a member of one local church over a considerable period?
- Do my spiritual gifts, and the result of their use, demonstrate that I could fulfill a missionary calling?
- Have I a burning vision of the glory of God being fulfilled in the salvation of unreached peoples, or is my desire to be a missionary more related to curiosity, a desire to travel or a longing for adventure?
- Have I shown that I can trust God for concrete situations?
- Do I have good health?

Asking oneself these questions will no doubt highlight many areas where growth is needed. Perfection, of course, is not a prerequisite for missionary service; humble awareness of areas that need the work of the Spirit is! If the answers to these questions are generally positive, they may indicate missionary potential. A potential missionary candidate should then proceed to seek godly counsel to confirm his or her own growing conviction.

SEEKING COUNSEL

Proverbs reminds us that "Plans fail for lack of counsel, but with many advisers they succeed" (Prov. 15:22). Neither in the local church nor on the mission field should we exalt Lone Rangers. The apostles themselves asked the Jerusalem congregation to consult and come up with the names of seven men. Later, the Holy Spirit appointed Barnabas and Saul as missionaries in the context of a prayer group of five. The two-by-two principle instituted by Jesus, and continued by the apostolic teams, reflects this need for mutual consultation and encouragement in any effort. Alone, we may deceive ourselves.

If married, the first person a candidate should ask for counsel will of necessity be his or her partner. Should the partner not echo the candidate's missionary vision, the door may be considered closed—at least temporarily. God does not lead a husband and wife in separate directions. It may take time for a couple to grow together in a missionary vision.

Candidates can also ask friends and family for their counsel. They must urge them to be frank; they know the candidates well, but without their permission they may gild the truth a bit to avoid hurting their feelings.

Counsel from within a local church is essential. Ideally, each missionary candidate should be a member of a local church. After some general counsel from family and friends, the person should seek counsel from the church's pastor, elders or deacons. Church leaders will have had the opportunity to view the candidate in the context of church life. They may either affirm gifts and character or recognize potential problems that need resolution. (This pattern should also be adopted by those who seek guidance concerning the pastorate.) The time to seek counsel is not after, but before, taking college or seminary training. Too many missionary candidates come to their church boards seeking their affirmation *after* they have already completed their Bible training and applied to a mission board. The time to seek counsel is before the missionary—or pastoral—training process begins.

Next steps in confirming a missionary call

SHORT-TERM EXPERIENCE

In recent decades opportunities to evaluate one's calling by going to a mission field have expanded exponentially. Many churches have incorporated summer or Christmas mission trips into their youth ministries. Some send work teams to help construct or renovate schools, churches, camps, and so on. Most mission boards advertise opportunities for short-term workers to join their teams for periods of from three months to two years.

A glance through a brochure that recently came to hand disclosed that one mission has short-termers in Africa, Asia and South America. They are involved in evangelism, teaching English as a second language, secretarial work, teaching missionary kids, helping refugees, serving as nurses, doctors, pharmacists or dentists in hospitals and clinics, reaching university students using computers and English studies, and various building projects. The list goes on and on.

Before signing up for a short-term experience one needs to be aware of its limitations. (This is dealt with more fully below.) While the experience is often extremely positive, the opposite can also be the case. Political upheavals, inability to communicate in a local language, health problems, shortage of full-time missionaries to help supervise—all these can color the experience. Then, too, short-termers are apt to go to a nearby country with a similar culture where the English language can be used. As a result, short-termers' views of missions are usually skewed. As a consequence, fewer missionary candidates may apply to serve in the very places where they are needed most. More distant and culturally diverse countries, such as in North Africa, the Middle East and Asia, may become neglected.

Short-term experience is not a panacea. However, it does have the benefit of giving potential missionaries a taste of challenge without locking them into permanent situations that may prove disastrous.

TRAINING

Training requirements will vary widely. Translation work may require college courses on anthropology and linguistics. Technical courses may be essential for those involved in using media. Basic to all missionary work, however, is a solid foundation in the Bible—preferably at a seminary level: surveys of the whole Bible, exegesis of important books, theology, hermeneutics, original languages, homiletics, courses on methods of teaching, evangelizing and so on, spiritual-gift development, church history, church practice, music. Bible knowledge is critical.

While gaining an education, perspective candidates can begin to collect information on mission boards and mission fields. Opportunities should be sought to be involved through a local church in various kinds of ministry, especially evangelism.

CHOICE OF A MISSION BOARD

Except for exceptional circumstances, I would discourage anyone from going to a mission field without some connection with a reputable mission board (see Chapter 19).

The choice of a mission board, however, is not easy. Hundreds of missionary organizations of every variety exist. A potential candidate should go through the following questions.

- Does my home church have its own denominational mission board?

Does it prefer to support missionaries under that board? Are there boards that it will not support?

- Am I comfortable with the doctrinal position of the board? Is it too narrow? Is it too broad?
- Can I work well under the administrative structure of the board?
- Will my training be accepted or will more be required?
- In what areas of the world does the board work?
- What types of work does the board encourage? Is there a balance that gives priority to church planting?
- Does it give time and priority to language learning and acculturation?
- What is the financial system? How much support will I need to raise?
- Is the board accountable to sending churches?
- What is its policy on the family, the education of missionary children and the role of the wife?
- How big is the board? Is it too big to encourage a team spirit? Is it too small?
- How long has the board been in existence? Is it so traditional that it lacks flexibility? Is it so new that it values novelty above biblical balance?

Once a mission board has been chosen, under the guidance of the candidate's local church leaders, an application will be sent. Upon acceptance, the candidate will begin orientation, further training and deputation work to raise prayer and financial support. A year or more often elapses between acceptance and departure for a field of ministry.

A WALK OF FAITH

Once accepted as a missionary, a Christian does not become a superhero. In common with all Christians, the missionary is called to walk by faith, to overcome temptation and to contend for the faith. Throughout his or her missionary career, the challenge will remain to be devoted to Christ through a daily walk of faith.

Short-term missions versus career calling

During the last few decades there has been a phenomenal increase in short-term missionary opportunities. Seth Barnes wrote in *Mission Frontiers* that in 1970 "you could count on one hand the number of youth groups doing short-term missions. Now it has become a standard feature for thousands of youth groups across the country."[4] In the same issue, Rick Wood editorialized, "There are few subjects in the mission world as controversial as short-term missions and their impact on field mission work. Few would argue with the powerful impact that short-term missions are having in mobilizing pastors, churches and young people to support missions or go as missionaries themselves." He went on to point out, however, that there are many unresolved questions of whether they are beneficial or detrimental to "both the participants and the work on the field."[5]

According to Bruce Teichroew, Seth Barnes laid the groundwork for Adventures in Missions (AIM) which has sent out 25,000 young people and partnered with over 1,000 churches in short-term projects. In cooperation with churches, AIM provides intensive pre-field preparation.[6]

Dr. Monroe Brewer estimates that, if well-supported and prepared short-termers are sent out, "half will not go back long-term; a fourth will go back long-term, but not immediately; and about a fourth will go back long-term immediately."[7] That is a very high recruitment rate! I'm sure Operation Mobilisation has seen similar results.

Others, however, sound a cautionary note. Peter Hammond decries what he calls "the amateurization of missions." He writes,

> More and more Christians are pouring into the mission fields—but for very short periods of time and for very superficial goals. I have been astounded to come across large tour groups (calling themselves "missionaries") travelling across the world just to spend four or five days "in the field!" ... most of these short-termers have undergone no selection procedure and received no training, and thus are ill-equipped to benefit the local believers ... Most people understand that doctors, engineers, and, in fact, every other profession, need proper training to be able to do their work. Yet for some obscure reason, many Christians seem to think that any churchgoer can be a missionary. The flood of untrained, ill-disciplined, and unaccountable, lone-ranger, supposed "missionaries" into Third World countries is disastrous.[8]

He decries the short-termers he calls "religious tourists," who make serious cultural gaffes by the way they dress, how they relate to one another, what they demand of local missionaries and Christians and by their poor Bible knowledge.

Luis Bush takes a more moderate approach. He is concerned that some seem to be saying that the day of the long-term missionary is numbered at just the time when we need more and more long-term missionaries. He writes, "Short-term service is no substitute for the bedrock of long-term missionary commitment."[9] He goes on to list the virtues of long-term commitment:

- Career missionaries are enriched by learning the host country culture.
- Relationships have time to develop meaning and depth.
- Blessings flow to the next generation of missionaries.

He then lists the values of short-term workers:

- Inspired by their short-term they become better prepared to go long-term.
- They communicate their enthusiasm back home among their peers and in their churches.
- They contribute on site in prayer, medicine, teaching ESL, repairing, etc.
- They can free up full-time missionaries from routine duties.
- If young, they can relate to the youth of the country positively.
- If older, they adjust more readily, have more tact and are able to use their greater experience to benefit.

His list of the drawbacks of short-termers includes:

- Few can function without long-term missionaries alongside, which takes considerable time and effort on the part of long-termers, forcing them to curtail some of their ongoing work.
- Usually months of culture-shock limit their contribution.
- Lack of motivation to learn a language hinders their ability to relate to local people.
- They can be insensitive to the damage they do to relationships of nationals and long-term missionaries.
- A sense of Western superiority leads to being overly critical.
- Short-termers often rebel against the way women are treated, causing many misunderstandings and moral problems.[10]

Short-term involvement is not limited to Western Christians. A team of Ethiopians brought refreshment to Pakistani Christians through an extended period in their midst. Organized by Partners International, Mizo and Naga teams from India, as well as Indonesian teams, have greatly blessed Western Christians. We live in a new day of international cross-pollination.

Short-term missions is here to stay. We can't fight reality, but we must maintain our commitment to long-term missionary service. And we must be sure that those short-termers who do go to a mission field receive careful orientation.

Notes

1 Quotations in this paragraph are from **Garry Friesen** with **J. Robin Maxson,** *Decision Making and the Will of God* (Portland, OR: Multnomah, 1983), pp. 328–329.

2 **Floyd McClung,** "Apostolic Passion," in *Mission Frontiers*, Special Issue, January 2000, p. 17.

3 Ibid. p. 18.

4 **Seth Barnes,** "Ten Emerging Trends in Short-Term Missions," in *Mission Frontiers*, Special Issue, January 2000, p. 13.

5 **Rick Wood,** "MF Behind the Scenes," in *Mission Frontiers*, Special Issue, January 2000, p. 6.

6 **Bruce Teichroew,** "A Growing Vision: The Origins and Vision of Adventures in Mission," in *Mission Frontiers*, Special Issue, January 2000, p. 15.

7 **Dr. Monroe Brewer,** "Short Termers and the Future of American Missions," in *Mission Frontiers*, Special Issue, January 2000, p. 27.

8 **Peter Hammond,** "The Amateurization of Missions," Chalcedon Report, Oct. 1999, p. 14.

9 **Luis Bush,** "The Long and Short of Mission Terms," in *Mission Frontiers*, Special Issue, January 2000, p. 16.

10 Ibid. pp. 18–19.

By Kenneth D. MacHarg, LAM News Service[I]

Ceres, Brazil. "You must have the wrong fellow," was Alan Mullins' response when a missionary recruiter called him over thirty years ago. "I was teaching school in North Miami and working at Sears to pay off my college loan when the recruiter said that he had heard about what he called my 'tremendous interest in missions.' He said he would be in Miami and would take me out to dinner. Well, I never miss a free meal, so I went. I guess you could say that was my mistake," Alan jokes.

Now, thirty years later, Alan and his wife Ézia are working with Christian Camping International-Brazil (CCI-Brazil), training camp leadership along with writing and developing curriculum and training material in Portuguese for use throughout the country.

"We provide staff training manuals, write books on games, outdoor activities, musical games and camp history, and prepare material to tell how the camping movement came about," explains Ézia, a Brazilian from the state of Minas Gerais. "We have four books we have published being used in training courses and two other books distributed by a publishing company. Some of these materials are being used by missionaries in Portugal, Mozambique and Angola."

The couple are heavily involved in training camp counselors and leaders who direct two sessions of camping each year during Brazil's January and July school breaks. "We have to start from scratch every year and that is very challenging," Ézia explains. "We try to pass on to them the idea of Christian camping and its full potential. The idea is to reach the whole person, working not only in leading the person to Christ, which is our main goal, but working with the teenager or child in his or her life as a whole—emotionally, socially, mentally and intellectually, encouraging and developing the whole person."

Alan and Ézia travel over a large portion of Brazil to hold workshops and training sessions. "Most of the camps in Brazil today are under the Brazilian church," explains Alan. "There are still some denominational missionaries working with specific camps, but that's becoming less and less true in Brazil."

One of the camps is the Presbyterian facility at Ceres serving campers from all over central Brazil. When Alan first arrived in the country the property was a boarding school for missionary children. "The Lord knew what he was doing bringing me to Brazil. I came here for three years to teach missionaries' children, fully expecting to return to the United States. But God had prepared me through a ministry of camping in the States to be the one to start teaching camping to the Brazilian church."

The couple train leaders at four different camps, sometimes twice a year at each site.

"There are about 300–400 campers per camping season for a total of from 600 to 800 per year," Alan says. "Out of those, we experience nearly 150 first-time decisions for Christ."

"Camping is one of the best tools to reach people for the church," says Ézia. "Many unbelievers would not go to church but they will go to camp because it is a neutral environment. A camp has a tremendous opportunity to minister to a person who would never darken the doors of a church, and it has twenty-four hours a day to do it, rather than just two hours a week."

Ézia knows how some campers feel when they are away from home and need attention. "Being the youngest of twenty children, you can imagine that I didn't get much attention from my parents. I remember a missionary who read me the Bible and treated me as if I was a person. When I was seven she took me under her wings and paid my way to school. I always wanted to be a missionary like her."

The Mullins are also involved in community service near their home in Campinas. "We started a church in our home in the 1970s," Ézia says. "We started a church for children who would come for juice and cookies and to hear Bible stories. Now the local director and his wife work with a congregation of 150 members that started in our garage. It is rewarding when the Lord allows us to see this."

God has also given the couple a ministry of helping young people who could not live at home or had been abused and needed a place to stay. "We have taken in around fifteen of these," Alan says. "One stayed for ten years and became a part of our family. Many are involved in the church in some way. Some are pastors and camp directors."

Currently the Mullins are helping to pay for the construction of a church building in Campinas by selling used clothing. Meanwhile, Alan and Ézia are looking for other missionaries to join them in their camp training ministry. "We can use short-termers who would like to work at a camp for a month in the summer or in January," Alan says. "They do not need to speak the language, but would help in the kitchen, with cleaning, and be a part of a staff."

They are also looking for permanent personnel to work nationwide in the area of training. "We need people who have experience in camping and would be willing to come to Brazil for five to ten years to help develop courses and teach leadership," Alan says.

We never know how far the influence of our ministry will reach. Ézia recalls one thirteen-year-old camper who sensed a call to missionary service around a campfire in Brazil.

"Twenty years later I met Agripino and he was one of the leaders of Mission Aviation Fellowship (MAF)," she recalls. "He was training leaders in Angola using some material in Portuguese. He shared with us that he was in an airplane in Angola ready to return to Brazil when officials of that country came and stopped the plane. A high-ranking member of the Angolan government came to him and said, 'We've heard you have been training some of these people in how to be leaders. I want you to come back and teach our government people these courses.' It so happened that I was the one who had put together those courses in the Portuguese language," Ézia recalls.

Note

1 From LAM (Latin America Mission). Used by permission.

Part 5

Missionary teamwork

Chapter 18

Missions: a team effort

In Western nations, many of our most cherished institutions enshrine individual rights. Then, too, Western capitalism seems to be winning the world the way democratic ideals never have. Capitalism bows at the shrine of entrepreneurial individualism. Our heroes are great individuals like Henry Ford and Lee Iacocca, William Wilberforce and Churchill.

In Christian circles, God has used a galaxy of spiritual innovators and adventurers to powerfully influence believers for good. I vividly recall the impact on my young life of biographies about Hudson Taylor, Jim Elliot and Jonathan Goforth.

When we turn to the Bible we seem to find the same pattern: a galaxy of great men and women—Abraham and Deborah, Moses and Joshua, Ruth and David, Peter and Paul. Hebrews 11 exhorts us to follow in their footsteps.

If individualism masks independence and downplays teamwork, however, it betrays the model left by the Master. While pastor, I counseled and prayed with a number of young people desirous of serving God. One young man informed me that God had called him to serve as a foreign missionary in a pioneer setting. Subsequent conversations revealed that he saw no need to take missionary training nor be married. He felt that informing church leaders about what he had already decided to do was enough! Fortunately, he mellowed. Subsequently, he accepted advice in both areas.

Another, a young woman, informed our church board of her intention to serve in a para-church organization. Her letter made it clear that she was not asking for input on her calling but for financial support.

Without preliminary consultation, a missionary agency once sent our church application papers for a young man planning to engage in summer missionary work abroad. We were taken aback that the young man had not asked his own church for prayer and input during the decision-making process.

My experience is too common. The church I pastored during that period encouraged young people to seriously consider the Great Commission. Our policy paper clearly laid out the importance of church involvement in each step of a prospective missionary's preparation. But in spite of all our efforts, the main impression we were given by prospective Christian workers seemed to be, "Where I should serve Christ is a personal and private matter."

The independent spirit is alien to apostolic practice. From the very first chapter of Acts we find Christians meeting together. They made decisions corporately. Peter stood up in a gathering of about 120 believers to suggest that they choose another apostle to replace Judas (see Acts 1).

The fire of Pentecost fell when "they were all together in one place' (Acts 2:1). Although Peter took the lead in interpreting this amazing manifestation of the Spirit, he did so while standing up "with the eleven" (2:14). Obviously, the others were in agreement.

The complaint in Acts 6 over the neglect of Hellenistic widows in the daily distribution of food led to congregational deliberation; "the twelve gathered all the disciples together" and explained the importance of maintaining their own ministry in the Word and prayer, and then said, "choose seven men from among you who are known to be full of the Spirit and wisdom ... We will turn this responsibility over to them" (6:2–3).

From the church's infancy the apostles involved the whole congregation in decision making. In Acts 6 we read that the apostolic suggestion about choosing men to help with distribution "pleased the whole group. They chose Stephen, a man full of faith and of the Holy Spirit; also Philip" (v. 5). Obviously, the apostles trusted the whole congregation to exercise wisdom in the choice of seven men. They were not disappointed.

In Acts 13 we find the Holy Spirit communicating his missionary vision to a group of five church leaders. Out of the group of five, the Spirit set apart Barnabas and Saul. These first missionaries were sent out under the guidance of a group.

Consider, secondly, the role of teamwork in apostolic witness. The early church sent out its missionaries two by two. "Set apart for me Barnabas and Saul for the work to which I have called them" (Acts 13:2). Barnabas and Saul constituted a team during their first missionary journey. When they prepared to leave on their second journey Paul refused to take John Mark. Paul and Barnabas parted company. But instead of going off singly on their separate journeys, both maintained the team principle by choosing another companion: "Barnabas took Mark and sailed for Cyprus, but Paul chose Silas and left" (Acts 15:39–40).

Jesus also stressed teamwork. He "appointed twelve—designating them apostles—that they might be with him and that he might send them out to preach" (Mark 3:14). When he did send them out to preach and heal, he sent them out "two by two" (Luke 10:1). Even in his most glorious and grievous experiences—when transfigured on the mountain and sorrowing in the garden—he took disciples with him. Imagine! The Lord Jesus Christ—although eternally self-sufficient—was a team player.

Acts is replete with stories of missionary teamwork. "Judas (called Barsabbas) and Silas, two men who were leaders among the brothers," were sent by the church from Jerusalem to Antioch (15:22). Paul added Timothy to his team in Lystra (16:1–3). Aquila and Priscilla greatly aided Paul's ministry at various times (18:2, 18, 26).

George Murray writes, "The book of Acts reveals 17 different missionary teams that worked with Paul. In his New Testament letters, Paul identifies 34 individuals as team workers with him in the preaching of the gospel."[1]

Notice, thirdly, individual decisions and actions are necessary at times. The importance of teamwork does not mean we should suspend individual initiative.

When persecution fell on the Jerusalem church after Stephen's martyrdom, "Those who had been scattered preached the word wherever they went. Philip went down to a city in Samaria and proclaimed the Christ there" (Acts 8:4–5). Philip was probably alone in Samaria. He faced a dilemma. Up to this point evangelism had been restricted to the Jewish community. He must have wondered about the validity of witnessing to non-Jewish Samaritans. But he made an individual decision and embraced a Samaritan evangelistic mission with powerful results (8:6).

Reports of the astounding response of Samaritans to Philip's preaching led the apostles to send Peter and John (8:14) to check out Philip's ministry. When they arrived in Samaria, God used Peter and John as the channels through whom he poured out the Spirit on the Samaritans. Obviously, Peter and John quickly recognized the genuine nature of Philip's work. Individual efforts and ministries do need the evaluation and supervision of a larger group.

Not long after, Peter, alone, received the vision which taught him about the importance of Gentile evangelism. While waiting for food to be prepared, Peter prayed on the roof of his host's home in Joppa. There he received a vision of unclean creatures which God encouraged him to kill and eat. Immediately after the vision, he was invited to preach in Cornelius's household, with powerful effect. Peter interpreted this event to mean that "God does not show favoritism" (10:34). Against all accepted practice up to this point, Peter "ordered them to be baptized in the name of Jesus Christ" (10:48).

Jewish converts, however, soon called Peter to account for his actions. Upon arrival in Jerusalem, "the circumcised believers criticized him" (11:2). Much of Acts 11 describes Peter's defense of his actions. At the end of his defense we read, "When they heard this, they had no further objections and praised God, saying, 'So then, God has granted even the Gentiles repentance unto life'" (11:18). In spite of Peter's stature among the twelve, he willingly submitted to group evaluation of his actions.

Apostolic precedent demonstrates that individual actions and controversial decisions are always subject to group scrutiny. Paul called Peter to account in Antioch (Gal. 2:11–21). Lay Christians, Priscilla and Aquila, took Apollos, the eloquent preacher from Alexandria, aside "and explained to him the way of God more adequately" (Acts 18:26). Preachers, evangelists and missionaries can never rise to a position where they are not accountable to other believers.

Consider, fourthly, the role of families in evangelistic and missionary outreach. If you are wondering what a discussion of the role of the family has to do with evangelism and missions, please bear with me. The issues are important. Historically, some Christians have sought to exalt singleness and celibacy. A few have argued that missionaries ought to have no children, or small families. Let's look at some of the biblical data.

The list of qualifications laid down for elders and deacons assumes that marriage and children are the norm: "Now the overseer must be ... the husband of but one wife ... [who] must manage his own family well and see that his children obey him with proper respect ... Deacons, likewise ..." (1 Tim. 3:2, 4, 8; see also Titus 1:6).

Peter and the other apostles, with the exception of Paul, were married. So was Philip (1 Cor. 9:5).

God ordained that the marital union illustrate the relationship Christ bears to the church: "Husbands, love your wives, just as Christ loved the church and gave himself up for her" (Eph. 5:25; see the whole section, 5:22–33). In the light of its crucial significance in divine imagery, marriage and the family must never be considered a hindrance or economic burden. Indeed, the Christian family is one of the most important missionary (evangelistic) units conceivable. Its importance far outweighs that of any kind of organization or para-church group, outside of the church itself.

The relationship between a husband and his wife and between Christian parents and their children ought to illustrate gospel interaction. God designed the Christian family to demonstrate to a skeptical world love and forgiveness, humility and obedience, discipline and patience—all in the context of relational give and take.

The way men and women serve in world missions and in church life ought to reflect the positive way they apply biblical principles in family life. Good families make good Christians, gentle pastors, thoughtful deacons, wise evangelists and able missionaries. Good families create team players.

God designed the home to be a womb where we develop the qualities necessary in mature adults, including a propensity to favor cooperation over competition. Even Jesus "grew in wisdom and stature, and in favor with God and men" (Luke 2:52) in the context of his home. God gave to Mary and Joseph a crucial role in the human development of his Son. Given this divine model, any organization that fails to give to the family its rightful place fails to incarnate the gospel.

Sadly, I have frequently witnessed in Canada and Pakistan the fallout of those who failed to give family life its rightful place. Workaholic deacons and pastors often have children who grow up unable to get along with their own spouses or hold normal jobs.

When we fail in the home, we necessarily stumble in the church and in its worldwide mission. But when families do their job, they nurture servants who understand the value of teamwork.

But what about singleness? Some men and women, under divine guidance, have chosen the path of singleness in order to further the gospel.

In 1 Corinthians 7 Paul argues, "Because of the present crisis, I think that it is good for you to remain as you are. Are you married? Do not seek a divorce. Are you unmarried? Do not look for a wife" (1 Cor. 7:26–27). He argues that if a man is able to control his desires he may remain unmarried, for he will be more "concerned about the Lord's affairs—how he can please the Lord. But a married man is concerned about the affairs of this world—how he can please his wife" (1 Cor. 7:32–33). The Roman Church has used this passage to sanction a system of unmarried priests. They assume that singleness will always enhance priestly ministry. How terribly shortsighted!

Paul himself carried on a powerful ministry as an unmarried man. There have been many like him. Christ seems to teach that in some cases—for example, Paul—individuals may purposely renounce marriage for the sake of the kingdom (Matt. 19:11–12). Singleness remains a viable but rare option.

Examples of apostolic marriage clearly indicate that God wills marriage for most who serve him (1 Cor. 9:5). Singleness is an exception to a general rule.

Any attempt to evangelize a given culture has to consider the value that culture places on marriage and children. Pakistani society, in common with most of the world's cultures, exalts marriage and the family. It views single missionaries with curiosity, if not outright suspicion. Only divinely appointed singles can hope to overcome this prejudice.

Children open many hearts to evangelistic opportunities. Universally, people love children. May God deliver preachers, missionaries and evangelists from the terrible thought that their wives and children are in the way of their ministries! Nothing could be further from the truth. As long as Christian parents demonstrate a balanced devotion to both Christ and their families, their ministries will be blessed.

Why is teamwork so important? Let me give two reasons. Firstly, our individual limitations call for corporate enrichment. No one has all the spiritual gifts. No one can do everything. Indeed, none of us will be able to always avoid temptation or keep from error. No wonder the author of Hebrews, deeply concerned about stumbling Christians, wrote, "But encourage one another daily, as long as it is called Today, so that none of you may be hardened by sin's deceitfulness" (Heb. 3:13). Paul counsels, "Carry each other's burdens, and ... fulfill the law of Christ" (Gal. 6:2).

Solomon wrote,

Two are better than one,
    because they have a good return for their work.
If one falls down,
    his friend can help him up.
    But pity the man who falls
    and has no one to help him up!
Also, if two lie down together, they will keep warm.
    But how can one keep warm alone?
Though one may be overpowered,
    two can defend themselves.
    A cord of three strands is not quickly broken. (Eccles. 4:9–12)

When George Murray and his wife arrived in Italy as first-term missionaries, a couple who had been laboring fruitlessly in one city for twenty years told them bluntly, "You will never plant a church in Italy."[2] In spite of this dire prediction they became part of a team that not only planted a church in ten years but saw the development of national leadership as well. He writes,

> We attribute this to the fact that we were a part of a BCU (Bible Christian Union) church-planting team. As members of that team, we enjoyed the advantages of companionship, fellowship, incentive, accountability, multiple gifts, wise counsel, mutual encouragement, corporate witness, combined faith and group prayer—to name just a few.[3]

Murray is not alone in this emphasis. The OM *Europe Résumé* prayer letter quotes the visionary Indonesian church leader Chris Marantika as saying, "The world hasn't been evangelized yet because Christians are attempting to do it independently, rather than together." Instead of churches being simply self-supporting, self-propagating and self-governing he proposed the "'Three Ps': pray together, pay together and proclaim together. Only if the body of Christ world-wide worked together would Indonesia be won to Christ."[4]

Marantika puts his finger on one of the most glaring deficiencies of Western missions: the failure to emphasize teamwork. Most people in the two-thirds world know the value of community. Too often, Western Christians forget that demonstrating love in the context of relationships is the very essence of Christian living.

Love cannot develop in isolation. Hermits can learn little about relational love in a relational vacuum. Likewise, those who blaze independent paths run the grave risk of caricaturing the very message they bear. Maverick individualists tend to become cranky, inflexible and domineering. The very things Christ died to save us from grow like weeds wherever teamwork is curtailed.

In team ministry we are forced to get along. Team ministry helps us to learn compassion, kindness, graciousness, forbearance, forgiveness, genuine compromise, humility and a host of other virtues. The Spirit uses the abrasion we experience when we clash with other people to sanctify us. These priceless qualities adorn the team-worker, endearing his or her message to those who hear.

When unsaved peoples see Christians working together harmoniously in a world of strife and back-biting, they stop and listen to what they have to say. As Murray points out, "a church-planting team which practices mutual love and respect actually becomes a model of the local church it is trying to establish. Anything less than that borders on hypocrisy. We must be the church in order to plant the church."[5]

We need visionary leaders who are team players, not Lone Rangers who gallop off into a sunset of their own creation!

Notes

1 **George W. Murray,** "Church Planting by Teamwork," in *BCU Increase*, February/March/April 1987, p. 4.

2 Ibid.

3 Ibid.

4 **Chris Marantika,** mentioned in editorial in *Europe Résumé*, August 21, 1985.

5 **Murray,** "Church Planting by Teamwork," p. 4.

Chapter 19

Missions and the sending church

When we talk missions we very naturally think in terms of great missionaries and well-known mission boards. In reality, missionary vision and nurture are meant to develop in the womb of the church. Missionaries are sent out from local churches. They go planting churches and they return to report to their sending churches.

The New Testament mentions "church" 115 times. Jesus said, "on this rock I will build my church, and the gates of Hades will not overcome it" (Matt. 16:18). The church is the "household" of God and the "pillar and foundation of the truth" (1 Tim. 3:15). It is the mystery hidden from all ages; the divinely inspired organization dedicated by God to breaking down ethnic walls so that people from all backgrounds might be one in Christ (Eph. 3:10). It is the body of Christ (1 Cor. 12:12; Eph. 5:23; Col. 1:18, 24, etc.). Christ died for it (Eph. 5:23, 25) and he rules it as its Head.

As Peters comments, "The local congregation of believers stands in a unique relationship to Christ and that local assembly becomes the mediating and authoritative sending body of the New Testament missionary. This is a vital, biblical principle and we dare not weaken, minimize nor disregard it."[1]

The church occupies a central place in all Christ continues to do from his position at the right hand of God. In Luke and Acts, Luke records what "Jesus began to do and to teach until the day he was taken up to heaven" (Acts 1:1–2). Jesus Christ continues to do similar things through his worldwide missionary force today. And since the principles we discover in Acts reflect the work of Christ, we should be very reticent to embrace principles alien to this historic record.

In the previous chapter we established the following principles:

- Missions involves teamwork.
- God calls missionaries in the context of their local churches.
- Local churches send missionaries.

- Missionaries are accountable to their sending churches.

Clearly, the Great Commission is a church-centered mandate. Although God calls individuals to respond to his call for laborers, churches are primarily responsible for their nurture and training. Let us look at several further principles.

Organization is developed as needs arise

The New Testament records a process of organizational development in which leaders responded to needs as they arose. At the beginning of Acts 6 there does not seem to be any organization aside from apostolic leadership. The choosing of seven men to care for the neglected Grecian widows probably led to the institution of the diaconate. Later, the choosing of deacons seems to have become a routine part of church organization (see 1 Tim. 3:8–15). Elders too begin to come to the fore as the missionary work progresses (see Acts 14:23; 1 Tim. 3:1–7; Titus 1:5–9).

The precedent set by this developing process is a strong argument for allowing organizational freedom. John Thornbury, in a paper on the "Rationale for Missionary Cooperation," argues for the validity of mission organizations. He quotes A. W. Pink's commentary on Hebrews where he "argues that the New Testament provides no model for the churches comparable to the divine pattern for the tabernacle" but that some Protestants have become legalistic "in the demand for a text for everything they do in the church."[2]

It is helpful to quote Pink extensively in this regard.

> Rome has erred grievously by declaring that the Scriptures are not sufficient, that "traditions" must be added if we are to have a full revelation of what is absolutely necessary for us to know in this life that we may be saved in the next. But some Protestants have gone to another extreme, taking the position that the Scriptures contain such a complete revelation of God's will for the regulation of our lives, both as individuals and as churches, that to act according to any other rule (be it the prompting of conscience or the dictates of reason) is presumptuous and sinful.
>
> In keeping with the vastly different character of the two dispensations, the "liberty" of the Spirit has (2 Cor. 3:17) supplanted the rigid legality of Judaism, and therefore has

> Christ supplied us with general principles (e.g. 1 Cor. 14:26, 40), which are sufficiently broad to allow of varied modification when applied to the differing circumstances of His people, situated in various climes and generations—in contrast from what was prescribed for the single nation of Israel of old ... The New Testament ... supplies us with general rules and principles, which are sufficiently elastic as to allow for human discretion to be exercised in the application of them to particular instances of the church's outward conduct ... To condemn all that is of human invention is not only to fly in the face of the judgement of the wisest and most godly men, but is to go beyond what the Scriptures themselves permit.[3]

Pink also quotes John Owen in a similar vein: "It is utterly vain and useless, to demand express institution of all the circumstances belonging unto the government, order, and worship of the church; or for the due improvement of things in themselves indifferent unto its edification, as occasion shall require."[4]

Surely we must concur with Pink and Owen and assert that the New Testament grants us great leeway in developing organizations that promote biblical purposes without usurping the role of the church.

Churches should work together to promote missions

The believers in the Jerusalem church (3,000 plus) consulted together to choose the first seven deacons. Later, believers were called to a council in Jerusalem to sort through issues related to Gentile evangelism (Acts 15). After the decision had been made all the churches were informed of the results (Acts 15:23). Second Corinthians also shows that churches acted in concert to collect and dispense money to destitute saints through a committee chosen by them (2 Cor. 8). Besides the general principle illustrated—that New Testament churches worked together—it also demonstrates that they turned over responsibility for the use of money to workers to whom they had delegated such responsibility.

John Thornbury, in the paper referred to above, concludes that cooperative missionary endeavors encouraged by associations of churches are beneficial to both missionaries and their supporters: "The church that cannot cooperate with other churches, like an individual which cannot work with other people, can easily become unbalanced and freakish ...

There are few leaders, preachers included, who do not have some special shortcomings which need the buffering influences of mutual counsel."[5] Of course, in order for associations of churches, or missionaries, to work together there needs to be theological and functional agreement.

Missionary teams are to be given great freedom

The two dozen workers in the Pauline missionary team had enormous freedom of movement. Acts records three extensive missionary journeys. Considerable time elapsed before Paul was able to report to his sending church. Communication was difficult—but even if it had been up to today's standards, the principle of giving distant workers responsibility to act on their own without recourse to their home churches is valid. Sent workers are trusted workers.

This principle led Hudson Taylor to initiate a policy that ensured that the China Inland Mission would be administered from the field so that work decisions could be influenced more by field realities than by the preferences of a sending body in a distant land. There is still considerable wisdom in this policy.

Where missionary vision is defective, individual initiative is encouraged

The Bible is replete with examples of God choosing a new vessel to replace a vessel originally chosen but after some time become defective. Israel is the prime example. Kings were appointed only after the theocracy of Joshua and Judges failed. David replaced Saul. Jeroboam was set aside. In time the institution of the prophets gradually eclipsed the role of the Jewish monarchy as spokesmen for God. John the Baptist superceded the tradition-ridden Jewish establishment, as did Christ. The church superceded the nation of Israel—but the church has not always remained true to her mandate. John was called by God to warn a number of the churches in Revelation to repent otherwise their candlestick would be taken away.

The tardiness of the Jerusalem saints to leave Jerusalem to begin worldwide evangelism was overruled by divinely engineered persecution. And those who fled Jerusalem went everywhere preaching the gospel.

Philip used missionary initiative to evangelize Samaria. The same pattern occurred in Antioch. In each of these places a church was born—even though there was no sanctioned apostolic emissary. The situation in both Samaria and Antioch was later recognized by apostolic emissaries to be of divine origin.

This biblical pattern is reflected in the hundreds of para-church missionary organizations that have sprung up, often as a result of the sluggishness of home churches to embrace the Great Commission. Witness the resistance William Carey met from the established church.

THE PARA-CHURCH QUESTION

Are para-church organizations—whether mission boards, youth ministries or educational institutions—valid? Daniel Parker, an Old School Baptist from the nineteenth century, believed the answer was no!

> That missionary societies, not being formed and sustained by the authority of the churches of Jesus Christ, not under their control, but based upon the principle of the payment of a definite sum of money by individuals, acting independent of the churches, and who, by appointing the managing committee, exercise entire control, and thus take the appropriate work of the churches out of their hands. That in assuming to appoint missionaries and designate the fields of their labor, without direct responsibility to the churches, they usurp another of the church's prerogatives, in controlling a portion of the ministry.[6]

Dick L. Van Halsema points out that

> Some parachurch organizations exist and work in such a way that the prefix "para" is construed as "in the place of." In such instances the agency for all intents and purposes practically takes the place of the church as instituted. Such agencies, to one degree or another, essentially assume functions and prerogatives to which they have no right, because these properties belong to the church alone ... Again, there are parachurch organizations which ... define "para" as "alongside of" the church [but] ... ignore the church, act independently of it, and assume that God's work and His workers basically can by-pass the church ... Real advantages for the church and kingdom of God can arise only from Spirit-prompted and Spirit-prospered parachurch movements which

exist "for" ("para") the church and its welfare—not as a substitute for, or as independent from, the church.[7]

It is extremely important that para-church organizations operate "for" the church and are accountable "to" the church. Van Halsema laments those who "rarely worship in the fellowship of a local congregation, who hold no membership in a local church, and who subject themselves to no spiritual or churchly oversight."[8]

Our studies of the biblical material, as noted in the previous sections, demonstrate that organized teams of missionaries were sent out by churches and remained accountable to those churches. They regularly reported back to the churches. But since they worked at some distance from their sending churches, they were granted considerable operating freedom. They made ministry decisions without slavish recourse to some distant governing body.

Surely this would indicate that there is considerable leeway to develop structures that operate beyond direct local-church supervision. Where geographical distance separates the missionary from his or her home church, membership in a para-church team becomes necessary. Para-church organizations are also necessary when the church fails to live up to its mandate. And fail it has. We must grant that many of the para-church organizations that have been raised up throughout history have been raised up under the guidance of the Holy Spirit to offset failures in the church. The Spirit will not allow the missionary mandate to lapse for long without inspiring new approaches to outreach.

George Peters suggests a number of biblical principles that suggest the validity of para-church organizations:

- Organization, such as that found in streamlined missions, increases efficiency and effectiveness.
- Corporate action, as in the association of churches for joint action and service, also increases effectiveness.
- Delegation as practiced by Christ and the apostles suggests the validity of churches delegating missionary responsibilities to missionary societies.
- Where the corporate body, such as Israel or the church, fails to carry out

the purpose of God, he raises up individuals who respond to his mandate.[9]

We would be naive to pretend that para-church organizations do not have problems. They are led by people, and where there are people there are problems. They can become as calcified, as top-heavy with administrative red tape, and as introverted as the worst church that we can imagine. It has been suggested that a movement starts with a vision, becomes an organization and then ends up as an immobile monument. But in spite of their problems, para-church groups have much to commend them.

BENEFITS OF PARA-CHURCH ORGANIZATIONS

Peters writes, "The advantages of being a member of a respectable missionary society are so numerous and so evident that we strongly urge young people to associate themselves with a missionary sending agency."[10] To deny the validity of para-church organizations is to seriously hamper the fulfillment of the missionary mandate. Van Halsema lists a number of advantages that para-church organizations enjoy:

- *Single-mindedness:* "A parachurch organization usually focuses on its goal with single-minded determination, guarding itself against distraction and diversion to projects not directly aligned with its purpose."
- *Specialization:* Para-church groups dedicated to a specific task, such as literature production or Bible translation, can reach a degree of specialization beyond the capacity of an organization, such as the church, which has a multitude of functions.
- *Adaptability:* Para-church organizations possess flexibility to adapt to rapidly changing circumstances in diverse cultures that is impossible in more rooted organizations.
- *Simplicity:* A para-church organization is usually able to effect economies of time and resources by making plans without being subject to a ponderous ecclesiastical process.
- *Catholicity:* Para-church groups are often able to provide an atmosphere where Christians from diverse denominations or traditions can work together in the Lord. They are also able to plant churches less influenced by the culture of the sending churches.

- *Spirituality:* The para-church group may provide an opportunity for deeply dedicated and committed individuals to work together with a degree of holiness and devotion uncommon in a church setting.
- *Accomplishment:* Being strongly goal-oriented, a good para-church organization is marked by service and action. Continual measurement of goals fosters a growth climate that produces results.[11]

Cooperative missionary efforts

While a few churches support independent missionaries, most support cooperative efforts of one kind or another.

In some cases, local associations of churches commit themselves to cooperate in sending out missionaries from any or all of their churches. Missionaries benefit from being supported by a geographically limited group of churches. Instead of traveling all over a country or continent reporting about their work during their home leave, they can settle down in their local churches and visit other nearby churches. For example, a group of churches on Vancouver Island have banded together to send out missionaries from their own membership pool. They covenant together to jointly do what no single church can do alone.

Other denominations send missionaries through a board that is accountable to the annual convention of all member churches. Southern Baptists, Fellowship Baptists in Canada and Conservative Baptists follow this model, as do many other denominations. In these cases church delegates elect representatives to form a supervisory mission board. Between conventions the board and its executive direct the affairs of the mission. They remain accountable to the annual convention for each action they take. Of course, given the size of some denominations, such as Southern Baptists, accountability to local churches is mainly symbolic.

Another pattern is the independent denominational mission-board approach. Boards formed on this model reflect the ethos of a particular denomination but are governed independently from that denomination. For example, Baptist Mid-Missions and ABWE (The Association of Baptists for World Evangelism) are committed to Baptist distinctives and draw their missionaries from particular groupings of Baptist churches but remain administratively independent of those churches. Many Anglican boards—for example, CMS—reflect a similar approach.

A fourth permutation is the "approved societies" approach. According to this pattern, a given denomination compiles a list of "approved societies" that reflect its doctrinal beliefs and practices, and then agrees to support only missionaries who go with those societies. In the USA the General Association of Regular Baptists (GARB) takes this approach.

One of the largest groupings of mission boards is the Interdenominational Foreign Missions Association (IFMA). Boards with membership in the IFMA share a common commitment to the evangelical faith and an openness to accept missionaries from various church backgrounds. Most grew out of the "faith missionary movement," a movement spearheaded by Hudson Taylor that emphasized evangelism, interdenominational fellowship, field leadership and dependence on God alone for finances.

Some IFMA boards accept members from backgrounds as diverse as Anglican, Presbyterian and Baptist. Others are more baptistic in belief. Some are narrowly pre-millennial in belief. Some are general church-planting missions while others specialize in a particular facet of missionary outreach or service: radio, aviation, support of nationals, relief and so on. Each has its own distinctives.

Examples of IFMA missions are Arab World Ministries (formerly North Africa Mission), Intercristo (formerly International Missions), Africa Evangelical Fellowship, Mission Aviation Fellowship, Overseas Missionary Fellowship (formerly China Inland Mission), SIM (formerly Sudan Interior Mission) and Trans World Radio.

The Evangelical Foreign Missions Association (EFMA) resembles the IFMA in evangelical belief. However, while the IFMA is formed of missions that are interdenominational in approach, the EFMA represents denominational societies. In various countries around the world other groupings of societies exist to take advantage of the importance of cooperative effort.

Mission-board organization and finance

While the organization of mission boards varies widely, depending on the degree of autonomy they enjoy, most have some characteristics in common. Typically there will be a Board of Reference, a group of men and women who lend credibility to the board without being involved in administrative matters. Next would come an International Council or Board that oversees the worldwide work of the mission. This council would appoint or elect a General Director and Treasurer to oversee the day-to-day operation of the mission. Each sending country—for example, the USA—would have a national council with a national director and necessary officers, depending on the size of the mission (for example, a Candidate Secretary, Treasurer, Prayer Secretary, Deputation Secretary). If the mission is large it might have area directors responsible for groupings of mission fields (for example, a South America Director, an African Director, a European Director, an Asian Director).

In the various countries where a given board ministers, there would be a field administration accountable to the annual field conference composed of all missionaries on the field. In a field-run mission this annual conference will elect a Field Leader, a Field Council, a Field Treasurer and so on. The degree of autonomy of field missionaries varies widely depending on a mission board's view of how to balance freedom and accountability.

The cost of supporting foreign missionaries is very considerable, especially if the missionary target is a developed country such as Germany or Japan, where the cost of living is high. When working Christians hear about the cost of sending missionaries, they may be tempted to respond, "But their salary is so much higher than mine!" The high cost of sending and supporting missionaries has given impetus to the movement to support nationals in the target country. (We will consider this later.)

Commonly, church members fail to understand the diverse elements that make up the missionary support package. Typically the field salary—the actual money that a missionary receives to live on—is less than half of the support package. Let me list some of the expenses as a percentage of the total. Of course, expenses for medical needs, pensions, furlough travel, etc., can vary greatly:

- field salary—50% (housing, food, clothing, etc.)

- field work expenses—up to 12%, may be separately raised (literature, language-learning expenses, vehicle costs, evangelistic programs, etc.)
- field administration—2%
- furlough travel—7%
- furlough housing, travel, etc.—8%
- home and international administration of mission, pastoral care, etc.—9% (many boards require a higher percentage to cover worldwide administrative costs)
- medical—4%
- pension—8%
- children's education—2% plus extra expenses in each family.

To complicate the financial picture further, different mission boards operate according to diverse support and distribution policies. Boards connected to historic denominations often pay their missionaries a specific salary, similar to the salary paid to their ministers. Many North American "faith mission" boards expect their missionaries to trust the Lord for the total amount of their support. As a result, they receive only what is specifically designated for their support. If one month several churches fail to send in their support, the missionary's salary is cut by this amount. This method is called "the personalized support system."

Other mission boards, notably in the United Kingdom, have a "pool system." Originally, almost all "faith missions" were financed through the "pool" system. Under this approach, missionaries are expected to trust the Lord as a group for the needs of the whole group, and as a group they share equally. Thus, if donations are low one month, the resulting "pool" of funds is divided equally among all—so all receive less. Besides these policies there are various approaches to the receiving of individual gifts for personal or work needs. Some missions allow an unlimited amount in personal or work gifts. Other boards require personal gifts to be offset against salary in some way.

How missionary societies operate varies widely—usually due to historical precedents set to ensure accountability and fairness. Careful financial and ministry accountability is crucial if sending churches are to be encouraged to entrust their missionaries to an organization external to their own structures.

Responsibilities of sending churches

Without vibrant sending churches, the whole missionary enterprise falters. The local church is the nursery where missionary vision is nurtured, the base from which missionaries are sent and the home to which they return for encouragement and rest. Local churches and mission boards are partners in the great missionary task. Among the responsibilities of local churches are the following.

NURTURE MISSIONARY VISION

If, as we have seen, missions is a central facet of biblical revelation, then wherever the Scriptures are faithfully preached God's people should find missionary passion bubbling up within them. Unless the pastor deliberately avoids certain Scriptures, a careful attention to the message of the Bible will underline God's missionary vision. Care should be taken to ensure that this vision is not sidelined by the modern penchant for messages that deal only with felt needs and issues. Missionary information and vision should be woven into the Sunday school curriculum, Bible studies for home groups, the organization of the church year as well as the preaching schedule.

Encouraging missionary vision requires regular exposure to missionaries: young people full of excitement about their calls, furloughing missionaries telling stories about what God is doing, national pastors and evangelists providing a concrete demonstration of the worth of missions. Every church must have a healthy missions' budget. The cry should not be, "We can't afford it!" but rather, "For what amount does God want us to trust him?" Care should be taken to plan well-conceived missionary conferences, seek gifted missionary speakers, encourage believers to offer hospitality to visiting missionaries, maintain missions as a priority in the weekly prayer meeting, give book reports on missionary biographies and keep the congregation up to date on missionary trends and happenings.

The key to local vision will be the attitude of the pastor. The prospective pastor's view of missions should be one of the central questions asked before a man is called to a given church. Churches should seek to encourage the development of pastoral missionary vision by arranging for their pastors to visit mission fields—even nearby ones—as often as is feasible. Cost is not the issue. Nothing creates more missionary fire than actually witnessing firsthand what God is doing in another culture. Of course, missionary passion ought to be powerfully enhanced in the seminaries and Bible schools where pastors acquire their training. Lamentably, that is not always a priority.

Another way to increase missionary vision is to send lay teams to established mission situations. Although there are disadvantages to this practice, benefits usually far outweigh anything negative. Teams sent to Mexico, Turkey, Haiti or Bosnia return excited about what God is doing. Other members of their home churches catch their excitement.

DISCIPLE BELIEVERS

Earlier we saw the crucial importance of character. Normally, local churches foster the skills and habits necessary to growth in grace. Discipleship produces missionary potential among those who maintain a commitment to daily devotions, believing prayer, church attendance, witness and service. Missionaries must be those who, though imperfect and subject to the realities of temptation, have made demonstrable progress in overcoming temptation and living lives marked by the fruit of the Spirit. The local church is the place where future missionaries are mentored in a process of one-on-one discipleship.

DEVELOP GIFTEDNESS

Successful missionary service requires more than determination, commitment and character; equipment is required—the gifts of the Spirit. No more should we send a surgeon to operate without dexterity than we should send a missionary without some of the essential missionary gifts of mercy, faith, church planting, preaching, shepherding, teaching or evangelism. I have seen too many sincere men and women laboring to do that for which they are not gifted. The resulting waste of resources and time coupled with its attendant frustration are hurtful to the missionary task.

A prospective missionary's gifts should be discerned within the local church long before application to a mission board. There, in the supportive context of a loving spiritual family, potential ministry gifts can be tested. Disciples can be asked to do a variety of tasks that demonstrate whether or not they have latent gifts in a certain area. For this to happen, church leaders must first believe in the importance of development through delegation. They must be willing to endure imperfections of speech and duty for the greater goal of helping people grow in confidence.

Disciples can be asked to read the Scripture, lead in prayer, tidy the church, usher, cut the grass, visit the sick, care for accounts, lead a Bible study, teach a Sunday school class, give their testimonies, distribute flyers for a local outreach, help at a summer camp, go on a short-term work team, lead a service, preach a sermon—the list is almost endless.

Capabilities for service begin to become apparent as people attempt to serve. Passivity is the enemy of gift discovery and development. Wise church leaders give growing disciples simple tasks and then more challenging jobs to do. When growing Christians exhibit spiritual abilities that show potential for pastoral, evangelistic or missionary service their churches should take steps to encourage their further development. Perhaps enrolment in a Bible college is called for. Perhaps experience at a camp, in a new church, in a work project will further the person's development. Church leaders can watch for retreats or conferences that might enhance the person's skills or clarify his or her vision. (See Chapter 17 concerning the development of a missionary call.)

Our Western societies are increasingly pagan. As a result some people are converted and discipled beyond the reach of a local church. In such cases, requiring home church experience may be impractical. Such exceptions to the rule that missionaries should have church experience will be rare.

SET APART MISSIONARIES

The link missionaries are to maintain with their local churches is further forged by a formal process in which those churches set the people apart specifically for missionary service. As the leaders in Antioch were worshiping and fasting the Holy Spirit said, "Set apart for me Barnabas and Saul for the work to which I have called them" (Acts 13:2). With

Barnabas and Saul thus commended by the church in a time of fasting and worship, "they placed their hands on them and sent them off" (v. 3).

Church leaders should earnestly seek the mind of God about prospective missionaries. When they discover the will of the Spirit, they should convene a church meeting in which the serious implications of missionary service—for the candidate and for the sending church—are outlined and in which the prospective missionary is publicly commissioned.

SUPPORT MISSIONARIES

The missionary's home church should become his or her supporting church. In reality, however, many missionaries are supported by a combination of individuals and churches. It is natural that friends and relatives get behind a new missionary. Although occasionally one church will provide the full support for missionaries that are raised up from their ranks, usually financial support is drawn from many churches and many individuals. This is often due to the inability of any one church, at a given time, to provide all of the support a missionary couple needs. Some missionary strategists point out that, since the spiritual prosperity of churches ebbs and flows, being supported by one church is dangerous. Mission boards overcome this danger in various ways.

The ideal support system toward which missionaries, churches and boards should aim would see missionaries supported by a few churches in a limited geographic area. Scattered support will mean long and tedious travels during furlough at just the time when missionaries need rest and refreshment. It will also mean that on home leave, they cannot immerse themselves in the life of any one or two churches. This lack will increase the understanding gap people already have about the missionaries they support.

PRAY FOR MISSIONARIES

Both sending groups and missionaries are responsible to maintain vigorous intercession. Missionary work, as well as church work, is the special target of the enemy. Frustration, discouragement and persecution, along with a host of other problems, face missionaries at every turn. The prince of darkness will not yield territory easily. Peerless training and awesome human skill can do nothing to blunt his attacks. Spiritual warfare—intense intercession—is necessary. After his amazing description of our warfare and God's armor Paul concludes by writing, "And pray in the Spirit on all occasions with all kinds of prayers and requests. With this in mind, be alert and always keep on praying for all the saints" (Eph. 6:18).

Although pastors should keep urging their people to pray for missionaries, the missionaries themselves must provide the fuel. Too often, missionary letters and emails are boring, trite, hopelessly general and infrequent. One of the best things that happened to my wife and I as missionaries was to have the pastor of one of our supporting churches sit us down and inform us gently, "We will support you—if you promise to send us regular letters that give us specific prayer requests for each week's prayer meeting."

The responsibility we felt to that one church led us to make it a habit of sending monthly, or bi-monthly, letters to all our supporters, with as interesting a description of our work as we could write. We also included a list of specific prayer requests for each week during the month or so that followed. When we returned for home leave we discovered that people were amazingly informed about the work and very grateful for specific prayer requests. And we never lacked financial support!

Veteran missionary Jo Anne Dennett writes, "My experience in serving on mission councils has impressed on me the direct link between missionaries' support and their correspondence with home churches. Those who faithfully keep their home churches informed about their ministry usually receive abundant prayer and financial support. Those who are not diligent in this matter are often poorly supported."[12]

Dennett suggests that it is helpful to have someone at home to produce and send out the letters. Here is a vital ministry that can be fulfilled by the home church. I've added my own to a few of the suggestions she makes about prayer letters:[13]

- Be interesting and creative, and write in an informal, personal way.
- Be varied in format and content.
- Include personal-interest stories of people, their conversions and struggles.

- Have Scripture and spiritual messages—but not a full sermon! (I would urge writers not to begin letters with Scripture. It will be skipped, not because it is not important, but because it is such a common practice.)
- Identify foreign words and acronyms.
- Warn about people writing back using sensitive material. Use initials or disguised names to protect nationals.
- Use photographs as often as possible.

HOLD MISSIONARIES ACCOUNTABLE

Although most missionaries serve under a home and field council, it is wise to monitor their ministries and hold them accountable—and not only when they return home to report their work. Certainly, at that time, the church board should sit down with the missionary and review his or her ministry with the aim of gaining as much understanding as possible. Missionaries should be willing to give their home churches a well-written report of their work—yearly, if possible.

Churches should not feel they are intruding by lovingly monitoring their missionaries' work during the time when they are overseas. I have known missionaries who deviated from their primary calling by becoming involved in distracting activities, missionaries who became lazy, and missionaries who drifted from the doctrinal parameters under which they were sent out. During the last few years several pastors have asked me what to do about missionaries whose theology has become aberrant. The looser the field administration—which is made up of the missionary's own peers—the more the sending church will need to monitor the work.

CARE FOR MISSIONARIES

The mission agency bears considerable responsibility for the care of missionaries. A lament we heard throughout our missionary career was, "Please send us a missionary pastor who will give himself to the counsel, encouragement and comfort of missionaries." Shortage of workers and money usually meant that this request had to be ignored. And yet, the importance of spiritual shepherding is pervasive in the Bible. I have no doubt that some missionary casualties could have been avoided by paying more attention to missionary care. The rebellion of some missionary kids could also have been spared. Always under stress, field and home administrations do what they can. If a board or churches cannot provide a missionary pastor, field missionaries must take it upon themselves to appoint someone from their number to offer this ministry.

Supporting churches can be of immense help here even though at considerable distance. Writing regular letters, sending magazines and books, and sending tapes of services and the occasional parcel of goodies will remind the missionaries that they are not forgotten. If at all possible, the church should send its pastor to visit its missionaries with a view to their encouragement and spiritual uplift. (Care should be taken not to disrupt crucial ministry plans.) Another way to be of help is to avoid putting undue pressure on missionaries for "results." We must bear in mind that the greatest missionaries—from Jeremiah to Judson—have had lengthy periods of seeming unfruitfulness. Some fields, such as the Muslim world, require decades of patient sowing before any fruit is evident—if then. Faithfulness to God has priority over Western ideas of church growth and success.

When missionaries return home, mission agencies and home churches should cooperate in their care. The perception that a mission agency has the resources to completely care for a furloughing missionary is a chimera. Dennett rightly suggests that the following questions need to be addressed—often by supporting churches:

- Who will meet the missionaries' plane?
- Where will they sleep and eat upon arrival?
- What about an early holiday and rest?
- Where will they set up their home base? Housing, furnishings, transport, medical coverage, etc.?
- What about scheduling meetings with home churches?
- Where will children attend school, and will extra funds be needed?
- What further training will they need for future ministry?[14]

Missionaries are trained to expect, and deal with, culture shock. Often, however, they fail to prepare for the tremendous adjustments they face when they return to their home countries. In our experience, after our initial adjustments to life in Pakistan had been made, the greatest culture shock we faced was returning to Canada. The severing of bonds with missionary co-workers who had become family, the loss of a sense of fulfillment through engagement in exciting ministries, the shock of facing accelerating materialism back in Canada, the preoccupation of so many Christians with what seemed to us to be irrelevant issues—all these routinely led to some measure of depression.

Since such reverse culture shock is routinely felt, the question of spiritual refreshment during furlough is a crucial one. Will the missionaries be given the funds to attend a retreat, a conference, buy uplifting books or get the counsel they need? Will there be funds to update their wardrobe so they don't look old-fashioned?

There will need to be a carefully structured counseling and debriefing procedure to ascertain the spiritual temperature of the missionary family, any wrong behaviors or attitudes, ongoing conflicts, hurts, fears and so on. Jo Anne Dennett has an excellent section in her book *Thriving in Another Culture* in which she gives advice and an evaluation form that can be used by a confidential counselor.[15] She points out that "the attrition rate of missionaries could be reduced with relevant counseling at all stages of their lives."[16]

Clearly, missions is a team effort that requires a partnership of sending churches and missionary agencies. The ACMC (Advancing Churches in Missions Commitment) is a North American organization that provides a great variety of resources designed to help local churches make their missions' commitment more interesting and informed.[17]

Notes

1 **George W. Peters,** *A Biblical Theology of Missions* (Chicago: Moody, 1972), p. 219.

2 **John F. Thornbury,** "Rationale For Missionary Cooperation," *Missionary Update* (newsletter of the Reformed Baptist Mission Services), Nov. 1984.

3 **A. W. Pink,** *An Exposition of Hebrews*, vol. iii ([n.p.]: Bible Truth Depot, 1954), pp. 329–333.

4 Ibid. p. 333.

5 **Thornbury,** "Rationale For Missionary Cooperation."

6 Cited by **Thornbury,** "Rationale For Missionary Cooperation," p. 1.

7 **Dick L. Van Halsema,** "Parachurch Organizations: Some Advantages," *Missionary Monthly*, March 1982, pp. 9–10.

8 Ibid. p. 10.

9 **Peters,** *A Biblical Theology of Missions*, pp. 224–226.

10 Ibid. p. 224.

11 **Van Halsema,** "Parachurch Organizations: Some Advantages," p. 11.

12 **Jo Anne Dennett,** *Thriving in Another Culture: A Handbook for Cross-Cultural Missions* (Melbourne: Acorn Press, 1998), p. 85.

13 Ibid. p. 86.

14 Ibid. p. 102.

15 See **Dennett,** *Thriving in Another Culture*, chapter 13.

16 Ibid. p. 113.

17 Visit: acmc.org.

In fiction, Tom Sawyer and Huck Finn drifted down the Mississippi—but in real life Luke, Matthew and Joel Dixon explore the sandy reaches of Burkina Faso, in mysterious and far-away Africa. It's a true story about cabbages and the King. Although time marches on, it's a capsule true to situations all over the world.

South of the shifting Sahara sands, north of the legendary Ivory Coast and east of teeming Nigeria lies the little-known country of Burkina Faso. As a part of the crescent of arid countries scorched by the southern reaches of the terrible Sahara, drought and famine often stalk the land. Tribes bearing strange names populate its scattered villages: Fulanis and Mandingos, Mossis and Gourmas.

In the isolated south-eastern part of the land, the Gourmas eke out an existence at the bottom of the social scale. Far from important population centers, the tribe live in villages without electricity or running water. In a dusty little provincial town called Diapaga, Alan and Alison Dixon, with their three boys aged nine, eight and five, live in the midst of the Gourmas.

Belief in a pantheon of spirits affects every aspect of Gourma life. Like others in Burkina Faso, their animistic practices are often overlaid with a patina of Roman Catholicism, the legacy of French colonialism. In a land rife with mystery and superstition, the isolated Gourma are not only looked down upon, but are also feared by other tribes.

The Dixon family don't fear the Gourmas, their friends. Luke, Matthew and Joel, like boys anywhere, laugh and play with their Gourma neighbors. Their mom and dad work to improve tribal agriculture and hygiene.

After more than a decade of missionary service, Alan Dixon's thoughts have been occupied by an acute tribal problem. Food is short and income is critically low. Intermittent rains and deteriorating soil, combined with increasing human and animal populations, have put an intolerable burden on the Gourma people.

In this part of Africa, two seasons prevail. The people plant sorghum and peanuts during the rainy season between June and September. In October, they prepare to grow a variety of dry-season vegetables suited to the cooler weather from November to March. Until the rains return they depend on wells for irrigation. But water is scarce and the soil is deteriorating. The people find it harder and harder to make ends meet as crop failures become more common.

Alan has been doing research on the best crops to grow under these conditions. He has found that certain varieties of cabbages grow well. Potatoes can be harvested and sold in the market to supplement the farmer's income. The potatoes not only provide some cash, they also improve the Gourmas' diet. When he finds a viable species, Alan searches for good seed and makes it available to his neighbors at cost.

Without demonstrating how to care for new crops, however, his efforts would be fruitless. No wonder Alan enlisted his three boys to help show the Gourmas how the cultivation of vegetables on plots as small as 100 feet square can supplement their diet and income.

Each of the Dixon boys accepts responsibility for a small plot of ground where they care for a variety of vegetables. Last year, nine-year-old Luke grew an abundance of cabbages. In fact, he grew so many that he was able to earn extra pocket money by making the surplus available for sale in the market. Tousle-headed Luke grins as his mother, Alison, explains, "He is the businessman of the family!"

Alison has her own projects. Teaching the three boys comes first. She had two choices: either to send them away to a boarding school in a neighboring country, or to teach them at home. When she considered the age of her children, the problem of travel and the difficulty involved in getting visas, she decided to home-school the boys.

Home-schooling requires discipline. She sets aside mornings from 8:30 until noon for teaching. When other duties intrude, as they invariably do, she must schedule an alternative time. Of course, with the heat so intense in the afternoon, Saturday morning is the usual alternative. From time to time her SIM colleague and neighbor, Jeanette Friesen, takes a turn. Jeanette is home-schooling her own three girls.

The Dixons find home-schooling overwhelmingly positive. Some critics of home-schooling worry about lack of social interaction. Alison responds, "They are always around children from the church; they play with African children all the time." She goes on to point out the priceless opportunity they have to experience real cultural immersion. She adds, "They have come to feel such a part of our work." She realizes that, later on, boarding school may become a more attractive option.

With medical needs on every hand, Alison also has opportunity to use her nursing skills. Most opportunities arise when people come to the back door for treatment. Many suffer from malaria or dysentery. Some, discouraged by the help they receive at more formal dispensaries, come looking for sympathy.

Adults and children show up at their back-door clinic with scratches or cuts—sometimes even infected ulcers. Alan points out how involved the whole family is in offering medical help as well as demonstrating an agricultural model. He explains that they give Matthew and Luke "responsibility for particular children who have to come back every day, or sometimes twice a day, for treatment."

Fortunately, Alison Dixon is able to do more than treat medical problems. She and Jeanette Friesen teach a class on hygiene in a nearby girls' school established by the church. Teenage girls come for six months to learn reading and writing, Bible and the basics of health. Not to be outdone, many of the young men requested a class. Consequently, provision was made for them to come during the season when the girls go home. Surprisingly, the young men have shown even more interest than the young women.

Alison and Jeannette use diagrams, drama and role-play to teach about health. They stress proper diet, dramatize the reality of germs, and teach about malaria, cholera and AIDS. They explain how to use pills and injections and what to do with diarrhea.

By popular request they added another class to their regimen of hygiene. The girls begged for help with sewing and knitting. The treadle sewing machine proved to be quite a challenge. Knitting, however, really caught on. Here again the Dixon boys have shown their value.

Alison often took the three boys with her when she went to teach in the girls' school. Before long, Luke became adept at knitting! He did so well that he began helping the girls to learn. When asked if the Gourma girls resent the help of the missionary kids, Alison replied, "Oh no, they love it! The kids are really well accepted anyway. In fact, they open a lot of doors for us."

From time to time the family visits a clinic in another town, called Mahadaga. They concentrate on teaching some pre-teen polio victims basic skills as well as showing them how to do crafts. When the Dixons visit, Luke pitches in to teach the kids how to knit.

But what about evangelism? What about the church? In some 200 locations around the country, Gourma Christians gather for fellowship and praise. The Gourma church in Diapaga is small but growing. Alan has been heavily involved in village evangelism around Diapaga, with students responsible for most of the witness. The greatest encouragement has come in the French work.

From its origin as a student-led ministry, the French worship service has evolved into a congregation of a hundred or so. Teachers, those in government service and students in the high school make up the bulk of the group. Alan helped them to restructure and become self-supporting. Meanwhile, the student whose original burden had led to the establishment of the French service returned from Bible school to become the pastor. Things are going well.

Burkina Faso may be unique, but the pattern God is duplicating there can be found in every corner on earth. Compassion and concern are being translated into health care and agricultural improvement, evangelism and church growth.

At the heart of what God is doing you will invariably find Christians being what committed Christians are meant to be all over the world: good neighbors. Most don't have high-profile ministries. Many like the Dixons have an added plus—the family factor! Of course, not all missionary kids are as involved as the Dixons'. Nevertheless, it is not unusual to find kids like Luke, Matthew and Joel thrilled by the privilege of being part of God's unfolding purpose—whether that involves knitting or cultivating cabbages. Tom Sawyer ... Huck Finn ... eat your hearts out!

Part 6

The missionary and culture

Understanding culture

Few issues generate such controversy among evangelical missionaries as debates on how to adapt missionary work to particular cultures. In the last few decades a new word, "contextualization," has been coined to describe the process in which a missionary sets aside the cultural baggage of his or her home culture and adapts to a host culture. This process, which used to be known as acculturation, is not easy.

From childhood we unconsciously adopt an approach to living that includes how we speak, what we eat, how we dress and how we relate to other people. Culture is part and parcel of who we are as individuals. We are Texans, New Englanders or Liverpudlians, Québécois or Koreans, Filipinos or Egyptians, Latinos or Germans.

When we are forced to adapt to a new culture, we feel a shock to our system. As new missionaries to Pakistan, Mary Helen and I enrolled in language school in the mountains of northern Pakistan. We stayed with a couple from the UK. He was a Scot and she was English. I can still remember the disbelief on his face as we sat down to our first breakfast together. We brought out a special treat, all the way from Canada—peanut butter to put on toast for breakfast.

They appeared shocked. Later we learned that our new friends felt very strongly about what constituted a good breakfast—its content and its order. They believed that first there should be eggs and toast with butter. Until the eggs were consumed, neither jam nor marmalade should be spread on the bread. Once the eggs had been eaten, jam—they called it jelly—or marmalade could then be used. Peanut butter didn't even come into the picture. Tea had to be made in a certain way and milk was to be put into the cup before the tea was poured.

This clash of cultures from different sides of the Atlantic created stress. Later we joked about it, but that morning we could cut the tension with a knife—and we didn't understand why. As the weeks passed, we adapted to one another. Ironically, their children learned to love peanut butter for breakfast. One of their boys would hardly eat anything else!

What does it mean to adapt to those of another culture? Does it mean to dress like the Chinese, as modeled by Hudson Taylor, founder of the China Inland Mission? Does it mean learning language and literature as well as appreciating the local flora and fauna, as exemplified in William Carey, the father of modern missions? Does it mean utilizing "Allah" as a suitable translation for "God" in Arab cultures? Does it mean dropping baptism by immersion as an ordinance in countries where such a practice lights a firestorm of opposition? Does it mean modifying church government to accommodate local patterns of leadership? Does it mean using drums in worship? Does it mean building churches shaped like mosques?

The issues are crucial. Some professing evangelicals have been so concerned lest missionaries overshadow the biblical gospel with Western cultural accretions that they have reduced their message to the person of Christ as interpreted by each culture. In the process they have avoided those elements of the biblical message that contain commandments and principles that might distract hearers from a focus on Christ alone.

Are we left with something so ambiguous? Are beliefs and commandments to be completely shaped by culture rather than by revelation? If so, what is truth? Are there any trans-cultural truths? Before we can respond to such a wholesale abandonment of biblical distinctives, we must come to understand culture as a real and dynamic part of every person's experience.

Defining culture

Lyman Reed, in his book *Preparing Missionaries for Intercultural Communication*, notes that anthropologists have given varied definitions of "culture": "It has been a long pilgrimage in the process of reaching consensus (among anthropologists)."[1] He lists some of the viewpoints that have been expressed over the years. Culture is, for example:

> The complex whole which includes knowledge, belief, art, morals, law, custom, and any other capabilities and habits acquired by man as a member of society. Taylor (1871)

> The sum total of the knowledge, attitudes, and habitual behavior patterns shared and transmitted by the members of a particular society. Linton (1940)

(All the) historically created designs for living, explicit and implicit, rational, irrational, and non-rational, which exist at any given time as potential guides for the behaviour of men. Kluckhohn and Kelly (1945)

The mass of learned and transmitted motor reactions, habits, techniques, ideas, and values—and the behavior they induce. Kroeber (1948)

Patterns, explicit and implicit, of and for behaviour acquired and transmitted by symbols, constituting the distinctive achievement of human groups, including their embodiments in artifacts. Kroeber and Kluckholn (1952)[2]

Webster defines culture as "the concepts, habits, skills, art, instruments, institutions, (language, values), etc. of a given person in a given period."[3]

At Willowbank, the Lausanne Committee defined culture as follows: "Culture is an integrated system of beliefs, of values, of customs, and of institutions which express these beliefs, values, customs, which binds a society together and gives it a sense of dignity, security, and continuity."[4]

THE CHARACTERISTICS OF CULTURE

Lyman Reed lists five basic characteristics of culture. Firstly, it consists of *learned behavior*. Culture is not transferred genetically. It is learned through "parental upbringing and interaction within a particular socio-cultural setting."[5] For example, we learn from childhood whether to eat with a spoon or chopsticks.

Secondly, culture is not peculiar to one person but *shared by a group* of people. An entire group will share a common approach to things such as dress, food, the building of homes and the playing of games.

Thirdly, culture involves *a shared set of ideas* about how to behave and what to value.

Fourthly, culture is *cumulative and changing*. A particular culture does not spring suddenly into existence but is the result of patterns of behavior learned over many generations.

Finally, culture is not a haphazard conglomeration of traits, but *an integrated system, a way of living*. Each system includes ideas and ways of speaking as well as material products and behavior patterns.

It should be noted that in any given culture many sub-cultures may exist. "A subculture is a cluster of behavior patterns related to the general culture and yet at the same time distinguishable from it."[6] For example, people from a basic Anglo-Saxon background who live in North America can be classified into a bewildering variety of groups: Southerners, Texans, Okies, Québécois, Maritimers, Newfies, Westerners, and so on. Singles, bankers, blue-collar workers, pub-crawlers, city-dwellers, farmers, and even sports enthusiasts such as golfers, fishermen and baseball fans, may each—in some sense at least—form sub-cultures.

Even different generations can be distinguished as sub-cultures. In Western culture we talk of the Depression generation, the post-war generation, Baby Boomers, Generation Xers, Baby Busters, Echo Boomers and even Tweeners.

Culture must be distinguished from *society*. A society is formed of people who occupy a particular geographic location, while culture is formed by a set of shared values and practices. One society—for example, the American society—may play host to quite a diversity of cultures.

HOW CULTURES DIFFER

Values, although not often recognized, vary widely from culture to culture. In her helpful handbook *Thriving in Another Culture*, Jo Anne Dennett contrasts the values to two representative cultures (see Table 4).[7]

Values such as these translate into practices that become very valuable to the people in the particular culture. Missionaries must be especially careful to observe and put into practice these modes of behavior in their host cultures. For example, an African field worker in Swaziland explained to Eddie Askew,

> It is very important to take time when you are meeting people; time to make the right greetings, to listen to them, to show respect. If you only have time to rush into a home, put the medicine on the table, and rush out with an apology for being busy, it's better to go at another time when you can be more relaxed.[8]

Culture A	Culture B
Individual; independence valued	Group-oriented; family honor valued
Time/work-oriented	People/events-oriented
Criticism seen as honesty	Criticism brings shame
Direct settling of differences	Indirect; use of mediator
Equality; consensus decisions	Authority; patriarchal decisions
Values zeal of youth	Values wisdom of elders
Progress in technology best	Traditional ways are best
Materialism; values possessions	Spirit world; values blessing of spirits

Table 4

Dennett lists six examples of these culture practices:[9]

- Greetings are prolonged and extensive in many cultures.

- With whom are you allowed to be friendly in this society, and from whom should you keep a respectful distance? Do you stand or sit in the presence of others, especially of the elders and chief?

- Which group is inaccessible to you? In Muslim countries males are not allowed to associate with women outside their family group.

- "Body language" is very important in many cultures. Eye-contact or not? Stand close or at some distance? Bowing? Shaking hands?

- Showing anger is offensive to some people and they are quick to discern signs of emotion. A national worker in our clinic told me, "When you are angry your neck turns red; the nurse's eyelids twitch."

- The manner in which food is eaten will differ. Slurping or burping to show enjoyment? Use of right hand only? Scraping plate clean or leaving some? Eat quietly and not talk?

From the biblical perspective, we must inject also the idea of a *counter-culture*. The Scriptures recount history from the perspective of a counter-cultural movement. In the Old Testament, Israel was a divinely appointed counter-culture given the task of wooing the pagan nations from their idolatrous cultural customs to the worship of Jehovah. In New Testament revelation, the kingdom of God is the counter-culture. We are called to establish visible outposts of that counter-culture—churches—among every people. Each church must reflect divine culture as revealed in the Scripture, and yet each church will also reflect some of its own culture. What it keeps and what it discards, however, is the crucial question. As Christians we are not satisfied with culture as it is because culture is never completely neutral in the struggle between darkness and light.

Culture and the demonic

It is a fact too little recognized by many missiologists that every culture falls within the parameters of the biblical concept of the "world." Evil, anti-God forces, far from being neutral, insinuate their way into all cultures. Missions exists to call men and women from the sinful ways in which they have lived to embrace the Christian *way*. We are called to teach people to deny "the ways of this world and of the ruler of the kingdom of the air, the spirit who is now at work in those who are disobedient" (Eph. 2:2). We are to rescue people who are bound by the rudiments of this world (Col. 2:8).

The world is the sphere in which Satan operates. He is the prince of the world who operates a kingdom of darkness (John 12:31; 14:30; 2 Cor. 4:4). The "friendship with the world is hatred toward God," because the whole world lies under the influence of the devil and is corrupted through lust (James 4:4; 2 Peter 1:4). All of us must struggle against "the rulers, against the authorities, against the powers of this dark world and against the spiritual forces of evil in the heavenly realms" (Eph. 6:12).

Jesus warns us against seeking what the Gentiles seek (Matt. 6:32). Paul urges us to "'come out from them and be separate' … Touch no unclean thing, and [the Lord] will receive you" (2 Cor. 6:17). John exhorts us, "Do not love the world or anything in the world. If anyone loves the world, the love of the Father is not in him. For everything in the world—the cravings of sinful man, the lust of his eyes and the boasting of what he has and does—comes not from the Father but from the world" (1 John 2:15–16).

Cultural systems, in so far as they encourage human lust and pride, are influenced by the devil. Paul lays out the terrible litany of evil present in the world's cultures in Romans 1–3 and Galatians 5, for example. Idolatry, rebellion, sexual perversion, and depraved and twisted thinking characterize people in every culture.

The Bible could not make it clearer that in missionary evangelism we call men and women to confess their cultural and personal sins and abandon those cultural ideas and practices that reflect animosity toward God and submission to Satan. The mission of missions is to invade all cultures, to call out a counter-cultural group, the church, which—as salt and light—will become a center of cultural change. Neither Christ nor his disciples, however, did away with Jewish clothing, language or food. Nor did they refuse to travel on Roman ships or use Roman roads and passports. Not everything that is cultural is evil.

How do we distinguish between morally neutral elements of human culture and demonic elements? It is helpful to classify cultural beliefs and practices into four categories. Various facets of culture can be classified as positive, neutral, morally evil (ethically wrong), or theologically heretical (untrue, false). In a very broad sense, Table 5 illustrates what I mean. I have used Canada and Pakistan, two countries that I know well. You may wish to classify the beliefs and practices of a third country or society in the final column.

Culture and our churches

While all authentic Christian churches claim that the Bible is their one source of authoritative teaching on the nature of the church, churches vary widely in their interpretation of it. Part of the reason for this can be traced to genuine differences of interpretation. For example: Does the New Testament teach a congregational or episcopal form of church government?

	Canada	Pakistan	(Culture of your choice)
Positive	• Freedom for church organization • Immigration from all over world • Technology for evangelism	• Importance of family • Hospitality • Respect for books	
Neutral	Dress, food, transportation, housing, system of government	• Dress in shalwar kameez • Curry and chapaties, etc.	
Morally evil	• Legislated abortion support • Easy divorce • Homosexuality	• Polygamy • Bribery • Revenge • Law of apostasy	
Theologically heretical	Belief in evolution, humanism, New Age, relativism, etc.	• Muhammad as God's prophet • No need of a Savior • Man not born in sin	

Table 5

We are separated not only by differences of interpretation but also by differences in culture. Much of the diversity in church forms can be traced to their roots in a particular culture at a particular period of church history. The most obvious examples of this would be the Mennonites, the Hutterites and the Quakers. We would also have to include the various ethnic expressions of the church: the Coptic Church, the Orthodox Church, the Latin Church (Roman Catholic), the Armenians, the Syrian Orthodox, the Mar Thoma Church and so on.

Most Western evangelicals trace their origins to the Reformation or post-Reformation revivals. Considerable similarity can be found among a Southern Baptist church, an Alliance church, a Pentecostal church—aside from charismatic distinctives—and an evangelical Presbyterian or Anglican church—aside from matters of church government. Differences do exist. But the big question when missionaries go to a foreign land to plant a church is: Which distinctives will they insist on? Will the shape of the church that they plant reflect the culture in which it is planted or the culture of those who plant it?

In a survey of over 500 Fellowship Baptist churches in Canada, it was discovered that 65 percent were stalled in a state of institutionalization. One of the main reasons for this can be traced to their failure to grapple with the challenges and opportunities of a new era. They act as if their way of "doing church" is the only way. Whenever members of a church insist that "This is the way we have always done it," they are usually referring to past cultural patterns of worship and organization that older people find comfortable. They may view change as compromise, when what is envisioned has nothing to do with threatening any biblical truth. Usually, suggested changes relate to practices that are morally neutral.

All this is understandable. No one wants to worship in a style that makes us feel uncomfortable. But when missionaries go abroad they must carefully distinguish between the wheat and the chaff in their own church practices. Place the church practices that follow in the empty Table 6 according to whether they concern biblical essentials or reflect cultural customs: timing of services, Bible reading in services, singing in services, singing psalms in services, using piano or organ in services, two services on Sunday, Sunday school, home Bible studies, Women's missionary society,

Culturally derived practices	Biblically essential practices

Table 6

men's breakfast meetings, young people's meetings, visitation, one-hour services, church picnics, church buildings, evangelistic meetings, preaching, prayer meeting on Wednesday night, dressing in suit and tie, standing to sing hymns, celebrating the Lord's Table, half-hour sermons, invitation after sermon, choir, soloists, pulpit on platform, seats in rows facing pulpit, baptizing in water, etc.

Having considered culture from the standpoint of the demonic and the sacred, let's move on to try to identify the ways we react to cultural differences in others. One way to demonstrate the power of culture is to observe reactions.

Reactions to culture

Since we are immersed in culture from birth, its presence is inescapable. It shapes the way we interact with others. The cultural differences that exist between people are more profound than the distinctions of color, hair, eyes and stature. They are not confined to ethnic and linguistic differences but include, for example, everything that makes urban Latin professionals distinct from rural farmers, or rural Punjabi sharecroppers distinct from city dwellers in Karachi.

When new missionaries meet people who are different, most react in some way or other. Positive reactions may take the form of curiosity, interest, appreciation or respect. Negative reactions may lead to resistance, suspicion or resentment. Reactions reflecting prejudice gravely hinder missionary work. After all, missionaries are called to bring a message of reconciliation to alienated peoples.

APPRECIATION

One of the best ways to avoid prejudice is to approach diversity in human culture with interest and curiosity. An eagerness to learn will prepare us to appreciate either curry or kippers, to admire American enthusiasm rather than criticize it, to appreciate British doggedness, Canadian reserve, Latin warmth, French *joie de vivre* and Indian ingenuity.

Approaching diversity in this way has immeasurably enriched my life. I've marveled at the quiet serenity of a Japanese garden and the unbelievable patience of a rug weaver in Pakistan. Spanish, Roman, Greek and Mogul architecture have held me spellbound. I have savored food in thirteen different countries, from Spain to Thailand. The world is a fascinating place full of things to interest and amaze. Without the ability to appreciate cultural diversity, our lives may become narrow and boring.

COMPARISON AND CULTURAL RELATIVISM

Someone has said that comparisons are odious, and nowhere is this more true than in comparing one culture with another. We have a tendency to get into an *us* versus *them* mentality through unfavorably comparing other cultures with our own. When we do compare cultures, we tend to use a series of lenses that magnify the strengths of our own culture while highlighting the weaknesses of others.

Cultural realities are not served by using comparisons made on the basis of superior versus inferior, civilized versus uncivilized, advanced versus underdeveloped, moral versus degenerate, technological versus primitive. If we base our comparisons on standards of living and amount of technology, for example, and fail to evaluate such things as the strength and stability of the family, we will be off the mark. Is a culture such as the Canadian culture, where a high percentage of people are computer-literate, really superior to a culture in which there is little literacy but a highly developed sense of community? A fair weighing of all the positive and negative factors that distinguish cultures is extremely difficult.

One approach to this issue can be called *cultural relativism*. In this view, all cultures are equally valid. We must not let the word "relative" throw us off. It does raise a red flag in a day when absolute truths are denied and anything and everything is tolerated. By the term "cultural relativism," however, we mean that—with the exception of demonic elements—one culture has as much validity as another. It is just as valid to dress in a suit as in a shalwar kameez. It is just as valid to use an organ as a sitar or a guitar. It is just as valid to eat manioc as mangoes.

But you may ask, "What about the Jewish culture as reflected in the Scriptures?" Since key elements of the Jewish sub-culture developed after the Exodus were revealed by God through Moses, it was superior to surrounding cultures—in important ways. And yet God did not reveal a totally new culture. He gave them inspired patterns of worship and distinct standards of moral behavior which were to be superimposed on the culture they already had, displacing demonic elements but not superceding neutral elements. The Israelites had many cultural characteristics, such as dress, food, agriculture and so on, which were not to be changed. They shared many of these elements with surrounding cultures.

Or consider the Christian church. Even though a biblically normative local church—in as much as it gathers a group of genuine disciples to worship and serve God according to biblical directives—provides its adherents with a lifestyle superior to that of the culture at large, it is not complete as a culture. Different local churches, equally true to biblical directives, will vary widely in habits of dress, food, music, speech and architecture.

Are all cultures equally valid? In their neutral and non-demonic elements, we must say, "yes!" If we don't, we will be found validating our prejudices and resting in a false sense of cultural superiority.

PREJUDICE

Prejudice leads a person to view other cultures as inferior. North American history ought to scare us away from any form of prejudice (the slavery of blacks, British atrocities toward the Indians and Acadians, Canadian treatment of the Métis, etc., etc.). And yet we hear people making brash statements that tar everyone with the same brush. "Americans are brash." "Asians are unemotional." "Canadians are critical." "Blacks are violent." "The English are cold." "The French are immoral." Unfortunately, prejudice exists in all cultures. The only thing true about generalities such as these is that since any population is almost infinitely diverse, they cannot be true.

ETHNOCENTRISM AND CULTURAL IMPERIALISM

Ethnocentrism is a polite word for prejudice. Reed quotes Taylor as saying that ethnocentrism "is defined as the practice of viewing alien customs by applying the concepts and values of one's own culture."[10]

Missionaries who fail to identify their own ethnocentrism may keep right on viewing everything through the rose-colored glasses of their own culture. Depending on our background we may unconsciously promote American or Canadian, French or British methods, with the result that we create resentment in the host culture.

Cultural imperialism is the term often used for earlier missionaries who went into the world to spread the supposed superiority of the white man's civilization: Dutch, British, French, German, Spanish. As a result we see the stamp of their colonial practices on many of the institutions and much of the infrastructure of countries such as Mexico, South Africa, Kenya, India, Pakistan, Indonesia and the Philippines.

CULTURAL SUICIDE

Modern missionaries, naturally, are horrified by these acts of cultural genocide. Some react so dramatically against their home culture that they "go native." They abandon their own culture and adopt everything in the host culture, including dress, food and ideology. While at first glance this might seem to endear them to their new hosts, it often produces suspicion. Nationals may ask themselves, "Why is this person being so radical? Why is he so disloyal to his own culture?" Some missionaries go to this extreme to cover up their failures to learn a local language. It becomes an easier way to impress a new culture than the hard road of disciplined language study.

CULTURE SHOCK

It is widely recognized that changes in our lives such as moving to another location, changing jobs, marriage, death, having a child, and so on, create stress. Too much stress can lead to sickness or malaise. According to a scale devised by Dr. T. H. Holmes, 300 life-change units, as he calls them, can lead to serious sickness or mental illness. Change of job rates 36 units. Change of living conditions: 25 units. Using his scale, Dennett has calculated that "entering another culture, new country, language, life style, job, relationships, etc." means that a new missionary faces over 400 life-change units![11]

Stress such as this can lead to grave reactions. A missionary working in Karachi slipped into severe culture shock and retreated from his ministry. As a result, he spent an inordinate amount of time gathering sea shells from along the shore of the Indian Ocean! And when he traveled through the city, he blew his horn incessantly and shouted insults at other drivers.

In another case, a worker suffering from culture shock in Bangladesh got up in the early hours of the morning and went out and killed the neighbor's rooster that had been annoying him every morning.

Clearly, all those who live in a foreign culture, whether they be immigrants arriving on our shores or missionaries living abroad, need to be forewarned about the very real danger of culture shock.

CULTURAL COMPROMISE/SYNCRETISM

Some adapt so thoroughly to another culture they incorporate moral and theological elements contrary to the Scriptures. Since this area continues to generate considerable controversy, let me quote rather extensively.

Ruth Tucker, for example, writes of E. Stanley Jones, a missionary to India around 1910:

> Jones was convinced that if the educated Indians had the opportunity to see Christ, without all his Western garb, they would gladly receive him. But Jones went further than merely disassociating Christ from Western civilization: he also disassociated him from the Old Testament: "Christianity must be defined as Christ, not the Old Testament, not Western civilization, not even the system built around him in the West,

but Christ himself." Eliminating the Old Testament from his preaching was naturally controversial, but Jones defended his action on practical grounds.[12]

By declaring up front that the Old Testament was imperfect, he avoided questions from his opponents dealing with Old Testament textual problems.

Tucker explains about his movement,

The Christian Ashram movement that Jones founded was also an accommodation to Indian social life—and alternative to the Western church ... The setup of the Christian Ashram was very similar to its Hindu counterpart. The "family" was required to rise at 5:30 a.m. and spend its day in a combination of activities, including private devotions, manual labor and group discussions, the latter being eliminated on the one day a week that was specified a day of "complete silence" ... Only God, as seen through Jesus Christ, Jones argued, was absolute. "The church is a relativism."[13]

Certainly, many things about how we organize the church and conduct worship vary according to culture—but is the church itself, as constituted by Jesus Christ, a "relativism"? While we must avoid Jones's extremes, we can learn something from his creative adaptations to Indian culture.

Charles Kraft comments positively on what Eugene Nida, a well-known missionary linguist, calls "relative cultural relativism." Kraft writes,

This position does not deny the presence of absolutes but relates all absolutes to God, who stands outside of culture, rather than to any cultural expression, description or exemplification of a God–man relationship (be it American, Greek or Hebrew). "The only absolute in Christianity," says Nida in what may be an overstatement, "is the triune God. Anything which involves man, who is finite and limited, must of necessity be limited and hence relative."[14]

Seeking to explain his position, Nida writes in another context,

Biblical relativism is not a matter of inconsistency, but a recognition of the different cultural factors which influence standards and actions. While the Koran attempts to fix for all time the behaviour of Muslims, the Bible clearly establishes the principle of

> relative relativism, which permits growth, adaptation and freedom, under the Lordship of Jesus Christ ... The Christian position is not one of static conformance to dead rules, but of dynamic obedience to a living God.[15]

Nida seems to question whether the New Testament, including the Epistles, is a revelation of both universal principles and absolute standards on moral issues. Nida goes too far and is too fuzzy to be practical in the day-to-day ministry of today's missionaries.

Phil Parshall has written many books on Muslim evangelism, most dealing with issues of contextualization. In *New Paths in Muslim Evangelism* he makes many helpful suggestions about building bridges to Muslim neighbors. But in the section on problematic Christian practices he writes, "In view of the fact that baptism is so misunderstood in Muslim lands, would it be feasible to construct a functional substitute for baptism that would retain the biblical meaning, but change the form?"[16]

Parshall mentions that in some circumstances secret baptism, self-baptism or delayed baptism have been practiced. He asks whether there is precedent for an alternative in the bar mitzvah ceremony that thirteen-year-old Jewish boys go through, or in the confirmation ceremonies that a number of denominations use. To be fair to Parshall, it should be noted that he is raising questions in the interest of more effective Muslim evangelism. He is not proposing that biblical baptism be forgotten. Even so, his book raised a storm of controversy.

Many more examples of contextualization could be cited. Some missionaries have clearly crossed the line that separates adaptation from compromise, while others have rescued themselves from syncretism just in time.

ACCULTURATION

Clearly, adapting to another culture is no easy matter. The challenge provokes different reactions. The difficulty involved leads some to avoid doing anything at all. Inertia sets in. Or insecurity might lead us to keep on doing things the way we have been brought up rather than make adjustments. We may feel threatened by another culture and worry about losing our identity. Pride may give us a smug sense of superiority.

Ignorance may stifle any attempt to change. Perhaps, since we have never had to adapt to people from a different culture before, we just don't know where to start. Alternatively, we may misunderstand the biblical doctrine of worldliness and damn all other cultures as worldly while we naively hold onto our way of doing things as the most "Christian" approach.

Whatever we do to stall the adaptation process strikes at a basic Christian principle. Acculturation is a biblically mandated practice exemplified by Christ and by the apostles. If we live and work in another culture, we must either adapt or become insular. It will help to remember that while people seem very different on the surface, they are basically the same the world over. A. R. Tippett quotes Goldschmidt to say that "People are more alike than they are different."[17] We all come from one father, Adam, through one Creator, God. We all bear his image, suffer from the same problem, sin, share a common destiny and judgment, and need the only Savior, Jesus Christ. We all share a common potential through the gospel to be one in the Body of Christ. "There is neither Jew nor Greek, slave nor free, male nor female, for you are all one in Christ Jesus" (Gal. 3:28).

Tippett summarizes Goldschmidt's conclusions:

> Goldschmidt then goes on to specify a series of generalizations concerning cross-cultural human similarity which suggest (among other things) that they may be universals:
>
> 1) The presence of deep dissatisfaction, selfishness, exploitiveness and conflict in every culture and
>
> 2) a longing for escape from all of this into "some kind of symbolic eternity."
>
> Furthermore, he asserts, the presence of communal groupings which involve individuals in patterns of activity in which they share with other persons is not (as Montague and others have suggested) to be interpreted as indicating "that man is … fundamentally a loving creature," but rather, as indicating that humanity needs institutional devices, "to preserve society against the essential self-interest of the human individual."[18]

Remembering that we are all more alike than we are different, missionaries should approach their new neighbors with a desire to discover what they have in common. In the process, a throng of interesting cultural practices will be discovered that can safely be adopted without the danger of compromise.

We are now in a position to define "contextualization" (or "acculturation") as *the process of adapting, without compromise, to another culture in such a way that the Christian faith can be conveyed in words and methods that take into account the whole cultural situation.*

Unfortunately, as we have seen in the quotations above, in some missionary circles contextualization refers more often to adapting the missionary message and theology to the culture of a given people in ways that compromise that very message. As always, we need to return to the New Testament for guidance in this area.

Notes

1 **Lyman E. Reed,** *Preparing Missionaries for Intercultural Communication* (Pasadena, CA: William Carey Library, 1985), p. 14.

2 Ibid.

3 *Webster's New World Dictionary of the American Language* (New York: Avenel Books, 1978).

4 From "The Willowbank Report" of the Lausanne Committee for World Evangelization, 1978.

5 **Reed**, *Preparing Missionaries for Intercultural Communication*, pp. 14–17.

6 **Grunland** and **Mayers,** cited by **Reed,** *Preparing Missionaries for Intercultural Communication*, p. 16.

7 **Jo Anne Dennett,** *Thriving in Another Culture: A Handbook for Cross-Cultural Missions* (Melbourne: Acorn Press, 1998), p. 25.

8 Quoted in **Eddie Askew,** *Many Voices, One Voice: Meditations and Prayers* (London: The Leprosy Mission, 1985), p. 76.

9 Adapted from **Dennett,** *Thriving in Another Culture*, pp. 25–26.

10 **Reed,** *Preparing Missionaries for Intercultural Communication*, p. 21.

11 **Dennett,** *Thriving in Another Culture*, pp. 26–27.

12 **Ruth Tucker,** *From Jerusalem to Irian Jaya* (Grand Rapids, MI: Academie Books, 1983), pp. 283–284.

13 Ibid. p. 285.

14 Charles Kraft, "Toward a Christian Ethnotheology," in A. R. Tippett, (ed.), *God, Man, and Church Growth* (Grand Rapids, MI: Eerdmans, 1973), p. 124.

15 Eugene A. Nida, *Customs and Cultures* (New York: Harper & Row, 1954), p. 282.

16 Phil Parshall, *New Paths in Muslim Evangelism* (Grand Rapids, MI: Baker, 1980), p. 195.

17 Tippett, (ed.), *God, Man, and Church Growth*, p. 124.

18 Ibid. p. 136.

Chapter 21

Missionary acculturation in the New Testament

Missionary acculturation involves adaptation without compromise and flexibility without relativism. To maintain that balance we need a biblical model.

The role of Scripture

Scripture challenges that which is demonic in a culture while offering principles that enable a disciple to live in the world as an American or a Brazilian without being worldly. This model includes a framework of explicit truths, including moral commands, and implicit principles. It also gives us case studies of cultural adaptation.

Many truths are *explicit* and clear. They include revelation about the nature of God, the nature of man, the dimensions of the moral law and the way of salvation. For example, the Ten Commandments give us ten objective moral standards that can be used in all cultures to measure behavior.

Examples of *implicit principles* include how we are to relate to one anther, the nature of marriage, the role of parents, the servanthood of disciples and the necessity of avoiding debt. Romans 13–14, for example, provides general principles on how to get along with those who differ.

The Bible, peopled as it is with characters, also provides us with many *case studies*. In the area of missions we have the examples of Christ as well as of the apostles.

Using these biblical sources (explicit truths, implicit principles and case studies) to define contextualization, we must consider three steps that we need to take in adapting to a foreign culture. Step One: Identification with the people among whom we live. Step Two: Discernment of what is good, bad or neutral. Step Three: Adapting language, customs, values and so on. Let's consider these in turn.

Identification

The incarnate Christ is our ultimate model of how to identify with those in a foreign culture. In Chapter 2 we saw the ways in which his incarnation demonstrates the ideal missionary:

- He was sent by God.
- His calling was rooted in the Father's will.
- His calling was totally voluntary.
- His incarnation involved leaving his own "culture" (within the Godhead).
- Although infinitely superior, he adopted a servant role.
- He identified with those to whom he was sent as a man and as a Jewish person.
- He demonstrated compassion.
- He adopted a sacrificial lifestyle.
- He communicated a message in terms people could understand.
- He directed his focus to a limited group, the lost sheep of Israel.
- He maintained a vision of reaching the whole world.

In Philippians 2 Paul uses the example of Christ to teach us how to identify with one another. In relationships, attitude is one of the most important factors: "Your attitude should be the same as that of Christ Jesus" (Phil. 2:5). And the most basic ingredient of his attitude was *agape* love. Missionary passion should arise from a love for others, an interest in others, a concern for others above oneself: "Each of you should look not only to your own interests, but also to the interests of others" (2:4). This kind of love is not self-centered nor proud. It is characterized by humility and a reticence to promote oneself. "Do nothing out of selfish ambition or vain conceit, but in humility consider others better than yourselves" (2:3).

Personal ambition, while valued in the business world, is anathema in missions. Missionary service should not reflect an ambition to advance one's career but rather to advance the cause of Christ and the spiritual well-being of men and women. Setting aside our own ambitions we need to become "one in spirit and purpose" with others on our team (Phil. 2:2).

Conceit is also tolerated in powerful business executives but is extremely harmful among Christians. This is especially important in cross-cultural ministries. The missionary must repudiate a feeling of superiority, whether it be cultural, educational or technological. An attitude of superiority is what doomed the cultural imperialism of some colonial missionaries.

God has a marvelous way of equalizing things: "opposing the proud" (James 4:6) and "choosing the foolish things of the world" (1 Cor. 1:27). In light of the infinite and real superiority of Christ, it makes no sense for saved sinners such as ourselves to profess superiority over others. Indeed, missionaries who go to other cultures need to face the fact that there will be much in those cultures that is superior to their own sending cultures. This was not true in the case of Christ, and yet he emptied himself. "Who, being in very nature God, did not consider equality with God something to be grasped [held onto]" (Phil. 2:6).

This last verse, and the verses that follow it (Phil. 2:7–8), capture an astonishing act of identification. Christ emptied himself! Although he was the Son of God, Jesus surrendered the independent exercise of his divine attributes in order to live among us as a man. Whatever he did, he did through the Holy Spirit after seeking the will of the Father: "I always do what pleases him" (John 8:29). When missionaries go to other cultures, they need to avoid clinging to the trappings of their own cultures. For example, they will not display the flags of their home countries, nor brag about their countries. They will be careful about an ostentatious display of what may be looked upon as wealth in the host country. They may avoid using household furnishings that seem alien, and will avoid wearing clothing that might be fine back home but give offense in the new culture.

Besides leaving behind cultural practices that flag them as foreign, missionaries will seek to adopt as many cultural practices as possible. Christ not only emptied himself of something, but he also took on something. He was "made in human likeness. And being found in appearance as a man …" (Phil. 2:7–8). While missionaries are not expected to deny their cultures of origin, they should seek to adopt the practices of their host cultures as much as possible. This will certainly involve speech. It may involve dress, food, living conditions and social patterns.

For example, when Mary Helen and I served in Pakistan, we sought to dress as Pakistanis did. Mary Helen wore a long-sleeved shirt (kameez) over baggy trousers (shalwar) and always in public covered her head with a long scarf (dupatta). This was essential for Mary Helen, lest her dress give offense. While many of the men had begun to adopt Western dress, I often wore the men's version of the shalwar kameez. (On trains, I was sometimes mistaken for a Pathan from the Northwest Frontier province.) We used Urdu forms of address. Rather than living in a mission compound, we rented a house in a Pakistani neighborhood. We used Pakistani furniture—even in the bathroom. We tried to decorate with Pakistani crafts, rugs and pictures. We ate Pakistani curries more often than Western food. We tried not to use the left hand in eating, since it is considered unclean in that culture. As a family we loved to clap our hands to keep time as we sang Urdu hymns and choruses. And yet, in spite of our efforts at identification, I have often wished we had done more through seeking to understand Pakistani forms of music and literature.

Paul next emphasizes the importance of following the example of Christ the sacrificial servant. Although he was God, he "made himself nothing, taking the very nature of a servant ... he humbled himself and became obedient to death—even death on a cross!" (Phil. 2:7–8). The whole passage revolves around the role of the sacrificial servant—the role that the Messiah was predicted by Isaiah to fulfill. And this is a role that all his followers are called to adopt. God does not send missionaries to the ends of the earth so that they can rule over others and become bosses, masters, sahibs—but to become servants. Missionaries, like Christ, are to "look to the interests of others" (Phil. 2:4). That will involve the sacrifice of personal interests, comforts, plans and maybe even health and safety.

Missionaries should constantly ponder, "What can I do to further the kingdom by contributing to the good of others?" Unfortunately, missionaries can easily become drunk on the elixir of power—power they did not wield at home but are often given by the very nature of being highly trained foreigners in a host culture. If they are not careful, the innate respect many cultures afford to guests will go to their heads. They may begin to believe in their own superiority and begin to subtly boss others around. Pastors back home face the same temptation.

When Jesus took the towel and basin of the servant and washed the disciples' feet he not only repudiated the leadership models of his day but also gave us a universal example: "Now that I, your Lord and Teacher, have washed your feet, you also should wash one another's feet. I have set you an example that you should do as I have done for you" (John 13:14–15). Servant leadership is desperately needed in every culture to overcome endemic patterns of competition and domination.

Identification arises from an attitude that reflects that of Christ and is worked out in the day-to-day life of the missionary servant who seeks immersion in the culture. How can the missionary be sure, however, that his or her immersion does not involve moral or theological pollution? Discernment is needed.

Discernment: cross-cultural problem solving

The record of the Council of Jerusalem in Acts 15 gives us further principles concerning the limits and forms of contextualization. The council was called after explosive church growth among Gentiles in Syrian Antioch, Cyprus, Pisidian Antioch, Iconium, Lystra and Derbe. In many of these cities Jewish people had been scandalized by the sight of uncircumcised Gentiles being welcomed into the church. As a result, "Some men came down from Judea to Antioch and were teaching the brothers: 'Unless you are circumcised, according to the custom taught by Moses, you cannot be saved.' This brought Paul and Barnabas into sharp dispute and debate with them" (Acts 15:1–2).

As a result the church in Antioch sent a group of representatives with Paul and Barnabas to Jerusalem. While there, some believers from the party of the Pharisees stood up and said, "The Gentiles must be circumcised and required to obey the law of Moses" (Acts 15:5). A meeting was called. After much discussion Peter arose and addressed the assembly, asserting that "God, who knows the heart, showed that he accepted them by giving the Holy Spirit to them, just as he did to us ... Now then, why do you try to test God by putting on the necks of the disciples a yoke that neither we nor our fathers have been able to bear?" (15:8, 10).

Peter, Barnabas and Paul rehearsed the wonderful things that God was doing. Finally, James stood up and said,

> It is my judgment, therefore, that we should not make it difficult for the Gentiles who are turning to God. Instead we should write to them, telling them to abstain from food polluted by idols, from sexual immorality, from the meat of strangled animals and

from blood. For Moses has been preached in every city from the earliest times and is read in the synagogues on every Sabbath. (Acts 15:19–21)

The decision suggested by James reflects an ideal way to discern between what is acceptable and what is not in a given culture. Using Richard Baxter's helpful dictum, we can chart their decision as shown in Table 7.

This deliberation shows, firstly, that *some adaptation to culture is necessary*. The assembly recognized the great difference between Jewish and Gentile cultures. Peter pled for them not to require the Gentiles to keep Jewish rules. James reduced to a minimum the things they would urge on the Gentiles.

Secondly, it demonstrates that *in essentials there must be unity*. The group recognized that Gentiles, no less than Jews, are saved by the "grace of the Lord Jesus" and by the cleansing of hearts through faith (Acts 15:9,

In doubtful things (non-essentials)—liberty Freedom of worship style and organization	"We should not make it difficult for the Gentiles" (Acts 15:19)
In necessary things (essentials)—unity Unity in theological essentials	"We should write to them, telling them to abstain from food polluted by idols" (Acts 15:20a)
Unity in moral essentials	"From sexual immorality" (Acts 15:20b)
In all things—charity (love) Avoidance of potential stumbling-blocks	"From the meat of strangled animals and from blood" (Acts 15:20c)

Table 7

11). Both groups depended upon the reception of the Holy Spirit (15:8). Both were "a people for [God]" (15:14). And both needed to keep the moral dimensions of the law—but not those injunctions which were temporary: ceremonial laws given to Israel as part of their covenant (15:5, 20).

They were required to keep themselves from immorality. Fornication was singled out, not to minimize other commandments such as the prohibitions to steal or murder, but because fornication was epidemic in the pagan world. It was often involved in pagan idol worship, and of course it was essential that they maintain the reality that there is only one God, that idolatry is evil. This reality represented all the other theological truths revealed by God in the Scriptures.

Thirdly, the council's decision encouraged *freedom of worship form.* Their deliberation shows that flexibility did not extend to the message of the gospel, but to the ways in which people were allowed to worship. The mass of Jewish religious ritual was completely set aside for Gentile believers. The council did not require Gentile believers to pray toward Jerusalem, to make a pilgrimage to the temple, to perpetuate sacrifices or to keep feasts, and, especially, they were freed from the requirement of circumcision.

From the rest of the New Testament we may also draw the conclusion that there is considerable latitude in adapting worship form to a local culture. The importance of incorporating teaching, preaching, prayer, celebration of the Lord's Supper, fellowship, collection for the needy and other universal church givens is made clear in Acts and in the Epistles.

Two of the prohibitions demonstrate that the essential biblical content is maintained in force. Idolatry was prohibited, even by association with meats sacrificed to idols, because to turn from idols was as essential an element of being a Christian as it was of being a Jew. Fornication, as already mentioned, was also prohibited as representative of the other moral commandments. (The rest of the moral law is enhanced by the Sermon on the Mount and upheld and heightened by the Epistles.)

Fourthly, *contextualization is moderated by love.* The freedom to adapt is moderated by the requirement to avoid what is abhorrent to a brother or sister of a differing culture. The New Testament teaches that eating meat of strangled animals and blood is allowable under certain conditions. The vision of the sheet let down before Peter and the teaching of Romans 14 enforce this view. And yet, in spite of this essential Christian liberty, the Council of Jerusalem forbade these things. Why? Jewish Christians requested Gentile Christians to abstain from these practices because they were particularly abhorrent to Jews living in their vicinity (15:21). The continuation of practices such as these by believing Gentiles in close proximity to Jews would damage the witness of the gospel and foment dissension with immature Jewish Christians.

This illustrates an important principle. When churches are established in a new culture, practices should not be carried on which give unnecessary offense to a neighboring culture. Otherwise, cross-cultural evangelism, fellowship and even communication will be hindered. If, for example, missionaries working among Punjabi Christians insist on eating pork, outreach among Muslims who abhor pork could be nullified.

In summary, discernment according to the following principles should guide the cross-cultural missionary:

- In moral and theological essentials we must enforce unity between all cultures.
- In non-essential matters there should be liberty to develop practices that suit a given culture.
- In all things there should be loving restraint to avoid practices that might cause non-Christians or neighboring cultures to stumble.

Adaptation

The early missionaries, after overcoming the objections of the Judaizers, began to follow the pattern laid down by Christ. They took advantage of every providential circumstance and difference in audience to tailor their message to the context of their hearers. It was this adaptability which made the apostles' ministry and message so relevant and searching.

This flexibility grew out of their sense of the reality of God's ongoing kingdom. Since God's kingdom exists, they knew that every providential event was ordered by him for some spiritual reason. As "providential evangelists," they adapted their ministry to providential elements in the culture of the audience itself and in the context in which they lived.

Whether we call it walking in another's shoes, acculturation or contextualization, adaptation to a host culture is a Christian ideal. In his first letter to the Corinthians Paul explains his commitment to adapt:

> Though I am free and belong to no man, I make myself a slave to every one, to win as many as possible. To the Jews I became like a Jew, to win the Jews. To those under the law I became like one under the law (though I myself am not under the law), so as to win those under the law. To those not having the law I became like one not having the law (though I am not free from God's law but am under Christ's law), so as to win those not having the law. To the weak I became weak, to win the weak. I have become all things to all men so that by all possible means I might save some. I do all this for the sake of the gospel. (1 Cor. 9:19–23)

Consider the way Paul and other early missionaries contextualized the gospel message. Care is needed here if compromise is to be avoided. Several principles can be isolated.

LANGUAGE

They preached in the languages and dialects of their audience. Paul spoke at least three languages: Hebrew, Aramaic and Greek. He used these as appropriate. "When they heard him speak to them in Aramaic, they became very quiet" (Acts 22:2).

Language adaptation is vital but often tough. Jimmy Walker, a new missionary in the Philippines, describes that difficulty in a loose paraphrase of Numbers 13:25–14:9. He compares the report of the spies returning from Canaan to the grumbling of new missionaries about language study:

> When they returned from trying out the language at the end of six months, they proceeded to come to their director and to all of their team in the city of Cebu of the Philippines. And they brought back word to them and to all of the team and showed them the dictionary of the land. Then they told them and said, "We went into the land where you sent us and it certainly does flow with strange vocabulary and complex suffixes and these fill our grammar notebooks. Nevertheless, the people who live in the Philippines speak very many languages and Cebuano is difficult, with strange *nga* sounds and unasperated vowels; moreover, we cannot understand them. The Filipinos

are living on an islandous country and the Tagalogs and Illocanos are in the North and the tribal people dwell in the mountainous regions. Languages, languages everywhere!"

Then the language school director quieted the people before the teachers and said, "You should by all means take up your section notebooks and study the grammar notes and practice the drills and listen to the tapes for you surely shall learn it." But the new missionaries who were being attacked by Satan said, "We are not able to learn this language for it is too difficult for us!"

So they gave out to the missionaries a bad report about the language which they had spied out in the Central Visayas region saying, "The language which we have heard on the streets is a language which devours and confuses its students, and all the Filipinos whom we heard are speaking it very fast! There we also heard the idioms (sons of the dialect) and we became like preschoolers in our own sight and so we were in their sight."

Then all the new missionaries lifted up their voices and cried out and the people wept that night. And all the new missionaries grumbled against their respective directors, and all the missionaries said to them, "Would that we had stayed at home or that we had died while discovering our support. And why is the Lord making us learn this language? To frustrate our minds? And our wives and little ones will not understand how to shop. Would it not be better to go home where we can find chocolate chips and strawberry milk shakes?"

So they said one to another, "Let us appoint a leader and return to our homeland!" Then the language school director fell on his face in the presence of all the missionaries. And the language school graduates tore their diplomas. And they spoke to the new missionaries saying, "This language can be learned and is an exceedingly beautiful language. If the Lord is pleased with us, then He will help you learn this language given to you—a language filled with strange vocabulary and complex sentence patterns. Only do not rebel against the Lord and do not fear the language of the people, for we shall tell them the GOOD NEWS. Their ears will be opened to understand your speaking in their language because the Lord is with you. Therefore, do not fear, but learn their language."[1]

Language frustrations abound whenever someone is immersed in another culture! The pressures are intense. The profit from disciplined patient study is, however, immense.

TERMINOLOGY

The apostles also used terminology appropriate to the culture which they were addressing. To the Jews they spoke of the Messiah, the hope of Israel and the kingdom of God. Among the Gentiles, where the term "kingdom" was inflammatory, they used the same content but in other terms, emphasizing Christ as Judge, Prince and Son of God. God was described as the Giver of the seasons and all good gifts, and Creator of the universe, rather than as the God of Abraham, Isaac and Jacob.

John Alkire relates how some Pume Indians of Venezuela translated the story of redemption: "I believe that the True Chief is the True Creator ... I cannot do anything in myself for my sin. The True Chief will send the Buyer, Jesus, to take care of it ... I am going to tell the folks upriver that our ancestors rejected the True Chief. The spirit rocks have no value."[2]

LITERARY HERITAGE

Apostolic missionaries made use of their listeners' literary and religious heritage when they spoke. The use of the Old Testament in preaching to Jews needs no elaboration. In reaching the Gentiles they demonstrated a sensibility to their religious prejudices and made use of their poetry. For example, "in him we live and move and have our being" and "We are his offspring" (Acts 17:28) are quotations from Greek poets (see also Titus 1:12 concerning the saying of a Cretan prophet). The foolishness of idolatry was contrasted with the glory of the true God whom they presented as living, eternal and creative. Paul referred to a specific inscription to the "unknown God" in his address on Mars Hill (Acts 17:23).

The apostles grew up in a time and place where knowledge of Greek and Roman culture—even Samaritan culture—was widespread. Pioneer missionaries today rarely have that advantage. A strenuous effort to master as much of the host culture as possible will be required. William Carey excelled in this regard. Although an uneducated cobbler he distinguished himself by mastering a number of Indian languages. He became Professor of Oriental Languages at Fort William College in

Calcutta and wrote a massive dictionary. He also collected information on Indian flora and fauna.

Ruth Tucker writes that "Carey was ahead of his time in missionary methodology. He had an awesome respect for the Indian culture and he never tried to import Western substitutes, as so many missionaries who came after him would seek to do."[3]

ADAPTATION OF MESSAGE CONTENT

Lastly, and most importantly, the apostles spoke to the context of their hearers by selecting from revelation those truths that would be most relevant to their situation and spiritual preparation. Let me explain.

To the Jews, who were in a sense pre-evangelized, they preached about Jesus using lengthy direct quotations from the Old Testament. These quotations proved that the prophets had foretold a Messiah who would be rejected, would suffer and would rise from the dead, and that Jesus was in fact this very one. They proclaimed the gospel as a fulfillment of the things that "God foretold through all the prophets" (Acts 3:18, 21, 24–26).

To Gentile proselytes and God-fearers from among the Gentiles who were attracted by Jewish monotheism, they made some references to the Old Testament witness but did not use direct quotations (see the accounts of the witnesses to the Ethiopian and Cornelius in Acts chapters 8 and 10 respectively).

To Gentiles who knew little or nothing of Jewish monotheism, Paul went right back to the elemental truths of who God is and what he does. As already mentioned, Paul's message in Athens about the unknown God followed this pattern (see Acts 17). Paul described the "unknown God" as Creator of all men, the one who is self-sufficient, the source of all things including life and breath, the sovereign ruler of the universe, the one who is omnipresent, and the one who will judge ignorant practices such as the worship of images made by men. In a sense, Paul was going back to Genesis to teach basic truths about God. The only mention he made of Jesus occurred at the end of his discourse.

Clearly, the apostles varied the content of their message relative to the preparation of their hearers. The less prepared the audience, the earlier was their starting point in biblical truth.

Contextualization on the part of the early missionaries meant the use of appropriate language, terminology and literary allusions. It meant, too, the giving of that portion of biblical content appropriate to their hearers' degree of preparation.

NO MODIFICATION OF DOCTRINAL ESSENTIALS

Let us be clear, however, what contextualization was not. There is not a shred of evidence that in their gifted adaptation of the message to their hearers, the apostles took liberties to cut out parts of the essential biblical message as irrelevant to this or that group. As we have seen, all the Old Testament concepts became part of the essential context in which the message of Jesus was given. The particularly Jewish aspects of the Old Testament concerning ceremony and the nation itself are fulfilled, *not* abrogated, in the New Testament's fuller revelation of Jesus's incarnation and atonement, and in the church as God's new nation or kingdom. (Otherwise why do we have Hebrews in our New Testament?)

The New Testament Epistles demonstrate that, ultimately, all believers, whether Gentile or Jewish, were fully instructed in the whole of biblical revelation. Paul, in summarizing his ministry to the leaders of the Ephesian church, stated unequivocally that he had declared to them the whole counsel of God. In 1 Corinthians 10:1–13 Paul states emphatically the relevance of Old Testament history in the lives of New Testament Gentile Christians. They were written, he writes, "as warnings for us, on whom the fulfillment of the ages has come."

New Testament contextualization involves being sensitive to the providence of God as reflected in culture and circumstances. It means:

- granting almost absolute freedom as to form of worship and manner of life under the moral law
- use of appropriate language and terminology
- use of culturally relevant literary and religious resources to make the message understandable and commanding
- leading converts to an extensive knowledge of all the essentials of biblical revelation.

Observations

ACCULTURATION AND VALUES

Not only must missionaries adapt linguistically, they must also moderate their lifestyles to reflect more closely the host culture. This may involve becoming more people-oriented and less task- or work-oriented. It may involve shunning personal independence to embrace a group-oriented approach to decision-making. It may involve settling disputes through a mediator rather than in person. It may involve de-emphasizing youth and valuing the wisdom of elders. Most probably, the Western missionary will have to seriously moderate his or her hurry-up, just-do-it impatient approach to group tasks.

BONDING

Acculturation is essential to missionary success. For this reason some mission boards immediately immerse new missionaries in the culture to which they are appointed. Jo Anne Dennett writes,

> They are placed in a national's home, or near vicinity, and eat, sleep and communicate only with nationals. The atmosphere certainly is conducive to learning the language and customs! The aim is to encourage *bonding* with the nationals and prevent the formation of a "missionary ghetto" mentality. The concept works best where there is an established church. It fosters a sense of responsibility in the church members to care for the new missionaries who have come to work among them. For some missionaries, such a program is overwhelming and causes harmful stress overload. A more gradual approach to culture may be required.[4]

BI-CULTURAL MISSIONARIES

Paul, and others of his era, had a great advantage over many of us who are mono-cultural. He was multi-cultural. Although steeped in Jewish customs and learning he was also immersed in the Greek and Roman cultures. His hometown was Tarsus, far from Judea, a place that was a cultural melting pot where indigenous Cilicians mingled with those whose ancestries could be traced to Hittites, Greeks, Assyrians, Persians and Macedonians. As a result Paul had a fluent command of Greek, Hebrew, and probably Aramaic, along with a working knowledge of Latin. His multi-cultural background made him an ideal missionary.

Concerning recruiting bi-cultural missionaries, Ian Downs writes,

> One strategy we feel should be illuminated again is using bicultural people to advance the mission faster and further. These are people who have already breached the cultural barrier at least once. They are a bridge between two distinct cultures. Because bicultural people are very familiar with more than one cultural pattern, they are potentially more effective at transferring the Gospel from one culture to a new, previously unpenetrated culture ... Becoming sufficiently bicultural [the missionary ideal] takes time—sometimes decades. Is there a way to speed up the process? ... Look for people who are already bicultural and nurture them.[5]

Here is an idea well worth promoting!

FLEXIBILITY

In our day, the message is too often presented in inflexible packages or in culturally harmful phraseology. Sensitive as they were to the context of their audience, the apostles did not use set formulae nor demand adherence to Jewish cultural forms of religious expression.

By contrast we find the proliferation today of inflexible packaging for the gospel message. The gospel is being widely shared in places like Mumbai and Buenos Aires in the form of hastily translated tracts and booklets that may have been relevant in New York or London but fail to communicate in India or Argentina. Yet these are often presented for use along with pre-packaged Western approaches to evangelism.

We need to be much more conscious of the cultural trappings of the message we present. The worldwide cry for contextualization has rightly underscored real weaknesses in missions. A survey in India of 5,000 Christian workers, including some missionaries, has brought to light an astounding problem. Over half of those interviewed said that it was not necessary to know anything at all about Hinduism or Islam to be an effective Christian worker in India! How strange.[6]

Sadly, similar views have not been uncommon among missionaries working in other parts of the world. Many fail to notice how laden their evangelistic approach is with Western stereotypes which obscure the essential message of the gospel. Too often, missionaries have been so busy, careless or smug that they've failed to take the time and effort necessary to master national language and literature. Urgency must not make us careless or impatient. Language ability and cultural sensitivity take time to develop.

Unfortunately, just when the need for long-term commitment to missions is becoming more acute, emphasis seems to be shifting to short-term service. Short-termers can never adequately contextualize.

THE DANGER OF SYNCRETISM

On the opposite side of the coin another danger rears its ugly head—syncretism. Syncretism blurs theological distinctives and blunts the gospel sword. The apostles' model grants us leave to contextualize as noted above, but never to change the basic content of the message.

Kenneth Cragg and Charles Kraft, in papers on Muslim evangelism that provide some helpful insights, undervalue the Old Testament as culturally skewed. At the same time they overvalue the Koran. Missing the unique relationship between the Old and New Testaments, Cragg argues that "There is precedent in the Christian reception of the Old Testament itself," encouraging us to value the Koran. He goes on to state that "the gloom of Ecclesiastes ... and the raw nationalism of psalms such as 68 and 137 are not compatible with the gospel"![7]

Charles Kraft blurs the line between the inerrant truth, which God revealed to the Hebrews, and the very fallible Hebrew culture itself. Kraft's arguments concerning the two Testaments show a fuzzy understanding of their relationship. He writes, "I deduce from this [Old and New Testaments] that God is pleased to accept expressions of organization, worship, witness and even belief and behavior that differ considerably from what we [prefer]."[8] Kraft talks as if God adapted his message to Jewish belief, behavior, views of sin and morality. He suggests that God adapted the message to Israel through using anything in their culture as a starting point and only demanding a basic allegiance.[9]

Glossing over its demonic aspects, Kraft views culture as basically neutral. He also fails to emphasize the culture-transforming influence of the gospel. He does argue legitimately for a more Semitic expression of the faith in line with Islam's Semitic roots. However, he goes too far, claiming that our concept of truth and knowledge is culturally Greek rather than Hebrew.

Kraft writes, "I contend that it is not pre-Christian to define faith as faithfulness, knowledge as experiential rather than intellectual and truth as relation-centered rather than fact-centered as Hebrews did ..."[10]

Has truth been defined in propositional terms only in the Greek Epistles? He carries on this theme by lamenting the undue notice given to Greek Epistles, such as Romans and Galatians, as opposed to those couched in Hebrew terms.[11]

Other examples of this worldwide trend to blur the line between culture and truth could be cited from South American Liberation Theology, movements to develop an African theology or from the women's liberation movement. It also seems to be present in the postmodern Emergent Church movement promoted by the likes of Brian McLaren. While we must resist this trend, we do need to encourage biblical acculturation.

Notes

1 From a missionary prayer letter from **Brent and Chris Ralston,** CBInternational, October 1994.

2 **John Alkire,** "My Father," undated article from New Tribes Mission.

3 **Ruth A. Tucker,** *From Jerusalem to Irian Jaya* (Grand Rapids, MI: Zondervan, 1983), p. 121.

4 **Jo Anne Dennett,** *Thriving in Another Culture: A Handbook for Cross-Cultural Missions* (Melbourne: Acorn Press, 1998), p. 23.

5 **Ian L. Downs,** "Their Day Dawns Again," *Mission Frontiers Bulletin*, Sept.–Dec. 1998, p. 30.

6 **Henry H. Presler,** "The Christian's Knowledge of Non-Christian Religions," *International Review of Missions*, 1 (April 1961), p. 184, cited by **James O. Buswell III,** "Contextualization: Is it Only a New Word for Indigenization?", in *Evangelical Missions Quarterly*, Jan. 1978, p. 14.

7 **Kenneth Cragg,** "Islamic Theology: Limits and Bridges," The North American Conference of Muslim Evangelization, Research Paper, 1978, p. 2.

8 **Charles H. Kraft,** "Dynamic Equivalence Churches in Muslim Society," The North American Conference on Muslim Evangelization, Research Paper, 1978, p. 2.

9 Ibid. p. 4.

10 Ibid.

11 Ibid. p. 3.

Ancient Nubia and the legendary Nile come together in modern Sudan. The history of this land is bound up with that of Egypt. The converted eunuch, spoken of in Acts 8, might have been the one who brought the Christian faith to this area in the first century. By the end of the sixth century northern Sudan had become largely Christian. Then followed a millennium of gradually increasing Islamic influence. By the 1600s the Arab north had become fully Islamicized.

Although Arabic is the official language, English is widely spoken. Fifty-six distinct ethnic groups and 600 sub-groups speak 132 languages, of which thirty-two are spoken by 50,000 people or more. The main diversity occurs in the Black African South. One third of Sudanese, speaking Arabic, control the country's destiny from their power base in the Arab North. Besides Arabs, other major groups include the Beja, Dinka, Fung, Nubians, Nuba and Nuer.

Arab and Black Muslims, who comprise 65 percent of the population, try to impose a brand of Islam strongly influenced by Sufism on any remaining non-Islamic peoples. Eleven percent of the population still adhere to African traditional religions, while 23 percent profess to be Christian.

Hostilities between the Muslim government in the north, who tried to impose Islam on the nominally Christian groups in the south, ravaged the southern portion of the country for at least two decades. Since 1983 there have been over two million deaths from war, genocide and famine. Beside these casualties, over two million displaced southerners fleeing strife and starvation tried to eke out a precarious existence in camps around Khartoum, a city of ten million straddling the Nile. With a peace agreement in place, an uneasy truce exists between north and south.

At that point, hostilities broke out in Darfur on the west side of the country. Untold numbers of subsistence farmers, Muslim in orientation—but black—were forced to flee bands of Arab marauders. Relief agencies created huge camps across the border in Chad. In spite of worldwide outrage, no solution has been found at the time of writing. In 2001 this troubled land was classified as number five on the world persecution index.

What of the church? Early devotion to Christ disappeared after the Muslim onslaught during the Middle Ages. Roman Catholic missionaries, beginning work in 1842, were able to establish a church which now makes up almost 6 percent of the population. Since 1916, the evangelical Anglican presence has enabled the Church Missionary Society to establish the second-largest church in the Sudan. SIM work, begun in 1937 among the Mabaan, spread to several other tribes, resulting in the establishment of thirty-eight SIM-related churches. By 1988 all but two of these congregations, known collectively as the

Sudan Interior Church (SIC), had been closed as southerners were forced to flee the rape and pillage of their villages. And yet new churches among displaced southerners in the northern camps continued to rise from the ashes during the civil war.

Even in the terrible days of famine and dispersion that characterized the last decade of the twentieth century, Uduk Christians exemplified the love of Christ by helping to relieve suffering and working with international relief agencies. They sowed the gospel seed from camp to camp. During the height of their misery, seven churches worshiped God regularly without any buildings, simply meeting in squares they marked off in the dust.

The history of the Sudanese church is one of triumph in persecution. Paul Rasha Angwo, a Uduk tribesman, chose to endure the scorn of his people and follow Christ. As a new Christian he braved censure to rescue the first twins who ever lived in his tribe. Sensing the call of God, he gave up his farm in order to translate the Scriptures into his mother tongue. Rasha Angwo developed into a Sudanese Paul; through his fearless leadership churches were established both in Uduk country and among other tribesmen as well.

In one of the cruelest strokes of all, many pastors were forcibly separated for years from their wives and children. Pastor Paul's wife, Hannah, and three of their children lived for five years in the northern Nodeng camp without ever being allowed to see him. In spite of these hardships, Hannah carried on her ministries among women and children in the camp, where her beautiful smile inspired many. Then she died.

Meanwhile, in a distant city, her husband Paul suffered his last days in a hospital. True to his calling, his concern even on his death-bed was to arrange for the appointment of an evangelist needed to help establish a new church in an unreached tribe. Now he is reunited with Hannah in the presence of the Lord he loved so well. In the absence of Hannah and Paul, others have taken up the torch of evangelism.[1]

Note

1 Supplemented from material provided in early 1992 by Becky Welling and Betty Cridland.

Part 7

Missionary strategy

Chapter 22

Choosing a mission field: the importance of strategy

With billions living and dying without exposure to the gospel, the vastness of the unfinished task strains our faith! Wherever we turn we face opportunities for evangelism. It hardly seems the time to be discriminating about whom we seek to win to the Master.

Strategic thinking, however, calls for the setting of priorities. Actually, the greater the task and the more limited our resources, the more important it is that we embrace careful planning. And before we can outline a plan we need to answer a range of important questions: Do we focus on the immediate needs for famine relief? Do we seek the re-evangelism of our own cities? Do we target those in our prisons or wandering our streets, or the elite of society or youth? Do we concentrate on training nationals or pioneer church planting? Should we focus on mass evangelism by radio, TV and the Internet or on one-on-one witness?

Globally, a lamentable failure to strategize has left us with what some call "the 10/40 window." Luis Bush writes that "most of the unreached people groups 'live in a belt that extends from West Africa across Asia, between ten degrees north to forty degrees north of the equator. This includes the Muslim block, the Hindu block and the Buddhist block.'"[1] Two-thirds of the people in the world reside in sixty-two different countries in this window. The most resistant peoples can be found here. While missionary efforts in this block have left their mark, greater success in other areas has tended to beckon many candidates to countries beyond this unreached belt.

In an article entitled "Missionaries Need to Battle Disturbing Bulge" Mark Orr reflects on the shocking findings of David Barrett, a well-known mission researcher who set out to discover where missionaries worked. He remembers overhearing conversations between his parents and friends when he was a ten-year-old missionary kid. They discussed

> the large numbers of missionaries living in a big Brazilian city ... It didn't seem right then—and it still doesn't. In our "global village" world there are 285,000 active cross-cultural Christian missionaries ... Amazingly, about 91 percent of the missionaries work with and around Christians; about eight percent work with evangelized non-Christians and one percent, or just under 3,000 missionaries, work with the unevangelized. Like those missionaries in Brazil years ago, today's missionary force is huddled together.[2]

Something is seriously out of balance!

In order to develop a set of priorities, in the following chapters we'll consider how the apostles chose their evangelistic audiences. Temple devotees, a beggar at the gate, despised Samaritans, Jews and Romans, Greek philosophers and slaves—first-century missionaries touched a diverse audience. Was their choice consciously planned or were they swept along by providence? How did they deal with such diversity? Specifically, we'll ponder whether to concentrate missionary efforts among: (1) resistant people; (2) responsive people; or (3) in building up national churches.

Audience: resistant, responding or redeemed?

Christ commanded the apostolic band to "Go into all the world and preach the good news to all creation" (Mark 16:15). The scope of the words "world" and "creation" underscores the universality of the evangelistic task. Every person in every place is to hear the good news.

The mandate, however, particularized the task in terms of "all nations, beginning at Jerusalem," "and in all Judea and Samaria, and to the ends of the earth" (Luke 24:47; Acts 1:8). Obviously the whole world could not be reached in the first day. Proclamation of the gospel was to proceed from a crucial location, Jerusalem, outward to increasingly less Jewish audiences.

The book of Acts tells how the apostolic bands reaped an abundant harvest of souls. Their success can be traced, in part at least, to the indwelling power of the Holy Spirit and their simple submission to him. It can also be traced to the distinctive ways God prepared the New Testament world for the harvest to come. The apostolic missionary bands labored during a harvest epoch. Four reasons may be advanced to buttress this claim.

Firstly, Acts describes preaching "in the fullness of time" (Gal. 4:4, NKJV). The covenant with Abraham came to fruition at this time. In conscious awareness of this Jewish connection, the apostles went preaching the "good news" and "What God promised our fathers" (Acts 13:32) at a time when Jews had a highly developed Messianic expectation. Centuries of sowing prepared the way for their success. We must not despise the apparently fruitless ministries of prophets like Jeremiah. (Would he be characterized as a "search theologian" today?[3])

Secondly, the preparatory ministries of John the Baptist and Christ made this epoch unique. Angelic beings heralded Christ's coming. Miracles followed him. And yet, in spite of his breathtaking life, teachings, death and resurrection, he won few genuine disciples during his sojourn among us. He did prepare the way, however, for a bountiful harvest.

Thirdly, the establishment of Jewish synagogues throughout the Mediterranean world prepared the way for apostolic missions. At the Council of Jerusalem James could say, "For Moses has been preached in every city from the earliest times and is read in the synagogues on every Sabbath" (Acts 15:21).

Almost every city of the Roman Empire had its synagogue. Each synagogue had its contingent of faithful Jews plus clusters of Gentile proselytes and God-fearers. Upon arrival in a new town, the apostles invariably went first to minister in the local synagogue (see Acts 9:20; 14:1; 17:1–2, 10, 17, etc.). In each location, these missionaries reaped a ready harvest in spite of arousing persecution (see Acts 13:43; 14:1–2; 17:4, 12).

The predominant task of the apostles, as described in the book of Acts, was preaching and reaping. Where the presence of Jewish ideas had not prepared the way, they reaped a proportionately smaller harvest. We see a progression in the numbers of those converted: 3,000 at Pentecost, the number of men soon growing to 5,000 (4:4), increasing until we read, "The number of disciples in Jerusalem increased rapidly, and a *large number* of priests ..." and "a great number" of Jews and Gentiles in Iconium and Thessalonica were converted through their ministry in synagogues (6:7; 14:1; 17:4). Then there is a gradual change: instead of numbers being mentioned it is said, "the *churches* ... grew daily" (16:5), *many* Jews believed and "a *number*" of Greeks in Berea (17:12). In Athens "*A few* men became followers ... and believed" (17:34). These Athenians all appear to have been Greeks. Where there was less preparation, there was less response.

Lastly, the whole cultural and political context of that era served to prepare the way for a great missionary movement. The preparation afforded by the Greek culture and language and the Pax Romana has been so well documented elsewhere that it needs no further elaboration.

We conclude that two millennia of divine preparation preceded this harvest epoch. The Jewish people themselves were the most prepared and thus the most receptive. From their communities there spread a widening but weakening ripple of preparation. Since this groundwork was divinely inspired, the early missionaries' strategy was not self-consciously adopted but rather the result of divine leading to minister where the harvest was ripe. I call this *providential evangelism*.

We can conclude that preparation, sometimes very lengthy preparation, is generally necessary before a harvest of souls. Preparation can be equated with sowing. Wherever Jewish influence extended, the apostles were harvesters, reaping where they had not sown. As Jesus expressed it, "the saying 'One sows and another reaps' is true. I sent you to reap what you have not worked for. Others have done the hard work, and you have reaped the benefits of their labor" (John 4:37–38).

Moses and all the prophets had sown the seed that the apostles were commissioned to reap. We must not give in to a "success" or "harvest" mentality—often present in modern evangelism and missions—that would minimize the importance of sowing. To do so would be to minimize the ministry of men such as Jeremiah, the Lord himself and many missionaries now working among presently "unresponsive" groups.

Even the first-century missionaries readily gave themselves to sowing gospel seed where there had not been the preparation of Judaism to ripen the harvest. Paul described it as his ambition to be a sower in virgin territory: "It has always been my ambition to preach the gospel where Christ was not known" (Rom. 15:20). Paul was preeminently the apostle to the Gentiles. He was wonderfully successful in the long run, but he did not immediately harvest as great a number among Gentiles as among Jews. He faced great difficulties and discouragements in his ministry. And yet he did not lose heart because his strategy came from God (see 2 Cor. 4:1).

Even though he ministered in an astounding harvest era, Paul moved to areas such as Lystra and Athens where the results were much more meager. This example, plus the thrust of the whole Old Testament, the universality of the Great Commission, together with the established need for there to be preparation preliminary to harvest—all lead to the inescapable conclusion that sowing, as well as reaping, must have priority in missionary strategy. And yet the neglect of the Muslim world and other hard areas demonstrates that this is not happening.

Prospective missionary candidates are often urged to "Go where the action is." Such an appeal resonates with our natural instincts, brought up as we are to be familiar with marketing strategy. Why knock your head against a brick wall ministering where it is hard and few people are converted, when accepted missionary theory allows you to go where there are results?

Many places in the world today could be compared with Israel's shattered kingdom during the Babylonian captivity—a time in Jewish history that prepared the way for the great Messianic harvest epoch. Isaiah and Daniel, among others, ministered with little immediate effect. The question is not just "Where is the action?" but "Where is God preparing the way for future action?" Surely failure to take this into account is responsible for the disproportionate number of missionaries serving where there are already established churches.

Consider an example. Bruce Bell had a fruitful ministry in Latin America. Then he shared with some of his Latin friends the needs of the Arab world, where he planned to begin work. When asked whether mission-minded people shared his conviction about the needs of the Muslim world, he replied,

> One "expert" told me we should pull out what missionaries we have in the Arab world and put them where the harvest is ... I say, however, that this harvest is taking place

> only because some daring souls sowed the seed in days gone by when things were a lot tougher and when it took a lot of courage and when results were not being seen ... We've got to start sowing the seed if there is ever going to be a harvest ...[4]

How right he is! Sowing the precious Word is just as honorable in God's sight as reaping a harvest of souls.

This leads to several other questions. Does reaping only involve men and women coming to faith in Christ through the proclamation of the message? Or is the edification of converts also part of the missionary's job description?

We cannot deny that missions in the early church included the intensive training of believers: "... strengthening the disciples and encouraging them to remain true to the faith. 'We must go through many hardships to enter the kingdom of God,' they said. Paul and Barnabas appointed elders for them in each church and, with prayer and fasting, committed them to the Lord, in whom they had put their trust" (Acts 14:22–23). "I have not hesitated to preach anything that would be helpful to you but have taught you publicly and from house to house ... the whole will of God ... Remember that for three years I never stopped warning each of you night and day with tears" (Acts 20:20, 27, 31).

The apostolic evangelists spent varying amounts of time in different churches: in Ephesus, Philippi and Antioch, for example. But whether their time was short or lengthy, they were very thorough in the way they followed up converts. They visited them regularly, organized them into functioning churches and wrote follow-up letters. They appointed men such as Timothy and Titus to ensure that believers were carefully shepherded.

The New Testament shows absolutely no trace of the extreme compartmentalization of functions common in our day. There is little or no biblical precedent for some men restricting their ministry exclusively to "bringing men to decision" while leaving their edification to others. New Testament evangelists were committed to the follow-up of converts. The mandate was to make *disciples*. If they were with us today, the apostles would no doubt be horrified by how modern evangelism has been divorced from church planting and edification.

Unfortunately, another extreme has flourished. The importance of discipling converts has become an excuse to justify missionaries staying forever in close proximity to the very churches they have established. With few exceptions, the apostles itinerated; they did not reside forever in the midst of the churches they established.

The original question was, "Where should an evangelist or missionary minister?" In summary, I would propose the following principles:

- The whole world needs the ministry of the gospel.
- Urgency in choosing where to minister may be given to areas where there has been providential preparation—where the harvest is ripe.
- Sowing is part of the God-appointed preparation that must be considered if there is to be a harvest in the future. Hard places today need to be prepared for harvest tomorrow.
- New converts must have priority. Evangelists are responsible to disciple converts and settle them in a church fellowship. One person may be a sower and not a reaper, but a person *cannot*, in a biblical sense, be a reaper-evangelist without making provision for converts to become part of vibrant churches.
- When strong evangelists or missionaries remain too long in the same church, or in the close proximity of converts, they tend to stunt the development of other believers.

In conclusion, let me make a couple of personal observations. The widespread missionary neglect of Asia in general and the Muslim world in particular is nothing short of criminal. Besides the 10/40 window, there are other places that have been neglected due to their resistance to the gospel: parts of Europe, our cities, our aboriginal peoples and so on. We need to be constantly on the search for unreached peoples.

Then, too, biblical missionary imperatives call for the thorough follow-up of converts. Since we in the West live in a day blighted by a superficial knowledge of Christian things, a case could be made for ministries committed to dispelling biblical ignorance. Vast segments of Western societies are functionally pagan or nominal.

Evangelistic and missionary organizations should minister among: (1) the unresponsive who need a sowing ministry; (2) the responding who need harvesting; and (3) the redeemed who need edification.

Notes

1 **Luis Bush,** "Getting to the Core of the Core: The 10/40 Window," Partners International, Brampton, Canada, private circulation, c.1990.

2 **Mark Orr,** "Missionaries Need to Battle Disturbing Bulge," *Christian Week*, Dec. 1999, p. 6.

3 "Search theology" is a somewhat derisive term used by some Church Growth proponents to describe those who labor for years among resistant peoples with little or no visible fruit. It is used to highlight the need, in their view, to go where the harvest is white—to minister among responsive peoples.

4 **Bruce Bell** (an interview), "Where the Action Isn't," *Christianity Today*, Oct. 7 1977, p. 23.

Chapter 23

Missions: planned or providential?

God is a God of order and planning. Since he expects us to mirror his character, careful planning and organization should be a part of biblical missions. And yet, apostolic missionaries seemed to be more reactive than creative—they reacted to circumstances more than they created their own strategy. Why?

We've already mentioned the millennia of preparation that preceded the outreach of the apostles. This preparation was part of God's strategy long before the apostles were born. The nation of Israel, the spread of synagogues, the preaching of the prophets and the spread of Greek culture and Roman political power—all contributed to "the fullness of time" (Gal. 4:4, NKJV) in which Jesus was born. These factors constitute different facets of God's sovereignly orchestrated preparation of the Mediterranean world for a great harvest epoch. Jesus was born. He preached. He taught disciples. He died, rose from the dead, and commissioned believers to go and harvest a great ingathering that had been sown by others. In reality they didn't choose a field of service; God chose it for them.

Acts 1:8 exemplifies God's basic strategy: that apostolic bands should fan out from Jerusalem to the ends of the earth, one province at a time. When the early missionaries were either slow to adopt his plan or sought to follow their own devices, God redirected them back into the center of his purposes. He often did this through circumstances he ordained: "... a great persecution broke out against the church at Jerusalem ... Those who had been scattered preached the word wherever they went. Philip went down to a city in Samaria and proclaimed the Christ there" (Acts 8:1, 4–5). Clearly, God overruled the negative impact of persecution to positively extend his kingdom and get his disciples out of Jerusalem into Samaria and beyond.

Consider several other examples. God interrupted Philip's Samaritan ministry to command him to go to the Ethiopian (8:26–39). Persecution led scattered believers to bridge an even greater cultural chasm than that between the Jews and the Samaritans. "Now those who had been scattered by the persecution in connection with Stephen traveled as far as Phoenicia, Cyprus and Antioch, telling the message only to Jews. Some of them, however, men from Cyprus and Cyrene, went to Antioch and began to speak to Greeks also, telling them the good news about the Lord Jesus" (11:19–20).

Christ directly intervened in the life of Saul to call him to the Gentiles. Later, he again intervened in the form of a dream to direct Paul to Macedonia. Time and time again, persecution in one city forced Paul and his band to go to another city. Persecution, however, was but one of the factors used by God to direct his missionary bands.

Providentially prepared political, cultural and geographic factors were also recognized by the apostles as an indication of where they should minister. They were influenced by Roman roads, Roman citizenship and the Greek language. The natural concentration of people in cities served as a magnet to keep them from focusing on scattered peoples in the great deserts of Arabia and Africa. Rome, as the capital of the empire of that day, greatly affected the direction of missionary advance. The movement of evangelists in the opposite direction, toward Persia and India, is not documented for us in anything but tradition. These journeys appear to have occurred later.

Since these "natural" factors occur in a world over which God exercises sovereign control they must necessarily be an integral part of his strategy. For this reason, missionaries committed to following the King will search for evidence of providential activity in the world and make that an important part of their missionary planning.

Providentially arranged circumstances, however, do not fully account for apostolic strategy. Divine intervention also occurred. God interrupted the ongoing programs of his servants in extraordinary ways. It took revelational dynamite to jar Peter from the mono-ethnic approach that prevailed in the early church, to get him to risk Jewish censure by going to the home of a Roman (see Acts 10).

Samaritan, Roman and Ephesian Pentecosts were necessary demonstrations of God's purpose to bless all the families of the earth. (It is a mistake to claim that these remarkable "Pentecosts" define normative

Christian experience. They were extraordinary events made necessary by Jewish cultural pride and isolation. Without them they might never have accepted Gentile Christians as genuine disciples.)

Paul's Damascus Road conversion is another example of how God unfolded his strategy in extraordinary ways. God told Ananias, "This man is my chosen instrument to carry my name before the Gentiles and their kings and before the people of Israel" (Acts 9:15). Later, the Holy Spirit supernaturally revealed to the church in Antioch that Paul and Barnabas were to be specifically set aside for Gentile ministry. Paul's natural inclination to plan campaigns in Asia and Spain was at least temporarily derailed by God: "... having been kept by the Holy Spirit from preaching the word in the province of Asia ... they tried to enter Bithynia, but the Spirit of Jesus would not allow them to" (16:6–7). It was at this time that a specific vision came which changed their plans.

Paul's lengthy stay in Corinth was due to a vision (18:9–10). His plan to go to Spain (Rom. 15:24, 28) was probably aborted by his imprisonment in Rome. The apostolic pattern of evangelism owes more to extraordinary divine direction than to conscious apostolic planning.

Should we, then, de-emphasize strategic planning and just trust God? Trust is certainly crucial. Without the guidance of the Holy Spirit we will be spinning our wheels. Without the regenerating power of the Holy Spirit no one will be converted, no matter how persuasive an evangelist might be.

However, this cannot be the whole answer. How can we ignore the need to plan when we are created in God's image and God is the ultimate planner? History isn't an accident, but the outworking of God's divine plan. Salvation isn't a rescue operation hastily put together by a divine committee, but a carefully designed plan that took thousands of years to come to fruition in the person of Jesus Christ.

If we need more encouragement to strategize, we need but turn to the book of Proverbs, where the folly of failing to plan is repeatedly taught. Clearly, maintaining a balance between prayerful waiting on God's direction and thoughtful planning will always be a challenge. Discovering where we should minister must be approached with the same delicate balance that we see in apostolic practice.

Balance involves a clear view of the providential factors that may have been at work for some time, plus a sensitivity to the immediate direction of Almighty God. To provide the former, we should research what is happening among the peoples of the world. This will require a study of population movements, the rise of cities, shifts in technology as well as a host of cultural, political and religious factors. Such observations will help us determine the direction we should go in. History records the close relationship between events and trends in the first century and missionary success.

God equipped the apostles with the background necessary to respond to the people to whom they were sent. The Galilean apostles, steeped as they were in Judaism, were prepared for their ministry among Jews. Paul, as a missionary sent primarily to the Gentiles, was equipped with an extensive background in Greek culture and language.

Since God is sovereign, we can be sure that there are tribes and segments of population already prepared for the gospel. There are other groups, such as the Muslim peoples of the world, that God would have us help prepare for future harvest. Indeed, the rise of terrorism and extreme Islam is already creating a climate of revulsion toward their own faith among many Muslims. Some credit the astounding growth of the Iranian church, now some 1 million strong, to this revulsion. In China, persecution has led to explosive church growth. A study of providential factors in the world around us—cultural, political, educational, economic, technological—must become part of the preparation required of missionaries choosing a field of service.

We should be prepared, however, to respond personally to the Divine Strategist. He may direct us where our common sense would tell us not to go. He may direct us to play down one popular medium or to utilize another. He may redirect us to a hard place or move us into an area where the harvest is ripe.

God directed Philip to go to the Ethiopian, Peter to the Roman and Paul to cross over to Macedonia. No one consciously planned the Protestant Reformation or the Evangelical Awakening, the movement of outcasts in India, the growth of the Ethiopian church during World War II or even the harvest in South Korea. A myriad of similar examples could be listed. It is out of the context of a balanced and God-centered life that missionary planning evolves.

Guidance is so susceptible to individual interpretation and distortion that a word from Proverbs would not be amiss here: "For lack of guidance a nation falls, but many advisers make victory [safety] sure" (Prov. 11:14). These advisers must be godly.

I am not arguing that we devalue the advice of anthropologists, linguists and missiologists; far from it—we need to approach the missionary task from many directions. Counsel that is many-sided, and yet rooted in the experience of men who walk with God, is the most important of all.

The image of the Body of Christ provides us with a model of healthy interaction. We need the variety of gifts, training and insights of others! Why, then, do we have such a plethora of movements founded and energized by the vision of single individuals? We must realize that strategy, while it is often inspired by the vision of one man, runs amuck if it remains isolated from "many advisers." Wise visionaries gather around them a team of men and women who can not only put feet to their vision but also put on the brakes when necessary. Mission fields are littered with the wreckage left by individualists who were not team players. Balance requires corporate reflection on the vision of individuals.

In summary, missions and evangelism involve planning and research. That research should involve a careful study of providential factors—evidences of God at work in his world—supplemented by earnest prayer.

Birds of a feather: bane or blessing?

Our studies of apostolic strategy have led us to recognize the validity of ministries to resistant, responding and redeemed audiences. We have also noted that apostolic evangelism owes more, in its choice of an audience, to its sensitivity to divine providence than to strategic planning. In this chapter we come face to face with another element of strategy: the targeting of homogeneous groups of people.

The Homogeneous Unit (HU) principle was formulated largely by Dr. Donald A. McGavran of the School of World Missions at Fuller Theological Seminary in California. It is a modern missionary formulation of the observed phenomenon that like attracts like.

Parents of pre-schoolers naturally gravitate to those in a similar situation. Fishermen love to get together to share fish stories. Nurses talk with other nurses about medical concerns.

We ought not to be surprised, then, that believers often gather with those who most resemble them in faith and practice. As a consequence we have, for example, Dutch churches and Chinese churches. Even among English-speaking Christians, some churches attract professionals while others draw blue-collar workers.

This phenomenon has led thinkers like McGavran to promote the HU principle. They assert that establishing churches that reflect the characteristics of homogeneous units of people enhances church growth. Church Growth proponents theorize that churches grow best when their members share common interests and backgrounds. In its extreme form, the HU principle would seem to sanction separate churches for the young, for athletes, for seniors, for bankers—the list is endless.

Art Glasser explains the HU principle as follows:

Dr. McGavran is continuously on the lookout for the separate characteristics of each section of society, whether ethnic, linguistic, political, geographic, economic, social. Why so? Because the church never grows among mankind in general; it always grows in a homogeneous unity and according to the specific pattern of that homogeneous unit.

Nothing is more important than identifying the homogeneous unity (or units) that make up a specific congregation. If a congregation is conglomerate, the probability is that it is growing slowly. The more each homogeneous unit congregation is encouraged to maintain its own distinctives, the more attractive it will be to members of that homogeneous unit yet to be converted. An important principle of church growth is that "discipling" each homogeneous unit out to the fringes is more desirable as a rule than establishing conglomerate congregations in many continuous HUs. Dr. McGavran sees the picture: "When each unit has a cluster of vigorous congregations in its midst made up exclusively of its own folk, then becoming a Christian involves neither denying one's own HU, nor traitorously joining a strange people. The decision to become a disciple of Christ is then solely a religious decision."[1]

How should we react to the HU principle? Let me present some pros and cons.

In Acts 1:8, a verse we have referred to frequently, Christ gave the apostles an overview of his evangelistic strategy. He commanded them to preach the gospel "in Jerusalem, and in all Judea and Samaria, and to the ends of the earth." Jesus mentions specific peoples, HUs, in strategic order: first Jerusalem—a city; then Judea—the surrounding province; then Samaria—an adjoining but ethnically diverse people. The mention of Judea and Samaria as distinct targets in this formula gives some validity to the claim that we must carefully focus our evangelism on HUs.

As the early evangelists fanned out through the Mediterranean world, they made a point of first contacting the homogeneous Jewish groups gathered at the synagogues of the dispersion. Jewish audiences had been extensively prepared by God to give the gospel a hearing. Then, too, the apostles were themselves Jewish, and they spoke the Jewish language.

Language alone renders targeting a homogeneous unit, such as the Jewish people, a valid strategy. People must hear the gospel and go on to worship God in a language they can understand. The New Testament mention of Greeks and Hebrews as distinct linguistic groups would seem to validate their treatment as HUs.

The HU principle recognizes cultural realities and human tendencies. People tend to prefer those similar to themselves. Deep-rooted prejudices condition people against accepting representatives of those they despise. Tribal rivalries boil beneath the surface in many countries. In evangelism one would be unwise, for example, to commission a Christian from an outcast background to evangelize high-caste Hindus.

Its prevalence in human society, however, does not mean that the HU principle should be perpetuated in the family of God. The Scriptures cannot be twisted to show that the apostles established mono-ethnic churches. The HU principle has value as an evangelistic starting point, but to promote it as a principle of normal church life would be disastrous. Let me give several reasons for my rejection of the HU principle in any situation other than that which occurs in new churches.

Firstly, the HU principle does not sufficiently recognize the heterogeneous nature of most societies, including the Jewish culture. Jewish society was broken up into a bewildering array of diverse and sometimes hostile groups: fishermen, merchants, artisans, farmers, tax-collectors, city and village dwellers; Pharisees, Sadducees, scribes and Zealots; Palestinian and non-Palestinian Jews; ignorant and learned men; Hebrew and Hellenistic Jews; priests and laymen, and so on. In spite of this diversity, we find no evidence that the apostles sub-divided the Jewish church into separate worshiping HUs corresponding to the different segments of Jewish society.

Although most of the apostles were from a provincial Galilean HU, they did not found a Galilean church. Neither did they make provision for other HU churches. They had opportunity to do so: "In those days … the Grecian Jews among them complained against the Hebraic Jews because their widows were being overlooked in the daily distribution of food" (Acts 6:1). This dissension could have been readily avoided by dividing into two groups, one Hebrew and one Hellenist. Separate organizations could have cared for the needs of each. Instead the apostles went out of their way to handle the problem in such a way that unity would be promoted.

The text makes clear that Hellenistic Jewish converts worshiped with

Hebrew believers: "All the believers were one in heart and mind" (4:32) and "All the believers were together" (2:44). It would appear that the divisions that fractured Jewish society disappeared where Christian fellowship occurred.

Secondly, notice the composition of the churches established throughout the Roman world. In their travels, the apostolic bands first went to Jewish synagogues to preach the gospel. As a result of their preaching some Jews and some Gentile proselytes in these synagogues believed. But in spite of the fact that they won converts from at least three distinct cultural groups—Jews, Greeks and Romans—they only established one church in each center.

Writers from the Church Growth school of missionary strategy paint a different picture. They try to maintain that each center, for example Ephesus, had separate ethnic churches where different HUs would feel comfortable. There is, however, no evidence for this view. The New Testament appears to describe churches that were heterogeneous not homogeneous units.

The word "Gentile" does not represent one HU. It is an umbrella term used to encompass a very broad mixture of contrasting cultures. It included both the Greek and the Roman. Even among those who spoke the common Greek language a diversity of cultures and dialects was represented.

Consider, too, the chasm that separated slaves from their masters. If ever there was a legitimate ground for distinct HU churches, we have it here. But the New Testament contains no evidence to support the contention that the apostles established separate churches for slaves and for free men and women. The Epistles record the opposite: Philemon and Onesimus were members of the same church!

Thirdly, apostolic practice calls for the members of diverse cultures to modify their practices in the presence of one another. At first, many Jewish believers reacted antagonistically toward Gentile believers from Antioch. They demanded conformity to Jewish customs: "Some men came down from Judea to Antioch and were teaching the brothers: 'Unless you are circumcised, according to the custom taught by Moses, you cannot be saved'" (Acts 15:1).

Because of the error of such a demand, "This brought Paul and Barnabas into sharp dispute and debate with them" (15:2). The issue, as it surfaced in Antioch, compromised church teaching on salvation by grace. It spawned serious theological error which Paul took pains to remedy.

Circumcision was but the tip of the iceberg of Jewish cultural pride. As we note from the text that follows in Acts 15, these Judaizers expected Gentile believers to adhere to Jewish cultural practices. The church in Antioch decided to take the matter before the mother church in Jerusalem (Acts 15).

At Jerusalem, leaders convened a council to settle the problem. In the council Peter demanded to know why Judaizers wanted to burden Gentile believers with religious duties when their own Judaistic religion had been "a yoke that neither we nor our fathers have been able to bear?" (15:10). After much debate, the Jerusalem Council decided that Jewish duties should not be imposed on Gentile believers.

Actually, believers from both cultures came to understand the need to accommodate themselves to each other to minimize friction. The Gentiles were specifically requested to refrain from blood and from things strangled (15:20) in order to avoid offending Jewish believers. Jewish believers, in turn, were to wholeheartedly accept the genuine nature of Gentile faith in Christ.

Paul clearly understood the principle of cultural accommodation. In Antioch, Jerusalem and in his letter to the Galatians Paul fought relentlessly against requiring circumcision. But when accommodation would not compromise grace he had no qualms about having Timothy circumcised (16:3). In this case, accommodation to Jewish cultural practice rendered Timothy's ministry more acceptable.

When believers from two cultures come together in the church, God expects both sides to change in order for them to draw closer to each other. Far from maintaining cultural distinctives through worshiping in distinct HUs, the Master expects believers to moderate their cultural practices to reduce friction and enhance unity. While the world at large spawns prejudice and ethnic tension, Christians must shed offensive practices that drive them apart. (This does not negate the fact that language differences necessitate some separation in worship.)

Fourthly, contrary to Church Growth policy, the apostles did not evangelize homogeneous units of society out to the fringes before they moved on to new groups. Apostolic witness kept spilling over from one HU to another. Philip broke out of his Jewish isolation to evangelize Samaritans and an Ethiopian. Through the vision of the sheet, Peter received instruction on scaling the wall that separated his countrymen from the hated Roman occupiers. Jewish converts from Cyprus and Cyrene, part of the Hebrew dispersion, came to Antioch and broke tradition by speaking to Greeks.

Church Growth theorists would tell us that one HU should be thoroughly evangelized before a new group is tackled. This did not happen with the Jews. The gospel spread to the Gentiles while the Jewish church was still in its infancy.

To be fair to McGavran, he does recognize the importance of what he calls "cross-cultural bridges" across which the gospel leaps from one culture to another. Church Growth theorists would urge us to not only define HUs but also search for bridges.

Finally, there is the matter of walls. The Berlin Wall has fallen! The Iron Curtain has crumbled into the dust of history! How much more must every cultural barrier fall under the assault of the gospel! God specifically designed the gospel to be the dynamite he uses to break down the walls of prejudice and cultural isolation that divide us!

At this point we come face to face with theology. The HU principle seems to minimize one of the very purposes of redemption. Concerning Jews and Gentiles, Paul stated, "For he himself is our peace, who has made the two one and has destroyed the barrier, the dividing wall of hostility." He went on to write, "His purpose was to create in himself one new man out of the two ... in this one body to reconcile both of them to God ... you too are being built together to become a dwelling in which God lives by his Spirit" (Eph. 2:14–16, 22). Paul declared, "There is neither Jew nor Greek, slave nor free, male nor female, for you are all one in Christ Jesus" (Gal. 3:28). Redemption reconciles us not only to God, but also to one another!

When we conform to the Word, our faith inevitably moves us closer to one another. The Holy Spirit breathing through the gospel unleashes a force that shatters prejudice and minimizes differences. We become brothers and sisters, instead of English and French, men and women, black and white.

Anything that encourages the continuation of prejudices and unbiblical divisions must be viewed as sub-Christian, whether it be hallowed as denominationalism, nationalism or culture. The HU principle can be twisted to justify isolation. Indeed, in past years proponents of South African apartheid buttressed their nefarious policies by reference to this theory.

Interestingly enough, when this principle came up in a mission class I taught, a South African Christian reacted with some outrage. He felt that catering to group instinct leads to superficial professions of faith and syncretism. He pointed out that industrialization, urbanization and education were having a profound effect upon South African society, causing rural communal life to disintegrate and creating, in effect, a new culture and lifestyle. "Even when the government divided the people according to their ethnic groups, they did not leave their churches. The churches were a unifying force." Although the Christians he met in Soweto, Pretoria or Durban came from many tribes, this student adamantly maintained that they enjoyed worship in heterogeneous churches.

Let us not misunderstand. We should encourage variety of expression in worship. Indeed, the perpetuation of separate denominational expressions of worship and organization is not evil as such.

Nevertheless, differences must be minimized if the beautiful mosaic of Christian unity is to shine forth from the dust and debris of human differences. While the HU principle may be valid as a missionary starting point, we must not allow it to become a pretext for maintaining the status quo. In the light of the five problems we have seen with the HU principle, heterogeneous is beautiful!

And yet, in spite of its problems, the HU principle does give us some helpful insights in how to more accurately target our communication to the needs of a particular audience. We can use it as a tool to increase our sensitivity to the cultural differences that render one group distinct from another. Without this sensitivity, we may present a cultural mélange that suits no one.

People groups

Hence we come to the crucial issue of *peoples* or *people groups*. The picture of kingdom success sketched for us in Revelation describes a time when "a great multitude that no one could count, from every nation, tribe, people and language, standing before the throne and in front of the Lamb" cry out in a loud voice of worship (Rev. 7:9). Ethnic, linguistic or cultural characteristics are identifiable. These characteristics will cause groups to stand out as distinct even around the throne of God.

It is helpful, then, to identify distinct people groups. Without doing so we may fail to understand the missionary task that remains. For example, if we look at the results of missionary endeavor in terms of the *nations* reached we may feel that the task is almost complete. And yet missiologists tell us that at least two billion people live culturally distant from any viable gospel church. Missionary strategists call these unreached people groups "hidden peoples" or "frontier peoples." In identifying these "hidden peoples," the HU concept is helpful.

Steve Hawthorne explains how the Lausanne Strategy Working Group sought to bring clarity to the remaining missionary task by defining people groups:

> A people group is "a significantly large grouping of individuals who perceive themselves to have a common affinity for one another because of shared language, religion, ethnicity, residence, occupation, class or caste, situation, etc., or combinations of these." For evangelistic purposes it is "the largest group within which the Gospel can spread as a church planting movement without encountering barriers of understanding or acceptance." An unreached people group is "a people group within which there is no indigenous community of believing Christians able to evangelize this people group."[2]

There are approximately 24,000 people groups in the world. Of these, 10,000 are unreached people groups that are "part of five large blocs of humanity: Muslim, Buddhist, Hindu, Chinese, and Tribal." Although many of these are tiny groups and do not live a huge distance away from already existing indigenous churches, they will not be reached without purposeful strategy. As already mentioned in an earlier chapter, the bad news is that only between 1 and 13 percent of the world's missionaries are devoting themselves to pioneer church planting. Most are serving already existing churches.[3]

Hawthorne points out, "The only reason to doubt that this generation will see a church for every people is the lack of resolve to finish the task and a blindness to see clearly the variety of peoples of the earth. We are better at distinguishing 20,000 different kinds of butterflies than we are in detecting human communities."[4]

In conclusion, identifying the specific characteristics of unreached people groups (HUs) is a crucial missionary task. Once a significant number of indigenous churches has been established in an unreached people group, however, maintaining a mono-ethnic church loses its merit. It may even be harmful to the spiritual vitality of the church.

In an article entitled "Should the Church Be a Melting Pot?" three men debated the HU issue. Ray Stedman stated,

> What you're calling a homogeneous principle is really a characteristic of the flesh. It's a reflection of the innate selfishness of human beings who want to be with our own people in our own group to feel comfortable ... People should grow in their ability to reach out across gaps and chasms to other people of different backgrounds and cultures, to show love and understanding.
>
> When you evangelize you almost always will do it on a homogeneous principle. But its purpose is to introduce new Christians to a larger group with a much more diverse background. When you look at the church you should see what the world is unable to create ... Disciples are those who have learned to love and live together despite differences. Diversity in unity is the great hallmark of the church as distinct from the world.[5]

At the end of the article, C. Peter Wagner of Fuller Seminary, representing the proponents of the HU principle, admitted, "The HU principle is a starting-point. If it's an ending-point it's sub-Christian."[6]

Some very illuminating letters came to the editor of *Christianity Today* after this article appeared. Here are a couple of excerpts:

C. Peter Wagner's "homogeneous unit principle" sounds to me like a subtle form of spiritual apartheid.[7]

Churches may grow better when everybody is alike, but since everybody is not alike we may have to sacrifice church growth for Christian growth, which in the long run may be the best way for church growth.[8]

We need discernment to choose what is helpful and discard what is harmful in this debate. We may, for example, enlist the HU principle to develop sensitivity to the needs of a particular people group. And, of course, differences in language must be freely acknowledged. Nevertheless, our goal should be a heterogeneous celebration of the diversity that is the Body of Christ.

Notes

1 **Arthur F. Glasser,** "An Introduction to the Church Growth Perspectives of Donald A. McGavran," in **Harvie M. Conn,** (ed.), *Theological Perspectives on Church Growth*, (Nutley, NJ: Presbyterian and Reformed, 1977), p. 70.
2 **Steve Hawthorne,** "Laying a Firm Foundation for Mission in the Next Millennium," *Mission Frontiers*, Special Issue, January 2000, p. 10.
3 Ibid. pp. 11–12.
4 Ibid. p. 12.
5 "Should the Church Be a Melting Pot?", *Christianity Today*, Aug. 18, 1978, p. 11–16.
6 Ibid.
7 **Steven J. Cole,** Letter to the Editor, *Christianity Today*, Oct. 6, 1978.
8 **Floyd J. Sanders,** Ibid.

Climbing the discipleship ladder in Pakistan: a grass-roots revolution

In Pakistan over 1,000 men and women are learning what discipleship means through an innovative country-wide program of in-depth Bible training. While in Pakistan several years ago, Mary Helen and I kept running into these eager disciples. Their real-life stories inject a dynamic new dimension into an equation overburdened by pathos and poverty. Let me give an example.

In a village twenty miles south of Lahore, a young man named Rashid loaded and unloaded trucks. He tried to supplement his meager income by selling toys off the handcart that he pushed up and down the dirt alleys of his village.

Although Rashid was nominally a Christian, he had never come to know Christ personally. He had never attended school. He could not write his own name. But a thirst for knowledge burned within. Sensing this, the local pastor helped him to make a start at reading Urdu, the major language of the country. Rashid learned quickly.

At the urging of a German missionary, he joined the local extension Bible class, where a young man was assigned to help him. However, when his helper discovered his lack of education and weakness in Urdu, he advised him to drop out.

Disheartened, he poured out his frustration to his German friend. Instead of commiserating, Wolf Munzinger replied, "You can do it! Here, sit down and I'll help you with this lesson." With Wolf's encouragement, Rashid began to progress by leaps and bounds. Since that time Rashid has completed thirteen Bible courses, taught three courses himself, and now even pastors three small congregations!

The vehicle Wolf Munzinger used to propel Rashid out of the grip of illiteracy and into a shepherding orbit was the Open Theological Seminary (OTS). Similar to the UK's Open University, OTS utilizes an extension model called TEE—Theological Education by Extension. Students continue with their occupations while they use special home-study courses to prepare for weekly seminars at extension centers.

The extension model of discipleship and ministry training came to Pakistan in 1972. Faltering experiments were mounted at Gujranwala Seminary, a residential Presbyterian school, and in the rural town of Rahim Yar Khan in Southern Punjab, where I ministered. In those days I worked frantically to write self-teaching courses and supervise their translation and publication before dashing off to teach waiting students.

Shortly thereafter, the Pakistan Committee for Theological Education by Extension (PACTEE) was formed to coordinate the development of TEE programs throughout the country. Soon Mary Helen and I moved to Lahore to supervise PACTEE. From the beginning we worked closely with Russ Irwin and Zafar Ismail from a small bungalow on the campus of a Christian college.

Climbing the discipleship ladder in Pakistan: a grass-roots revolution

Zafar and Russ illustrate the mix of international and Pakistani staff that have made the Open Theological Seminary such a success. Converted from Islam after dabbling with communism, Zafar injected the problem-solving ability of an engineer and the skill of an Urdu wordsmith into our struggles with the Urdu language. Russ commuted from a distant tribal area, where his wife served as doctor in a mission hospital. Russ's linguistic skills, combined with his optimism and patience, kept us moving ahead. Before Mary Helen and I returned to Canada, we saw PACTEE slowly expand nationwide.

Then, thirteen years later, we were reunited with this creative duo. Years out of touch dissipated like the early-morning mist as Russ and Zafar laughed about long-forgotten episodes and rejoiced in the current triumphs of the King.

We were seated around the same battered dining-room table where we used to collate and staple TEE courses! I could almost hear the protesting clank of our old mimeograph from the back verandah. They had already given us a tour of the offices. Instead of part-time helpers, a full-time staff now supervises the far-flung centers, keeping track of the progress of each of the 2,000 registered students. Advanced computers and copy machines speed the process. Instead of a handful of roughly bound courses, at least twenty-three attractively printed courses line the shelves.

"Eric, do you remember dashing for the train to Rahim with a bundle of TEE courses?" Zafar laughed. Did I ever—and how thankful I had been for Zafar's help! Russ reminded me of our futile attempts to translate courses ourselves before Zafar came to translate and advise.

"Zafar, what has happened to the students we taught in those early TEE classes in Lahore?" I asked.

"Almost all the students have a fellowship group meeting in their homes," he replied. "Irfan has gone on to head up a Pakistan-wide student movement. Shifait Ullah has planted a new church near the airport where he serves as part-time pastor. God has used Robert Otto in unusual ways.

"Robert, you will remember, served as an engineer in the agricultural department. He was in our first class and became our first TEE graduate. He went on to receive his Bachelor of Theology degree from Gujranwala Seminary. God has given him a burden for invisible Christians."

"Invisible Christians? What do you mean?" I interjected.

"Some authorities claim that up to 50 percent of the nominal Christian population has been neglected on the census. They are the poorest of the poor. Illiterate and disenfranchised, they drift from village to village in search of work. Many labor in the brick kilns that fringe our cities. They are overlooked by the traditional churches and missions. They trace their origins to the mass-movements in the early part of the century but today remain totally ignorant of Christ.

"Now retired, Robert has become a village missionary. He bounces over the dirt tracks on his motorcycle as he searches for these 'invisible' people. With his own funds he has constructed eight simple church buildings in outlying villages. Preaching, teaching, conducting literacy classes, Robert fights for the souls of these forgotten people.

"Wherever he has put up a simple building, a cluster of people have put up simple huts and put down roots. Instead of an endless cycle of migration after elusive work, they have found stability in their 'church.' Slowly, children are gaining access to education and parents are discovering the reality of Jesus Christ."

"An amazing story! Obviously, Robert Otto is unusual—but have the TEE courses made any great difference in the lives of students in general?" Mary Helen asked.

"Absolutely," Zafar replied. "It has been a blessing in so many ways. The family lives of our students have improved. As you know, women in our society suffer under a patriarchal system. The unity and intimacy God intended married couples to enjoy is rarely seen. Among our TEE students, however, we have seen a marked improvement in the love that husbands and wives show to each other.

"Not only that, but TEE students have learned how to substitute biblical discipline for a haphazard approach to child training. Their studies in the Scriptures have also given them a new sense of community. There are exceptions, of course. Generally, however, we find our students busy in ministry—not church politics. Indeed, many have heard the call of God and become full- or part-time shepherds.

"We've also seen a revolution in their attitude toward their Muslim neighbors. Love for their neighbors has overwhelmed the insecurity and resentment they normally feel. Evangelism grips them in a new way."

"Zafar, I know that many churches and missions use OTS expertise to run extension centers. The staff here supervise centers from Karachi to Islamabad. Tell us about some of the most encouraging centers."

"Well, of course, there is Rahim Yar Khan. Your SIM missionaries stood behind John Masih as he concentrated on discipling an ever-increasing circle of students. He trained many to help him as tutors for his expanding centers."

John had been one of the first students in the Rahim Yar Khan area. Like Amos of old, God called this diminutive farmer from following oxen to become a shepherd of souls. Early in his ministry he moved to the town of Khanpur, where he pastored a struggling church for twelve years. We opened one of the first TEE centers in his church. From the beginning, John excelled both as a student and as a man of God. I vividly recall him interrupting his studies on Ephesians to apply its teaching on forgiveness. He cycled over to an estranged family, where he asked forgiveness for a wrong he felt he had committed.

John took every extension course available before going on to Gujranwala Seminary. (At that time the Open Theological Seminary had prepared twenty-three courses.) After graduation he returned to head up TEST, the SIM TEE program, which he saw grow from fifty to one hundred students.

Not content with ministry in the Christian community, John has moved on to a new challenge. His God-given love for Muslims has led him into a "faith ministry" aimed at sharing Christ with those who follow Islam. God has given John and his family some amazing opportunities to discuss Christ with interested lawyers and doctors.

Today the Open Theological Seminary feeds solid biblical courses to over 1,000 active students studying in some sixty extension centers around Pakistan. Instead of the restrictive entrance requirements most traditional seminaries require, the OTS is open to all. As a result it helps even poorly educated students—like Rashid and John—blossom. Ten certificate-level courses lead struggling students gradually up the ladder to biblical competence. In turn, ten diploma-level courses increase the degree of difficulty until finally students face ten university-level courses.

OTS is an Asian success story. When well-known Bible teacher and writer Michael Green visited Lahore, he said, "I am profoundly impressed by the influence of the Open Theological Seminary and the quality and appropriateness of the training it supplies. It combines sound academic education in basic Christian theology with regular and practical local supervision on the ground."[1]

Notes

1 This capsule describes the progress of OTS through 1995. It continues to thrive and grow.

Part 8

Missionary work proper

Chapter 25

Missions: worship before work

In this final section we come to the actual work of missions—which we have alluded to throughout the book. Even here we find a multitude of choices. Missionary work is enormously diverse! Bazaar evangelism and radio ministry; evangelism using newspapers or through correspondence courses; prison ministry, health work, agricultural improvement—over the years, missionaries have tried almost every method imaginable in a laudable effort to become all things to all men, that by all means they might reach some.

If you're a pragmatist, you may react at this point, "Finally we have something to sink our teeth into—something we can *do*." Yet I'm not quite ready to counsel our plunge into the methodology of missions.

After all, life has its priorities. We have to put on our socks before we put on our shoes. Cultivation precedes planting. January comes before June. Spiritually speaking, the first commandment lays down our priority: "Love the Lord your God with all your heart and with all your soul and with all your mind" (Matt. 22:37).

Worship and prayer

In evangelism and missions, first priority must be given to worship and devotion, prayer and praise. Vertical communication with our heavenly Father precedes horizontal communication with people. Jesus responded to Satan's temptation with exactly this emphasis: "Worship the Lord your God, and serve him only" (Matt. 4:10). Worship comes before service.

God called Paul and Barnabas to missionary service during a time of worship: "While they [the leaders in the Antioch church] were worshiping the Lord and fasting, the Holy Spirit said, 'Set apart for me Barnabas and Saul for the work to which I have called them'" (Acts 13:2).

This incident was not isolated. Prayer and worship routinely preceded evangelism. Pentecost burst upon them when "they all joined together constantly in prayer" (Acts 1:14). Those converted at Pentecost quickly adopted this pattern. Believers "devoted themselves to the apostles' teaching and to the fellowship, to the breaking of bread and to prayer" (2:42). Warnings to stop witnessing about Christ, intended to silence them, moved them instead to lift up "their voices together in prayer to God" in order to request boldness to carry on (4:24).

They appointed deacons, not in a conscious attempt to organize, but to help the apostles maintain the priority of preaching and prayer: "Brothers, choose seven men from among you ... We will turn this responsibility over to them and will give our attention to prayer and the ministry of the word" (6:3–4). (Incidentally, their practice demonstrates that smooth organization should foster prayer. Disorganization often robs a group of time to pray.)

Prayer was involved when the gospel spread from the Hebrew to the Roman culture. The first step in this watershed in cross-cultural communication occurred after Peter received a vision while praying on a house top (10:9). Cornelius himself saw a vision of an angel who said, "Your prayers and gifts to the poor have come up as a memorial offering before God" (10:4). Obviously, the Lord of the evangelistic harvest communicates many of his major moves to his people when they are at prayer.

Priority given to vertical communication ensured that the apostles' horizontal communication with sinful men and women took place in the right context of reverential awe and joyful expectancy. No wonder "everyone was filled with awe" (2:43). Dr. Luke describes the increase of the church in Judea, Galilee and Samaria in these terms: "encouraged by the Holy Spirit, it grew in numbers, living in the fear of the Lord" (9:31).

While working on this chapter, I was reading a new book on the importance of discipleship and evangelism. Much that I read struck a responsive chord. Unfortunately, however, in common with so many other books, it viewed evangelism as the fundamental purpose for which the church exists. Evangelism and missions become ends in themselves.

The early disciples avoided this emphasis by focusing on God. They cultivated a deep devotion to the risen Christ. Instead of time spent in prayer leading to a decline in evangelistic fervor, we can trace an increase in zeal corresponding to their heightened sense of the presence of the living God. This lively impression of "God in the midst" overflowed as worship. It made witnessing more natural. They expressed the seriousness of their sense of dependence on and love for God by fasting (13:2–3; 14:23).

John Piper, in his writings, has done much to call us back to the centrality of worship. He writes,

> Missions is not the ultimate goal of the church. Worship is. Missions exists because worship doesn't. Worship is ultimate, not missions, because God is ultimate, not man. [Missions] is a temporary necessity. But worship abides forever. Worship, therefore is the fuel and goal in missions. It's the goal of missions because in missions we simply aim to bring the nations into the white-hot enjoyment of God's glory. The goal of missions is the gladness of the peoples in the greatness of God.
>
> Missionaries will never call out, "Let the nations be glad!", who cannot say from the heart, "I rejoice in the Lord … I will be glad and exult in thee, I will sing praise to thy name, O Most High" (Psalm 104:34; 9:2). Missions begins and ends in worship … When the flame of worship burns with the heat of God's true worth, the light of missions will shine to the most remote peoples on earth. And I long for that day to come.[1]

The early church teaches us that *worship must precede work, and prayer precede programs, if sterility, frustration and fruitlessness are not to result.* Of course, professing Christians all render lip service to this principle. We would not think of commencing our meetings without prayer. Too often, however, we offer little more than a token prayer. If we succumb to this temptation, we may fall into the trap of seeking to press the missionary battle without missionary weaponry.

Missions is spiritual warfare. Prayer and worship lead us to the forge where the divine smithy crafts our spiritual armor. We dare not engage the foe without putting on the helmet of salvation and the breastplate of righteousness and taking up the shield of faith. We dare not press the battle without the Spirit putting a keen edge on our sword.

Too often we shop in the world's mall for technological fireworks instead of retiring to the divine smithy. As a result we empower committees, develop programs and prepare hardware designed to evangelize the world. We seek to organize our way to evangelistic success. Eventually, we become weary and faint. Our faith becomes rusty, our breastplate tarnished, our sword dull and our helmet dented. We try to leap right into evangelism without going to Christ, the great Evangelist.

From the apostles we learn that missionary success cannot be attributed to a particular technique, since variety and flexibility were hallmarks of their ministries. We cannot even trace their success to their saintliness. Many besides the apostles before and since have been Christlike without their success. The secret of the harvest is the presence of God. Where the Lord is not at work, any amount of organization, or excellence of technique or intensity of effort, will not yield results.

Harold Cook studied movements to Christ among five groups widely scattered from one another, both geographically and historically: the Armenian church, the Celtic church of Ireland, the Hawaiian church, the Karen church of Burma and the Batak church of Sumatra. After searching for some common pattern he concluded,

- There is no one simple explanation for church growth.
- The application of sound principles does not itself explain church growth.
- Certain local circumstances helped to prepare for church growth.
- A dominant personality played a prominent role.

Cook went on to discuss factors totally beyond the control of human evangelistic ingenuity. He concludes, "It seems to me that all too often we leave him [the Holy Spirit] out of our discussions of church growth."[2]

Strategic missionary planning, if we would follow the apostolic pattern, must give first priority to seeking the mind of the Spirit. God alone knows where he has already prepared the soil for harvest. Conversely, he alone knows where we need to invest energy in preparing for a future harvest. Since successful missionary work depends on God's providence and power, strategizing ought to begin in the presence of the King.

Humility

Although the apostles had more cause for pride than others of their time or ours, they manifested an admirable humility. They refused to brag about being "eyewitnesses of his majesty" (2 Peter 1:16) and recipients of the power to perform miracles. Their Christo-centric faith kept them from the idolatry of self-promotion.

Peter rigorously denied that his own personal power or piety had any bearing on the healing of the lame man. Instead he directed the crowd's attention toward the God of their fathers who had raised up Jesus, through whose name this healing took place (Acts 3:12; 4:10). When Cornelius knelt in homage before him, Peter immediately raised him up with the words "Stand up. I am only a man myself" (10:26). When a pagan mob in Lystra mistook Barnabas and Paul for Zeus and Hermes and sought to sacrifice to them, they tore their robes and rushed out to restrain them (14:14). They might have been tempted to seize on this adulation as a way to enhance their ministry. Thankfully, humility prevailed.

In the early church era, church names did not advertise distinctives or personalities. There was no St. James's Church or St. Peter's. Distinctive names, such as First Christian Church of Antioch, do not appear. It was simply "the church in Antioch." They didn't label the first missionary organization "the Antioch Missionary Society." They abhorred cults of personality. Paul denounced attempts in Corinth to move in this direction (see 1 Cor. 1:10–17). They had learned that Christ must reign over all his servants and their ministries.

How easily ego intrudes on evangelism and missions! How much organizing and advertising betray a spirit of unhealthy competition only the Lord knows. Admittedly, church history has produced a jumble of confusing groups. In this jumble, naming an organization by its distinctives has merit. But too often, organizational labels hide subtle competition and group pride. We must ask the Lord to protect us from a desire for fame and the longing to be remembered by posterity. Lord, teach us humility!

Authority

Not only humility, but confidence and authority attend the ministries of those who give to praise and prayer their proper place. The apostles radiated a sense of authority because they carried over into their service the glow they had gleaned in God's presence. Words such as "declare," "prove," "refute," "exhort," "proclaim" and "preach" imply authority and confidence.

The manner in which they received their calling contributed to their authority. They were not the hirelings spoken of by Jesus (John 10:12). Jesus had called them, one by one, to follow him. Later he had sent them out as his heralds. The Holy Spirit, in turn, had gifted them for ministry. As a result, even their enemies were astonished at the boldness of this band of uneducated men. We will never experience what they experienced. But God still calls men and women to be his witnesses. Those who have never been divinely called cannot witness with divine authority.

Evangelism and missions flower in the soil of worship and prayer. When we become God-oriented in our devotional lives, we shall become God-directed in our ministries. Short-circuiting this divine order dooms us to trying to organize missions without unction. If we would follow the pattern of the apostles, we must learn to discover the general shape of our ministries in private and corporate prayer, in personal and congregational worship, and in devotional and theological study of the Word. Anything else is, practically speaking, baptized humanism. Humanism, a disease we fault in others, all too easily infects our practice. Humility and authority fall victim to egotism and manipulation. Let us flee such a consequence by retreating often to the place of prayer.

Prayer support

No wonder, then, that missionaries repeatedly seek to engage a team of people at home to uphold them in prayer. Although "please pray for us" is such a common request of missionaries that we scarcely take any notice of it any more, this trite phrase represents a genuine plea. As the following story recounted by Peter Ackley reminds us, happy is that missionary who not only learns to pray himself, but also has serious "prayer warriors" behind him:

HOW I DISCOVERED A PRAYER-PARTNER AT A FUNERAL!

As I stood by the grave of Roberta Marder, I was startled to have her husband turn to me and say, "Ever since you and Sadie left for Africa in 1949, Roberta and I have prayed for you every day." Speechless, I could only mumble words of appreciation as I mused about his words.

Sadie and I had never dreamed that the promise they made to us so many years ago would be literally fulfilled. We had just completed 43 years of service. The Marders' prayers had been with us all that time! I thought of the hot dusty years in Sudan—years in poor war-torn Liberia—Bible classes in Sierra Leone. My mind was boggled by the sudden realization of the strategic place, all unknown to us, they had played in our missionary service. To think that Roberta Marder's funeral occurred the very day we retired ... It was as if her passing was delayed until our years in Africa came to a close.

Sadie and I hadn't known them that well. When I was a young teen our family moved to Dallas, Texas. In Dallas my mother became quite involved in the Scofield Memorial Church where she and Roberta Marder became good friends. They taught Sunday School and led Women's Bible classes together.

In 1949 the Scofield Church commissioned Sadie and me for missionary ministry. That very day Ed and Roberta Marder vowed to pray for us every day. Ever since, Scofield Church had been one of our main supporters. Obviously, the Marders too, had fulfilled a crucial role in our missionary service.

Far from the spotlight, Ed and Roberta Marder lived lives of quiet faithfulness. They never visited Africa. Roberta was something of a home-body. They had not supported us financially through the years, indeed they were not able to support many missionaries. Writing letters too, was not their forte. But when Roberta sent us a birthday card, she assured us that they were praying for us and our children.

And pray they did, but behind the scenes. They prayed daily. They prayed for a host of missionaries.

Married 62 years, Ed and Roberta Marder were a quiet but loving couple who fulfilled a hidden role in missions. I wondered, "Do we tend to take people like the Marders for granted?"

As the graveside service concluded, my astonishment turned to concern. I realized that the church's prayer base is eroding. Old-time prayer warriors are dying off. Although the need for intercession surpasses anything that I have ever known, this kind of commitment is rare today.

As we turned to leave the graveside, I said, "Ed, you and your dear wife will one day meet a host of Sudanese pastors and believers. They will be there in heaven because of your prayers. Your intercession has watered the seed we sowed in the Sudan, in Liberia and in Sierra Leone."

As we drove home, I pled with God to raise up more *Prayer Marders*.[3]

Notes

1 **John Piper,** *Let the Nations Be Glad! The Supremacy of God in Missions* (Grand Rapids, MI: Baker, 1993), pp. 11–12.

2 **Harold R. Cook,** *Historic Patterns of Church Growth* (Chicago: Moody, 1971), p. 104.

3 An event recounted by Peter Ackley, an SIM missionary, in 1993.

Chapter 26

Missionary adaptability

Apostolic methods were legion. The apostles communicated the gospel wherever they could find a hearer. Variety stands out as the first principle that impresses a student of their methods.

Variety

As proof, note the terms used in Acts for apostolic communication. Table 8 summarizes apostolic nomenclature and gives the approximate frequency of each term's occurrence in the NASB.

This table demonstrates apostolic variety by drawing attention to the varied terms they used to describe their evangelistic and teaching ministries. Since most of the messages record opportunities to speak to the unconverted, the majority of terms relate to that activity. However, there is no hard and fast division of usage between words used for evangelism and those used for the edification of the saints.

Flexibility and lay involvement

Both church leaders and lay persons were equally involved in communicating the gospel. The main emphasis focuses on what the apostles did. Nevertheless, we read that lay Christians went everywhere preaching (Acts 8:4), witnessing (1:8) and speaking the Word (11:19). Stephen and Philip were appointed to distribute food to widows, yet they gradually gravitated to other ministries. We must infer that no communication technique or activity was the property of only one office in the church. For example, preaching was not the exclusive domain of those called to the pastorate.

Flexibility allowed all disciples to grow by exercising their spiritual gifts. From the earliest days of the church, God led the apostles to decentralize authority and delegate responsibility. By so doing they involved a broad cross-section of believers. This encouragement to minister did not produce disrespect for church leaders. Freedom did not generate independence but a warm sense of mutual interdependence. The flexibility developed by the early disciples encouraged innovative outreach.

Terms	Use	Terms	Use
witness	6	refute	1
testify	7	demonstrate	1
declare	5	exhort	2
speak	17	instruct	1
teach	9	guide	1
proclaim	11	bear the name of	1
preach	17	this ministry	6
prove	1	mission	1
reason	7	admonish	1
explain	5	encourage	2
persuade	6	strengthen	4
give evidence	1		

Table 8

Too often in history, authoritarianism has stifled freedom and inhibited outreach. The apostles exhibited strong leadership without dominating the saints. They encouraged believers to serve the Lord. As a result, believers manifested both adaptability and mobility.

ADAPTABILITY

In an earlier chapter we noted how the content of the apostles' messages manifested variety and relevance. They were not dependent on one communication technique. As far as ministry location was concerned, they spoke in law courts and in the temple, in private homes and in schools, in cities and villages, in synagogues and on the beach, in prison and in the market place, on board ship and in a governor's palace.

Consider the ethnic diversity of their ministries. They touched Jews and Samaritans, Greeks and Romans, slaves and masters, highly educated philosophers and uneducated commoners, merchants and soldiers.

The heterogeneous nature of the human situation necessitates a varied response. When appropriate, the apostles declared the gospel authoritatively. When reasoning and persuasion were needed, they adapted their method to suit that need. Events such as a healing, an imprisonment or an impending shipwreck became springboards for witness. No wonder their ministry was so relevant!

The importance of using one's own personal testimony can be mentioned here. Skeptics may deny doctrine but they cannot ignore your life story. On six occasions between Paul's third missionary journey and his trip to Rome, he stood before different audiences—many of them hostile—and presented Christ. In these cases he did not debate or preach but gave his own testimony. Among postmodern Westerners and pre-literate peoples the power of an oral story can hardly be overemphasized. As proof of this contention, we need look no farther than the parables of Jesus.

If we would pattern our evangelistic and missionary endeavors on the apostles we must cultivate flexibility, variety and adaptability. People represent differing cultures, live in the midst of changing circumstances and face personal challenges that vary from day to day. G. Campbell Morgan notes "... the glorious regularity of the irregular in the work of the church by the Holy Spirit. It is a powerful argument against the stereotyped in Christian organization and method!"[1]

The following examples demonstrate this point. Peter and Paul broke Jewish tradition by going and eating with Gentiles. The Jerusalem Council authenticated the spread of the gospel among Gentiles without imposing Jewish cultural practices on new Christians. Paul himself accommodated lingering Jewish prejudice by circumcising Timothy (Acts 16:3), having his hair shorn for a vow (18:18) and undergoing a Jewish purification ritual in Jerusalem (21:20–26).

Paul took advantage of a deep division between the Sadducees and the Pharisees over belief in the supernatural (26:6–10). He used the privileges of Roman citizenship to escape unjust sentencing (22:25; 25:8–12).

God prepares the world for evangelistic sowing and harvest by acting upon the cultures of the world through his providence. The biblical evangelist who understands this reality will always be ready to adapt and modify methodology.

Of course, it is much easier to have one standard approach, one media package. Learning the values and practices of another culture and reading the ebb and flow of human events require effort and time. But time must be taken, as canned and imported approaches to evangelism do more harm than good.

Failure to adapt to local customs and culture creates evangelistic failures. Some years ago an American evangelist was invited to speak to a large Christian convention in Karachi. Pakistani Christians are usually eager to have an outsider present God's Word. However, this poor fellow did not have a clue about how to speak in another culture. While speaking in that meeting about the necessity of "standing on the promises of God," he put his Bible on the floor and stood on it to illustrate his point. That was the end of the meeting. An uproar erupted.

This man of God probably came to teach God's Word and inspire disciples to be more like Christ. Instead, his action appeared to defame the Word. And his listeners turned violently against him. His actions ended his ministry in Pakistan.

Why? In Pakistan, in common with many parts of the world, failure to care for a holy book creates scandal. Probably the evangelist had never considered the importance of being sensitive to other cultures. Many of us from the West assume wrongly that our cultures are superior. And yet many of our practices scandalize people from other places. This insensitivity to others can usually be traced to cultural pride.

The evangelist barely escaped with his life. He learned in a disastrous way what every cross-cultural missionary must learn carefully: that methodology must be adapted to the local culture without compromising the message.

Sensitive missionaries observe what happens around them, listen, ask questions, adapt their approach and only then do they get up and speak!

Zealous but insensitive Westerners create many problems. How could harm not result from co-educational youth teams sent to a culture where mixed groups are considered risqué? How can Sunday school material illustrated by reference to supermarkets, baseball and snow hope to speak to children who know only bazaars, cricket and sand? Appeals for young people to repent of their rebellion against parents may lose their force where children have grown up with a lifelong respect for their elders.

Mailing Bibles to every telephone number might have merit in Atlanta, Georgia but not in Lahore, Pakistan, where piles of unclaimed Bibles ended up being torn apart to make paper bags—to the discredit of the whole Christian community.

Many examples of how a passionately held belief in a particular evangelistic elixir leads to failure could be cited. Some promote literature as the answer—but what to do where 80 percent are illiterate? Others claim that radio alone can reach the world for Christ—but how can those be reached who have no radios, or who only listen to popular music? The limitations of using Campus Crusade's *Four Spiritual Laws* as a universal evangelistic tool have already been noted.

Door-to-door witness may be just the ticket in one place. But in Muslim countries, where men do not converse socially with women, door-to-door visitation by men leads to scandal. Muslim men will become livid with anger if they return from work to hear about Christian men visiting their wives. What we need is the flexibility to adapt evangelistic materials and methods to suit each particular situation.

Consider technology. Genuine love fosters empathy and concern. Empathy demands that we take the trouble to approach people creatively. Each person rises from a unique set of experiences. We will never be able to develop a computer or machine to do our evangelizing for us because each person needs to be approached personally. Oh yes, let's use technology to enhance creativity, but not to stifle innovation! Variety, in evangelistic methodology as in food, is the spice of life.

MOBILITY

Apostolic evangelism manifested not only an adaptability to local cultures, but also mobility. Acts is a book of travels. Paul and Barnabas march through its pages on one journey after another. The Jerusalem church sent Peter and John to evaluate the work of Philip in Samaria (8:14). After encouraging the saints in Antioch, Peter and John "returned to Jerusalem, preaching the gospel in many Samaritan villages" (8:25). In chapter 9 "Peter traveled about the country" (9:32). God sent Peter from Joppa to Cornelius's house in Caesarea (ch. 10).

Some of the early church's movements occurred because of persecution

(8:2, 4; 11:19–20). And yet, although they were hounded from one place to another, persecuted saints played out God's sovereign evangelistic strategy by taking the gospel wherever they went.

Early believers came to realize that God overruled the negative effects of persecution to further his positive missionary strategy. Instead of becoming the victims of their oppressors they rode a tide of outreach superintended by God. When persecuted, they neither fought back nor courted martyrdom. Instead they moved on to another field of service. Paul escaped Damascus in a basket (9:25) and fled from Iconium to Lystra (14:6). After being stoned in Lystra he went on to Derbe (14:19–20).

Rejection of their message also contributed to apostolic guidance. The apostles did not continue to proclaim the gospel to those who remained deaf to its appeal. Shaking off the dust from their feet, as a testimony against those who rejected them, the apostolic evangelists moved on to more fruitful towns (see 13:46, 51; 18:6).

Barnabas and Saul desired to move into Asia but were blocked by the Spirit. The resistance and blasphemy Paul encountered in Corinth might have moved him to pack up had not the Lord assured him in a night vision to stay (18:9–11).

Indiscriminate blanket witness, so common today, did not characterize these early missionaries. Intensely mobile without being thoughtlessly random, they targeted synagogues and Gentiles who had been prepared by Mosaic teaching. Repeatedly we read, "they entered the synagogue" (e.g. 13:14, 43; 14:1). Realizing the strategic importance of cities, they focused their efforts on centers of commerce and philosophy such as Corinth and Philippi, Colosse and Ephesus. As a result of this wise approach the Word of the Lord spread through the whole region.

What a balance we find in the apostles between an intense dependence on the guidance of the Spirit and a careful attention to strategic effort! Their efforts rested not so much upon intense planning as upon developing a sensitivity to the leading of the Lord. They were Spirit-led, providentially guided evangelists.

Mobility, however, can have its own dangers. A commitment to itineration may hide a love of adventure. A desire to escape the hard work of discipling converts until they become productive members of healthy churches may move some evangelists to slip away too quickly. The early missionaries planted strong and stable churches in each center. Trained believers carried on useful lives as salt and light in their communities. The travels of Acts should not be made the basis for flitting from church to church without putting down roots anywhere.

From the apostles we should learn to be ready at any time to move through opening doors or to shift personnel into ripening harvest fields. We must be willing, too, to leave those who decisively reject the message. Thinking back over my years of service in Pakistan, I sometimes wonder why we kept on trying to teach nominal Christians who repeatedly rejected basic Christian principles such as forgiveness.

Does the apostolic pattern imply that we should shake the dust off our feet in Muslim lands, just because they are so resistant to the gospel? Should we write off one-fifth of the world's population? No! Bruce Bell has already been mentioned in Chapter 22 as an example of the right kind of missionary mobility. Leaving a fruitful ministry in Latin America, he moved into the hard Arab world. We cannot fault the patience of Jeremiah, who obeyed God and persevered in a thankless and fruitless ministry. We need to be mobile, but only when such mobility is consistent with overall strategy. There is also a time to be immobile while we strengthen believers.

Balance! How easily we tend to push principles to the extreme, to formalize, to institutionalize, to fossilize. Evangelism and missions do not escape this tendency. We have all heard how easy it is for a vision to develop into a movement and for a movement to degenerate into an institutional monument. Many evangelistic relics celebrate the creative mobility and marvelous adaptability of their founders while their modern managers keep slogging along according to formulae that were innovative fifty years ago!

Apostolic precedent calls us to be flexible and adaptable. Every culture is distinct. Every age has its own diversity. Evangelism requires all the powers of creativity we can bring to bear. Canned approaches and stilted prose may totally miss the mark. We should encourage believers to develop a spirit of evangelistic freedom to tailor their witness to suit the individual eccentricities they meet.

This is not to say that we ought not to have a basic outline in our minds. Without being clear on the basics of what sinners need to hear and how they should respond, we will not be confident enough to adapt to the diversity we face from person to person.

Notes

1 **G. Campbell Morgan,** *The Acts of the Apostles* (New York & London: Revell, 1927), p. 6.

Chapter 27

Missionary methodology

Although missionary methodology reflects an enormous diversity, certain basic principles apply generally. Most we have already dealt with earlier in this book. However, several questions remain unanswered. To what degree should missionaries commit themselves to social programs such as famine relief? Is evangelism furthered by "signs and wonders"? Should we expect the occurrence of miracles as a normal part of church life? What role does testimony play in evangelism? As always, we turn for guidance in questions such as these to apostolic precedent. We must place our emphasis where they did, if we would achieve biblical balance.

Since the previous chapter highlighted the need for variety and flexibility, we might be left with the impression that in evangelism and missions "anything goes." Such is not the case. There is a recognizable biblical rhythm. Consider, firstly, the relative weight the apostles gave to biblical truth and to personal testimony.

The role of personal testimony

A missionary must experience the truth he or she proclaims. The apostles practiced what they preached. This correspondence between faith and practice rendered their ministry extremely practical and very personal. Two of the terms used in Acts bear out this contention: "witness" and "testify." Peter talked of the gospel of Christ as that to which "we are all witnesses" (Acts 2:32). He said, "For we cannot help speaking about what we have seen and heard" (4:20).

Their intimate acquaintance with the risen Christ energized their witness, enabling them to boldly testify in his name. They commanded men and women to repent—a repentance that they had experienced. They urged their hearers to believe in Christ—a faith they daily exercised. They did not preach about that of which they had no personal knowledge. Their sincerity, coupled with the transparency of their lives, stamped their preaching as authentic. No wonder their words had a profound effect on their hearers.

Let me interject a word of caution at this point. While their faith was intensely personal, they did not base their preaching upon their own experiences. Peter did mention his own experience in his message to Cornelius. In a court setting, when testimony became necessary to authenticate their ministry, the apostles did refer to their experiences. Court requires testimony! Likewise, Paul described the general dimensions of his ministry when he addressed the Ephesian elders for the last time. The vast bulk of their preaching, however, did not contain personal testimony.

The apostles did not use their own personal experiences as a lever to persuade others to believe. Nor did they seek to prove gospel principles by appealing to experience. They did not allow their own, very real and very exciting experiences to usurp the place reserved for gospel fundamentals. They did not go around saying things such as, "I received Christ by doing such and such, therefore you too should respond in this way," or "The Holy Spirit came upon us at Pentecost after we tarried in prayer; therefore all should tarry in prayer to receive the Spirit." They did not preach about their own conversions, their own faith, their own repentance, their own reception of the Spirit or, except in a tangential sense, the blessings they had received.

The apostles preached Christ, not themselves. They focused on the experiences of Christ. They turned people's attention to objective, historical facts and the theological truths derived from them. Surely, if anyone had a right to point to personal experience, they did. Paul echoes the apostolic pattern when he says, "For we do not preach ourselves, but Jesus Christ as Lord, and ourselves as your servants for Jesus' sake" (2 Cor. 4:5). The apostles wisely refrained from expecting others to reproduce their experiences.

A comparison of apostolic restraint with our modern preoccupation with the existential ought to alarm us. Christendom in our day is more enamored with personal experience than with theological content. Whole movements, such as the charismatic and Vineyard movements, rest on an experiential rather than an exegetical foundation. Although there is much in these movements to admire, I find their appeal to experience unwise when they say, "I spoke with other tongues," "I was healed," "I felt the Spirit descend on me."

This tendency toward a pragmatic focus on experience is not confined to the charismatic movement. Those who have the organizational genius to successfully promote their formulae become the latest evangelical standard bearers. As a result, some organizations build their strategy around "coming forward" in a mass evangelistic rally, others on literature distribution, others on door-to-door witness, others on seeker sensitivity, others on sports outreach and still others on a purpose-driven formula.

This kind of reasoning, when applied to follow-up and discipleship, produces a whole array of specialty organizations—often spectacularly successful in appearance. However, we cannot base our strategy on their success—nor should we discount them out of hand. Careful sifting of modern "successes" may yield some valuable insights. Nevertheless, only apostolic practice is normative.

Consider another example of our penchant to exalt experience. In North America "star" converts are widely exploited for evangelistic purposes. When God converts a well-known football player or politician, actress or criminal, the fact is widely publicized. New converts with star quality quickly find themselves in demand to "give their testimonies." I'm not denying the joy, both in heaven and in the church on earth, when any man or woman becomes a true brother or sister in Christ. But the overuse of converted "stars" puts them in spiritual danger and promotes the idea that evangelism will be more successful when we parade the experiences of famous people.

Is it not strange that unpretentious early Christians turned the world upside down? Is it not a wonder that the uneducated Galilean apostles impressed highly educated priests and powerful politicians by the mere force of truth? Let us avoid the danger of overemphasizing the experiences of prominent people or shaping our evangelistic strategies to fit our existential experiences.

Face to face vs. evangelism from a distance

Apostolic communication was personal, not because they talked a lot about their personal experiences, but because their lives were consistent with the objective gospel truth they preached. It was personal, however, in another way as well. Their ministry was face to face. Paul "taught ...

publicly and from house to house ... I did not cease to warn everyone night and day ..." (20:20, 31). In every recorded instance, they were personally present among those they sought to reach. The letters they wrote are an exception to this rule. But even their epistles are full of personal detail. They used these letters either to follow up previous face-to-face ministry or to prepare the way for the personal visits they planned.

Gospel communicators ought to not only *present* the gospel but also *represent* the message by their attitudes and actions. People need to see salvation demonstrated in lives of converted friends and neighbors. Peter, Andrew, James and John impressed the Galileans who saw in their lives the difference Christ made. No wonder their network of Galilean friends and relatives fed a great stream of disciples into the early church.

Biblical strategy generally requires that the gospel communicator dwell among those he or she seeks to reach. The presence of the communicator means his or her conduct will be observed.

Modern technology has vastly improved our ability to communicate the gospel globally. The availability of radio, television, films, CDs, the Internet, correspondence courses and literature encourages us to believe that the missionary task can be accomplished quickly. These multiplied means do enhance missionary outreach. Subtle dangers, however, lurk in the shadow of our love affair with media technology. Their use to accomplish distance-evangelism may tend to siphon off resources and personnel needed for person-to-person evangelism. It may shift our trust away from the Holy Spirit to marketing techniques. It may relieve the sense of responsibility individual Christians feel for personal evangelism.

I am not denying that God has given us powerful tools to use in the extension of his kingdom. But on no account should any person involved in these media fail to demonstrate a careful commitment to a local church. He or she must live a life of accountability, not only to the ministry organization, but to local Christians as well. But other less obvious dangers surround the issue.

One-on-one witnessing is the bread and butter of personal evangelism. Media can only supplement, never usurp, the place of men and women sharing Christ over back fences.

Christ could have chosen to be born in an era when TV and radio would broadcast his gospel far and wide. In spite of all the options before him, he came among us and pioneered a very labor-intensive method of evangelism. He spent three years training twelve men. And yet, within a few years, his well-trained few turned the world upside down. There is no better evangelistic method than people reaching people face to face.

What will happen if we listen to the siren song of technology? We will overlook the need to mobilize ordinary Christians to do lifestyle evangelism. Both local-church outreach and foreign missions will suffer. The pool of candidates for general missionary work will dry up.

Training disciples and sending them out to evangelize is the method of the Master. More than anything else, the kingdom needs a host of missionary foot-soldiers out on the front lines doing unglamorous missionary evangelism. In spite of this crucial need, there has never been a time when it has been harder to recruit the "general missionary." True, specialists fill an important place in the missionary program. Nevertheless, general missionaries committed to church planting through face-to-face, culturally sensitive evangelism are vital. The same is true on a local level.

Theological thoroughness and the importance of the mind

We have already underscored the importance of theological truth over personal experience. As I studied the apostolic messages I also noted that, while they appealed to the whole personality—intellect, will and emotion—yet their main target was the mind. They appealed to sinners by directing their messages through the door of the intellect.

The place of the intellect in apostolic evangelism can be established in several ways. The terms used for apostolic communication—proving, reasoning, explaining, persuading, giving evidence, refuting, demonstrating, teaching and instructing—confirm that the apostles grappled intellectually with their hearers. This kind of terminology could apply to a scientific lecture! Not surprisingly, we find Philip asking the Ethiopian, "Do you *understand* what you are reading?" (Acts 8:30).

We have also previously noted the immense breadth of content present in their communication. Why tell their hearers so many facts if an emotional appeal would suffice? While the apostles called for repentance, this was not simply a feeling. Repentance literally means a "change of mind."

We discover Paul describing Christian living in terms of the destruction of "arguments and every high thing that exalts itself against the knowledge of God" (2 Cor. 10:5). "Those who are perishing" have had their minds "blinded" by "the god of this age ... lest the light of the gospel of the glory of Christ ... should shine on them" (2 Cor. 4:4). The gospel illumines the mind. (Transformation, of course, never stops with the intellect but moves on to touch the wills and the hearts of men and women, leading them to submit to Christ.)

Apostolic precedent, it would seem, directs us to reach human personality through the door of the intellect. Unfortunately, as evangelicals, we have too often shied away from intellectual pursuits. With irrationality parading its seductive wares all around us, let us not jettison careful reasoning to buy into excessive visual or emotional appeals. Sinners may be darkened in thought and deed, but they are not dunces. If we would follow the apostolic pattern we must challenge the minds of our generation with culturally relevant, clearly focused, interestingly presented, mentally challenging truth. The apostles did not aim to arouse temporary interest by sensationalism, but to effect permanent personality change by assailing the intellect of darkened sinners. We are called to preach, teach, persuade, reason and explain!

POSTMODERNISM

What of postmodernism? As I write, the Emergent Church movement, motivated by leaders such as Brian McLaren, is making headway in North America. Emergent churches seek to reach postmoderns without using the dogmatic, formulaic evangelistic approaches of the past. They aim to be flexible and open to people in a relational context. As you can tell from what I have already written, I have some sympathy for this approach.

We cannot deny that, in the West, the rationalistic, modern age inspired by the Enlightenment is giving way to a relativistic, subjective approach to reality. People are much more mystical today. Making absolute truth claims is problematic in this new context. In McLaren's view, the church is unfortunately stuck in a time-warp, believing that evangelism still requires the presentation of facts and evidence and reason. For McLaren the gospel is not primarily informational but relational.

As we have seen, however, the gospel as information, truth, reason and argument precedes the Enlightenment by 1,600 years. While we need to carefully study the postmodern person and tailor our approach to his or her context [the process of contextualization], I do not believe that requires us to jettison the use of reason. Christ had a lot to say about truth and falsehood. The Emergent Church movement deserves ongoing scrutiny.

THOROUGHNESS

Consideration of the way in which the apostles assaulted the mind leads us also to note the thorough nature of their evangelism. Both their range of content and their variety of technique reveal their thoroughness. In the thirteen different evangelistic messages and testimonies in the book of Acts, I have isolated thirty-three distinct content elements which range over the whole of biblical revelation. They were painstaking in their preaching!

Those who would make radical distinctions between evangelism, teaching and preaching fail to notice the overlap of these activities in apostolic practice. Preaching and teaching are closely linked in seven different references (see Acts 4:2; 5:28, 42; 13:5, 12; 15:35; 18:25; 28:31). An evangelistic message given to people in the temple is described with the words "taught the people and preached …" (4:2). The Jewish authorities viewed the apostles' work as a teaching ministry (5:28). The apostles demonstrated thoroughness in the way their preaching included teaching and their teaching included authoritative declaration—preaching.

Too often, evangelism is superficial. The artificial distinction many have made between teaching, preaching and evangelism may really be a smoke-screen thrown up by evangelists too impatient to do thorough follow-up, or by teachers too lax in evangelism, or by preachers unwilling to prepare thoroughly. God's work today calls for both flexibility and thoroughness. In some cases evangelists will need to persevere where the harvest is slim, building precept upon precept, truth upon truth as if they were teachers. And evangelists are always responsible for the careful edification of converts. I find no support in Acts for modern mass evangelistic efforts that sweep into town, stay a week or two and then head off to some other center. Dare I say it? Mass evangelism is hardly church planting!

Signs and wonders

Since the rise of the charismatic movement and the spread of John Wimber's ideas about the importance of signs and wonders for evangelism, we need to ask another question: What is the role of miracles and healing in the evangelistic equation? The Lord used the apostles to heal many. Astounding miracles, similar to those Christ had demonstrated, attended their ministries. Nevertheless, as time passed in both the ministry of Christ and that of the apostles, healing and miracles tapered off. Once the gospel message had been authenticated by signs, the need for attesting miracles ceased.

The twenty-five different Greek words used to describe the verbal communication of the apostles overwhelmingly support the preeminence of communication and the minimal importance of miracles in general and healing in particular.

The Great Commission, recorded five times, contains no mandate to go into all the world healing and doing miracles. It stresses preaching, teaching and baptizing. True, the passage in Mark 16 does mention that signs will follow apostolic witness. During the apostolic period, signs and miracles did enhance and authenticate their ministries. There is no doubt, however, that the salvation and transformation of sinners far outweighs the importance of healings and miracles in the divine economy.

Christ had warned about the danger of a preoccupation with the miraculous: "A wicked and adulterous generation looks for a miraculous sign, but none will be given it except the sign of Jonah" (Matt. 16:4). In Matthew 24:24 Jesus cautioned about paying attention to the lying signs and wonders of false prophets. In John 6 and 12 we can easily trace how the crowds were fascinated with the miracles but rejected Christ's call to faith and repentance. "Even after Jesus had done all these miraculous signs in their presence, they still would not believe in him" (John 12:37).

As we survey biblical history we must conclude that signs and miracles occurred sporadically. We do find a pattern, however. Miraculous signs occurred when God ushered in a new epoch in redemptive history: during the time of the Exodus, during the period of the Jewish kingdom, and at the initiation of the gospel epoch. The historical Protestant position, that God granted signs and wonders to attest his revelation and inaugurate new eras, fits well with what we see in Scripture. The apostolic period merited demonstrations of the miraculous both on the grounds of inaugurating a new era, the church age, and attesting a new revelation, the gospel.

Scripture documents the purpose of signs and wonders. Peter took up the theme at Pentecost when he stated that Jesus was "accredited by God to you by miracles, wonders and signs, which God did among you through him" (Acts 2:22). In Iconium Paul and Barnabas were "speaking boldly for the Lord, who confirmed the message of his grace by enabling them to do miraculous signs and wonders" (14:3).

In the apostolic period, the people of God needed proof that two fundamental changes in the dispensation of God's grace were divinely instituted and not human constructions. The first concerned a change of focus from Moses and the Law—centered in the temple—to Jesus and grace—centered in the ministry of the church, his body. While the connection between the new covenant under Christ and his apostles and the old covenant under Moses and the prophets was constantly affirmed, nevertheless a fantastic change in focus was demonstrated. "The apostles performed many miraculous signs and wonders among the people" (Acts 5:12).

In the second place, the dramatic change from a narrow faith centered in one nation—Israel—in one place—Jerusalem—to a faith for all peoples required a dramatic demonstration that it was sanctioned by God. No wonder a series of special manifestations occurred as God authenticated the spread of the gospel from Jewish enclaves to Gentile peoples. Cornelius's Roman household evidenced their new faith in Christ by speaking in tongues. Similar manifestations occurred among mixed-race Samaritans and in the pure Greek setting of Ephesus. These outpourings of the Spirit demonstrated to the apostles that Gentile conversions were genuine. God attested the entrance of Gentiles into the Jewish congregation by "giving the Holy Spirit to them, just as he did to us [the Jews]". God also granted other signs as evidence of his work among the Gentiles (15:8–12; 10:44–48).

No one can deny that the radical change from the old to the new covenant required some kind of dramatic confirmation. Signs and wonders provided this attestation. Why, then, do many still insist that signs and wonders continue as part of normative church life, when the very reason for their occurrence has disappeared?

In our age we possess, in the Bible, a complete and attested revelation of God's will for mankind. As long as the Bible remained incomplete and uncollected the confirmation of its message by signs and wonders was necessary. Now it is confirmed as God's Word, we don't need continual confirmation by extraordinary physical signs. Instead, the miraculous regeneration of rebel sinners and the ongoing sanctification of redeemed individuals—the most astounding miracles of all—attest the veracity of the gospel. The conversion of sinners, the planting of churches and the advance of missions constitute the signs of God's presence in this age.

If we try to resurrect a ministry of healing, for example, as an adjunct to evangelism, we run the serious danger of de-emphasizing the major human problem. The essential human problem is not sickness, but sinfulness. The excitement that healing generates tends to draw attention away from tough realities like depravity, repentance, sacrifice and discipleship. Today, just as in the time of our Lord, the spectacle of supposed miracles draws a crowd that quickly thins when the stern demands of discipleship are explained. Many followed Jesus only because of the loaves and fishes he had multiplied.

Children run into the front yard when they hear a fire engine. People like to be present when momentous things occur: the fall of the Berlin Wall, the opening of the Olympics, the visit of a championship soccer team, the occurrence of miracles. But is it excitement or conviction we need to generate?

Let me add a word of caution here. Whether or not signs and wonders actually occur today is, of course, totally beyond our control. God is the sovereign source of the miraculous. It may be that in pioneer situations among largely illiterate people, or in the midst of highly resistant peoples such as Muslims, God may do unusual things: communicate through dreams or visions; demonstrate miracles.

God's ways are not our ways. He cannot be put in a box. Experience and observation indicate that he works in unpredictable, uncontrollable ways. People may claim to have the power to heal. But they cannot manufacture genuine miracles. Let us leave their occurrence in the capable hands of God.

Social uplift

To take the discussion one step further, we need to ask ourselves about the role of social-uplift programs in missions. The apostles expressed their concern for the plight of widows by arranging for their care. Acts records the concern of early Christians for those suffering from famine. Gentile churches were urged to collect an offering to alleviate the suffering of those in Jerusalem. The compassion of apostolic missionaries is not in question.

We must ask ourselves, however, whether the works of mercy demonstrated in the early church occurred as the natural outworking of Christian love or as the result of strategic evangelistic planning. I am convinced that the former is the case.

In Acts 6 the apostles came to a crossroads. They were faced with the choice of either creating a full-scale ministry to widows or of maintaining their preaching ministry. They concluded, "It would not be right for us to neglect the ministry of the word of God in order to wait on tables" (Acts 6:2). They were not trying to avoid servanthood. They didn't think that serving tables was beneath them. The image of Jesus washing their feet had burned into their subconscious a commitment to servanthood. No, they based their conclusion on an analysis of priorities. They realized what modern missionaries must also realize: We must "give our attention to prayer and the ministry of the word" (6:4) without overlooking the needs of others. To care for the widows, the apostles suggested that "seven men from among you who are known to be full of the Spirit and wisdom" be put in charge of this task (6:3).

The apostles wisely chose not to be diverted from their primary task. As a result of their conscious choice, evangelistic outreach continued at a dynamic pace. The apostles knew what we often forget: that Jesus's mandate called for church planting not philanthropy.

Missionary church planting is not the enemy of works of mercy. These are not two competing preoccupations. But they must be addressed in a specific order of priority. When we evangelize according to the apostolic model, local churches spring up where converted sinners can gather to worship, pray and fellowship with one another (Acts 2:38–47). Once established, they become centers of salt and light. As outposts of the kingdom of God, they radiate, in a dark and selfish world, a new climate of love and concern. As sinners grow in grace they increasingly manifest both love for God and love for their neighbors.

The love found in growing Christians becomes the catalyst for all kinds of individual and corporate social programs. It is no accident that Christians have fought against slavery and child labor, have started orphanages and homes for battered women, have initiated schools and colleges. Love for others moves some African churches to collect grain to help alleviate the suffering of their community during the yearly round of drought. Love moves churches in Khartoum to take in refugees and prairie churches in North America to collect grain to ship to Sudan and Ethiopia.

Authentic churches demonstrate social concern. But churches must first be planted! If we do not give priority to the planting of organized churches then centers of compassion and concern cannot be established in needy places. The apostles clearly understood their priorities—that evangelism precedes, and produces, social action. In this area at least, the Church Growth school of missionary thinking has done us the valuable service of challenging God's people to get their priorities right.

God has not called us to go into all the world and improve agriculture, relieve medical distress or build schools. He has called us to go and plant churches, which in turn become centers of improved agriculture, health and education. Educational, relief and medical work must take their place behind church planting in order of priority.

Please understand that I have the greatest respect for Christian works of compassion: hospitals, schools, literacy programs, relief projects, agricultural efforts. But we must never again allow social action to usurp the place of evangelistic ministry. Ambivalence here spawned the social gospel of a previous generation. Fuzzy thinking in church and missionary circles is once again beginning to obscure the exact nature of our mission.

Thus far I have argued that the proclamation of God's Word in verbal form must take priority over personal testimony, over healing and miracles and over social uplift and works of mercy. Priority prevails, or chaos reigns.

Let me summarize the principles that we have considered in this chapter on apostolic methodology:

- The apostolic example forbids the proclamation of truth that has not been experienced. Evangelists and missionaries must have a living relationship with the Lord and demonstrate in their lives the impact of truth.
- Missions (and evangelism) must concentrate on communicating the theological truths of the Christian faith and not the experiences of the evangelist. Any ministry shaped by the personal experiences of the founder is suspect and must be restructured to reflect biblical balance.
- The silent witness of a godly life must be buttressed by verbal witness consistent with the witness's own spiritual gifts. Presence evangelism, without proclamation, is never enough.
- Personal face-to-face evangelism should take precedence over impersonal or distance evangelism such as that which leans heavily on media.
- Biblical ministry should be characterized by an appeal to the content of the Word of God and not to signs, wonders or miracles.
- Works of mercy and compassion must never take strategic precedence over the crucial task of church planting. Growing believers and established congregations become the base from which Christian love reaches out in social concern.
- Biblical communication should be directed to the human soul primarily through the door of the intellect, rather than by an appeal to the emotions or the will.
- Evangelism ought to manifest thoroughness both in conception and application.

Principles such as these, if adopted, could revolutionize evangelism and missions and greatly enhance the extension of the Kingdom by redirecting our efforts to the core task of missions!

Church planting: the central task of missions

As John Piper has reminded us, "missions is not the ultimate goal of the church, worship is."[1] Jesus explained to the woman at the well that God seeks worshipers. At Pentecost God converted 3,000 self-centered sinners into God-centered worshipers. The Spirit gathered these converts into a church. In Psalm 47 the sons of Korah call upon all the nations to "shout to God with cries of joy ... sing praises to our King" (vv. 1, 6). The only way this vision can be fulfilled is through church planting among all the nations. As groups of believers gather into churches—large and small—they raise their joyful voices in worship, albeit in a multitude of languages.

There is nothing quite so uplifting as joining together with a group of redeemed saints in the worship of our glorious Triune God. I remember vividly being in a worship service in Thailand where I didn't understand a word but felt uplifted to the throne of God by the congregational worship. This is uncommon, but not unheard of.

While our goal is worship, the pathway to that goal is church planting. Fortunately Jesus is totally involved in this process. In this chapter I want to consider the steps we can take as we seek to partner with Christ and the Holy Spirit in church planting.

Defining a biblical church

First of all we need to be clear on the nature of the biblical church.

Churches are made up of disciples. As we noted in Chapter 8, *a disciple is a sinner who has been regenerated by the Holy Spirit, justified by faith in Christ's atoning death, and who is being progressively sanctified through following and serving Jesus Christ and his church.*

Those sinners who become disciples need to be gathered into churches. As Acts 2 demonstrates, *a church is a local group of baptized believers who come together in an organized way under biblically qualified leadership.*

An authentic local church maintains commitment to apostolic doctrine and practice by celebrating two ordinances: gathering to worship, pray, hear the Word and fellowship; and demonstrating a growing godliness and love in personal and community life and outreach.

Church-planting models

Since missions is essentially church planting among unreached people, pioneer missionaries work in a church-less vacuum. Even though they start from scratch, they need to have in mind a general pattern of the church to be planted. Will it be similar to a church in a nearby city, or like a denominational church back home, or something completely different? Without a model, unforeseen circumstances will tend to shape the organization of the infant church in ways that might be harmful. And patterns established in a church's infancy prove almost impossible to eradicate later.

Veteran missionary Abe Wiebe mentions five models he has encountered. One approach is to adopt a pattern from one's own denominational background. For example, "Brethren, Baptist, Presbyterian or Anglican missionaries tell the national believers what the church looks like and how it is to function."

A second method "is to develop an over-all plan for the national church that includes a doctrinal basis and practical aspects of church and body life. Each city adapts this to its situation but essentially follows the biblical outline. A third approach is to insist on contextualizing the Gospel in its social and religious context." This approach adheres to the basics but tries to incorporate what people are used to in their culture when they join a group.

"A fourth approach focuses on cell groups of four to five believers only. This model develops leaders and is much less visible in a hostile environment. The fifth model calls for house churches" that gather in the home of a person known in the community as a man of peace. Through his family and neighborhood connections the gospel can readily spread.[2]

The first approach should be rejected. The third approach is probably the wisest in most contexts. Approaches four and five could be merged into the third, the contextual approach. These last two have the great benefit of enabling a church to start with just a few converts, multiply converts naturally and avoid the crippling costs involved in making building construction an essential part of the goal.

Essential qualities of a healthy church

For almost a generation Church Growth theory has promoted a certain approach. As I've already noted in previous chapters, my own study of the Scriptures has led me to question many of the principles of this approach, a methodology that seems to exalt quantitative growth at the expense of quality.

Research now shows that what the Scriptures teach about qualitative characteristics actually promotes church growth. We need not allow technology or the sciences of sociology, anthropology, linguistics, and so on, to dictate missionary policy.

In his extremely helpful book *Natural Church Development: How Your Congregation Can Develop the Eight Essential Qualities of a Healthy Church*, Christian A. Schwarz lists eight essential qualities that characterize healthy churches. Schwarz has conducted a scientific survey of 1,000 churches in thirty-two countries on six continents. These churches range in size, denominational affiliation and cultural background. He concludes that too often, church-growth studies have highlighted models that seem successful, often those of large churches, but with characteristics that may not be transferable. His study discovered principles that apply to churches everywhere—not surprising, since the Bible highlights these attributes.

The eight essential qualities are:

- empowering leadership. "Leaders of growing churches concentrate on empowering other Christians for ministry … they invert the pyramid of authority so that the leader assists Christians to attain the spiritual potential God has for them."
- gift-oriented ministry. "When Christians serve in their area of giftedness, they generally function less in their own strength and more in the power of the Holy Spirit"; recognizing the priesthood of all believers.

- passionate spirituality. Churches that are not legalistic or tradition-bound but where members find times of prayer inspiring and who are enthusiastic about their church. Joy and enthusiasm rather than duty.
- functional structures. "Wherever God breathes his Spirit into formless clay, both life and form spring forth." The presence of department leaders responsible for certain areas of church life indicates a presence of structure.
- inspiring worship service. Instead of attending boring services out of a sense of duty healthy churches have inspiring worship that draws people to their services. The "seeker service" is not a universal growth principle.
- holistic small groups. "The continuous multiplication of small groups is a universal church growth principle. They must "go beyond just discussing Bible passages to applying its message to daily life"; place where one is free to discuss one's personal problems.
- need-oriented evangelism. Every Christian is not an evangelist. Healthy churches "distinguish between those Christians who have the gift of evangelism and those who do not have this gift." All Christians already have an existing network of relationships with non-Christians. "The key to church growth is for the local congregation to focus its evangelistic efforts on the questions and needs of non-Christians."
- loving relationships. "Growing churches possess on the average a measurably higher 'love quotient' than stagnant or declining ones … unfeigned, practical love has a divinely generated magnetic power far more effective than evangelistic programs …" Healthy churches have a lot of laughter.

Since Jesus often talked of natural growth—fields, seeds, weeds, birds, etc.—Schwarz relates many of his quality principles to the way things grow in creation. These principles bring us much closer to biblical expressions of church health.[3]

An overview of the typical steps of a church planter

While it's impossible to develop a plan that will work in all situations, typically, a missionary just arriving in his or her field of service will progress through the following steps.

BONDING WITH FIELD TEAM

Believing in the importance of team ministry, new missionaries will give themselves to developing relationships of understanding, openness and love with their colleagues on the field team. They will expect differences of background, training, culture and temperament. They will pray for loving patience to rescue them from being critical or annoyed by differences. Few things can hinder missionary outreach more than disunity among missionaries. Any lack of harmony will likely be reproduced in the churches that are planted.

Experienced missionaries can't expect new recruits to be the only ones to adjust. They need to be sensitive to their ideas and problems. Teams that embrace a consultative approach usually function much better than those led by authoritarian leaders. Newer and younger missionaries, on their part, need to keep their ideas on ice until they have come to understand the culture in which they will be working.

SETTING UP A HOME

Missionaries should generally set up their homes among the people they are trying to reach. Where conditions are extremely primitive, this may be next to impossible. Renting a basic, lower-middle-class house in a nearby host culture is the next best option. Living in the midst of a typical neighborhood will create many opportunities to make friends and learn about the new culture. As for living in mission compounds, avoid them like the plague. Compounds inevitably have walls, and walls symbolize separation rather than identification.

ACCULTURATION

Acculturation is the first ministry priority: learning to speak the language, adapting cultural practices and understanding the culture. New missionaries need to adopt appropriate dress, and learn ways of greeting people and how to avoid offensive body language. For example, modest head covering and full-length clothing may be required in Muslim countries. Men will not be allowed to visit or talk to women outside their family groups.

Missionaries will ask the Lord to keep them from making the typical comparisons one tends to make with one's home culture that results in classing other groups as inferior, uncivilized, underdeveloped, primitive or degenerate. With the help of more experienced missionaries and new converts, new missionaries will seek to identify cultural practices that are positive or neutral and avoid those that reflect moral evil or theological falsehood.

If the new missionaries feel undue stress, or suspect the onset of culture shock, they should share this with their missionary teams. A vacation or break may be needed. Conversely, the temptation to adopt everything in the target culture must also be resisted, lest compromise result. During this period of extreme adjustment, care needs to be taken to maintain balance in family life, in health, and in time given to leisure. Adapting to another culture takes great reserves of emotional and physical strength. There is no easy way to linguistic or cultural fluency.

FAMILY EVANGELISM

Family life is a gift of God's common grace. Everyone loves children. Children are a heritage of the Lord. Far from feeling that children inhibit missionary work, Christian families should realize that they are one of God's secret weapons. The presence of children opens doors far better than most evangelistic programs. And the presence of a missionary wife naturally attracts the interest of other women. How missionary parents treat their children can also demonstrate parenting skills unknown in the host culture. The Christian balance of discipline and love, and of teaching children responsibility and respect, is revolutionary in many cultures.

The home is the natural base from which to demonstrate the Christian lifestyle. The curiosity of people about a missionary's family life creates opportunities to share Christian values—and ultimately the gospel. Instead of viewing family responsibilities as something to detract from time spent in "the work," missionaries should embrace their home life as one of the most basic missionary methods.

The relationship between a husband and wife is a model of the relationship between Christ and the church. What better way to lay down church principles than through demonstrating in the home practical love, forgiveness, respect and teamwork? Of course, the feminist view on the role of women will not go down well in most cultures. Women must take care to avoid appearing controlling or independent. Men, too, must avoid the chauvinism so prevalent in the world.

Hospitality is an important Christian virtue. A Christian home is the ideal place to deepen friendships with neighbors and new acquaintances. An openness here will go a long way to offset the perception that missionaries feel themselves to be superior (1 Peter 4:9).

WIDESPREAD EVANGELISM

In the early years missionaries will spend much time close to home acquiring language and culture skills. Often the contacts made during these early years develop into an extended network of potential converts. In most cases, however, the evangelistic net needs to be thrown far and wide to harvest prepared hearts. Jesus sent his disciples out two by two throughout Judea and Galilee, and so missionaries in the early stages of church planting will probably need to itinerate with the gospel. The method employed will vary greatly depending on the culture, the individual missionary's own gifts and unusual opportunities that arise.

The following methods have proven useful:

- Selling or distributing literature such as Gospels, gospel tracts, books, Christian magazines, etc. Charging a small amount for literature increases its value in the eyes of buyers.
- Distributing invitations to study the Bible by correspondence. This will depend on the presence in the country of a Bible correspondence school.
- Newspaper advertisements offering free literature.
- Arranging special evangelistic meetings with a visiting preacher who is gifted in the host language.
- In a free society, if permission is granted, using a market or park as a venue in which to preach or give illustrated talks using object lessons or chalk drawings.
- Door-to-door visitation with basic literature, in a culture that allows this.
- Showing gospel films such as the *Jesus* film (while not all Christians favor using a medium which portrays visual images of Christ, there is no doubt that the *Jesus* film has been an effective stimulus for missionaries

to engage with people from many different cultures on the person and work of Christ).

- Setting up a literacy program to teach illiterates how to read and write.
- Offering courses in English, ESL.
- Offering to teach a basic course in computers, crafts or car mechanics, etc.
- Setting up a weekly medical clinic. (Care needs to be taken. Institutions tend to mushroom to meet demand and then gobble up all a missionary's time.)
- Operating a demonstration agricultural farm.
- Promoting Christian radio or TV programs.

Church-planting missionaries often use a mixture of methods during this stage in an attempt to discover those hearts which God has prepared for the gospel. In some cultures this stage may be short, in others it may take decades to gather a group of inquirers.

PERSONAL EVANGELISM

Friendship evangelism is probably the most basic and most needed of all missionary methods. Missionaries who seek to follow Jesus's pattern will be flexible and adaptable, and able to respond to people wherever they may be—at a well, arriving at night, by the roadside, at a bus station. Missionaries will aim to be friendly to all, except to those of the opposite sex. Repeated visits with merchants in the bazaar, taxi-drivers, a milkman, a car mechanic, a gas-station attendant or a student curious about English may often ripen into friendly contacts. Repeated contacts are usually necessary to overcome the prejudice people have toward foreigners.

Of course, one can't be friends with everyone. And even the best friendships may not ripen into converts. Yet friends are valuable as friends, whether or not they become Christian. After all, God calls us to love people in general, not just to promote our agenda.

FOLLOW-UP OF CONTACTS

Careful note needs to be kept of those who respond positively for later follow-up. As contacts multiply a time will come when it is more fruitful to cultivate the connections one already has rather than make new ones.

Repeated friendly contact is often what bears eternal fruit. James Engel has identified some ten to sixteen stages converts go through before they achieve a measure of maturity in Christ.[4] Veteran missionaries to Muslims have commented that Muslim converts often require fifty contacts before they become committed to Christ. Some have labored for fifteen years before seeing the first convert baptized. Remember, God is not in a rush.

DISCIPLING OF CONVERTS

As the Holy Spirit converts people to Christ, the missionaries begin to concentrate on their discipling—one of the central foci of the Great Commission: "make disciples ... teaching them to obey everything I have commanded you."

Even before this stage, missionaries will need to prepare themselves for the appearance of converts by asking serious questions. How much of the Bible is translated and available for follow-up? Are there discipleship materials to use in teaching converts what it means to follow Christ?

The missionaries will spend time with individual new converts, instructing them in the gospel; showing them how to pray; training them in how to deal with temptations, the importance of confessing sin, the ready availability of forgiveness, and the need to rest in the finished work of Christ; explaining how to share their faith and how to put on the armor of God. The missionaries will seek to understand converts' unique temperaments and spiritual gifts so they can become part of viable new churches.

As soon as there is assurance that a conversion is genuine, baptism should be arranged. In some cases delay may be wise.

As the group of converts grows, the missionary team will begin to give them more and more responsibility. Delegation of tasks creates a sense of responsibility and leads to gift development.

ESTABLISHING A CHURCH

As soon as a few converts can be gathered together in one location, a church should be established. While in some cases five or six may be enough, usually six to twelve are needed to form a viable church. If possible, these new believers should not all be from one family.

At first the missionaries may lead the meetings, but even then they will seek to involve converts in arranging the worship location, reading, praying, and so on. Missionaries should avoid setting up the new churches as meetings in their own homes. What will happen when they move on to another location? Far better to meet in the home of a convert—no matter how simple the home. Weather permitting, the church could meet under a tree or in a courtyard or school. From the very beginning it is crucial that converts learn that they, not a building, are the church. A building may only be erected as the converts themselves can arrange financing and help to build it.

Services should involve the basics that the missionaries want to see in the growing church: reading, preaching/teaching, prayer, celebration of the Lord's Table, collection of offering, perhaps even a fellowship meal.

In order to ensure the church becomes self-sustaining it is essential that believers be taught to give. The compassion missionaries may feel for the poverty of the people among whom they work must not move them to deny converts the privilege of giving. Failure here has doomed many missionary churches to dependency. (See the following chapter for a fuller treatment of this subject.)

The patterns that are adopted at the beginning become carved in stone, almost impossible to change. Generally, converts should not become paid pastors or evangelists unless their own church can pay them. Lay involvement is best. Missionary money can become one of the most disruptive forces in missionary work. The whole Indian sub-continent and much of Africa has suffered much from dependency on Western funds and expertise. And yet all was done with the best of intentions.

In 1995 Steve Saint, son of martyred Auca missionary Nate Saint, returned to visit the Auca churches that had been established in Ecuador. He found that some of the most seemingly innocent actions had hindered the indigenous development of this church. He discovered that their need for protection was not so much from government agencies and oil companies but from the "overbearing, over-indulging outside Christian community."[5] The Aucas had become spectators, expecting foreign Christians to take the initiative. Instead of holding their own Bible conferences they waited for outsiders to initiate a conference. "The outsiders would bring rice and sugar, and it would be a big festive occasion. But the Huaorani [Auca] couldn't afford rice and they couldn't afford sugar, so they figured this is something that the outsiders do."[6]

Nineteen years previously a work team had come down and built a church with concrete posts, a board floor and walls with a tin roof—fairly simple by Western standards. Since that time, however, Steve discovered that they had not built another building to be used for worship. When Steve asked them why, they said, "Oh, the outsiders build churches." They found Steve's contention that a thatched roof was adequate very novel. They had assumed that the outsiders didn't think them sophisticated enough to build anything. Ultimately, Steve helped them to take more and more responsibility by using chainsaws to make boards, running dental equipment, and so on.

We must be very careful what we do for people. As Steve Saint points out, unintentional benevolence can create "dependency, but people come in with good intentions to do things, not understanding the context in which they're doing them. This undermines the initiative of the people."[7] (This is not to say that foreign Christians should not offer short-term help in times of great crisis—floods, earthquakes, famines. But even in these situations there is danger that short-term help becomes long-term aid.)

DEALING WITH DEFECTS THAT APPEAR IN A CHURCH

Missionaries must be prepared to see problems arise in any new church. The New Testament epistles prepare us to expect this. Consider Corinth, Galatia and the seven churches of Asia Minor.

When a problem arises, missionaries may be tempted to personally step in, bypassing local leaders, out of a laudable desire to see the church maintain purity. Since training leadership is their key role, however, they should endeavor to maintain a certain distance from the decision-making process by urging the new church leaders to deal with issues as they come up.

Many missions and denominations retain hierarchical control over new churches to—as they contend—ensure purity of life and doctrine. For this reason, the purse strings may be held by the missionary or denomination. Unfortunately, instead of ensuring purity, this ensures dependency.

Missionaries must learn to trust in the Holy Spirit. What they can do is teach the whole counsel of God and pray that Christ, who is the Head of the church, may apply the Bible to any situations that arise. Surely the missionary goal is to see a church planted that is dependent on God and not on a foreign missionary organization. This entails a very delicate self-discipline on the part of the missionaries. Often they will have to bite their tongues to avoid speaking out. Much will depend on how thorough has been their discipling of new converts.

As part of the discipling process missionaries will have taught new converts that, while perfection is our goal, it is never completely possible in our fallen world. An essential part of growing in Christ is confessing our sins and being forgiven. Missionaries will have taught about our responsibility to one another in the body of Christ that requires us to carry one another's burdens and to watch out for brothers or sisters who become ensnared by sin (see Gal. 6:1–2). The missionaries will have taught that restoration is to take place in the context of love and gentleness (see Eph. 4:2; Phil. 2:2–4). They will also have taught Christ's four-step procedure for dealing with a brother caught in sin (see Matt. 18:15–17).

The missionaries will have taught church leaders that a caring fellowship is a fragile flower. When the integrity of a fellowship is compromised by the actions of one member, the body must take action. That action, though compassionate, must be decisive and disciplinary whenever entrenched sin is perceived: "you must not associate with anyone who calls himself a brother but is sexually immoral or greedy, an idolater or a slanderer, a drunkard or a swindler. With such a man do not even eat" (1 Cor. 5:11). The Scriptures require us to take disciplinary action in at least the following cases:

- immorality (1 Cor. 5:1–5, 9, 11)
- behavior that creates conflicts and divisions. "Warn a divisive person once, and then warn him a second time. After that, have nothing to do with him" (Titus 3:9–11)
- dishonesty (stealing, lying, swindling) (1 Cor. 5:11)
- materialism or greed (1 Cor. 5:11)
- slander, backbiting, gossip (1 Cor. 5:11)
- false teaching (2 John 10–11; 1 Tim. 1:19, 20)

- false religions (idolatry) (1 Cor. 5:11; Titus 1:10–14)
- laziness (2 Thes. 3:6–15)
- addiction (1 Cor. 5:11).

The missionaries will encourage church leaders to deal with flagrant sinners, first individually and then as a leadership group, before taking any matter to the whole church.

If the new church fails to act or seems to tolerate evil, the missionaries may need to step in. Paul did this in Corinth when the Corinthians were tolerating an immoral man. He told them to "hand this man over to Satan, so that the sinful nature may be destroyed and his spirit saved on the day of the Lord" (1 Cor. 5:5). Recently, a missionary friend wrote about having to step in when a pastor, converted from an idolatrous tribe, married off his daughter to a notorious idolater in the tribe.

THE CHURCH-DEVELOPMENT SIDETRACK

Once a new church is developed the desire to see that church grow in healthy ways can sidetrack the missionary. A whole cluster of missionary temptations arises at this point: a tendency to want the church to be perfect before surrendering control to local leaders, and authoritarianism—the desire to control, the proud-parent syndrome that unconsciously keeps the new child dependent. The new church itself, out of a deep sense of appreciation for the new life mediated through the missionary, may expect or appeal for an almost permanent missionary presence. This tendency can lead missionaries into the church-development sidetrack—a never-ending succession of programs geared to developing the church.

It is only natural for missionaries to feel loath to leave young church plants. They have gone through so much. They arrived with a vision to evangelize and plant churches. As people in the target culture were converted, they spent enormous energy on discipling them. They baptized them. They organized the church. They wept and agonized over the vicissitudes of new converts. Breaking off to move into a new church-planting field is akin to the agony a parent feels over a young person leaving home. And so, to alleviate the pain of separation, they convince themselves that more nurture is needed. Bingo; they become ensnared in the church-development sidetrack.

This syndrome, widespread in missions, will be dealt with in some detail in the next chapter. From the very initial stages missionaries must fight this tendency by teaching new converts the Great Commission, the central role of church planting among unreached peoples. They should make it clear that they have arrived to work themselves out of a job—to raise up a church that will become independent of their presence.

STARTING DAUGHTER CHURCHES

Of help in escaping the church-development sidetrack will be an emphasis from the very beginning on enlisting growing converts in visiting new towns and new villages with the aim of planting new churches. A vision must be encouraged of not just one church, but of a whole group of churches being planted. As the original churches mature missionaries should spend less and less time with the new churches and more and more time in unreached areas.

CROSS-CULTURAL CHURCH EXTENSION

Since the missionaries have included in the discipling of new converts an understanding of the Great Commission, it should come as no surprise to new churches when missionaries suggest cross-cultural church planting. Resistance may be felt. Near but distinct cultures are often viewed with prejudice or even hatred. The missionaries will pray and teach intensively on the unity of the human race, the universal lostness of mankind and the need to proclaim the gospel in all the world.

When there is a group of indigenous churches in an area, thought of reaching another people group should be considered. Converts in the first group may have relatives in a nearby culture, or language skills that suit them to communicate cross-culturally. If at all possible missionaries should enlist the help of established converts in a new cross-cultural outreach. In some cases, local prejudices may render the missionaries from distant cultures much more acceptable than Christians from near cultures. Indigenous missionary societies have become extremely important to cross-cultural missions: South Korean societies working in Pakistan and India; South Indian societies working in the Muslim north of India; Spanish missionaries working in North Africa.

Although I have described in general terms the stages in missionary work, there is probably no place on earth where this will be exactly duplicated. Mission fields and missionaries are diverse. As an ideal, however, we would be wise to adapt the general principles delineated here.

Notes

1 **John Piper,** *Let the Nations Be Glad! The Supremacy of God in Missions* (Grand Rapids, MI: Baker, 1993), p. 11.

2 **Abe Wiebe,** "Church Planting in an Islamic Context," *Doorway* (Arab World Ministries), Winter 2000/01.

3 **Christian A. Schwarz,** *Natural Church Development: How Your Congregation Can Develop the Eight Essential Qualities of a Healthy Church* (South Winfield, Canada: The International Centre for Leadership Development and Evangelism, 1998).

4 **James F. Engel** and **H. Wilbert Norton,** *What's Gone Wrong with the Harvest?* (Grand Rapids, MI: Zondervan, 1977), p. 45. (See an updated version under 'Engel Scale' at: en.wikipedia.org.)

5 **Rick Wood,** "Fighting Dependency Among the 'Aucas': An Interview with Steve Saint," *Mission Frontiers*, May–June 1998, p. 8.

6 Ibid. p. 9.

7 Ibid. p. 10.

Missionary specialists

Although church planting is the basic missionary method, many missionary specialists undergird this fundamental enterprise. Among the most basic specialties are Bible translation, literature production, medical work and relief efforts. Others include missionary agronomists, engineers, radio broadcasters, writers and publishers, dentists, builders, accountants, teachers and house parents for missionary boarding schools, teachers of ESL, musicians—the list is endless.

Rather than describe each specialty in detail, let me give some examples in vignette form. These vignettes describe real mission situations that represent the continuing contributions of missionary specialists up to the present day.

Missionary linguists[1]

Where there is no translation of the Bible in the language of a target people, missionary work is seriously hindered. Wycliffe Bible Translators provide the worldwide missionary force with invaluable help. Many other missions also encourage linguists. Consider one example in Ethiopia.

Ministry of Education officials praised Bruce and Betty Adams for their help in developing the Wolaitta system of writing. The presiding official told newly trained elementary-school teachers how the Adamses had assisted in developing a system for writing Wolaitta using Roman script letters rather than Ethiopic characters.

Earlier, when the Ministry decided to teach the Wolaitta people in their own language, they had come to the mission for help. The Adamses had assisted them in drafting a writing system based on the mission's years of experience in translating the Bible into Wolaitta. The Ministry was so impressed, it adopted their suggestions and invited their help in training elementary teachers. The mission in turn donated 2,000 copies of the Wolaitta writing rules they had printed.

One day, a Ministry of Education official came to the Adamses' home and said, "Today we are completing the training of 1,100 teachers to write the Wolaitta language and use it in the elementary schools throughout

Wolaitta. Please come round with me to the three towns where the teachers have gathered. Tell them how the missionaries produced Scriptures in the Wolaitta language many years ago, before the Emperor decreed that books should be produced only in the Amharic language. We have a literary history and heritage. Also tell them how your studies at the University of London have made our language known as a world language."

Bruce and Betty were glad to oblige. Thinking back over the way God had worked, Bruce commented, "This all ensures that the government way of writing Wolaitta does not clash with the way we write the Bible. God brought us both together. Amazing!"

With Wolaitta material rolling off the mission press, the translation team could push ahead with its work on the Old Testament. On the weekends Bruce and Betty Adams happily threw their boxes of books into the four-wheel-drive Toyota to bounce over the trails from village to village selling literature. The Wolaitta churches got the Bible in their own tongue ... and Wolaitta children received an education!

Missionary medical ministries[2]

Patients travel miles to Raxaul to get treatment at the Duncan Hospital in northern India. Many find more than healing for their bodies. During one two-and-a-half-month period thirty-one were baptized at the Raxaul Christian Church. Twenty-three of these came from across the border from the Himalayan kingdom of Nepal. Besides this group, another twenty-one were baptized at one of the daughter churches in Nepal itself.

The Raxaul Christian Church grew up out of the ministry of the Duncan Hospital. Located in the north-Indian state of Bihar, this church had been busily reaching out to the villages round about. One January the church commissioned an evangelist to go to Singhasini village to teach believers. A month after his arrival local believers there erected their own tiny thatched church, where they gathered for prayer, fellowship, singing and Bible study. A team from Raxaul regularly supported the evangelist by going to Singhasini to help in teaching women.

On Easter Sunday that year Christians from Raxaul joined local Christians to witness the baptism of ten Singhasini believers. Six men and four women rose from the dirty, black water to vividly demonstrate the power of the resurrected Christ.

Even when medicine fails, the dedicated nurses and doctors often see the Kingdom advance. One busy clinic day, a distressed father carried his ten-year-old daughter, Kuadari, into the hospital. She had a high fever and convulsions. She responded well to treatment for meningo-encephalitis and was released. Later, when the outreach team visited her village, they found a grinning girl wanting them to sing "the songs of Jesus Christ." On a return visit, however, the staff were shocked to learn that she had had a relapse and died. But their tears were moderated by the joy of knowing that this child was now with the Lord of whom she loved to sing.

Another man cycled sixteen kilometers to bring his son, Allowadine, to the hospital. Suffering from advanced heart disease, Allowadine found it difficult to breathe. Even after ten days of treatment the long-term prognosis was not good. But when he returned to his village, his dramatic improvement caused such a stir that thirty new patients trekked the sixteen kilometers to the hospital for treatment. When the outreach team followed up with a Sunday visit to Allowadine's village, it received an enthusiastic reception.

A Christian Literature Center with two full-time staff members furthered the spiritual ministry of the hospital. Staff members conducted open-air preaching during clinics, showed film strips and held ward services on Sundays. The Reading Room they maintained sold Bibles and gave away thousands of gospel packets and tracts.

In a new venture, the hospital opened the Duncan Academy, an English-medium Christian school that soon had one hundred students.

Relief/missionary aviation[3]

Through the window of the Bell helicopter, the snowclad mountains of northern Albania presented a pretty sight. North of the border, in fractured Yugoslavia, Serbs pounded Bosnian positions. It wasn't the plight of suffering Yugoslavia, however, that brought Jerome West to the remote mountain valleys of Albania. Jerome involuntarily shivered as he guided the chopper toward a rude village of draughty stone huts. He thought of the grim winter ahead for the poorly clad farmers eking out a living from the stony soil below. As the chopper touched down, barefoot children came running toward him, shaking from the cold.

By the time the rotors stilled, the Helimission chopper was surrounded by a crowd of men and women bundled up in a motley mix of garments. On their feet they wore a pathetic array of torn sneakers and rough leather brogues stained by mud and rent with holes. As Jerome and his crew unloaded the shoes, socks, winter clothes and Bibles they breathed a thankful prayer for the European Christians who had collected their precious cargo.

Jerome West first flew as an agricultural pilot in New Zealand before joining SIM. The Kiwi branch of SIM promptly seconded Jerome to Helimission. This band of Swiss-based innovators fields a small fleet of helicopters scattered at various bases in Africa. They use their airborne chariots to whisk missionaries doing pioneer evangelism into remote places inaccessible by fixed-wing aircraft. As needs arise they also pitch in to help with relief work.

Helimission had already used Jerome's skills in their East African operation. Isolated missionaries on remote stations in Kenya, Zaire, Tanzania, and more recently Ethiopia, looked forward to hearing the sound of his chopper. Leaders in the mission's work there commented about Jerome's spiritual perception and his way with people. No wonder his services were requested in Albania.

With Helimission fielding its third foray into the poorest nation in Europe, Jerome headed north to take the controls of XRAY, LIMA, LIMA (XLL). The Bell 206B helicopter had been badly damaged in a 1987 crash in Ethiopia. When repairs proved too costly in Europe, the helicopter had been shipped to New Zealand for major reconstruction. Resurrected, as it were, XLL served for sixteen months in Papua New Guinea before being flown back to headquarters in Switzerland. Jerome picked it up there and flew it down to Albania, where it became the workhorse for Helimission's October airlift.

After offloading their cargo of shoes and winter clothes, the Albanian villagers showered the chopper crew with tokens of their immense gratitude. In one village they pressed on the crew a gift of two sheep and 200 kilos of walnuts. Eight different villages insisted they accept a gift of a sheep. Not only thankful, the villagers proved hungry for the gospel. Jerome reported, "The most isolated and poorest villages seem to be the most attentive ... The men will sit and listen to every word spoken and the New Testaments that are distributed are eagerly read." Another member of the team commented, "These people are so open, you can see right into their souls."

What had begun as a one-shot foray among the neglected villagers of Albania early in 1992 had become a continuing program bringing both physical and spiritual solace. During the first flights, Helimission had flown in food, medical supplies and Bibles for 4,000 families. During that first foray, they quickly realized that more must be done. The sight of unplanted fields made them realize that starvation would stalk the hills during the coming year if seed could not be found. The government and the people pled for help. Helimission responded with a second series of flights in May bringing in tins of seed corn and 100 tons of seed potatoes.

Jerome quickly spotted the results of that second airlift when he flew into the same villages in October. Two of the peasant families proudly displayed the 600 kilos of potatoes they had harvested from the fifty kilos of seed potatoes provided in May. The precious harvest was carefully stored for the coming winter in the families' bedrooms!

The Word was bearing fruit as well. Time and again, villagers pled with the chopper team to stay and tell them more about the gospel. In one place they insisted that the team come back the following Sunday for a wedding. Of course, not everyone was happy with their presence. Jerome wrote, with typical Kiwi understatement, "Unfortunately, somebody took a dislike to our presence in the country and popped two rounds through the rotor blades, grounding us for a week. We had to go to church in Tirana, the capital, instead of attending the village wedding."

While waiting for the arrival of the replacement rotor blade, Jerome wandered the streets of Tirana. International Red Cross surveys had underscored the need for urgent assistance in the mountain valleys, but the needs were real enough even on the streets of the capital. Jerome wrote, "The crowds outside the bakeries have more resemblance to a riot than to customers queuing up for one of life's necessities." The wheat for this staple of life had been donated by Italy. Commenting on his impressions of

Tirana, Jerome exclaimed, "There is less food available on the streets of Tirana than on those of any capital city I have seen in Africa."

Africa had left an indelible mark on his heart, and with the third Albanian airlift complete Jerome headed back to Ethiopia to take up where he had left off. He knew there would be medical emergencies to respond to and mobile clinics to hold. As he flew across the cerulean waters of the Mediterranean, he was reminded of his flights with Dr. Sam Kanata.

He had flown Dr. Kanata across the steep ravines and over the rocky crags north of Addis Ababa to reach scattered Ethiopian villages. The ten-minute chopper ride normally took villagers eight hours or so by bone-rattling mule-back down the precarious mountain tracks. When news of the coming doctor circulated, hundreds would gather. As soon as the rotors stilled, Jerome would pitch in to prepare packets of pills. In these inaccessible villages, even aspirin was almost impossible to obtain.

Their reception usually left them with a glow of satisfaction. Occasionally they shook their heads in disappointment when villagers greeted the gospel presentation with cool disapproval. Sometimes the local priest agitated against the team's work, leading the people to complain that praying outside the Orthodox church was forbidden. In those villages people might sullenly demand medicine and treatment for their cattle at no cost.

Jerome found himself particularly looking forward to flying with the SIM missionaries pioneering outreach in the "Valley of Death" in south-west Ethiopia. The communist government, during its rule, had banished missionaries from this dangerous area where continual tribal wars had left deep scars. The Helimission team helped the mission to re-establish a presence at Metser in the infamous "Valley of Death."

Using the helicopter, Jerome was able to help missionaries not only reach remote and inaccessible villages but also to cross tribal boundaries stained by centuries of blood. Three tribes were within easy access by helicopter. The Mali, although a relatively pastoral tribe, were distinguished as the only tribe in Ethiopia known to use poison-tipped arrows. The hardworking Dimi tribe, living around the Metser station, stand out among others because they are one of the few remaining tribes that actually smelt iron. In contrast to the Mali and Dimi, the sadistic Bodi tribe raid and massacre their neighbors.

Chapter 29

An evangelistic and nutritional survey among the pastoral Malis uncovered shocking privation. The Malis, makers of poison-tipped arrows, faced an even deadlier enemy—starvation. The chopper-assisted team discovered that during the past three years most, if not all, of their animals had either died or been sent away to find grazing as the drought steadily tightened like a noose around their lives.

In one Mali village they found that three people had gone into their homes, closed the door and lain down to die. Throughout the area, the Mali were subsisting on grass and leaves. But even in their weakened state, the Mali showed an astonishing openness to the gospel. In one village four asked Jesus to become their Lord. With few churches in the whole area, the church-planting opportunities opened up by the helicopter team were encouraging. But first, dire physical need had to be cared for. The team made immediate plans to airlift in food and seed.

The Dimi, who live in the area around Metser station, smelt their own iron to forge tools and craft spears and jewelry. Although used to raising livestock, the hardworking Dimi have been forced to give up husbandry because of the depredations of their fierce neighbors, the Bodi. Among the Dimi, the gospel has begun to take root.

Earlier in the year, Jerome had already flown missionaries and evangelists into the village of Gerfa to conduct the first baptism in the whole area. When they heard about this threat to their domain, witch doctors had warned that if anyone went under the water they would not come up alive. In spite of the threats, twenty-eight new believers were baptized in a muddy water hole. How ironic that the witch doctors' warnings highlighted the true significance of this epochal step!

The new converts came up out of the waters very much alive in Christ. So alive, in fact, that a few months later Jerome returned with SIMer Jimmy Cox and several evangelists to conduct the baptism of twenty-one more believers. These new Christians became enthusiastic to start churches in other villages.

The cruel Bodi tribe presented a different challenge altogether. In March of that year they raided a tribe north of them and killed over 200 before the remnants of their target village could flee. But after missionary Jimmy Cox met with the Chief of the sadistic Bodis and asked for permission to establish evangelists in their territory, he agreed. The Chief said, "We will be observing the Dimi Christians, and if Satan didn't destroy the Dimi, then the Bodi would believe in Christ too!" Soon after this the helicopter crew were able to fly in two evangelists to work among the Bodi. It was not easy. With that kind of threat around, it must have been comforting to know that a helicopter pilot like Jerome was within call.

Jerome felt a deep sense of satisfaction at being able to participate in the extension of the Kingdom. He knew that the grace of God that led him so far from New Zealand was hard at work in the villages of Albania no less than among the craggy peaks of remote Ethiopia.

Time has passed, but pilots like Jerome West continue to save missionary time and effort, and open up new fields for the gospel.

Many specialties

Besides the three vignettes in this chapter, the stories of many other missionary specialists have been scattered throughout the book. We have read about:

- help from a Korean medical team for church planters in Paraguay
- musical ministry and film evangelism in Senegal
- a camping ministry in Brazil
- a literacy program in Pakistan
- an agricultural and health ministry in Burkina Faso
- a theological training program in Pakistan
- relief ministries
- aviation ministries
- medical ministries.

The most successful of these ministries are those that can be turned over relatively quickly to national believers.

Notes

1 The information in this vignette is culled from privately circulated letters and articles featuring the SIM missionaries Bruce and Betty Adams (no date).

2 Adapted from a report by **Dr. Aletta Bell,** *SIM UpDate*, July 30, 1992.

3 From SIM *UpDate*, June 3, 1992, and other privately circulated papers.

Chapter 30

Missions and the national church

Christ is building his Kingdom! Under the superintendence of the Holy Spirit, missionary work has been phenomenally successful. In spite of persecution in some quarters and spiritual retreat in others, an increasing host of believers gathers each week in churches large and small to worship God. As we shall see, the phenomenal growth of national churches is not without its problems. But we would expect that. None of our sending churches are free from problems, nor were any of the churches planted by apostolic missionary teams.

There is much to celebrate. In a special issue, *Mission Frontiers* pointed out that "Humble people committed to God, across the centuries, have constantly been gaining a higher and higher percentage of all the people on earth."[1] Too often we become distracted by the population explosion with its attendant increase in the net numbers of unreached Muslims, Hindus, Buddhists, and so on. Quoting figures compiled by David Barrett in the *World Christian Encyclopedia* this article pointed out that in a population of 181 million in AD 100 there was one Bible-believer for every 362 persons. By AD 1000 the proportion was reduced to 1 in 227; in AD 1500 to 1 in 85; in 1900 to 1 in 41; in 1950 to 1 in 31; and in 2000 to 1 in 9 among a population of 6.1 billions—an astonishing growth.

This study defined "Bible-believing Christian" in terms of Colossians 3 as those "who read, believe, and obey the Bible ... Bible-believing Christians today amount to at least 7 million congregations."[2] It has taken only seventy years for dedicated believers "to grow from 5 to 11.2 percent of the world population."[3] Even if we rigorously discount these figures to account for nominal Christians, mistakes in analysis or exaggeration, we are still left with a picture of the victorious advance of Christ's kingdom. Patrick Johnstone points out that, while Roman Catholics and Orthodox are growing slowly—even declining relative to population growth—evangelicals are advancing at three times the population rate.[4]

This growth can be seen on many fronts. Since 1600 the number of languages with the Scriptures has climbed from 36 to 2800.[5] A new translation is being completed every ten days. Since 1990 the *Jesus* film has been seen by an accumulated total of approximately 3.3 billion people! In spite of the deficient appeal at the end of the film, God has used it to touch many, many hearts. By the end of the year 2000, it was estimated that audio gospel recordings were available to 96 percent of the world's population.

Partnerships between radio ministries are blanketing much of the world. Of the 372 mega-languages identified by the World by 2000/World by Radio Vision, ninety-three had gospel broadcasts in 1985. Ninety further languages had been covered since 1985. Others have been found to have a program on air beyond these already noted. This cooperative radio group estimates that seventy-eight languages are still in need of broadcasts. Major broadcasters include HCJB, Voice of the Andes, FEBC, Far East Broadcasting Company and Trans World Radio (TWR). Although church planting has not been a primary focus of many of these programs, nevertheless TWR-India has seen 406 worship groups, gathered under the umbrella of India Believers Fellowship, planted during the decade mentioned.[6]

The Joshua Project "is a global cooperative strategy, focused on the least evangelized peoples of the world, that seeks to engage every church, agency, denomination and Christian from every country in the world in an effort to implement the goal of 'A church for every people and the Gospel for every person by AD 2000.'"[7] While that goal was not fully reached, nevertheless 88 percent of unreached groups were identified and targeted, and 66 percent of those had a church-planting team on-site by the end of 2000.

Another reality that must be acknowledged is the enormous growth of the Pentecostal/charismatic movement. From 2 percent of Christians in 1900 this group rose to become 6.4 percent in 1970 and 27.7 percent in 2000. In Latin America, for example, the number of Pentecostals has exploded.

While some of us might view this with alarm, and charismatics might argue that this demonstrates the validity of their emphasis on what they call "the full gospel," much more is going on below the surface. As Christian A. Schwarz has demonstrated through his massive study of 1,000 churches in thirty-two countries, there is little or no difference between charismatic and non-charismatics where they both emphasize the eight quality characteristics found in healthy churches, as discussed in Chapter 28.

I believe that charismatic growth is due to a neglect of important principles in older churches, such as: lay involvement and training, small groups, passionate spirituality, inspiring worship services, need-oriented evangelism and loving relationships. Too often our more traditional churches tend to be bound by their past, unable to innovate and flex, unable or unwilling to delegate tasks to any but trained clergy, and dull in the way they conduct worship and pray. Non-charismatic churches that demonstrate Schwarz's eight qualities, which are, in fact, biblical qualities, grow just as exponentially as do charismatic churches.

One of the most encouraging trends concerns the growth of indigenous mission societies. Statistics in the sixth edition of *Operation World* indicate a total of 201,928 missionaries at work in the world in 2000. Of these, 135,596 were from Africa, Asia and Latin America. Many of these have been working in cross-cultural situations either in their own countries or abroad. India alone had 40,713 missionaries serving in 174 agencies.[8] The growth in missionary passion among South Koreans, Singaporeans, Indians, Brazilians and many other groups is a foretaste of great things to come. Since 2000 the number of non-Western missionaries has continued to grow.

These encouraging statistics do not mean that the task is nearing completion, but they do demonstrate exciting progress. Mighty movements of God have exploded in places as diverse as South Korea, Ethiopia, India, Indonesia, South Vietnam, Russia and China. Without detracting from the optimism this generates, we must realize that untold millions remain unreached. We must also highlight some serious problems that affect the progress of the gospel. Several of these relate particularly to the relationship missionary organizations have with the churches they have established.

Church-development sidetrack and the loss of missionary vision

Many churches, whether in missionary-sending countries or those planted by missionaries, seem to quickly lose their missionary passion. Missions is church planting among unreached peoples. But once a church is planted, the excitement and joy of seeing new believers rejoice in their Savior may lead missionaries to settle down with a focus on feeding these hungry new

Christians. Peter Wagner calls this tendency the "Babylonian Captivity of the Christian Mission."[9] It is the church-development sidetrack mentioned in Chapter 28.

It is a historical fact that when the mainline denominations merged their missionary operations with their emerging churches, missions fell away. Giving was reduced, missionaries were laid off and missionary interest ebbed. The danger we face is to see this phenomenon reproduced in the evangelical world.

In his paper, Peter Wagner explores a theme I have frequently referred to in this book. (I don't often agree with him so fully!) His thesis is that "The Christian mission will enjoy good health and best fulfill the will of God to the degree that its vision remains on the fourth world [people beyond the gospel]."[10]

As we have seen, missionaries usually go out with a clear missionary vision: to evangelize and plant churches. As people in the target culture are converted they must be discipled. New believers must be baptized. The church must be organized. Care must be taken to feed these new believers with the milk of the Word so that the new church is healthy. Before long, this new task—church development and nurture—can tend to occupy most of the missionary's time and vision. If new priorities that continue to emphasize the importance of outreach are not established at this point, the missionary can become almost totally absorbed in church development.

It is Wagner's contention "that the tendency of missions at this point has been to give too much care to the emerging church." As new waves of missionaries are sent out, mission organizations adjust their job descriptions to utilize gifts that play down the role of the evangelist and play up the role of teaching and nurture.

The emerging churches usually find this focus attractive. Instead of carrying the torch of outreach to the ends of their cultures, they concentrate on perfecting those already won. They expect their missionaries to line up with this task. They may even become jealous of missionaries who spend their time in outreach. Indeed, as the new churches become organized, they may even discourage boards from sending church-planting missionaries. They may call for technicians to help with agriculture, media ventures, medicine, literacy and community-development projects. Of course, they usually welcome seminary professors.

Wagner explains,

> Nothing avoids the syndrome of church development more than a missionary out there in the fourth world setting the example of winning men and women to Jesus Christ, planting churches, turning the churches over to the national denominations and getting back to the fourth world as quickly as possible ... The best service that missions can render to the national church is not to be absorbed by the church, but rather to encourage the church to promote its own mission [organizations].[11]

Fortunately, God has often overruled the tendency of missionaries and church leaders to want to control younger churches. This occurred in the Jerusalem Council. More recently, this was demonstrated in the explosive growth of the Ethiopian church in the absence of missionaries. The same is happening in China. Unfortunately, crises have often done more to break this syndrome than self-conscious missionary policies.

Wagner points out that many Pentecostal missionaries in Latin America have avoided this syndrome due to their "willingness to turn the work over to the nationals as Paul and Barnabas did." He credits this willingness to their emphasis on the Holy Spirit. Whatever the cause, missionaries must pass on, not only the commands of Christ that relate to personal growth, but also the commands that relate to missionary passion!

The problem of dependency

A related problem concerns how to serve national churches without creating a cycle of dependency. Ray Wiseman, in a paper on dependency which I will later quote at considerable length, points out that this has a historical root.

> The concept of dependency as understood in traditional mission circles comes out of their own past. In the early days, as missionaries entered China and India, they often rewarded converts by giving them allotments of rice. The people who "converted" just to get the food earned the name "Rice Christians." As missions organizations matured, they overcame the Rice Christian problem but began paying converts to act as maids or

garden boys. Soon nationals began working in mission projects or as paid evangelists or pastors.

Employment by the mission meant they followed an overseas agenda.[12] Without paternalistic direction and overseas finances, the work they did soon collapsed. Without a doubt, the mission-dependent system has created a cycle of dependency. How did this come about? I believe the material success of the West and the inability of Western missionaries to escape the excesses of their own culture brought it on.[13]

In many cases dependency as described by Wiseman has sprung up as the natural result of missionary patterns used in the past. It may be perpetuated by the type of organizational setup imposed on new churches. Ongoing financial support can easily create dependency. Even patterns of discipleship can contribute to this blight, if the missionary is looked upon as the only expert who can truly disciple believers. Training nationals abroad, where they imbibe methods and ideas that are foreign to their own culture, is another subtle form of dependency, because they may return to their home cultures and expect churches to adopt the methods they learned—methods that cannot be sustained without foreign publications, seminars, experts, and so on.

Dependency is often the result of well-meaning foreign help. In Chapter 28 we noted Steve Saint's comments about dependency in the Auca church. They became dependent for help in evangelism, teaching and church construction. Since the Aucas' culture was being surrounded and powerfully influenced by a more technological culture that could have wiped them out, Saint helped them to become more independent and able to face the modern world without losing their identity. He helped them to identify a biblical church structure that worked for them, to even accept tourists and use the money to buy their own plane and, to the astonishment of missionary colleagues, to learn how to use dental equipment. He taught them how to use a chainsaw to cut their own boards. When people are not challenged, their innate abilities often remain hidden.

Steve Saint concludes,

I think it is critical that we keep sight of what the purpose of missions is. Missions is not

> to go in and create and control a church for other people nor be the church for them. It's not our job to ensure that it functions. It is simply and only to plant the church in every people group and nurture it until it is able to propagate, govern and support itself. When missions go beyond that, then they are imposing themselves in the area of responsibility that belongs to the indigenous people and then everything gets out of whack.[14]

Nevius's advice to the missionaries in Korea a hundred years ago was designed to protect the new church from this very problem. He urged the missionaries and Korean believers to: (1) have converts remain in their calling and work to support themselves; (2) develop church methods and organizational structures only as far as the Korean church could take responsibility for them; (3) call out full-time workers when the church was able to support them; and (4) have the Christians themselves build church buildings from their own resources and in their own style. When we look at the vigorous South Korean church today, we realize what wise advice he gave. If present trends continue, the South Korean church will soon send more missionaries than the USA.

Ironically, some groups use the indigenous principle to decry the sending of expensive foreign missionaries when national missionaries can be supported much more cheaply. Christian Aid, an organization committed to supporting national workers through raising foreign funds, asked the following rhetorical questions in a mailing I received:

> Do you believe most Canadian and U.S. based mission organizations are on the right track in spending $30,000 to $50,000 per year, per family, to send North Americans overseas, when over 100,000 native missionaries are already on the field reaching the "unreached" multitudes at a fraction of the cost? ... Knowing that native missions accomplish ten times what traditional North American missions are doing at less than 5% the cost—doesn't it make sense for anyone dedicated to world evangelism to help the well-qualified and effective foreign-based groups accomplish what they are better equipped to do?

The Christian Aid Mission then asked for $40 to $100 a month to support a native missionary.[15]

An Indian missionary responded to this kind of approach:

"$30 a missionary." In some publications that seems to be the published price of a national worker these days. A bargain ... Further we are told how the native missionary is more effective in reaching people in his or her nation. However, it just isn't true. I am an Indian with now over 20 years' experience in mission work in India. I am proud to be an Indian. To me, the notion of a cheap native laborer is ludicrous. Such language actually hinders the furtherance of the Gospel in lands like India ... It is simply not correct to call these folk, [receiving $30 per month] who are often new converts, missionaries.[16]

D'Souza went on to point out that most have only the briefest of training and live in simple conditions where they use this money as a supplement to their income.

They are certainly not cross-cultural missionaries, or even missionaries at all ... This numbers game, so essential in raising money, has its own drawbacks ... [In, for example, recruiting young people from South India to go to the north they are] ill-equipped to handle the massive challenge of a very complex and culturally rooted north India. To pit the foreign worker against the national worker is a destructive strategy which will only hinder the work of the Gospel.[17]

Dependency is a topic hotly debated in missionary circles today. The dangers that revolve around the issue engaged men such as Steve Saint, Patrick Johnstone and Robertson McQuilkin in writing extensive articles in the *Mission Frontiers* magazine.

Robertson McQuilkin, responding to adverts such as the one I quoted from the Christian Aid Mission, writes,

More than 140 organizations are now built on the premise of gathering and sending money, not people. One of the largest of the money-gathering agencies reports that it now supports 3,300 full-time workers in over 50 countries. But ... at least a billion of the lost live where there is no evangelizing church movement, often no witness at all. For these, by definition, someone must leave home to reach them ... There are no nationals to reach these billion people even if money were sent.[18]

McQuilkin points out that, although we exult in "the burgeoning Third World missionary movement," it cannot handle the remaining task. There are never enough missionaries. We need foreign and national missionaries. But the main problem with this finance-centered approach to missions is that "money is power ... power corrupts."[19]

McQuilkin quotes Jerry Rankin, President of the International Mission Board, Southern Baptist Convention, who points out,

> When North Americans subsidize the work of churches and pastors on the mission field: potential growth is stalled because of a mind-set that it can't be done unless an overseas benefactor provides the funds ... jealousy often develops ... People are deprived of growing in faith, learning to depend on God and discovering that he is sufficient for all their needs.[20]

He goes on to list the maladies that result in churches, or among church leaders, when a financial pipeline to the USA is secured. They become "mired in an ecclesiastical welfare state," with the result that:

- believers learn to depend neither on God nor on themselves
- leaders become preoccupied with raising North American funds
- those leaders who can't get to the "pipeline" become demoralized
- believers sue believers
- an independent and unaccountable higher class of Christian workers arises whose stylish lifestyles are envied by "unconnected believers"
- recipients become ungrateful
- organizations compete for workers, stealing trained leaders from new churches who had learned to be self-sufficient.[21]

After almost twenty years of missionary work, I can attest to the reality of the problems mentioned. But these questions do not have easy answers. Generosity is a mark of Christian living. Surely there must be some way to help financially—as the early churches did with the Jerusalem church—without creating dependency. Perhaps even that example is suspect. There is the possibility that the Jerusalem church died out, both because of an inability to throw off Judaism and because of its dependency on the burgeoning Gentile church. An intriguing historical question.

Avoiding dependency through partnership

In a paper responding to issues of dependency entitled "Partnership to

Avoid Dependency," Ray Wiseman addresses most of the questions surrounding this issue. In his reasoned response, he agrees that dependency has become a problem, but he identifies historic mission policies as precursors of spiritual, institutional and financial dependency. He further argues for true partnership among equals, showing that partnership as practiced under the principles established by Partners International replaces unhealthy dependency with dynamic interdependency.

With his permission, I here quote the full text of his analysis.

The prestigious missions publication, Mission Frontiers, of the US Center for World Mission dealt with "dependency" in a recent series of articles.[22] In over 40 pages mission representatives attempt to establish that "foreign funding" has created dependency among third-world churches. They argue that depending on outside money has crippled the overseas churches' capacity to give and seriously impaired their ability to reach out to others with the gospel. For the most part, they conclude that western churches and missions organizations must cease funding third-world Christians.

Will true partnership create dependency?

In a novel, *The Keys to the Kingdom,* Catholic author A. J. Cronin identified dependency as a major problem on the mission field. Nearly 60 years later evangelical missions have suddenly awakened to the dangers of unhealthy dependency. Why have evangelicals moved so slowly in recognizing a problem others identified decades ago?[23]

At age 39 I fulfilled a life-long dream. I became a career missionary, working among Africans who live in the huge townships bordering Johannesburg, South Africa. My commitment to historical or traditional missions dimmed when I realized that African Christians ministering among their own culture easily outperformed me and most of my expatriate co-workers. They did so because they spoke the languages, understood the polyglot culture and lived where the people lived. And then to clinch the argument, they did the job at a fraction of what it cost my mission board and supporters to send me.

Within five years I had returned home convinced that the church needed a new way to "do mission." Along with a host of other returned missionaries, I embraced the concept of supporting nationals. I soon began volunteering with Partners International, an organization founded separately in the USA in 1943 and in Canada in 1959 by former missionaries with the same dream.

In recent years churches and individuals in the western or developed world have also begun shifting their emphasis toward supporting nationals. According to *MARC*,[24] 2% of money committed to missions through US agencies goes to the support of indigenous mission workers while 47% supports traditional missionaries.[25] (Mission groups use the rest in projects and relief work.) Although not a large amount, the 2% has caught the attention of those who oppose "North American" money going to indigenous church or para-church ministries. They argue that we must wean the recipients from North American money to stop them from developing an unhealthy dependency.

A reaction by traditional missions?

Many people associated with traditional missions see the increase in support for indigenous ministries as a threat to conventional missions. They believe, with some justification, that too much "North American" money shifting to national support will shrink the piece of the pie claimed by regular mission organizations meaning fewer expatriate missionaries will go to the field.

Patrick Johnstone expresses "grave misgivings" regarding sending money to national workers, while at the same time he says, "I see this as an entirely valid way of enabling the missionary task to be completed."[26]

Johnstone expresses his grave misgivings, or arguments against funding indigenous ministries, in words often heard from other mission leaders:

1. Funding nationals appeals to the materialistic desire of western Christians. By giving money they do not need to go themselves.
2. Foreign money can damage the growth of missionary vision in other countries.
3. Foreign money can shift the agenda from the indigenous group to the supporters (he who pays the piper calls the tune).
4. Missionaries and nationals working separately suggests a division in the body of Christ. We are one body.
5. The use of the term "national" implies paternalism.

Certainly, most of his [Johnstone's] arguments have some validity when those who give and those who receive do not practice true partnership. Numbers 2 and 3 relate to the issue of dependency, the major topic of this paper. Arguments 1 and 4 really anticipate the conclusion of this paper, interdependence. Argument 5 strikes me as a "red herring." When I live and work in Canada, I am a national worker. When I worked in South Africa, people called me an expatriate. I consider both names technically correct. They have nothing to do with my position in the family of God; they describe my place of origin or national allegiance in the family of man.

The origin of dependency

Dr. Jon Bonk in his book, *Missions and Money: Affluence as a Western Missionary Problem*, reviews the last 200 years of missionary enterprise and identifies the affluence or prosperity of western missionaries as the greatest hindrance to world evangelism. Bonk argues: "that this insular prosperity, while enabling the western church to engage in numerous expensive, efficient and even useful activities overseas, has an inherent tendency to isolate missionaries from the cutting edge of missionary endeavor, rendering much of their effort either unproductive or counter productive, or sometimes both."[27]

Even though poor by the standards they knew at home, missionaries have tremendous wealth when compared to the people on the field. When they import the comforts of home: cars, refrigerators, generators, air travel, health insurance and special education for their children, they create a desire in the hearts of the nationals for similar things. The missionaries have few options: renounce their wealth and live like a national; share with the nationals; or refuse to share and attempt to foster a western-like materialistic culture among the nationals. Sadly, only the first option could have overcome the path to dependency.

The cycle of dependency

Dependency has roots much longer and deeper than the financial ones that have become the center of focus today. Spiritual dependency often develops between the missionary and the convert. A proper approach to discipling can go a long way in correcting that problem.

Institutional dependency occurs in missionary situations when the target people begin taking on characteristics of the evangelizing group. It begins when they adopt methods or organizational structures that might seem appropriate in a western culture, but won't work in a third-world climate. Most of the methods and structures borrowed from the West are money-intensive. The newly-evangelized group soon finds itself trying to support extensive and costly outreach, training programs and complex church organizations and buildings.

Only the West can afford to run programs imported from the West. So westerners feel the need to lavish funds on their overseas spiritual progeny. Not to support would bring about the collapse of the things missionaries had worked toward for generations. And so the specter of financial dependency has entered.

Many of the costly programs imported by mission personnel involve theological education and discipleship training. This further strengthens the spiritual dependency and so completes the cycle. Because the converts of the westernized church in the third-world know only the system bequeathed to them, breaking the cycle of dependency becomes difficult if not impossible.

Where traditional missions have helped create a cycle of dependency, they should address the problem. But in so doing they need to guard against throwing out the baby with the bath water.

A biblical perspective

The scriptures stress we must help those in need. Jesus gave very specific instructions to those with wealth. I walked through the city of Manila with Arsenio Dominguez, a key Filipino Christian leader. Each time he passed a beggar on the street, he pressed a coin into the outstretched hand. He didn't stop to preach or reproach; he expected nothing in return; he just gave. Although not a rich man, and able to spare only a tiny coin, he gave each gift as though dropping it into the hand of Jesus. In my own missionary experience fellow missionaries instructed me not to give; always expect the recipients to work for everything they get. What a contrast. We in North America know little of Dominguez's kind of giving.

Jesus and the Apostles John and Paul come down solidly on Dominguez's side. Jesus said, "All men will know that you are my disciples if you love one another" [John 13:35]. Then John enlarged on that by letting us know that the expression of love involves more than abstract feelings. It touches our total lives and modifies our culture. He said it this way: "If anyone has material possessions and sees his brother in need but has no pity on him, how can the love of God be in him?" [1 John 3:17]. Paul echoed John, even broadening the concept when he said, "as we have opportunity, let us do good to all people, especially to those who belong to the family of God."

New Testament Christians didn't just enunciate biblical principles; they lived them. They gave to others in need across cultural and national boundaries. When drought struck Jerusalem, the disciples in Antioch "decided to provide help for the brothers." They did it by sending aid by Barnabas and Paul [Acts 11:28–30]. In another passage we read that Paul commended the Corinthian church for its desire to help others [2 Cor. 9:2].

Alan Finley has pinpointed a major deterrent to supporting other Christians across cultural and national boundaries. He says:

> The church was born in a Jewish society and needed to be delivered from the sin of racc and culture from its beginning. Unfortunately this sin also afflicts the church in the West. Pride of race and culture causes self-centeredness. We accept members of our local church or even our denomination as "foreigners" who should be responsible for their own needs.[28]

In very simple words, we don't support others across cultural and national boundaries, because we have ethnocentric or racist attitudes.

During our term in South Africa, my wife and I stirred up a controversy among fellow missionaries and suffered a degree of criticism when we increased the salary of our part-time maid and gardener. Attitudes toward us worsened when we chose to welcome people of other races to our house and dinner table. Did our fellow workers react from feelings of ethnocentricity, racism, selfishness, materialism, fear of creating dependency, or from sound missiological principles? You decide.

We really can't use the specter of cultural superiority or dependency to escape our personal God-given responsibility to those in need. And we shouldn't assume that by collectively giving financial help to our poorer brethren in the less-developed world we will always make them dependent.

Another view: interdependency

Those of us from western nations, especially North America, make independence a cultural imperative. We tell our children to stand on their own feet. We relate myths of brave settlers standing alone against the wilderness. We admire the self-made man. Unfortunately, as missionaries, we attempt to impose that standard on other cultures that prefer a collective lifestyle to individuality.

In contrast Dr. Chris Marantika of Indonesia stresses the concepts of interdependency—he firmly believes we need each other. His concept of the "three Ps" proposes that nationals and missionaries, third-world peoples and westerners, practice interdependence. He believes we should pray together, proclaim together and pay together.[29] This concept assumes we can accept each other as equals and work together in partnership.

Dr. Marantika's view of interdependency much more closely approximates the biblical position than does our North American view of independence. The key biblical statement appears in the passage "Now the body is not made up of one part but of many " found in 1 Corinthians 12:14–23. David Howard says of this scripture:

> This is the most significant passage in the New Testament about our interdependency. It is impossible for us to say, "I do not need you." An eye cannot hear. An ear cannot see. If the ear is going to see, it needs the help of the eye. If the eye is going to hear, it needs the help of the ear. Interdependency within the Body of Christ is absolutely foundational to our work.[30]

Charles R. Taber suggests some features that should characterize a successful model of interdependence:

- mutual trust—fundamental to any success is a climate of mutual trust, respect and genuine love.
- Christian love (i.e., love shorn of its paternalistic, condescending dimension), based on the *koinonia* God intends for the whole body ...
- local decision making—it is crucial that decision making be focused in the place and on the persons who will be most directly involved ... As long as westerners remain effectively in charge of designing the program, there will continue to be difficulties with the model of development used, and with the mode and priority of aid ...
- encouraging local initiative—we need to encourage nationals to take the lead in determining the most fundamental goals and methods of operation.
- giving without strings—this principle is underlined by a deeply felt statement by Byang Kato: "If foreign aid is to help rather than deeply hinder the work of the Lord, it must be given as unto the Lord and received as God's money ..."[31]

Taber says it well, although his third point, "Encouraging Local Initiative," could, if handled badly, smack of western paternalism. With Partners International, most partner ministries establish goals and prove their methods long before partnering with PI.

True partnership involves interdependence

Could dependency become a problem among the partner ministries of Partners International? Yes, if we as an organization and individuals failed to observe the rules of true partnership and interdependence.

In true partnership indigenous ministries ably do the work that westerners cannot do; we at PI join with them by channeling funds they would not otherwise have. In true partnership the agenda belongs to the partner ministry, not to PI. They know the culture and needs of the target people and make all ministry decisions. They establish goals, salary, expense schedules and working conditions for their workers. They arrange core support for their ministry within their own country. The finances that come through PI expand existing ministries enabling them to reach a wider group.

We (PI and western supporters) depend on them to reach into their storehouse of spiritual gifts, cultural knowledge and abundant manpower to send out laborers. They depend on us to tap our financial riches, pray for them and provide expertise only when asked. As members of the Body of Christ, we depend on each other to fulfill the great commission. We couldn't do it alone and neither can they.

Interdependence begins when all of us individually and collectively admit that we need each other.[32]

While I cannot agree with everything that Ray Wiseman has written, nevertheless, the approach he outlines—the approach of Partners International—is among the best I've seen. We would be unwise, however, to ignore cautions outlined in an earlier period by John Nevius and more recently by Robertson McQuilkin, Steve Saint and the *Mission Frontiers* magazine. The widespread animosity toward and jealousy of the USA, in spite of it being one of history's most generous nations, should be a warning to us. Money does strange things.

Some form of partnership, however, must be developed. In a recent OMF paper, I noted the relationship being fostered between an Ontario church and new churches among the Tai Dam people in Asia. Forward Baptist Church, allied with its missionaries Greg and Janet Short, embraced a partnership that involves corporate, family and small-group prayer specifically for the salvation of the Tai Dam people. This will involve sending a team from Forward to Thailand to visit, pray for and observe this unreached people group in order to communicate a vision back home.

In the article there is no mention of money or of building. Instead the linking strategy included "organizing a vision trip to the people group; linking the church with other interested churches; providing timely, concise and informative prayer requests and any other communication that will bring these people to life and cause them to be an integral part of the local Canadian church."[33] The goal is to see self-supporting and self-reproducing churches established in this people group. This goal seems a wise approach to partnership that avoids creating dependency. Time will tell. The church will be mightily tempted to send Canadian goods and dollars in lieu of their sons and daughters.

In spite of the dangers, money is an essential ingredient in missionary work. Those whom God has entrusted with wealth will be called to account for how they have used it to extend the Kingdom. And where discipleship is engendered money will be used responsibly. No wonder the fundamental task Christ called us to was to make disciples. True disciples can be trusted.

Although missionaries face the danger of creating a pattern that produces either diminished missionary vision or dependency, this challenge is small compared with the potential for joy that comes from being involved with Christ in the extension of his Kingdom.

Notes

1 **Ralph D. Winter** and **Bruce A. Koch,** "Finishing the Task: The Unreached Peoples Challenge," *Mission Frontiers*, Special Issue, January 2000, p. 22.

2 Ibid.

3 Ibid.

4 **Patrick Johnstone** and **Jason Mandryk,** *Operation World* (6th edn.; Waynesboro, GA: Paternoster USA, 2001), p. 3.

5 **Winter and Koch,** "Finishing the Task," p. 14.

6 **Richard S. Greene,** "Words of Hope," *Mission Frontiers*, Dec. 2000, p. 13.

7 **Winter** and **Koch,** "Finishing the Task," p. 17.

8 **Johnstone** and **Mandryk,** *Operation World*, pp. 747, 749.

9 **C. Peter Wagner,** "The Babylonian Captivity of the Christian Mission," paper circulated from Fuller Theological Seminary, Dec. 1972.

10 Ibid. p. 3.

11 Ibid. pp. 6, 9.

12 For further thoughts on the source of the agenda in missions, see the article by **Ray Wiseman,** "The Fundamental Question in Mission-national Partnerships," *Didaskalia* (The journal of Providence Theological Seminary), Fall 1997.

13 **Ray Wiseman,** "Partnerships to Avoid Dependency," paper circulated.

14 **Rick Wood,** "Fighting Dependency Among the 'Aucas': An Interview with Steve Saint," *Mission Frontiers*, May–June 1998, pp. 8, 11.

15 Unsolicited mailing received from Christian Aid Mission [n.d.).

16 **Joseph D'Souza** with **Susan Hill,** "National Versus Foreign Missionaries?", in *Windows* bulletin (Operation Mobilization Canada), Summer 1996, p. 1.

17 Ibid.

18 **Robertson McQuilkin,** "Should We Stop Sending Missionaries?," *Mission Frontiers*, Aug. 1999, p. 38.

19 Ibid. p. 41.

20 Cited by **McQuilken,** "Should We Stop Sending Missionaries?"

21 Ibid. pp. 39–40.

22 See *Mission Frontiers* for Jan.–Feb. 1997 and May–June 1998.

23 Like all great novelists, Cronin used fiction to make insightful comments on the human condition and the failings of society.

24 A publication of World Vision USA.

25 Based on data collected from 702 US agencies and reported in the *MARC* 1998–2000 Mission Handbook.

26 *Mission Frontiers*, July–Aug., 1998, p. 8.

27 **Jonathan J. Bonk,** *Missions and Money: Affluence as a Western Missionary Problem* (New York: Orbis Books, 1992), p. xix.

28 From **Alan Finley** and **Lorry Lutz,** *The Family Tie* (Nashville, TN: Nelson, 1983), p. 49.

29 **Ray Wiseman,** *I Cannot Dream Less* (Brampton, Canada: Partners International, 1998), p. 69.

30 See **David Howard** in **Daniel Rickett** and **Dotsey Welliver,** (eds.), *Incarnational Presence: Dependency and Interdependence in Overseas Partnerships Supporting Indigenous Ministry* (Wheaton, IL: Billy Graham Center, 1997), p. 26.

31 **Charles R. Taber,** "Structures and Strategies for Interdependence in World Missions," in Rickett and Welliver, *Incarnational Presence*, p. 65.

32 **Ray Wiseman,** *Will True Partnership Create Dependency?*, paper passed on by Wiseman to author [n.p.; n.d.].

33 "God cares about the Tai Dam—So does this church," *OMF Heart for Asia*, Issue 12.

Conclusion

God is moving history toward its dynamic conclusion when "the Lord himself will come down from heaven, with a loud command, with the voice of the archangel and with the trumpet call of God" (1 Thes. 4:16). Missions culminates in the return of Christ.

We've traced the missionary purpose of God from creation to new creation, from its source in the mind and nature of God to its concrete fulfillment in the growth of the church worldwide. From "all peoples on earth will be blessed through you" (Gen. 12:3), through "I will pour out my Spirit on all people" (Acts 2:17), to the multitude around the throne from "every tribe and language and people and nation" (Rev. 5:9) who sing the praises of Christ, the Lamb of God.

Revelation pictures for us both the triumph of missions and the deadly conflict missionaries face during the whole church age. Clearly, missions is the most taxing task of mankind and yet its most thrilling and hopeful venture. As we read the book of Revelation, we cannot help but be sobered on the one hand while being transported into the heavenlies on the other. Every demonic clash, however, only makes the doom of the old serpent more certain and the conquest of the Lamb more triumphant.

We stand at this juncture of history before him who proclaims, "I am the First and the Last. I am the Living One; I was dead, and behold I am alive for ever and ever! And I hold the keys of death and Hades" (Rev. 1:17–18). He is the one whose eyes are like blazing fire, whose feet glow like bronze in a furnace, whose voice is like the sound of rushing waters, in whose right hands are the seven stars, out of whose mouth proceeds a double-edged sword, and whose face is like the sun shining in all its brilliance (Rev. 1:14–16).

The Lamb calls us to take the eternal gospel, held by the angel flying in midair, to all "who live on the earth—to every nation, tribe, language and people" (Rev. 14:6). He commissions us to proclaim "the name that is above every name, that at the name of Jesus every knee should bow, in heaven and on earth and under the earth, and every tongue confess that Jesus Christ is Lord, to the glory of God the Father" (Phil. 2:9–11).

As we individually and corporately, in churches and in missions, work to fulfill the Great Commission we know that many witnesses are looking on. There are the four living creatures and the twenty-four elders

who sang a new song:
"You are worthy to take the scroll
  and to open its seals,
because you were slain,
  and with your blood you purchased men for God
  from every tribe and language and people and nation.
You have made them to be a kingdom and priests to serve our God,
  and they will reign on the earth." (Rev. 5:9–10)

"Thousands upon thousands" of angels, the martyrs under the throne and all the creatures of heaven and earth sing of the worth of the Lamb and wait with bated breath until the curtain falls on the triumph of missions. Then a great multitude in heaven will shout, "Hallelujah! For our Lord God Almighty reigns. Let us rejoice and be glad and give him glory! For the wedding of the Lamb has come, and his bride has made herself ready" (Rev. 19:6–7). That bride is composed of the unnumbered multitude "from every nation, tribe, people and language" who cry with "a loud voice: 'Salvation belongs to our God, who sits on the throne, and to the Lamb'" (Rev. 7:9–10).

Can we do more than pray expectantly, "Even so come, Lord Jesus—come quickly!" Yes, we must do more, because Satan "is filled with fury, because he knows that his time is short" (Rev. 12:12). We must "overcome him by the blood of the Lamb and by the word of [our] testimony" (Rev. 12:11). As Luther so ably described it, "That word above all earthly powers, no thanks to them, abideth."[1] It is the word of the gospel. It is the message of Christ's death, burial, resurrection and triumph. It is the message of missions, and it will prevail.

While signs of Christ's coming multiply—signs over which we have no influence—there is one thing we can do to speed his coming (speaking of human agency, not of times and seasons which are fixed in God's decree). What is that? Jesus said, "... this gospel of the kingdom will be preached in the whole world as a testimony to all nations, and then the end will come" (Matt. 24:14). The end of the age, the coming of Christ, is linked to the fulfillment of God's missionary purpose.

How glorious to be active participants in the unfolding drama of missions! The time is hastening on. The Kingdom is coming. The gospel is spreading. The church is growing. Hallelujah!

Notes

1 **Martin Luther,** "A Mighty Fortress is our God," 1529.

Other books by Eric E. Wright

Josh Radley Suspense Novels

The Lightning File

Captives of Minara

Non-fiction books

Tell the World

Church—No Spectator Sport

Strange Fire?

Revolutionary Forgiveness

Through a Country Window

Down a Country Road

For information see his web site: www.countrywindow.ca

About Day One:

Day One's threefold commitment:

- TO BE FAITHFUL TO THE BIBLE, GOD'S INERRANT, INFALLIBLE WORD;
- TO BE RELEVANT TO OUR MODERN GENERATION;
- TO BE EXCELLENT IN OUR PUBLICATION STANDARDS.

I continue to be thankful for the publications of Day One. They are biblical; they have sound theology; and they are relative to the issues at hand. The material is condensed and manageable while, at the same time, being complete—a challenging balance to find. We are happy in our ministry to make use of these excellent publications.

JOHN MACARTHUR, PASTOR-TEACHER, GRACE COMMUNITY CHURCH, CALIFORNIA

It is a great encouragement to see Day One making such excellent progress. Their publications are always biblical, accessible and attractively produced, with no compromise on quality. Long may their progress continue and increase!

JOHN BLANCHARD, AUTHOR, EVANGELIST AND APOLOGIST

Illuminated preaching
The Holy Spirit's vital role in unveiling his Word, the Bible

JEFFREY CROTTS

978–1–84625–166–5

All true expository preachers want to experience the illumination of the Scripture in their hearts when they study and preach. Sadly, today's preaching culture promotes an imbalance in the discussion of the Spirit's role in preaching. In this Bible-soaked study, Jeffrey Crotts defines and applies the seemingly forgotten doctrine of illumination. Preachers who long for illumination during their personal study and preaching will be enriched as they read and apply this scholarly yet pastoral work on the priceless doctrine we call illumination.

I'm thankful for Jeff Crotts' balanced and sharply focused emphasis on the Holy Spirit's illuminating ministry ... Here is a sound, biblical antidote to the shallow superficiality and silly pragmatism that have commandeered so many pulpits today.
John MacArthur, pastor-teacher of Grace Community Church, Sun Valley, California, USA

A commendable balance characterizes the author's efforts and product ... May this book rescue many contemporary preachers from theologically aberrant methods by the Spirit's illumination of God's words from his Word. May they come to understand where the power of true change comes from and be liberated from ultimately ineffectual tactics.
George J. Zemek, Academic Dean, The Expositors Seminary, USA

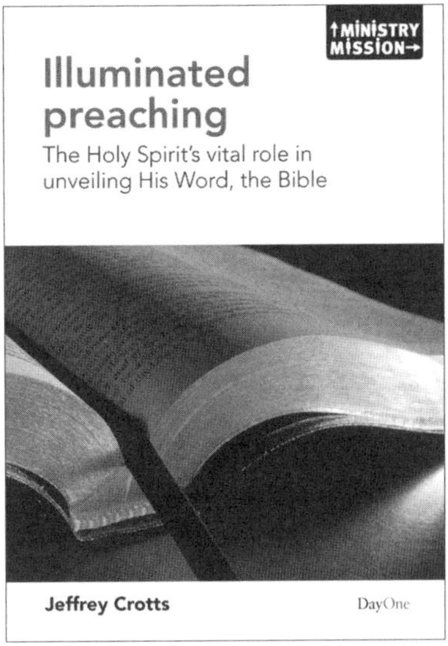

Jeffrey Crotts was raised in a Christian family in Virginia Beach, Virginia. At the age of 17 he became a Christian, and at 18 sensed a call to preach. He trained at Liberty University and The Master's Seminary, as well as a variety of ministry internships. In 1994 he met Judith, a Biblical Counseling and English major at The Master's College. They were married in 1997. They moved to Little Rock, Arkansas in 1998 when Jeffrey joined the pastoral staff of the Bible Church of Little Rock. He now ministers as senior pastor at Anchorage Grace Church in Alaska. They have been blessed with six children.

Exemplary spiritual leadership
Ministry and mission
Its dynamics, dangers and development

JERRY WRAGG

978–1–84625–200–6

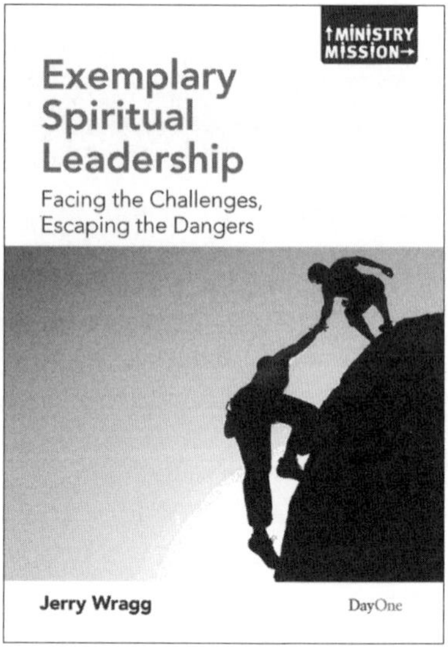

What is it that compels a group of people to follow the leadership and vision of one person? Why are the insights and pursuits of certain individuals more persuasive than those of others?

In this book, Jerry Wragg investigates how leadership should be characterized in the church, and how biblical leadership must differ from the kind of leadership promoted in the world. He explores the dynamics of leadership, particularly the character traits that need to be built up or eradicated in leaders, the dangers that leaders face and temptations to which they are particularly prone, and the development of future leaders: how to recognize leadership potential and encourage leadership gifts in the next generation. Throughout, Jerry Wragg writes honestly and offers pastoral encouragement and practical guidance that will help all men placed in church leadership positions.

Jerry Wragg was born and raised in California. Although exposed to Christian training through his parents' example and his own involvement in church, he didn't come to faith in Christ until after he was married and serving in the United States Air Force. After he was discharged, he graduated from The Master's Seminary with a Masters degree in Ministry and served as an associate pastor and personal assistant to Dr. John MacArthur at Grace Community Church, California. In 2001, he accepted the call to be pastor-teacher at Grace Immanuel Bible Church in Jupiter, Florida, where he is currently ministering. He has taught on church leadership, biblical counseling, theology and Bible survey courses, marriage and family, and parenting. In addition, Jerry serves as Board Chairman for The Expositors Seminary, Jupiter, Florida. He and his wife, Louise, have four adult children and are the proud grandparents of three grandsons and one granddaughter.